I0161032

This book is part of the Historical Collection of Badgley Publishing Company and has been transcribed from the original. The original contents have been edited and corrections have been made to original printing, spelling and grammatical errors when not in conflict with the author's intent to portray a particular event or interaction. Annotations have been made and additional content has been added by Badgley Publishing Company in order to clarify certain historical events or interactions and to enhance the author's content. Photos and illustrations from the original have been touched up, enhanced and sometimes enlarged for better viewing. Additional illustrations and photos have been added by Badgley Publishing Company.

This work was created under the terms of a Creative Commons Public License 2.5. This work is protected by copyright and/or other applicable law. Any use of this work, other than as authorized under this license or copyright law, is prohibited.

ISBN 978-0615501895

Memoirs of the Early Pioneer Settlers of Ohio

With Narratives of Incidents and Occurrences in 1775

Originally Written by

S. P. Hildreth

In the year1852

Re-Created, Re-edited Re-indexed and Re-published
With
Additional photos, illustrations and annotations
By

C. Stephen Badgley

In the year 2011

PREFACE

INTRODUCTION

COLONEL ROBERT OLIVER

PREFACE

This is the second volume of the Early History of Ohio, prepared by Dr. Hildreth of Marietta, and published under the auspices of the Ohio Historical Society. It is composed of a series of Biographical Notices of the early settlers of Washington County, who were also the early settlers of Ohio. Among them are some names celebrated in American history, whose active life commenced amid the most stirring events of the Revolution, and whose evening days were finished amid the fresh and forest scenes of a new and rising State. So various and eventful lives as theirs have scarcely ever fallen to the lot of man. They were born under a monarchy,—fought the Battle of Independence,—assisted in the baptism of a great republic,—then moved into a wilderness,—and laid the foundations of a State,—itself almost equaling an empire. These men not only lived in remarkable times, but were themselves remarkable men. Energetic, industrious, persevering, honest, bold, and free — they were limited in their achievements only by the limits of possibility. Successful alike in field and forest,—they have, at length, gone to their rest,—leaving names which are a part of the fame and the history of their country.

Among the biographies of such men will also be found notices of some women, whose characters deserve to be perpetuated among the memories of the State. The public and posterity will owe much to Dr. Hildreth for having so carefully preserved these memoirs of the early times. The Historical Society deeply regrets that it has no power to do more than merely introduce this interesting volume to the public.

Edward D. Mansfield, President of the Ohio Historical Society.

Dr. Samuel P. Hildreth
1783 -1863

INTRODUCTION

"The early history of the first settlements in the now great State of Ohio, not only ought to be preserved as an important epoch in the general history of our common country, but also the characters and public services of those men who were eminent in forming these settlements, have a claim to go down to posterity amongst the benefactors of mankind. The influence of their morals and habits has had a lasting effect on society, and is now perceptible in the general character of the communities in which they resided. The facts thus preserved, will enable the future historian to account for many things in our history which otherwise might appear obscure. The origin of an orderly, well regulated society, in any given district, may often be explained by tracing back its history to the influence exerted over it by some one or more individuals, who have imparted this character to it in its commencement: while the example of a few dissolute men, may have done much in placing a stigma on the name of a place, that will remain for ages." The settlements of the Ohio Company were fortunate in this respect; all the leading and influential men were on the side of good order, morality and religion; and the impress of their character is seen and felt to this day, in the well regulated, quiet habits, of a New England community, worthy the descendants of their Puritan ancestors. While many of the early colonies in the West, were composed of the ignorant, the vulgar, and the rude, those of Washington county, like some of the Grecian, carried with them, the sciences and the arts; and although placed on the frontiers, amidst the howling wilderness, and tribes of hostile savages, exposed to danger and privation, there ran in the veins of these little bands, some of the best blood of the country. They enrolled many men of highly cultivated minds and exalted intellect. There was at one time, in 1789, no less than ten of these, who had received the honors of a college course of education: a larger number than can now be found in the same district of country, if the professors in the Marietta College are excluded. The Hon. William Woodbridge, in his remarks before the Senate of the United States, on the question of the annexation of Texas, against which the citizens of Marietta, with thousands of others in Ohio, loudly remonstrated, when presenting that paper, gave the following sketch of the character of the men who first founded that place:

"It was on the 7th of April, 1788, that this settlement was first commenced; it was then that the first stone, the *corner stone,* of this great state was laid; and it was laid by these men, or by their immediate ancestors. The colony then consisted almost entirely of a remnant, and a most revered remnant, of your Armies of the Revolution—of officers and soldiers, who, at the close of that seven years' term of privation, of suffering, and of battles, found themselves let loose upon the world with their private fortunes, in general ruined, estranged almost from their own early homes, and with occupations gone! If they were of any of the learned professions, and there were many such, their professions were forgotten, and if their pursuits had been agricultural, commercial, or mechanical, why they had lost those business habits so difficult to acquire, but which are yet so indispensable to success; and such of their pay, too, as they may have been enabled to preserve, being old continental certificates, and become almost worthless in their hands, for all available purposes. In circumstances of so much gloom, the thought occurred of establishing themselves once more in a body, in the untrodden West. During many years they had camped together, and eaten together; they had fought and bled together; there was something pleasing in the plan of continuing still closer, their social and friendly relations. They had warrants which entitled them to public lands; many of them had continental certificates and other evidences of claim, which would go far to enable them to make their purchase. An association was formed; negotiations with the old Continental Congress and with the Board of War were commenced, and during the year 1787, a purchase was effected; and on the 7th of April, as I have said, 1788, the first and principal detachment of that interesting corps of emigrants, landed at the confluence of the Muskingum with the Ohio River. This was directly athwart the old Indian *war path;* for it was down the Muskingum and its tributary branches, that the Wyandots, the Shawnees, the Ottawas, and all the Indians of the north and northwest, were accustomed to march, when from time to time, for almost half a century before, they made those dreadful incursions, into western Virginia and western Pennsylvania, which spread desolation, and ruin, and despair, through all those regions. Being arrived there, they marked out their embryo city, and in honor of the friend of their country, the Queen of France, called it Marietta. They surrounded it with palisades and abatis; they erected block-houses and bastions. On an eminence a little above, and near the Muskingum, they constructed a more regular and scientific fortification. Thus did the settlement of that great state commence. Among these colonists were very many of the most distinguished officers of the Revolution, and of all grades. Gen. Rufus Putnam, and Gen. Benjamin Tupper, of the Massachusetts line were there. Gen. Parsons of the Connecticut, and Gen. Varnum, of the Rhode Island lines were there. Old Commodore Whipple, of Rhode Island, for whom the honor is claimed of firing the *first* hostile gun from on board a "Congress" vessel of war, and who during the whole war, was another Paul Jones and as active and daring, found his grave there; as did a near relative of Gen. Nathaniel Green. The sons of the "Wolf Catcher," Gen. Israel Putnam, and the descendants of Manasseh Cutler were there. Col. Cushing and Col. Sproat, Col. Oliver and Col. Sargent, and multitudes of others, distinguished alike for their bravery, for their patriotism, and for their skill in war, were there. Some few there are, some very few, still alive, and whose names I recognize, who constituted a part of this wonderful band of veteran soldiers. The rest, one after another, have dropped off. Many of the things I have adverted to, I personally saw. I was a child then, but I well recollect the regular morning reveille, and the evening tattoo, that helped to give character to the establishment. Even on the Sabbath, the male population was always under arms, and with their Chaplain who was willing to share the lot of his comrades, were accustomed to march in battle array, to their block-house church. And I take this occasion to remark, that it was not until the memorable victory of Gen. Wayne, that the War of the Revolution really ended, and Gen. Harrison was right when he made that assertion."

There is nothing more noble than to feel a deep interest in the honor of our country, our state, or the community in which we mingle. The history of these men belongs to the United States; their breasts were often the bulwarks, which, in the "time of trial," saved us from the enslaving power of Great Britain, and we are endeavoring to preserve their names and their characters from oblivion, by erecting this *historical monument* to their memory. For the materials on which it is founded, the author is indebted to many kind friends, generally the relatives of the persons, but in an especial manner to W. R. Putnam, Esq., Hon. Judge Cutler, Col. Joseph Barker, and William Slocomb: for Com. Whipple, to his grandson, Dr. Cornstock, of Boston, John Howland, Esq., of Providence, Rhode Island, and P. G. Robbins, M. D., of Roxbury, Massachusetts. The names of many other prominent men are omitted from a lack of the facts on which to found a written biography; and the larger number of those here given were obtained with much laborious search, amongst old letters, volumes of history, oral tradition, and numerous letters of inquiry written to the relatives of the deceased, in various and distant parts of the country. A full and well written biography of the late Gov. Meigs, who was one of the early settlers of Marietta, has been published in a posthumous volume of Sketches of the early Settlers of Ohio, by the late Alexander Campbell, Esq., and is not given here.* The present work has many imperfections, but may be the means of preserving some facts not generally known, for the use of a future and more able historian.

* That of General R. Putnam in the same volume is a brief sketch taken from a newspaper notice at the time of his death; and that of Paul Fearing, Esq., was written for Mr. Campbell, by the author of this volume, and is now republished with some additions.

Chapter I
PIONEER SETTLERS OF OHIO
RUFUS PUTNAM

Rufus Putnam
1738 - 1824
Founder of Marietta

General Rufus Putnam, the subject of this historical memoir, was a descendant in the fifth generation from John Putnam, who emigrated from Buckinghamshire, England, and settled at Salem, in the province of Massachusetts, in the year 1634. He brought over with him three sons, who were born in England, viz.: Thomas, Nathaniel and John. The father died quite suddenly, when about eighty years old. He ate his supper as usual, performed family worship, and died directly after getting into his bed.

Edward Putnam, the son of Thomas, and grandfather of Rufus Putnam, in the year 1733, made the following record: *"From those three proceeded twelve males, and from these twelve forty males, and from the forty eighty-two males;"* so that in 1733, there were eighty-two males by the name of Putnam, besides the females. All, of that name in New England, were the descendants of John.

With respect to their condition in life, he observes, *"I have been young, I now am old; yet have I not seen the righteous forsaken, nor his* seed begging bread; except from God, who provides for all; for He hath given to the generation of my father's Agur's petition, neither poverty nor riches; but hath fed us with food convenient for us, and their children have been able to help others in their need."

When this was written, he was seventy-nine years old. He lived after that fourteen years, and died when he was in his ninety-fourth year. This Edward was the grandson of John, the patriarch of the Putnams in New England. The males of this family were for many ages famous for longevity, numbers of them living to be over eighty years old, and several over ninety. The descendants of this good old man still inherit the promise and the blessing of the righteous; all of that name have had, and still continue to have, not only an abundance of bread for themselves, but also to spare to the poor and needy.

Elisha Putnam, the father of Gen. Rufus, was the third son of Edward Putnam, and his wife, Mary Hall, was born in Salem, Massachusetts, in 1685. Here he continued to live until manhood, and married Susannah Fuller, the daughter of Jonathan Fuller, of Danvers. About the year 1725, when forty years old, he moved, with his wife and family of three children, to the town of Sutton, Worcester county, Massachusetts, where he purchased a fine farm, and pursued the occupation of a tiller of the earth, as all his fathers had done. After his removal to Sutton, three other sons were born to him; of these Rufus was the youngest, and born the 9th of April, 1738.

The Rev. Dr. Hall, in his diary, says, that "Deacon Elisha Putnam was a very useful man in the civil and ecclesiastical concerns of the place. He was for several years deacon of the church, town clerk, town treasurer, and representative in the General Court, or Colonial Assembly of Massachusetts. He died in June, 1745, in the joyful hope of the glory of God."

Maj. Gen. Israel Putnam was also a descendant of Thomas, the oldest son of John, in the fourth generation, by Joseph, the third son of Thomas. Joseph had three sons, William, Daniel and Israel. The latter was born in 1717, and was the cousin of Elisha Putnam, the father of Gen. Rufus. At the death of his father, Mr. Putnam was seven years old. He was now sent to live with his maternal grandfather in Danvers, and remained in his family until September, 1747. During this period he was sent to school a portion of the time, and made some progress in reading.

In the course of this year, his mother married Capt. John Sadler, of Upton, Massachusetts, and he went to live with him, and remained under his roof until his death, in 1753. His mother was now again a widow.

In 1752, when fourteen years of age, Rufus made choice of his brother-in-law, Jonathan Dudley, of Sutton, as his guardian, and the certificate is signed by the Hon. Joseph Wilder, judge of probate for Worcester county. During the time of his residence with his step-father, all opportunities for instruction were denied him. Capt. Sadler was very illiterate himself, and thought books and learning of very little use, and not worth the time bestowed on their acquirement. The world is not destitute of such men to this day; they think and act as if they believed that the body was the only part to be provided for, and that the mind needed no instruction, or food for its growth, except what is acquired by natural observation and instinct. But young Putnam felt that he had another appetite to supply, besides that of the body; that his mind craved food and instruction, and would not be appeased without it. Notwithstanding the ridicule and obstructions thrown in his way by his step-father, he sought every opportunity for study, and examination of the books that fell in his way. Having no school books of his own, and this parsimonious man refusing to buy them, he soon fell upon a plan to get them himself. Capt. Sadler kept a kind of public house, at which travelers sometimes called for refreshment. By waiting diligently upon them, they sometimes gave him a few pence. These he carefully laid by, until he could purchase some powder and shot: with this ammunition and an old shot gun, he killed partridges, or pheasants, and sold from time to" time until the proceeds bought him a spelling book and an arithmetic With these two invaluable articles, the foundation of all, even the most profound learning, he soon made considerable progress in the rudiments of education, without any teacher but his own patient ingenuity. In the same way he learned to write, and make figures in a legible manner, progressing in a short time to the rule of three, guided only by the directions laid down in the book. How delightful must have been his sensations when he could put his own thoughts into tangible sentences on paper, and understand the rules of calculation, so important in all the concerns of life.

In March, 1754, when nearly sixteen years old, he was bound as an apprentice to the millwright trade, under Daniel Mathews, of Brookfield.

He was a man who had nearly the same opinion of the inutility of learning, as Mr. Sadler, and entirely neglected to send his apprentice to school. He, however, was more favorable in one respect, as he did not refuse him the use of candles for light, when pursuing his studies in the long winter evenings. His attention was chiefly directed to the acquisition of arithmetic, geography and history; while orthography, etymology, and the rules of grammar were neglected. Having no books in these branches and no one to teach him, his attention was chiefly directed to that which would be more immediately useful in the common affairs of life. In penmanship he had no aid from those nice copperplate engravings, published in after years, nor anyone to guide him in the art of neat handwriting, so that those two important branches, spelling correctly, and writing handsomely, did not receive that attention they otherwise would have done, and left him during all his future life to regret his deficiencies in these respects. Could he have looked into futurity, or had the least intimation of the public stations of trust and honor which he was destined by Providence to fill in manhood, he would doubtless have been better prepared for their arduous duties. The greatest wonder of all is, that with the discouragements and privations which environed him, he had the fortitude and perseverance to overcome these obstacles, and acquire so much really useful learning as he did. Ninety-nine boys in a hundred would never have made the attempt, but have lived and died in ignorance.

During this portion of his life, from sixteen to nineteen years, he was busily occupied under Daniel Mathews, in acquiring the practical art of the millwright, and in working on his farm. It required some knowledge of geometry, to form perfect circles, divide them into numerous equal portions, and lay out the exact angles necessary in the framework of the mill; thus gradually enlarging his knowledge of mathematics, for which he had naturally an ardent attachment, and a mind well fitted to comprehend. During this time his physical frame grew full as rapidly as his mind, so that when he was eighteen years old, he possessed the brawny limbs, the muscular power, and the full stature of a man six feet high. In all athletic exercises, he was renowned for his great strength and activity; and thus eminently fitted for the fatigues and privations of the military life he was destined so early to enter.

E Braddock

The war between Great Britain and France, in which the colonies were much more deeply interested than the mother country, commenced in the year 1754, when he entered on his apprenticeship. The accounts of the several battles, the defeat of Gen. Braddock, and the exploits of his martial relative, Capt. Israel Putnam, no doubt filled his youthful mind with ardor, and led him while yet only in his nineteenth year to enlist as a private soldier, in the Company of Capt. Ebenezer Learned, consisting of one hundred men, many of whom must have been his acquaintances or associates. The term of service was a little short of a year, commencing the 15th of March, 1757, and ending the 2d day of February, 1758. By the 30th of April the detachment was ready for marching, and that day left Brookfield, on their route for Kinderhook, on the Hudson River, about eighteen miles below Albany, which place they reached on the 6th of May.

In this and his subsequent campaign, he turned the art of writing, which he had with so much difficulty acquired, to a useful purpose, by keeping a regular journal of the events which took place; and without this precaution would have been lost or forgotten. He remarks that Capt. Learned prayed regularly, night and morning, with his men, and on the Sabbath read a sermon in addition—a proof of the general prevalence of piety amongst the New England people, and which if more common in this day, would suppress much of the profanity and wickedness so universal amongst the soldiery of modern times. On the 18th of May, they left Kinderhook, and marched the same day to Greenbush, opposite the town of Albany.

On the 21st of May, the company moved to Seaghticoke, a Dutch settlement on the banks of the Hoosick River, three miles from the

Hudson. It was deserted by the inhabitants on account of the Indians, and now lies in the north-westerly corner of Rensellear County.

On the 9th of June, the detachment joined Col. Fry's Regiment, at Stillwater, a spot subsequently famous for the battles at Bemis' Heights, which turned the tide of Burgoyne's success, and finally led to his surrender. On the 11th they marched to Saratoga, a place still more celebrated in military history, for the conquest of his army, thirty years after this time, in which Mr. Putnam acted a conspicuous part.

On the 14th of this month, Fry's Regiment, composed of seventeen companies of provincials, decamped, and on the following day reached Fort Edward. This celebrated military post, so often noticed in the events of the old French War, was built two years before this time, and was now in the pride of its strength. It stood on the east or left bank of the Hudson River, about fifty-two miles above Albany, and was constructed by a body of colonial troops under Gen. Lyman, and named after Edward, Duke of York, the eldest son of King George the Second, of England. It is thus described in Mr. Putnam's journal: *"The river washed one side of its walls. The form was somewhat irregular; having two bastions and two half bastions. The walls were high and thick, composed of hewed timber—a broad rampart, with casements, or bomb-proofs—a deep ditch with a draw-bridge— a covered way, glacis, &c"* In an after note, he says, *"I have been particular in this description, because in 1777, there was by no means so great an appearance of there having been a fortification here as we find in the ancient works at Marietta and other parts of the Ohio country."* It stood at the head of the carrying place, between the Hudson and Lake George, and also Wood Creek, a tributary of Lake Champlain. The village of Fort Edward stands near the site of the old fort, and serves to perpetuate its name. The tragic fate of Miss McCrea happened in this vicinity in 1777. White Hall, at the head of the Lake, the port from which steamboats now run to St. John, in Canada, was, in the Revolutionary war, called Skenesborough and was named after Maj. Skene, presently noticed by Mr. Putnam in his journal.

Being determined to see as much *as* possible of the adventures and hardships of a military life, he joined the Corps of Hangers, as a volunteer, and on the 8th of July, marched on a scout under Lieut. Collins, with twenty-two men, to reconnoiter South Bay, the southerly extremity of Lake Champlain, distant about twenty-five miles from Fort

Edward. On the 9th, having approached, as they thought, near the bay, the main party was halted, and three men, of whom Mr. Putnam was one, sent forward to learn its situation. Supposing it would occupy but a few hours, they left their blankets and provisions with the men that remained in camp. It proved to be much further than they had anticipated, and after fulfilling their orders, it was nearly night when they got back to the encampment. Much to their vexation and disappointment, they found that the Lieutenant and his men had left the ground, carrying with them their blankets and provisions. It seems that the leader had taken alarm at their long absence, supposing them either killed or captured by the Indians, and had hastily retreated in confusion. The deserted Rangers fired their guns, to give notice of their return, but no answering signal was heard. Two nights were thus spent in the woods, exposed, without their blankets, to the annoyance of gnats and mosquitoes, which swarmed in vast numbers over this humid region. The dress of the Rangers was similar to that of the Indians, leaving their thighs bare, and exposed to their attacks. They reached Fort Edward on the 11th, having been forty-eight hours without food, thus realizing a little foretaste of a Ranger's life. Lieut. Collins did not get in until the following day, and confessed that he heard their signal guns, but supposed them fired by the Indians. He, however, by various excuses, pacified Mr. Putnam and his comrades; yet he remarks on the transaction, *"It was extremely un-soldier like to leave us in the woods in the manner he did. If our long absence gave cause of alarm, he ought to have withdrawn but a short distance, placed himself in ambush, and posted two men under cover to watch for our return, or give notice of the approach of the enemy."*

On the 23d of July, about eight o'clock in the morning, a large party of Indians fired on the Carpenters', or Mechanics' Guard, within half a mile of the fort, and killed thirteen men, with one missing. This was the first view he had of Indian butchery; and says, *"It was not very agreeable to the feelings of a young soldier, and I think there are few who can look on such scenes with indifference."* In the afternoon, two hundred and fifty men, under Capt. Israel Putnam, were sent out in pursuit. They followed the trail until sunset, when the main body was halted, and three men, of whom Mr. Putnam was one, sent forward a mile or more, with orders to secrete themselves near the trail until after dark, watching closely for any scout that might be sent back, *"for,"* said the Captain of the Rangers, *"if they do not embark tonight in their boats, they will send a party back to see if they are pursued."* They went as ordered, but made no discovery. He remarks, *"It was a maxim I treasured up in my mind, as applicable, especially in the woods, whether you are pursuing, or are pursued by the enemy,"* and was the beginning of his military knowledge.

Capture of Fort William Henry

The Marquis de Montcalm, who commanded the French forces in Canada, was a man of intelligence and vast enterprise. After one or two ineffectual attempts to surprise the fort without the trouble of a regular siege, he finally concluded to collect all the troops in his power, and set about the work by regular approaches. This fort stood near the head of Lake George, distant fourteen miles from Fort Edward, and seventy from Albany, and was built by Gen. Johnson in 1755, who named it after one of the Princes of the reigning family. It was a square work, with four bastions. The walls were made of timber, filled in with earth and with a ditch on the outside. It was able, for a time, to resist a cannonade or bombardment. Having arranged his plan of operations, Montcalm came up the lake with a formidable array of boats; and on the 3d of August, 1757, landed an army of ten thousand men, and a large body of Indians, with a heavy train of artillery; and immediately commenced the siege. Col. Munroe, who commanded the fort, had arrived only the day before, with his regiment, from Fort Edward, to reinforce the garrison. He was a brave man, and made the best defense in his power; but the troops under his command were too few in number to hold out long against so formidable an attack. Many of his cannon burst, and the ammunition failed. After a spirited defense of six days, a capitulation was entered into for the surrender of the fort and troops, on the 9th of August. About half a mile east of the fort, separated from it by a swamp and creek, lay a body of fifteen hundred Provincials encamped within a low breastwork of logs. On these Montcalm made no serious attack; and they might at any time have made their escape, by forcing their way through the enemy posted in that quarter; but the next morning after the surrender, or the 10th of August, as the Provincials were paraded, to march to Fort Edward, agreeably to capitulation, the Indians attacked them, and a horrid butchery ensued. Those who escaped with their lives were stripped almost naked; many were lost in the woods, where they wandered several days without food. One man, in particular, was out ten days; and there is reason to believe, that some perished, especially the wounded. The number murdered, and missing, was some hundreds.

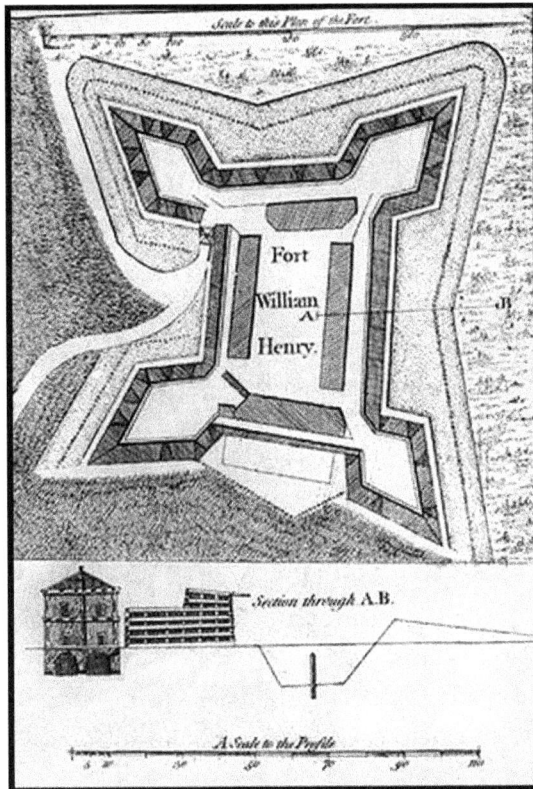

"Gen. Webb lay, all the time of the siege, at Fort Edward, with not less than four thousand men and for a considerable part of the time, with a larger number, by the coming up of the New York Militia. He was informed, every day of the siege, by an express from Col. Munroe, of the progress of affairs at the lake, and knew that the enemy had made an attempt on the fortified camp of the Provincials. It was the opinion of many officers, that he might have relieved the fort and that he was much to blame for not attempting it. The general opinion amongst the soldiers was that he was a coward; for he took no care to bury the men butchered in the manner mentioned, or to seek for the wounded, should there be any living among the dead. I was on the ground a short time after and saw the dead bodies as much neglected as if they had been wild beasts."

(Man. Jour.) He remarks, that the Provincials lost all confidence in Gen. Webb, and many of them left the army, and returned home. He was himself, at one time, being under great excitement at the dastardly conduct of Webb, on the point of leaving, but was providentially prevented.

On the 8th of October, the campaign being closed for that year, the Provincials, who composed the Corps of Rangers, were discharged. He, however, continued to do camp duty some days longer, and then attached himself to a company of artisans, who were employed, until the 10th of November, in completing the defenses of Fort Edward. On that day, the remnant of Col. Frye's regiment, himself, and the larger portion of his men, having been captured at Fort William Henry, marched down to the Half-moon, a post twelve miles above Albany. His providentially joining the Rangers, no doubt, saved him from participating in this slaughter and captivity.

On the 18th of November, three hundred and sixty men of the detachment were drafted into four companies, and ordered to different posts for winter quarters. This was a vexatious disappointment, as the Provincials expected to be discharged at the close of the campaign, although, according to their enlistment, they were to serve until the 2d day of February, 1758.

Capt. Learned's Company, to which Mr. Putnam belonged, was ordered up to Stillwater, on the east side of the Hudson; while he and several other mechanics were detained and employed in completing the King's works at the Half-moon, until the 29th of December.

The 1st of January, 1758, was celebrated by the men in great festivity, with an earnest looking forward to Candlemas, or 2d of February, as the period of their release from servitude.

From the movements of the commander of the stockaded garrison, Capt. Skene, afterward Major, and proprietor of Skenesborough, they began to suspect he intended to retain them in service beyond the time of their enlistment. The Provincials were quartered in huts by themselves, a short distance from the post, which was guarded by a company of British Regulars. Having decided on making a push for home, as soon as they considered themselves fairly at liberty, previous arrangements were made for the journey by preparing snow shoes for each man, as there was no possibility of marching through the woods where the snow was three or four feet deep, without this ingeniously contrived Indian apparatus, which had been adopted by the New Englanders from them. Capt. Learned, who had just returned from a furlough to Massachusetts, when made acquainted with the design of his men, approved of their plan, and said he would lead them, unless he could procure their regular discharge. Mr. Putnam observes on this transaction, that he thought well of the Captain at the time, but had since learned, that for an officer to desert his post is unpardonable.

On the 2d of February, Capt. Skene ordered the Provincials into the fort, and read a letter from Gen. Abercrombie, directing him to persuade the Massachusetts men under his command, to tarry a few days, until he could hear from that government and know their intentions in regard to them. To this they replied, that he is a good soldier who serves his full time, and that the Province had no farther concern with them; neither would they remain any longer. Capt. Skene threatened them with death if they departed without a regular discharge, and ordered them back to their barracks. He, however, took no forcible measures to detain them, nor did he search their huts for the *snow-shoes,* which they took the precaution to secrete under the snow. Their huts were sheltered by a high bank, out of sight of the fort, which screened their movements from observation.

Firm to their purpose, about three o'clock in the morning of the 3d of February, they marched off as silently as possible, seventy in number, under the command of Capt. Learned and Lieut. Walker; leaving Lieut. Brown, and a few invalids, who did not choose to join them. After leaving their barracks, they had a level piece of intervale, bordering the Hudson, about half a mile wide to cross, exposed to the artillery of the fort, had they been discovered by the sentinels, which was the reason of their departure in the night. They did not fear any opposition from the men in the garrison in the open field, as they outnumbered them. As to provisions for the march, they had provided as well as they could, by saving a portion of their daily rations for a week or two previous, and had hoarded up in this way, two or three days' allowance. The distance to Hoosack Fort, as it was called, a small stockaded garrison belonging to Massachusetts, was thirty miles, and was allotted for two days march. The snow in the woods was deeper than expected, and made the traveling laborious for the leading men of the file, while those who followed after had a pretty firm path. The second day of the march was in a snow storm; nevertheless, they bore manfully on, directing their course for Hoosack River, which was to be their guide to the fort; but during the snow storm they became bewildered, and falling on a westerly branch, instead of the main stream, it led them far out of their course, and at night they encamped without reaching their desired haven. Two turkeys were killed during the day, which aided their scanty stock of food. On the third day's march, they decamped very early, confident of reaching the fort before noon, but mid-day passed by, and the night arrived without the sight of it. One turkey was killed, and the camp formed with heavy hearts; which was done by kindling fires against a fallen tree, and lying down on the snow with their blankets, in the open air. Their provision was now nearly spent, and they were led, reluctantly, to believe, that they were actually lost in the woods. Several of the men, from the extreme severity of the weather, had frozen their feet; and one had lost a snow shoe by breaking through the ice.

On the fourth day the march was continued up the stream until noon, when they concluded to alter their course. This branch of the Hoosack, it seems, led up into the New Hampshire grants, afterward Vermont, where the town of Bennington was subsequently built. The direction of the march, by the advice of Capt. Learned, was now about south-east, over a hilly broken region, and the sun went down as they reached the top of a high mountain, which appeared to be the water shed, or dividing ridge between the streams which fell into the Hudson and Connecticut Rivers. The weather was excessively cold, and the snow five feet deep. On the morning of the fifth day, after a very uncomfortable night, thirty of the men, Mr. Putnam being one of them, breakfasted on a small turkey, without salt or bread. After traveling about five miles they fell on a small branch, running south-east, down which they followed until several tributaries had enlarged it, by night, to a considerable river. All this day they had no food but the buds of the beech trees, and a few bush cranberries. At night they encamped, weary and faint, but not disheartened. The sixth day's march was continued along the course of the river discovered the day before, which none of them knew the name of, in a broken, hilly region, not very favorable to the point of compass they wished to follow. The weather was cold and stormy, while the men were so feeble and lame from frozen feet, that only a few were able to lead the trail, and break the path in the snow. By marching on the frozen river, the lame men found a smooth path, or it is probable some of them would have perished. At night they encamped by tens in a mess. As it happened they had with them one dog, and only one. He was large and fat. At night it was concluded to kill him for supper. This was done, and his body divided into seven portions or one part to every ten men, the entrails falling to the butcher as his fee; and as he belonged to Mr. Putnam's mess, they made their supper on the fat. On the morning of the seventh day, his men breakfasted on one of the feet and a hind leg cut off at the gambrel joint, which being pounded and roasted in the embers, so as to separate the bones of the foot, made quite a palatable viand to a hungry stomach. That day the party confined their march to the river and about noon came to a spot where some trees had been recently cut for some shingles. This was the first sign of inhabitants they had seen, and it revived their drooping spirits. At sunset one of the men noticed a small stream putting in on the left bank, which he recognized as Pelham Brook and that Hawk's Fort, on Deerfield River, was not more than three miles distant. This latter river is a branch of the Connecticut.

Their leader now ordered two men to go forward to the fort, and make provision for the arrival of the party in the morning, which was a wise measure, and directed the most active men to make fires for the more feeble and lame ones, as they came up, which happily they all did by dark. That night Putnam's mess supped on the thigh bone of the dog, made into soup, with a small bit of pork and a little ginger, which made a very palatable dish. With respect to the flesh of a dog, he observes, *"since the experience of that day, I have believed it to be very good meat, and could eat it at any time without disgust."* This goes to confirm the experience of Lewis and Clark's men in their journey over the Rocky Mountains, who lived on it for weeks, and preferred it to any other meat.

On the eighth day's march, which was the 10th of February, early in the forenoon, they met some men from the fort, coming to their relief with slices of bread and meat, to appease their appetites and enable them to reach the post, where they were received with great kindness. Many of the men were badly frozen, and nearly exhausted with hunger. As a proof of the vigor of his frame, Mr. Putnam carried the pack of a sick man in addition to his own, and was always one of the leaders in breaking the path; although he felt the cravings of hunger, yet never failed in vigor or activity. One cause of this he attributes to the use of a little honey, which one of his mess had in a bottle, about a pound weight. Into this *honey bottle,* each man dipped the end of a rod and put to his mouth, and not like Jonathan into a *honey comb.*

On the 15th of February, he arrived at his former home, very thankful for his preservation amidst so many dangers. Capt. Learned was much censured for his conduct, and was not again commissioned during the war.

After passing the remainder of the winter at home and forgetting the sufferings of the last campaign, he again enlisted in the provincial service, for another tour of duty, in Capt. Joseph Whitcomb's Company, and Col. Ruggles' Regiment. The war, thus far, had been a continued scene of disasters, and disgrace to the crown; one army after another had been defeated or captured, and the French were in a fair way of overrunning the British possessions in America; and although the number of inhabitants in the Canadas was not more than one quarter as great as that of the colonies, yet their military commanders were much more able and energetic than the British, and carried conquest and victory wherever they turned their arms.

The regiment, to which he was attached, rendezvoused at Northampton, in Massachusetts, and marched for Albany on the 3d of June. On the 6th, they passed Pantoosac Fort, a small post on the Hoosack River, then within the boundaries of the province of Massachusetts. This was the station that Capt. Learned expected to reach on the second day after his unmilitary and disastrous desertion of his post at Stillwater, on the 2d of February. On the 8th, the regiment arrived at Greenbush, opposite to Albany. *"From Northampton Street to this place was through a wilderness, with but one house in the whole distance, except the little fort above mentioned."* This was in the year 1758; since that time vast changes have taken place in this region, and the railroad, in a few hours, would transport the whole regiment over the distance which occupied five days of steady marching.

On the 12th of June, he was detached with about eighty other artisans from the regiment under Lieut. Pool, and ordered on to the head of Lake George to erect works, in advance of the army. On the 5th of July, the troops being, assembled, embarked in batteaux, amounting to seventeen thousand men, under the command of Gen. Abercrombie, Lord Howe, the second in command, Gen. Gage, the third, and Col.

Bradstreet, quarter-master-general. The commander-in-chief was an old man, and entirely unfit for the post, as was proved by the result of the campaign. The army had but little respect for his abilities; while on the contrary, Lord Howe was their idol, and in him they placed their utmost confidence. He was remarkably easy and affable in his manners, mixing familiarly with the mechanics and common soldiers, inquiring into their condition and wants, displaying a real interest in their welfare, very different from those generally in high authority. This won the regard of the troops, and they would undergo any sacrifice at his bidding. Gen. Gage never acquired much reputation as a commander and the furious Bradstreet was hated by all the army. The batteaux moved down the lake until evening, when the troops landed at Sabbath Day Point for refreshment, and then rowed all night. On the 6th they disembarked at the northern extremity of Lake George, in two divisions, one on each side of the outlet. On the approach of the division on the right bank, a detachment of the enemy stationed there, retired without firing a gun. That division of the army on the left bank, was under the command of Lord Howe, and on its advance was met by a skirmishing party of the French, who, very unfortunately for the British, killed Lord Howe in the early part of the engagement. His death struck a damp on the spirits of the whole army, and no doubt had an influence in causing the defeat which followed. Mr. Putnam was left in charge of the boats but soon volunteered his service in the attack on the works and joined his regiment, which was posted with Col. Lyman's, of Connecticut, on the west of the mills, and was busily employed in erecting a breastwork. The attack on the fort at Ticonderoga, began at twelve o'clock, and was continued without intermission for several hours, without making any impression. At length the ammunition of the regular troops was exhausted, and a call was made on the Provincials to forward them a supply. Mr., Putnam again volunteered in this service. When they approached the scene of action, they found that the attacked troops had been effectually repulsed in their attempt to storm the enemy's lines, but did not consider it a total defeat, as it finally proved to be Col. Ruggles' Regiment remained in their breast-work until midnight unmolested, and then retreated to the shore of the lake, where they had landed on the 6th. On the morning of the 9th, Ruggles found his regiment in the rear of the army, which had retreated in the night, leaving them with the Rangers of the other regiment of Provincials near the French lines. In the forenoon of that day, all the troops embarked and returned to the south end of the lake, closing Gen. Abercrombie's expedition, which commenced with such high hopes, under a cloud of disgrace, and a loss of fifteen hundred men, in killed and wounded. Ticonderoga Fort was protected on three of its sides by water, and on the other for some distance in front extended a morass; the remainder was fortified with a breast-work, eight feet high, and planted with artillery. In addition to which the ground for one hundred yards in front, was covered with abatis. After reconnoitering the works, the engineer sent on this important duty, was so stupid as to report to the commander that they might be carried by musketry. The difficulty of advancing artillery over the morass and broken ground in front, led to the adopting of this fatal advice, and the defeat of the army. The post was defended by about four thousand men, and although their actual assailants amounted to twelve or fifteen thousand, and the attack lasted for more than four hours, yet they could make no impression on the garrison. The loss must have been greater than actually estimated, as twenty-five hundred stands of arms were picked up by the French. Mr. Putnam remarks that *"when he subsequently became acquainted with the strength of the works and the mode of attack, he considered it the most injudicious and wanton sacrifice of men, that ever came within his knowledge or reading."*

Nothing further of an offensive nature was attempted in that quarter, by Abercrombie, this season. A fort was commenced on the ground occupied by the fortified camp of the Provincials, in 1757, during the siege and capture of Fort William Henry, which was called Fort George, and stood half a mile east of that unfortunate garrison. On the 22d of July, the regiment to which he belonged was ordered to Fort Edward, and the men employed in repairing the roads from that post to Albany, until the 29th of October, when they were discharged.

On the 9th of November, he arrived at Sutton, his native place, where he passed the winter. On this campaign, in after life, he has these remarks: *"Thus was I carried through a second campaign, enjoying uninterrupted health, the friendship of my officers, and never charged with a fault. But, alas! In my journal, I cannot find any acknowledgment to my divine Benefactor and Preserver, nor do I recollect that I had any serious reflections on the subject."* This is in accordance with the natural heart, but when it becomes touched with the influences of the Holy Spirit, it is ready and willing to acknowledge its obligations to its rightful Lord and Benefactor.

On the 2d of April, 1759, he decided on again entering the military service, and enlisted into Capt. John Fibley's Company, as a substitute for Moses Leland, who had been drafted into the army, but did not wish to serve. For this enlistment he received fourteen pounds, thirteen shillings, Massachusetts currency, or forty-five dollars, fifty cents. The original receipt yet remains in the Leland family. He was finally transferred to Capt. William Page's Company, of Hardwick, in the Battalion of Lieut. Col. Ingersoll, in Col. Ruggles' Regiment; and was now advanced to the post of Orderly Sergeant; marching with the army by the old route, to the south end of Lake George.

On the 21st of July, they embarked in batteaux under the command of Gen. Amherst, *"a sagacious, humane and experienced commander."* Mr. Putnam notices his kindness and attention to the welfare of the common soldiers, as highly commendable. On the 22d, they landed at the outlet of the lake, in nearly the same numbers, as of last year, without meeting with any opposition. The following day they took possession of the breastworks, where they were so signally repulsed the year before, with little opposition, and think the loss of so many lives in the previous attack, attributable to the rashness of Col. Bradstreet. On the 24th, they began to open their trenches for a regular siege and bombardment of Fort Ticonderoga. This was a regular, strongly built, stone fort, erected by the French in 1756, and capable of resisting any common attack. The French had kept up a regular discharge of artillery, since the 23d, while their enemies were erecting their works for the batteries. That night, before any serious attack had been made, the garrison silently evacuated the fort, and embarked on the lake for Crown Point, a strong post, ten or twelve miles lower down on the west side of Lake Champlain. About three o 'clock in the morning of the 27th the fort blew up, with a tremendous explosion. The French did not make any resistance at Crown Point, but proceeded on down the lake to Montreal. The cause of their sudden desertion of these strong posts, was the news of General Wolf's approach to Quebec, so that no aid could be sent them from below; and rather than be captured they abandoned their positions.

Thus terminated the third campaign, in which Mr. Putnam had been engaged, with the total demolition of the French power on the lakes George and Champlain, leading to their final expulsion from North America. This was a glorious conquest for the British arms, in which the Provincials shared largely; but the greater good to them was the check it gave to the incursions of the savages, who for more than a century had invaded their frontier, assisted and encouraged with supplies of arms and ammunition from the French, plundering, murdering and carrying into captivity their exposed inhabitants, from Maine to Pennsylvania.

As the army was about to leave Ticonderoga in pursuit, greatly to his disappointment and vexation, he was ordered by the Brigadier-General to remain and superintend the building of a sawmill, at the lower falls on the outlet of Lake George, where it debouches into a bay of Lake Champlain. After the mills were completed, he obtained a pass to go to Crown Point, where his regiment then lay. When he arrived there, instead of going into the lines, he was ordered by Maj. Skene, the superintendent of the works then building for the enlargement of the garrison, to labor as a carpenter on the block-houses, promising him the fall wages for such work. After a few days he was ordered back to oversee the operations of the saw-mills, and retained until the 1st of December, some months after the discharge of his regiment. The engineer of the army, whose name is not given, when he was finally discharged, would not allow him the dollar a day as had been promised by Col. Robinson, the Quartermaster-General, but turned him off with fifteen pence, the pay of a private soldier; putting, no doubt, the extra pay justly due him into his own pocket.

On the 1st, in company with Col. Miller, Capt. Tate and others, eleven in number, he embarked on Lake George, to go up to the southerly end, in two batteaux. Expecting to reach Fort George the next day, they took but little provision. But the wind failing them, they passed the night four miles north of Sabbath Day Point, a noted head-land. On the 2d, the wind arose to a perfect storm, with intense cold, so that they were confined to the shore, and could not move at all. On the 3d, their provisions were expended. The wind and cold continued, and their situation was becoming alarming; but in rambling along the shore one of the men found an old provision bag, with about a dozen pounds of salted pork, which, with some damaged flour, brought by Col. Miller to feed two horses he had on board, made into dumplings, served well for that day. The 4th day was calm and they again embarked, but one of the boats being leaky, the ice formed so thick and heavy in it, that it was abandoned and the whole party entered the single boat. This additional burthen loaded her down within two or three inches of the top of her sides, and the least agitation of the water would have filled her. But, providentially, it remained calm all day, and they reached the fort at sunset without any accident. From thence he returned to Brookfield, in Massachusetts, on the 16th of December.

Disgusted with the treatment he had received in the service, in removing him from the duties of an Orderly Sergeant and placing him among the artisans, without any extra pay for his labor, he concluded not to engage any further in the army. The post of Orderly Sergeant is well calculated to improve the soldier in knowledge of military duty, which appears to have been his object and aim that he might finally be promoted. It was a good school to prepare him by these trials for the life intended for him by Providence. Beginning thus in the ranks, when he finally became a Commander, he knew well what to require from the private soldier. Nearly all the famous Marshals of Napoleon rose to this distinguished honor from privates, solely by their merit. He seems early to have acquired the respect and confidence of those under his command, and several anecdotes are related of their implicit obedience to his orders.

The winter of 1759 was passed in New Braintree, working on a small farm of fifty acres, which he had purchased from the avails of his wages and bounty.

In March, 1760, orders were issued by the Provincial Government to raise troops for another campaign. At the first muster of the militia he enrolled himself in the company of that town, and was by Capt. Page, presented with recruiting orders from Col. Ruggles. His well known character for bravery and soldierly conduct enabled him to recruit very successfully. While occupied in this service he received a commission as ensign, in Col. Willard's regiment, Ruggles having been promoted to a brigadier. On the 2d of June he left recruiting and set out for the army, taking with him one of the men as a waiter, and joined his company, which had marched some time previous, under Capt. Thomas Beman, at Ticonderoga, on the 18th. Here he found four companies of Provincials.

His own was stationed at the landing on the outlet of Lake George, where they remained to the end of the campaign, and he was thus deprived of the honor of partaking in the fatigues of the siege and capture of the garrison at Isle au Noix, which opened the way for the junction of the three British Armies before Montreal, and caused its surrender on the 8th of September, thus completing the conquest of Canada. On the 19th of November his company was discharged at Ticonderoga, and on the 20th they crossed Lake Champlain, and began their march through the wilderness, by way of Otter Creek, to Number Four, on the Connecticut River, a place often noticed in the early history of the country, and distant eighty miles from the lake; which place they reached on the 25th. On the 1st of December he arrived at his home in New Braintree.

In 1761, there being no further call for military service, he resumed his old employment of building mills and farming which he followed for seven or eight years. After which time, to the period of the Revolution, he was engaged in practical surveying for the neighboring landholders in that and the adjacent towns. This art he acquired under the direction of Col. Timothy Dwight, of Northampton, the father of President Dwight, of Yale College. The book chiefly, and perhaps only studied, was Love's Art of Surveying, printed in London in 1768, and now in the family. He was one of the best writers on that subject. Geometry was acquired from the same source, to which he also added the study of navigation. His own natural mechanical cast of mind, and habits of close observation, soon enabled him to practice the art of surveying with great accuracy and deserved credit. Mr. Putnam was a practical, matter-of-fact man, in whatever branch he engaged. First a millwright, then a soldier, next a surveyor, and finally an engineer; the principles of all which he acquired from a very few books, with but little instruction, and intent, close study of the subject before him. When a soldier, he stored his mind with military maxims, and a strict observance of discipline, which enabled him in after life to win the approbation of his superiors, and the love and good will of his equals, as well as of all under his charge.

In April, 1761, he was married to Miss Elizabeth Ayers, daughter of William Ayers, Esq., of Brookfield, an extensive landholder, and one of the first families in the place. In November following his wife died in childbed, leaving to the sorrowing father a little son, which God in his providence saw fit also to remove the following year. Nevertheless he bore these privations without murmuring against his Maker, and was enabled to ascribe righteousness to the Lord

In January, 1765, he was again married to Miss Persis Rice, daughter of Zebulon Rice, of Westborough, Massachusetts, with whom he lived in great harmony and happiness more than fifty-five years, and raised a numerous family of children. After this marriage he settled in the north parish of Brookfield, on a small farm of fifty acres, where his family resided during the war, until the year 1780, when he purchased a large farm and capacious dwelling-house in the town of Rutland. It was one of those confiscated estates belonging to the Tories, who had deserted their country and joined in league with the enemy for the subjugation of the Whigs. However we may now consider the justice of the policy pursued by our forefathers in those turbulent days, there is no doubt they considered it strictly honest and right to devote to the use of the country, the property of those who had thus unnaturally deserted the land which gave them birth and turned their hands, like parricides, against their own fathers and brothers. Many enormities were then practiced by the Whigs as well as the Tories under the excitement of party feelings, which time, and a more cool consideration of right and wrong, leads us to condemn.

In the year 1772, Gen. Lyman, one of the Provincial officers, returned from England, where he had been detained several years, in soliciting the British Government for a grant of land to the Colonial officers and soldiers, who had served in the late war against France. Soon after this, a meeting of the adventurers was notified to be held at Hartford, Connecticut, the same year. At this meeting the general informed them that an order was passed by the King in council, authorizing the Governor of West Florida to grant lands in that province in the same proportion and manner as given to his majesty's regular troops. Soon after the war was closed, in the year 1763, three new governments, or provinces, were established in their newly acquired American possessions, called by the names of Quebec, East Florida and West Florida; and an order was passed by the king and council, giving to the British troops engaged in the war, grants of land in these provinces; and the Governors were ordered to make the donations in the following proportions, of any unoccupied tracts, viz.: To a person of the rank of a Field Officer, five thousand acres; to a Captain, three thousand acres; to a Subaltern or Staff Officer, two thousand acres; to a Non-Commissioned Officer, two hundred acres; and to a Private man, fifty acres. The same was also granted to the officers and men in the navy; but nothing was said of any grant to the Provincial officers and soldiers, many of whom had served during the whole war, and were as justly entitled to the benefit as the regular troops. But the Crown seems always to have felt a coldness and want of regard for the interests of the colonists; treating them much more like menials and aliens than real subjects and children of the realm. One reason of this might have been their great distance from home, and the consideration of their dissenting and Puritan principles, no way in accordance with the established religion of the kingdom. It was with reluctance that the promise was made to Gen. Lyman, or they would not have been so long in granting it, and even then he brought no written document to substantiate the grant; but his word was so far credited that the meeting resolved to explore the lands, and appointed a committee for that purpose, of which Mr. Putnam was one.

On the 10th of December he left home on the mission to Florida, passing through Brookline, Connecticut, to accompany Col. Israel Putnam, who was another of the exploring committee. They took shipping at Norwich, and arrived at New York on the 20th of the month. The 10th of January, 1773, they sailed from the city on board the sloop Mississippi, chartered by the associates of The Military Company of Adventurers, as the company was styled. The exploring committee consisted of Col. Israel Putnam, Capt. Enos, Mr. Thaddeus Lyman and Rufus Putnam, accompanied by Daniel Putnam, a son of the Colonel, and a hired man. On the 30th of January they arrived at Cape Nichola Mole, a port in the north-west part of the island of Hispaniola. The harbor is an open bay, exposed to the north winds. The town contained about three hundred houses, situated in a mountainous portion of the island, with no plantations near it. He gives no particulars of the voyage, from the effects of sea sickness. Leaving the port, they sailed to Montego Bay, on the north side of Jamaica; and the 9th took their departure for the Bay of Pensacola, steering a westerly course. On the 11th Mr. Putnam took an observation of the latitude, and found it to be 19° 10' north. On the 12th, at night, they narrowly escaped shipwreck, by running on to a low sandy island, called the Grand Commanders. On the 18th, doubled

Cape Antonio, the west end of Cuba, and steered north-west. From the 21st to the 25th, the weather was very stormy, and on the latter day extremely cold for this climate; and when he returned to New England, found that this day was called "the cold Tuesday," showing the extensive range of this great depression of temperature. On the 28th they had soundings at forty-five fathoms, and soon after the first land made was their desired port, which was rather extraordinary after such tempestuous weather. On the 1st of March they entered the bay of Pensacola, and anchored at some distance from the town, the water being very shallow and landed from their boat. Gov. Chester and his council treated them very kindly, but no order for granting lands to the Provincials had yet arrived. This was a discouraging circumstance, but the hope that it might yet arrive, and a proposal being made of granting lands to the company on terms already within the Governor's power, induced the committee to decide on proceeding to reconnoiter the country on the Mississippi, and make such surveys as they thought proper. For this purpose Mr. Putnam was commissioned by Gov. Chester, as a Deputy Surveyor of the Province of West Florida, which commission is now in the possession of his son. The town of Pensacola, he says, contained about one hundred and fifty houses; and the country around, when viewed from the top of the statehouse, is covered with a pitch pine forest. The surface of the earth is white sand, and a few miles back bears a scanty supply of scrubby oaks, walnut and sassafras.

On the 18th of March they left the Bay of Pensacola, and steered for the mouth of the Mississippi. As they approached the father of American rivers, the broad surface of turbid, clay-colored, fresh water, floating for many leagues on the top of the salt water, led them to think they were running on to a sandy beach. However, they soon discovered their mistake, and continued their course into the clay-colored water. The surface was fresh for several feet down, but on sinking the bucket beyond a certain depth it brought up salt water. On the 20th of March, at five o'clock, P. M., the sloop anchored just off the mouth of the river, with the blockhouse, on Mud Island, bearing north-west. In the night a gale from the north drove the sloop from her anchorage, and she did not regain her position under twenty-four hours. Soon after a Spanish schooner anchored near them, and sent her boat on board asking for provisions. They stated that forty days ago, they were lying at anchor near where the sloop now lay, when a north wind drove them to sea as far as the bay of Campeche, and they had not been able to regain their lost ground until now. On this he remarks, *"How different our fortune! In the passage from Cape St. Antonio to Pensacola, in crossing the same bay, we had to conflict with storms and contrary winds for five days, lying at the mercy of the currents to carry us we knew not whither; yet Providence conducted us directly to our desired port!"* Thus acknowledging the kindness of that God in whom he trusted all the days of his life.

On the 22d of March they entered the Mississippi River, and proceeded up about ten miles from the mud bank at the mouth of the ship channel, called the French Balize. On the bar they found twelve feet of water. Here they were wind-bound for several days, and Mr. Putnam occupied the time in surveying the delta at the mouth, with the several outlets. As it will be very interesting to compare this survey with the present condition of the delta, and see the encroachment it has made on the gulf in the period of seventy-three years, which is doubtless very great, a plan of that survey is annexed, copied from the one made by Mr. Putnam, and preserved among his manuscripts relating to that exploration. There is also a plan of the Mississippi, as high up as they ascended, taken by measurement of each day's progress, and the meanders of the river. His well known accuracy in surveys of this kind would make his old sketches a valuable acquisition to science, to show the changes that have taken place in this ever wandering stream.

On the 26th they passed the first plantation, thirty-five miles from the mouth, on the left bank. On the 28th, they passed the plantation of Mons. de la Loira, about sixty-five miles above the mouth, which is the largest yet seen, and contained three hundred and twenty acres, French measure, and sixteen negro slaves. This man, while under the French government, valued his possession at twelve thousand pounds; but now, under the Spanish rule, was not worth more than one third of that sum. He was seventy-two years old, and said he was the first man born in Louisiana. He also stated that the river at that place never rose or fell over eight feet, and commonly only five or six feet, but that higher up it was different. Mr. Putnam observed that the French inhabitants looked as healthy in this settlement as the people of the northern colonies. On the 30th of March, they passed the English reach, and came to against a high bank three miles below New Orleans, where they found several English and other vessels, waiting for trade; not being allowed by the Spaniards to lay at, or opposite the town. In coming up he took the courses and estimated the distances, making from the mud bank at the mouth, eighty-five and three-fourth miles to the English reach, and from thence fourteen miles to New Orleans, which, added together, make ninety-nine and three-fourth miles. Thus far, he says, the river was about half a mile wide, with a gentle current. With the wind in a southerly quarter, a vessel could make the passage to English reach in a short time. At this point the river was seven hundred and fifteen yards wide, and seventy fathoms deep. On the 8th of April, the Captain of the sloop refused to proceed any further up the river, and the committee embarked in a small bateau; making use of oars, and a sail when the wind was favorable. He still continued, as they proceeded, every day, to take the courses and distances as before. On the 11th, they reached the Acadia settlement, seventy-one miles above New Orleans. It was composed of the inhabitants of Nova Scotia, removed to this place by the English in 1754, on the conquest of that country. They passed one day with the Acadians, and were treated hospitably. On the 13th, they passed an Indian village of twenty warriors. On the 15th, they passed the River Iberville, so called in the treaty of 1763, at the head of the Island of Orleans; and is one hundred, eighteen and a half miles from the town of New Orleans. It is a small outlet of the Mississippi, and was dry at the time of their passage. In high water it fills, and runs eastward,' discharging its waters, with the river Amite, into the lakes Maurepas and Pontchartrain, forming the island of Orleans. This outlet was subsequently called Bayou Manchac On the island side of the outlet was a Spanish garrison, with an officer and ten men. On the English side, called Manchac, was a small village, with good gardens, but no soldiers. A mile and a half above was a village of Alabama Indians, on the left bank. On the 18th they passed Baton Rouge, fourteen miles above Manchac. On the 19th, came to the fort and church of Point Coupee, a French settlement, extending about seven leagues on the river, and said to be as old, or older than New Orleans. On the 20th, they passed a village of the Tonica Indians, of about forty huts. On the 22d passed the outlet of the Opelousas, which flows into the Gulf of Mexico; at that time it was about forty perches wide, and by Mr. Putnam's measurement, three hundred, fifteen and a half miles from the balize, or mouth of the river, and ninety-seven and a quarter above the Iberville, or head of the Island of Orleans. The mouth of the Red River was then three miles above the outlet of Opelousas, and apparently about two hundred yards wide. On the 23d, they passed Loftus' Heights, now Fort Adams. The next day, a *few* miles above the mouth of the Homochitto Creek, they coasted a curious bend in the river, of eleven and a half miles, which at the isthmus or neck was only forty-seven yards across; and by a water level he ascertained the fall in the river to be two and a half feet in that distance. Their average progress against the stream was from twelve to fourteen miles a day. On the 26th, they arrived at Fort Rosalia, at the Natches, and half a mile below, he notes, *"is the first gravel stones we have seen on the shores of the river."* Fort Rosalia, or rather its ruins, was seated on the margin of an elevated plain or bluff nearly eighty perches from the river, and was approached by a winding road, not difficult of ascent. It was a regular heptagon, capable of containing four or five hundred men, built by the French in 1714. The English, after the peace of 1763, kept a garrison here until about four years before this visit; since which the barracks and outbuildings were burnt by the Indians in a drunken frolic. Here he took the latitude of the place with one of Davis' quadrants, and made the fort to be in latitude 31 deg. 50 min. N., and the variation of the needle 5 deg. E. The lands for several miles adjacent appeared to be old, worn-out, Indian planting grounds. The buildings were only one trader's hut, near the old fort. How vast the changes since that period! No appearance of civilized man but one solitary trader's hut, where the large and flourishing town of Natchez now stands. It had formerly been populated with a numerous tribe of Indians, who more nearly approached the Mexicans in civilization at the time of the conquest than any other tribe in North America, but they were totally exterminated by the French about the year 1729. On the 27th, the party visited a small settlement on Catharine's Creek, three miles from the river, and was informed that on Homochitto Creek, about twenty miles distant, were a number of settlers.

They had now ascended the river by Mr. Putnam's estimate, three hundred and eighty-eight miles, and in all that distance had seen no spring, or creek water, fit to drink. On the 28th they left the Natchez, and on the 3d of May, arrived at the mouth of Bine River, or Stone Creek, forty-six and a half miles above. About eight miles below is the Petit gulf, where now is the village of Rodney. The river is bounded for nearly a mile by a solid rock, at an angle of forty-five degrees, and about three hundred feet high. All the valuable lands on the Mississippi, below Bine River, having been already located, they here commenced their reconnaissance of the country on the left bank, or east side of the river, for a tract of land suitable for farming. They ascended Stony Creek in their boat, seventeen miles to the forks. The lands on the left side were low and subject to the river floods, and on the right broken, with soil rather thin and gravelly. About one hundred rods below the forks, they marked a tree, for the commencement of the location. On the 5th, they returned down the creek to the Mississippi. The town of Gibsonport now stands on this creek, which is known by the name of Bayou Pierre, and is in the midst of a rich, cotton growing country. The same day they ascended the river to Grand Gulf, to the residence of Thomas James, an Indian trader. The following day he engaged a Choctaw Indian to accompany them as a guide, and also to notify the Indians they might meet in the woods, who they were. Three miles above Mr. James' station, was the mouth of the La Fourchetto, or Big Black River. At this point two of the committee, with the Indian guide, left the boat, and proceeded across the country to the Walnut hills, while the others in the boat proceeded on to that place by water. The distance from Big Black, was estimated to be fifty-five and a half miles, and the boat reached there on the 8th of May. On the way up passed several high, handsome bottoms, as well as some that were flooded in high water. Here they met the party by land, who reported that their route was over a flat country, with some cypress swamps, and cane brakes so thick that it was impossible to explore any distance from the path. On this camping ground is now located the commercial and thriving town of Vicksburg, the second for population and business in the state, and will probably soon be the first. On the 9th, they proceeded on to the mouth of the Yazoo River, the same two gentlemen going by land as on the 6th, for the purpose of exploring the high grounds on this river, distance seventeen and a half miles. On the 10th, the boat ascended the Yazoo River nine miles to a high land, said to have been formerly a French post, where they met their companions, who had traversed the woods, at a fine spring, issuing from under the rocks.

By calculation Mr. Putnam ascertained that they were now north of the provincial line of West Florida, which was further confirmed by the angry looks of several Indians, who had met them there, and disapproved of their visit; this induced them to return without further examination. The Yazoo, he says, is about twenty-five perches wide, a dead stream, abounding in alligators. The Mississippi in floods backs high up this river. They descended that day six miles, and encamped. It was intended by Mr. Lyman and Col. Israel Putnam, to have gone by the Chickasaw path from Yazoo, across the country, to Big Black River, but their Indian guide refused to pilot them. From the 11th to the 13th, they explored the lands on the left bank, or south side of the Yazoo, and on the latter day Col. Putnam, Mr. Lyman and M. Putnam set out by land, to explore more carefully the ridge of high land stretching from the old French post to Walnut Hills. They traveled as near the hills as possible, on account of the cane brakes, discovered several small streams issuing from the high grounds, and found the soil very rich. In the afternoon they were taken up by a mighty cane brake. Here Col. Putnam climbed a tree, and saw high land about one hundred rods distant, which we were *two hours in gaining, on account of the difficulty of getting through the cane.* At this place, Mr. Putnam mounted a tree, and had a fine prospect of the country. The lands from the north-east round to the south, appeared hilly, but not mountainous or very broken. They descended part way down the hill, and encamped by a fine spring. This mount of vision must have been in the north-west portion of what is now Warren County, fifteen or twenty miles north of Vicksburg, in the midst of the present rich cotton plantations. On the 14th, they came, by a zigzag course, through the flat lands to their boat, which had descended to within one mile of the Walnut hills. This region was much injured by ponds, cypress swamps and overflowing of the river. The cane was chiefly confined to the uplands. On the 15th, Mr. Putnam and Lyman ascended to the top of the hills, where the former climbed two trees, and found the country still rising toward the north, and toward the east and south-east, soil rich, and covered with cane on the highest ridges, which extended over on to Big Black. Some miles above the mouth, near the foot of the hills, are some cypress swamps and dead water, but no brooks or running streams. Having completed the exploration in that quarter, they dropped down the river, landing several times to examine the bottom lands. They had intended to send a part of the committee by land, across the bend of the Mississippi above the mouth of Big Black, but were told it was impassable by reason of ponds and swamps. On the 16th of May they returned down the river to Mr. James' Station, who spoke the Indian language, and through him their guide informed them, that on the Yazoo, he met two of his chiefs, Chickasaws, who were opposed to the whites exploring any of the country above the Big Black, and that was the reason why he had refused to pilot them from the Yazoo to that river. The following day, Col. Putnam, Mr. Lyman, and Mr. Putnam commenced a further survey of the lands on the Big Black, in reference to a location. They found this stream from six to eight rods wide, and ascended it twenty-five miles, with the boat, to a rocky rapid, over which the water falls about a foot, and is a good mill seat. They saw much fine land on and near the creek, with several springs of water; on the left bank, it was hilly, but rich land.

On the 20th, they returned again to Mr. James', and there found Capt. George, a Chickasaw chief, waiting to see them. He showed them his commission from Gov. Chester, in which he is called Mingo Oumee, or Snakehead. He informed them, that at a congress of his people, it had been decided that no whites should settle on the Yazoo, but that they might do so on the Big Black, but not higher up the Mississippi. The Chickasaws have their towns on the Yazoo, and the Choctaws east of them. On the 21st they left the Indian traders' post, on their return down the river, and on the 24th of May reached the Natchez, where Mr. Putnam again took the latitude, and found it as before, to be 31 deg. and 15 min. N., and by an observation at sun setting, found the variation of the needle to be 5 deg. and 30 min. E. Here they were told that the country on the heads of the Homochitto, now in Franklin County, Mississippi, were hilly, much broken, and badly watered; therefore they did not explore that region, as formerly intended.

On the 2d of June, they arrived at Manchac, being delayed by explorations of the country at various points on the left bank of the river. A description of the region examined, is given by Mr. Putnam with minuteness. The climate in winter is so temperate that cattle need no fodder but live abroad all the season in the woods and yet the summer heat is by no means great. The intervals or bottoms he describes as very rich, but subject to be overflowed, and interspersed with ponds and cypress swamps, which will be difficult to drain. That the uplands back of the bottoms, are rich, but broken, and from several views taken from the tops of trees continue so for several miles into the country. The soil, rather thin but rich, based on clay; the undergrowth cane. The timber hickory, and oaks of various kinds; while on the bottoms he found locust, willow, cottonwood, copalm?, ash, mulberry, the royal magnolia, or high laurel, with cypress in abundance. As to the streams of water, he saw but few small ones, and none suitable for mills; and the only mill-seat he saw or heard of was on the Big Black. The feathered race consists of some turkeys, plenty of ducks, and in winter, geese and wood pigeons (Columba Migratoria.) The wild game were deer and bears chiefly. Reptiles not abundant, and those he saw, harmless. Fish of various kinds were plenty in the rivers, the chief of which were catfish and sheep's-head. Alligators swarmed in the Mississippi and were found in all the streams they visited. On the 3d of June they met the sloop, which brought them out three leagues below Manchac, and were detained until the 9th, by Mr. Ladle, the Supercargo, in taking in lading.

On the 12th, came to, at four miles above New Orleans, and remained until the 28th, repairing the vessel. On Thursday, the 1st of July, at 4 P. M., they passed the Balize, and sailed for Pensacola, but on account of head winds, did not arrive there until the morning of the 5th.

On the 6th, the committee waited on the Governor, who informed them that he had received letters from England by way of Jamaica, since their absence, but nothing further relating to a grant of lands to the Provincials. The following day they presented a petition to Gov. Chester and council, with a plan of the townships they proposed to locate; but so many objections were made to it, that the decision of the matter was laid over to the 9th. In the meantime, the surveyor-general requested Mr. Putnam to make out a new draft of the proposed townships. On that day the council presented the committee with their decision as to the lands, which limited the time of their taking actual possession, to the 1st of March, 1774. They appealed to the Governor for an extension of the time, but without success. On the 11th, they left the town of Pensacola, and fell down to Rose Island, from which place, on advice from Mr. Jones, one of the Council, Col. Putnam and Mr. Lyman went up to town, to engage Mr. Livingston, the Secretary, to make one more effort in council, for lengthening the time, but the result is not recorded.

Owing to head winds, they did not sail until the 15th of July. The latitude as observed that day was 29 deg. 11 min. N. From thence to the 22d, he kept a regular journal of the progress of the voyage, giving the daily latitude, currents, &c, with the tact of an old navigator. On that day, he was so prostrated by sea-sickness, that the observations are omitted until the 6th of August, when they arrived at New York. From thence he returned down the sound to Norwich and from thence by land, to his home in Brookfield, having been absent over eight months.

As to the result of this exploration, he says, *"So favorable was the report of the committee, as to the quality of the land, climate, &c, and moderate terms on which the Governor and council had engaged to grant them, that at a meeting of the military land company in the fall of 1773 at Hartford, they resolved to prosecute the settlement; and during that autumn, winter, and spring following, several hundred families embarked from Massachusetts, Connecticut, and other places, for the purpose of settling on the lands we had explored. But they were sadly disappointed. On the 6th of October of that year, Gov. Chester received an order from the King in council, prohibiting him from granting any more lands, either on family rights, or on purchase, until the King's pleasure be further signified to him. Thus the land office was shut before the emigrants arrived and indeed I believe before any of them sailed, and never opened afterward."* The poor Provincials were greatly disappointed, but were permitted to occupy any vacant land they could find. The emigrants of 1774 arrived generally so late in the season, that many of them sickened and died in this new climate, and the war which soon followed, put a stop to any further attempts to prosecute the settlement Thus early had that spirit of roaming and change of place infected the New Englanders, which appears to be natural to their Saxon blood, descending from their Puritan forefathers, who wandered early in the seventeenth century from their native land to find a new home in North America.

Mr. Putnam received only eighty dollars for all his expenses and loss of time in this trip to the Mississippi.

The annexed plan is an interesting relic of this affair, and shows the boundaries and forms of the townships located for the company, which was drawn by Mr. Putnam, and appended to the report of the committee. In his orders from Elias Dunford, Esq., the Surveyor-General of West

Florida, preserved amongst his papers, minute directions are given as to his manner of conducting the survey, requiring notices of important places on the river for landings, wharves, towns, &c The townships were in no case to exceed in width one third of their length, so that their base on the water courses should not occupy an over proportion of their banks, which accounts for their unusual shape. They were nineteen in number, and intended to contain about twenty thousand acres each, making the whole grant from Gov. Chester amount to three hundred and eighty thousand acres. The cost to the company was no more than the fees claimed by the officers of the government, amounting to five pounds sterling, or eighteen dollars, twenty cents, for every thousand acres.

In the Boston Weekly Newsletter, of December 4th, 1772, there is published a full account of the meeting of the Company of Military Adventurers, held at Hartford in November, with the origin of the company, their previous doings, and the names of all the various committees. In the preamble to this meeting, it is stated that Gen. Phineas Lyman was chosen as their agent to solicit the Court of Great Britain for a grant of land, in 1763, and that he had been detained at that court for nine years, to the great expense of the company in obtaining the grant. This was a fair specimen of the manner in which the mother country dealt with her colonies; and even then the pretended gift was a delusion, as they promised Gen. Lyman that the order to Gov. Chester, authorizing the grant, should be sent out so as to reach him by the time he arrived at Boston.

Several letters are preserved amongst Gen. Putnam's papers, from the adventurers who went out to West Florida. Amongst them is one from Capt. Michael Martyn on the river Amite, August 17, 1774. He had settled forty-five miles up that stream. His family had been sick, but he was pleased with the country. Gen. Lyman, with several other families, had moved on to the Big Black River, in the surveyed territory, and one man was about erecting a mill at the little falls on that stream; but that the prospect of making money by shipping lumber to New Orleans was blasted by the Spaniards forbidding that trade.

In the year 1802, the survivors of that company, about one hundred in number, reorganized themselves, and petitioned Congress for a confirmation of their old grant, but it does not appear that anything was done for them; and thus ended this famous land adventure, which at the time caused a good deal of excitement in New England.

The revolutionary storm, which had been gathering for several years, burst upon the colonies, the second year after his return from this expedition. Ever active to the service of his native country, he joined the army in the capacity of a Lieutenant-Colonel, in the Regiment of Col. David Brewer. His regiment was stationed at Roxbury, in Gen. Thomas' Division of the army, soon after the affair at Lexington.

In a short time after the Battle of Bunker Hill, the general and field officers of the Roxbury Division, met in council on the best course to pursue, in their present defenseless situation, exposed at any time to the attack of the enemy without any better protection than a board fence. It was decided that lines should be thrown up for the defense of the town. When this was determined, the difficulty arose where to find a man capable of directing the works in a military manner. Engineers were rare amongst a people who had never carried on a war but under the direction of mother Britain, who filled such posts with her own sons. At length it was mentioned to the general by some of Col. Putnam's friends, that in the late war against Canada, he had seen some service in this line; but on being solicited by the Commander to undertake the work, he frankly told him that he had never read a word on that branch of science, and all his knowledge was acquired by working under British engineers. The general would take no denial, and Col. Putnam reluctantly set about tracing out lines in front of Roxbury toward Boston, and various places in the vicinity, especially at Sewell's Point. It so happened that he was occupied at the latter post, when Gen. Washington and Gen. Lee, first came over to examine the situation of the troops, and state of the defenses on that side of Charles' River. The plan of the works met the entire approbation of Gen. Washington, and Lee spoke in high terms of that on Sewell's Point, when compared with those at Cambridge, which animated and encouraged him to persevere in his efforts. All the defenses at Roxbury, Dorchester and Brookline, were of his construction, and especially the fort on Cobble Hill.

**General
George Washington**

In the course of this campaign, at the request of Gen. Washington, he surveyed and delineated a map of the courses, distances, and relative situation of the enemy's works in Boston and Charleston, with the American defenses in Cambridge, Roxbury, &c, which must have been of great importance to him in arranging his plans for an attack on the former place. In December, he accompanied Gen. Lee to Providence and Newport, Rhode Island, and at the latter place planned a battery that commanded the harbor; also, a work on an elevation at Howland's Ferry, which secured the communication of the island with the main land. In the new organization of the army, made in the fall of 1775, he was appointed a Lieutenant-Colonel in the Twenty-second Regiment, commanded by Col. Samuel Wyllis. He, however, did not actually join that regiment, but was continued in the Engineer Department.

In the winter of 1776, Gen. Washington was deeply engaged in planning an attack on the British army in Boston, by crossing the troops on the ice, or else to draw them out from their stronghold, by erecting works on Dorchester Neck, that would not only annoy the town, but destroy their shipping in the harbor. In constructing the latter work, Col. Putnam, with his usual modesty, and constant reliance on an overruling Power, in directing the affairs of man, thus speaks: *"As soon as the ice was thought to be sufficiently strong for the army to pass over, a council of general officers was convened on the subject. What their particular opinions were I never knew, but the Brigadiers were directed to consult their Field Officers, and they to feel the temper of the Captains and Subalterns. While this was doing I was invited to dine at head-quarters; and while at dinner, Gen. Washington invited me to tarry after the company had departed. When we were alone he entered into a free conversation on the subject of storming the city of Boston. That it was much better to draw the enemy out to Dorchester than to attack him in Boston, no one doubted; for if we could maintain ourselves on that neck of land, our command of the town and harbor would be such as would probably compel them to leave the place. But the cold weather, which had made a bridge of ice for our passage into Boston, had also frozen the earth to a great depth, especially in the open country, like the hills on Dorchester Neck, so that it was impossible to make a lodgment there in the usual way, (that is, by excavating the earth.) However, the general directed me to consider the matter, and if I could think of any way by which it could be done, to make a report to him immediately."*

He then describes the events which he calls providential, and may evidently be referred to him who created, as well as rules the destiny of man, but which thoughtless and blind mortals attribute to the freaks of chance. *"I left headquarters in company with another gentleman, and on the way came by those of Gen. Heath. I had no thought of calling until I came against his door, when I said, "let us call on Gen. Heath", to which the gentleman agreed. I had no other motive than to pay my respects to the general. While there I cast my eye on a book which lay on the table, lettered on the back Muller's Field Engineer. Immediately I requested the general to lend it to me. He denied me. I repeated my request. He again refused, saying, he never lent his books. I then told him that he must recollect that he was one, who at Roxbury, in a manner compelled me to undertake a business on which, at the time, I confessed I had never read a word and that he must let me have the book. After a few more excuses on his part, and pressing on mine, I obtained the loan of it."*

He arrived at his quarters about dark, but was so much engaged in receiving reports of the progress of the works until a late hour, that he did not examine Muller until morning. On looking over the contents of the book, he came to the word chandelier. This was a new phrase to him, but on turning to the page where the article was described, and reading it carefully over, he was soon ready to report a plan for making a lodgment on Dorchester Heights. In a few minutes after he had decided on the feasibility of the plan, Col. Gridley, who had planned the works at Cambridge, and Col. Knox of the artillery, who had been directed to consult with Col. Putnam on this difficult subject, entered his room and acquiesced in his plan. The report was approved by Gen. Washington, and preparations immediately made to carry it into operation. The chandeliers were made of stout timbers, ten feet long, into which were framed posts, five feet high and five feet apart, placed on the ground in parallel lines, and the open spaces fitted in with bundles of fascines, strongly picketed together; thus forming a movable parapet of wood, instead of earth, as heretofore done. The men were immediately set to work in the adjacent apple orchard and woodlands, cutting and bundling up the fascines, and carrying them with the chandeliers on to the ground selected for the work on the night of the 4th of March, and on the morning of the 5th, the British troops were astonished to see a formidable battery, erected by their industrious Yankee foes in one night, where the evening before no appearance of such a defense was to be seen. The ground was so deeply frozen that the entrenching tools made no more impression on it than on a solid rock, and their old mode of excavating trenches, and throwing up parapets of earth, was utterly at a nonplus.

The providential visit of Col. Putnam at Gen. Heath's quarters was both the remote and immediate cause of the sudden withdrawal of the British troops from Boston. On the first sight of this barrier, mounted with artillery and frowning defiance, Gen. Howe decided on landing troops and carrying it by storm, and would have probably been another Bunker Hill adventure or something worse. The ice broke way soon after, and his boats being dispersed by a gale of wind, when the troops had embarked, he gave up the design, and sent word to Gen. Washington that he would leave the town with his army unharmed if he would not molest the shipping while the men and stores were removing. The evacuation of the place, and the relief of the inhabitants from British thralldom and abuse, being all that Washington sought, the terms were complied with, and this desirable object accomplished without bloodshed.

On the last day of March, 1776, he was ordered by Gen. Washington to proceed to New York, by way of Providence, Rhode Island, to aid Gov. Cook with his advice and assistance, in constructing works for the defense of that town. While on this tour of duty, he again visited Newport, and made additional defenses there. On the 6th of April he had an interview with Washington, at Providence, who felt a deep interest in his welfare, not only for his successful effort on Dorchester Heights, but also for the integrity, uprightness, and straightforward patriotism of the man; and not only during the war, but during his whole life, treated him with marked respect and friendship. He reached New York about the 20th of April, and was immediately authorized as chief engineer, to lay out and oversee the works of defense during that campaign at New York, Long Island, and their dependencies, with Fort Washington, Fort Lee, Kingsbridge, &c, the larger portion of which appears in the plan of New York Island, attached to Marshall's Life of Washington. This was a service of great fatigue, as it occupied all his time from daylight in the morning until night, and sometimes all night.

On the 10th of July, Gen. Washington, in a letter to Congress, notices the services of Col. Putnam: *"Gen. Mercer is now in the Jerseys, for the purpose of receiving and ordering the militia coming for the flying camp, and I have sent over our Chief Engineer to view the ground in the neighborhood of Amboy, and to lay out some necessary works for the encampment, and such as may be proper at the different passes in Bergen Neck and other places."*

In August, Congress appointed him engineer, which was announced by Gen. Washington to him, as follows:

"New York, August 11, 1776.

Sir: I have the pleasure to inform you that Congress have appointed you an Engineer, with the rank of Colonel, and pay of sixty dollars a month. I beg of you to hasten the sinking of vessels and other obstructions in the river at Fort Washington, as fast as it is possible. Advise Gen. Putnam constantly of the kind of vessels you want and other things, that no delay that can possibly be avoided may happen.

I am sir, your assured friend and servant,

G. Washington.

P. S.—Congress have just sent two French gentlemen here as engineers. Will either of them be of use at Fort Washington or Kingsbridge?"

A vast deal of labor and expense was bestowed by the Americans early in the war, in placing obstructions in the North River, such as chains, booms, chevaux-de-frise, sunken vessels, &c, to prevent the ascent of the enemy's ships of war to the highlands; but all of it was useless expenditure, for with a leading wind their large frigates and seventy-fours could with ease break through any obstruction of this kind, and only excited their derision. After a year or two of trial, this mode of defense was abandoned. Their entire control of all our harbors and mouths of rivers by their vast fleets, gave them a great advantage over their foes, in the transport of troops, munitions of war, &c, from one point to another.

On the 8th of September, 1776, a council of general officers had determined on holding possession of the city of New York. On the 12th, by order of Gen. Washington, Col. Putnam went out with Gen. Mifflin to reconnoiter between Kingsbridge and Morrisania, and on their return Washington met them near Harlem Heights, where they made their report. This led to a council of general officers, in which it was decided to abandon the city, and this measure was based on their report, being the means of saving the army from total destruction.

Col. Putnam remarks that his appointment by Congress as Engineer was wholly unexpected. That his first attempts in that department arose from pure necessity, in place of a better man, and that his continuance in that service was more out of respect to Gen. Washington, than a sense of his own qualifications. After his arrival at New York he had greatly improved his knowledge, by the study of writers on that subject; and his daily practice in that profound art for more than a year, had now made him a much more skillful engineer, yet his natural modesty had never led him once to think of being appointed to the first post in a corps of engineers. His observations on the deficiencies and difficulties which attended that department, led him, in September, to draw up a plan for a Distinct Engineering Corps, which was presented to Gen. Washington and by him laid before Congress, with the following letter, of November 5:

"I have taken the liberty to transmit a plan for establishing a Corps of Engineers, Artificers, &c, sketched out by Col. Putnam, and which is proposed for the consideration of Congress. How far they may incline to adopt it, or whether they may choose to proceed on such an extensive scale, they will be pleased to determine. However, I conceive it a matter well worthy of their consideration, being convinced from experience, and from reasons suggested by Col. Putnam, who has acted with great diligence and reputation in the business, that some establishment of the sort is highly necessary, and will be productive of the most beneficial consequences."

In his letter which accompanied the project, Col. Putnam disclaimed all pretensions to being placed at the head of the corps, but expressed a desire to serve in the line of the army. In this modest rejection of so distinguished a post, he was, no doubt, in some measure influenced by the well known deficiencies of his early education, but his love of country being greater than the love of self, led him to prefer the appointment of some better educated man. His judgment and practical skill in this branch, was no doubt equal or superior to that of any other man in the army, while his knowledge of surveying and drafting, with his mechanical turn of mind and sound judgment, rendered him a far better master of this branch of science than he was willing to admit.

On the 19th of October the enemy landed their army on Pells Point, and some skirmishing took place between a part of Glover's Brigade and the advance of the British troops, near East Chester. The following morning Gen. Washington directed Col. Putnam to reconnoiter their position. For this purpose he left Kingsbridge, in company with Col. Reid, the Adjutant-General, and a foot-guard of twenty men. From the heights of East Chester they saw a small body of the enemy near the church, but could learn nothing from the inhabitants, as the houses were all deserted. Col. Reid now left him to attend to other duties, and Col. Putnam requested him to take back the guard, as he thought he could better succeed in reconnoitering by himself. He then disguised his appearance as an officer, and set out for White Plains, a place he had never visited, nor did he know the road which led to that place. Directly a highway turned off to the right, which he followed a short distance, and came to a house, where a woman informed him that the road he was now on led to New Rochelle; that the enemy were there, and had posted a guard at a house then in sight. He now turned his course and proceeded toward White Plains, approaching within three or four miles of the place, when he discovered a house a little ahead with men about it. Before advancing, he carefully examined their appearance with his spyglass, and ascertained that they were not British soldiers. He then advanced and entered the house, which was a tavern; calling for some oats for his horse, and sitting quietly down, listened to their conversation. He soon discovered that they were Whigs, and ascertained the following valuable facts, viz.: that the main army of the British were lying near New Rochelle, distant from White Plains about nine miles, with good roads and an open level country between, and that at the latter place was a large quantity of American stores under the guard of about three hundred militia. That a detachment of the enemy was posted at Mamaroneck, only six miles from the Plains, while on the other side was the Hudson River, in which lay five or six of the enemy's armed vessels at a distance of only five miles, so that the main depot of provisions for the American army, which Gen. Washington had ordered here as a place of safety, was enclosed on three sides by his adversaries. Col. Putnam saw at a glance their hazardous position, and hastened back with his all important discoveries. The road from Ward's Tavern where he then was, led across the Braux, and was the most direct route for his return, but it passed so near the positions occupied by the enemy that it required great watchfulness to avoid detection. As he approached the highland west of the little River Braux, he saw it was already occupied by armed men, but on applying his spyglass, ascertained they were American troops and on his arrival found it to be Lord Stirling's Division, who had taken a position there since he passed in the morning. He announced his discoveries to the general, refreshed himself and horse, and set out for head-quarters, ten miles distant, by the mouth of Saw-mill River, a road he had never traveled before, leading through a noted Tory settlement. It was now dark, but he dare not inquire the way, lest he should be arrested. An overruling Providence guided his steps, and he arrived in safety at Gen. Washington's quarters, near Kingsbridge, about nine o'clock. He found him alone, and ready to receive his report, with a sketch of the country, which he hastily made, showing the relative positions of the different British detachments, and the stores at White Plains. This, like the clue of the labyrinth, at once led him to see the difficulties and dangers of his position, and the path by which he could be extricated. Gen. Washington complained very feelingly of the gentlemen of New York, from whom he had never been able to obtain a plan of the country: that it was by their advice he had ordered the stores to White Plains, as a place of safety. This was a serious difficulty under which he labored through the first years of the war, the lack of correct topographical descriptions of the country in which he was acting, often leading him into the toils of the enemy, when he thought he was escaping or out of danger. Such a man as Putnam was then an invaluable treasure who was fearless, but cautious in scanning the positions of the foe, and could delineate on paper, what he had seen with his eyes, making his descriptions both intelligent and practical. Washington immediately sent a messenger for Gen. Greene and Gen. George Clinton, since Vice President of the United States. When the latter entered, Putnam's sketch and report were laid before him, and the question asked as to the correctness of the topographical sketch. He confirmed its accuracy. In a short time he was charged with a letter to Lord Stirling, and orders to proceed immediately to his camp, which he reached by the same route, about two o'clock in the morning. Before daylight his division was in motion, in full march for White Plains, where they arrived about nine o'clock on the morning of the 21st of October and thus was the American army saved *by an interposition of Providence,* from a probable total destruction.

"It may be asked wherein this interposition of Providence appears? I answer first, in the stupidity of the British general, in that he did not early in the morning of the 20th, send a detachment, and take possession of the post and stores at White Plains; for had he done so, we must then have fought him on his own terms, and at such disadvantage on our part as must, in all probability, have proved our overthrow. Again, when I parted with Col. Reid, on the 20th, I have ever thought I was moved to so hazardous an undertaking by foreign influence. On my route I was liable to meet with some British or Tory parties, who would probably have made me a prisoner, as I had no knowledge of any way of escape across the Braux, but the one by which I came out; hence, I was induced to disguise myself, by taking out my cockade, lopping the sides of my hat, and securing my sword and pistols under my overcoat; and then had I

been taken under this disguise, the probability is that I should have been hanged for a spy."

It was as late as the 29th, before the enemy advanced in front of the American lines at White Plains. About 10 o'clock, A. M., Col. Putnam had arrived on Chatterton Hill, intending to throw up some defenses, just as they came in sight. As soon as they discovered the Americans, they opened a severe cannonade but without much effect. Gen. McDougal now arrived with his brigade, and seeing the enemy crossing the Braux below in large bodies, placed his men in an advantageous position behind the stone walls and fences to receive them. They were twice repulsed with great loss but by bringing up fresh detachments, they so greatly outnumbered the Americans as to turn their right flank, and cause them to retreat. Our loss was great but it was afterward ascertained that the British loss was much greater; they receiving the same pay as at Bunker Hill. After the Battle of the 29th, Col. Putnam was employed in examining the topography of the country in the rear of White Plains, toward North Castle, Croton River, &c, with a view to military operations, when, on the 5th of November, he received the following letter from Gen. Washington:

"Head Quarters, White Plains, Nov. 5, 1776.

Sir:

You are directed to repair to Wright's Mills, and lay out any work there you conceive to be necessary, in case it is not already done. From thence you are to proceed toward Croton Bridge, and post the two regiments of militia in the most advantageous manner, so as to obstruct the enemy's passage to that quarter. You are also to give what directions you think proper to those regiments, respecting the breaking up the roads leading from the North River eastward. After this you are to go up to Peekskill, and direct Lasher's detachment to break up the roads there; you are likewise to lay out what works will be advisable there, and order them to be set about.

Given under my hand,

Geo. Washington.

To Col. Putnam, Engineer."

On the 11th of November, Gen. Washington visited Peekskill and Col. Putnam accompanied him to Fort Washington. On the following day he crossed the North River, instructing him to ascertain the topography of the country, with the roads and passes through the Highlands which report he soon after made. A copy of this report is among his papers and gives a minute description of the different passes; pointing out such as would need protection with a skeleton map, containing valuable information for the defense of the passes in the Highlands of the Hudson, a point so important in the contest with Great Britain. On the 8th of December, he addressed a letter to the Commander-in-Chief, informing him that he had accepted the command of a regiment in the Massachusetts line, of the Continental Army, with his reasons for so doing, assuring him at the same time of his attachment and readiness to execute any service he should be ordered on. The following is an extract from his answer:

"Bucks County, Near Cayell's Ferry, Dec 17, 1776.

Dear Sir:

Your letter of the 8th, from Peekskill, came duly to hand. Your acceptance of a regiment, to be raised on continental establishment, by the state of Massachusetts Bay, is quite agreeable to me, and I sincerely wish you success in recruiting, and much honor in commanding it.

Your professions of attachment are extremely gratifying to, dear sir, your most obedient servant,

Geo. Washington."

In a letter to Congress, of December 20th, he thus speaks of Col. Putnam:

"I have also to mention, that for want of some establishment in the Department of Engineers, agreeable to the plan laid before Congress in October last, Col. Putnam, who was at the head of it, has quitted, and taken a regiment in the state of Massachusetts. I know of no other man tolerably well qualified for the conducting of that business. None of the French gentlemen, whom I have seen with appointments in that way, appear to know anything of the matter. There is one in Philadelphia who I am told is clever, but him I have not seen."

After closing his accounts as Engineer, in January, 1777, he returned to Massachusetts to recruit and fill up his regiment. In this he was quite successful. As early as May, three companies were filled, and marched from Worcester to Peekskill; and in June were ordered up the North River to Fort Ann. On the 3d of July, Col. Putnam followed with the rest of the regiment, and joined his brigade, at a point four miles above Fort Edward. This gave him an opportunity to examine the condition of the old fort which he had so often visited and worked on in the former war. He found that in the last seventeen years it had greatly decayed and was quite untenable as a work of defense; nevertheless it was shortly after occupied by the troops of Gen. Burgoyne for a few days, probably the last time the British flag will ever float near its walls.

The campaign of 1777 was big with events deeply interesting to the United States. Burgoyne with a large army had invaded New York from the north, pursuing the old route so often traversed in former years by the hostile bands of France and Great Britain. The hordes of savages which accompanied his army made the resemblance still more striking. A numerous body of men and shipping, under Clinton, assailed the same state on the south, by the way of the North River, intending to unite the invading armies at Albany, and thus divide the eastern from the middle and southern states. Ticonderoga, considered the key to the northern portion of the union, had fallen into the hands of the enemy but the lives and the liberty of the army which occupied it, were saved from the hands of the conqueror, by the good sense of Gens. St. Clair and Schuyler, who thought it useless to defend an untenable post, and thus served as a nucleus around which to rally the militia and continentals who hastened from all parts to arrest the progress of the enemy. New England was electrified at the threatened danger, and poured forth the thousands of her hardy yeomanry from her granite hills, to meet the coming storm.

Col. Putnam, with his brave Massachusetts men, again traversed the grounds he had so often visited in the "Old French War;" familiar with every part from Fort Edward to Stillwater, while few if any of his officers or men had seen this part of the country before. Although he was busily engaged in all the military operations of September, in the contests with Burgoyne, his regiment being the earliest on the ground, yet he has left no record of these events, except to correct some misstatements made by the historians of that period in relation to the storming the works of the German Reserve on the 7th of October, and a few other matters. In front of those works was an open field, bounded by a wood, at the distance of one hundred and twenty yards. In the skirt of this wood Col. Putnam was posted with the Fifth and Sixth Regiments of the Massachusetts line, under his command. Both the right and left of their work was covered by a thin, open wood, and the rear by a thick wood. The moment that orders were given to storm, he moved rapidly across the open field, amidst a murderous fire of grape and musketry, and entered the works in front, at the same moment that Learned's Brigade, in which Jackson's Regiment was stationed, entered on *the left and rear.* Col. Putnam immediately formed his two regiments, and moved out of the works, which were not enclosed in the rear, and advanced into the wood, toward the enemy's enclosed redoubts, on the right flank of their main encampment. Gen. Learned, as soon as he had secured and sent off the plunder taken in the German camp, withdrew all the other troops, without notifying Col. Putnam of his design, leaving him unprotected in the occupancy of the wood. Here he remained until toward morning, when he was reinforced with three regiments from the right wing of the army, under Gen. Glover.

The historian Marshall's account varies materially from this. He says, *"Jackson's Regiment of Massachusetts, led by Lieut. Col. Brooks, turned the right of the encampment, and stormed the works."* In this account no mention is made of Brig. Learned, who stormed at the same time with the other corps of the brigade, as well as Jackson's; nor of the two regiments under Col. Putnam, who stormed *in front,* under much greater exposure than Jackson. Again, Marshall says, *"Brooks maintained the ground he had gained;"* which is entirely contrary to the truth for, except the two regiments commanded by Col. Putnam, the troops which entered the works were in great disorder, so far as fell under his observation; nor did he see any of them formed in order for action, before he moved out with the Fifth and Sixth Regiments, as above stated.

At page 288, of the 3d volume, is a note from the historian Gordon, who says that, *"On the morning of the 11th of October, a report was spread in the American camp, and believed by the officers, that the main body of Burgoyne's army had marched away in the night for Fort Edward, leaving only a rearguard in the camp, which was to march as soon as possible, leaving only their heavy baggage. On this, it was decided to advance, and attack the camp in half an hour; and the officers repaired to their respective commands. Gen. Nixon's being the oldest brigade crossed the creek first. Unknown to the Americans, Burgoyne had formed a line behind a parcel of brushwood, to support the park of artillery, where the attack was to be made. Gen. Glover was on the point of following Nixon; just as he entered the water, he saw a British soldier malting across, whom he called and examined."* This soldier was a deserter, and communicated the important fact that the whole British army was in their encampment. Nixon was immediately stopped and the intelligence conveyed to Gen. Gates, who commanded the order for the assault and called back the troops, not without sustaining some loss from the British artillery.

Col. Putnam's account of this affair is as follows:

"Nixon's brigade was put in motion, and marched in close column to the creek, just as the fog broke away, when the whole park of British artillery opened upon us, at not more than five hundred yards distance. Finding we were halted, I rode forward to the head of the brigade, to inquire why we stood there in that exposed situation. But Nixon was not to be found, and Col. Greaton, who commanded the leading regiment, said he had no orders. I then advised the crossing the creek, and covering the troops under the bank, which was done. I then, at the request of Col. Stephens, advanced with my regiment across the plain, and posted them under cover of the bank of an old stockade fort, while Stephens advanced with two field pieces to annoy the British who were attempting to take away some baggage wagons standing about midway between us and the British battery. We remained in this situation about an hour, when I had orders to retreat and found Nixon near the church, and after some debate, obtained leave to send a party and cut away the British boats which lay above the mouth of the creek. Capt. Morse, Goodale, and Gates, with seventy or eighty volunteers, started on this service and effected it without any loss."

This plain statement puts the affair in a different position, and shows that but for the promptness and bravery of Putnam in this unexpected dilemma, the loss of the Americana must have been much greater. The bold act of cutting loose Burgoyne's store boats, in the face of his army was of his suggesting, and accomplished chiefly through the fearless activity of Capt. Goodale, who was noted for daring exploits.

Kosciusko, the philanthropic and brave Polander who volunteered his services in the cause of American freedom, was placed at the head of the Engineering Corps in Gates' army, and often consulted Col. Putnam in planning the works of defense and offense so necessary in the operations of hostile armies. He remained in the northern department until the surrender of Burgoyne which took place a few days after the last adventure, on the 16th of October; thus closing the career of this haughty Briton who fancied he could march his *invincibles* from Ticonderoga to Albany, in defiance of all the efforts of "the rebels," the common name for the Americans, and there unite his triumphant columns with those of Sir Henry Clinton. This was the most glorious event that had yet attended the arms of the United States, and infused new life into the desponding portion of the community. They learned, by actual experience, that British regulars were not invincible, while their enemies were taught to respect a foe they had heretofore despised. After the cessation of hostilities in this quarter, Nixon's Brigade, to which Col. Putnam belonged, went into winter quarters at Albany.

In January, 1778, he received a message from Gov. Clinton and Gen. Israel Putnam, requesting him to repair to West Point, and superintend the fortifications proposed to be erected at this American Gibraltar. He declined the offer unless his regiment was allowed to go with him, except at the express orders of Gen. Washington. A French Engineer had been sent by Congress to plan and execute the works proposed to be erected; but his views were not approved by Gov. Clinton and the general officers as suited to what they deemed necessary and hence arose the confusion and delay noticed in Gen. Washington's letter to Congress of the 13th of March, 1778.

In February he succeeded Col. Greaton in the command of the troops in the Northern Department, who went home on furlough. It seems that Congress, without consulting the Commander-in-Chief, had matured a plan for a winter campaign into Canada which was now left in a manner, defenseless. The chief duty of Col. Putnam was to forward provisions and military stores to Coos, on the Onion River, by which route the army of invasion was to pass, as early as the 20th of February. The sound mind of the Colonel at once perceived the fallacy and impossibility of the project. The country was covered with a deep snow and the soldiers, as usual, only half clothed, and entirely unprepared for a winter campaign. This was always a serious difficulty during the whole war; our armies were never decently clad, and the poverty of the country was seen in their tattered garments and shoeless feet. When men were required by Col. Hazelet, the Quarter-Master-General, to open a road, he had the firmness to refuse him on account of the inclemency of the weather and the destitute condition of his men.

About this time, the 10th or 12th of February, the Marquis Lafayette, who was to command the army of invasion, arrived at Albany with the Baron de Kalb. After a careful inspection of the troops he confirmed the views of Col. Putnam and the expedition was abandoned; and fortunate for the country was it that they did so, for this was not a war of offense, but of defense; and whenever the Americans left their own soil, disaster and defeat followed their steps; but so long as they confined their operations to justice and to right, the God of armies and of justice was on their side.

In March following, he was ordered with his regiment down to West Point, where his valuable services were required to lay out and superintend the construction of fortifications at that important place, and Gen. McDougal, who had been appointed to the command, arrived about the same time. Of all the foreign engineers who had been sought out and employed, not one had yet been found with the sound judgment and practical skill of this untaught American. The strong mind and calm considerate reflection of Putnam took in at once the commanding points of the positions to be fortified, and his practical skill soon accomplished what his genius had projected. He found the foreign engineers' main fort laid out on an extreme point next the river, and commanded by the adjacent high grounds. It was abandoned for this purpose and a simple battery placed there to annoy the enemy's shipping, should they attempt to turn the point and force the boom placed a little higher up. As a defense against an attack by land, a chain of forts and redoubts was laid out on the high ground bordering the plain which forms the point that gives name to the place. The principal fort was built by Putnam's own regiment and named by Gen. McDougal, "Fort Putnam." It stands on an elevated rocky eminence which commands both the plain and point. This rock slopes gradually on to the plain on one side, while to the assailants it presents a mural front of fifty feet perpendicular. It was subsequently strengthened with additional works and made a very formidable place. These defenses occupied him until June, when he joined the division of the army under Gen. Gates at Peekskill and on the 24th of July united with the grand army under Gen. Washington at White Plains. By his orders he reconnoitered the country about Fredericksburg, Quaker Hill, &c, making plans and sketches for the use of the Commander. On the 16th of September, the main army was broken into divisions and posted at different places. The division, to which he was attached under Gen. Gates, marched to Danbury, Connecticut. While here he was directed by Gen. McDougal to examine the roads and passes from New Milford, leading eastward, which service he accomplished, and made his report to him. Soon after this he received the following letter from Gen. Washington:

> *"Head Quarters, Oct. 9th, 1778.*
>
> *Sir:*
>
> *I have perused your report of this day to Gen. McDougal. You will continue your examination of the different roads, &c, reconnoiter the most convenient halting places on each; allowing the interval of one day's march from one to the other, and make report of the whole to me, that I may be enabled to regulate the different routes. The road toward Litchfield offers, from your account of it, to be worth attention, and Col. Hall should be directed to proceed on it accordingly.*
>
> *I am, sir, your obedient servant,*
>
> *G. Washington.*
>
> *Col. Putnam."*

In answer to this letter he made a lengthy and very particular report, exhibiting his tact and sound judgment in such services for which he was naturally constituted.

Previous to making the final arrangements for winter quarters, he made a tour of reconnaissance with Gen. Greene, in the vicinity of the Hudson River. Late in December Nixon's brigade took up their winter station in the Highlands, on the road from Peekskill to Fishkill. Nixon left the brigade on furlough, and it was placed under Col. Putnam for the winter. Early in February the brigade was ordered to leave their quarters. Col. Putnam's regiment was directed to march to Croton River and build a bridge across that stream, which was completed about the last of March and was all extra service for which no additional pay was given.

At this time he had a furlough to visit his family where he had not been since December, 1777. This was an inconvenience under which the most useful officers labored; they could not be spared from the service, while the less valuable procured leave of absence more readily. The families of many of the New England officers, high in command, were in poor circumstances, and required all the industry and foresight of their calculating wives to keep their families in comfortable circumstances during their absence. Mrs. Putnam and the children, the oldest not more than twelve or fourteen years, lived on a small farm of fifty acres of rather sterile land; while so poor and uncertain was the pay of the soldier and in 1779, so depreciated in value, that had it not been for the assiduous application of the needle by this patriotic woman, her children would sometimes have been very poorly supplied with food. It was common in those days which tried the souls of women as well as of men, for females in some of the best families to make garments gratuitously for the soldiers sent from their vicinity while many of them made also for their neighbors less skilled in the art, for which they received produce or continental paper in exchange. Mrs. Putnam was one of this class; and let it be remembered to her honor and praise, that she labored diligently with her hands, both at the distaff and needle, like the virtuous woman of old, for the support of her household while he who should have been their provider was absent, devoting his time to the cause of freedom and fighting the battles of his country. Many interesting anecdotes are yet remembered and related by the family of the frugality and industry practiced during this cruel war, for their support.

During his absence, Fort Fayette, on Verplank's Point, was taken by the British. It was commanded by Capt. Armstrong and surrendered to overwhelming numbers.

Toward the last of June, Col. Putnam returned to camp and in a few days received the following order from Gen. Heath:

"Highlands, Danforth's House, June 29, 1779.

Sir:

I am very desirous, if possible, to obtain the exact situation of the enemy on Verplank's Point, and of the vessels in the river. As you are well acquainted with the ground on both sides of the river, I would request that you would, tomorrow, reconnoiter the enemy with due precaution, and make such remarks as you may think proper. You will take a part, or the whole of your own light infantry company as a guard. Your knowledge of the country, and abilities, render particular instructions unnecessary.

Yours, &c,

Wm. Heath.

Col. Putnam."

To execute this order, he had to march through the mountains about twenty miles, by an unfrequented route, and to prevent discovery, conceal his men in the woods. This duty was successfully performed but the report is mislaid. Soon after his return he received the following note from his Excellency, the Commander-in-Chief:

"Col. Putnam has permission to take as many men as he chooses, of his own regiment, or any other, for special service, and to pass all guards.

G. Washington.
July 9, 1779."

The "special service" here intended, was to reconnoiter the posts on Verplank's and Stony Points previous to the meditated assault on those places. For this purpose, Col. Putnam left Constitution Island, opposite to West Point, in the afternoon of the 10th with fifty men and landed at Continental Village about sunset. Soon after dark he proceeded, by a back road, to a point near the scene of his intended observations and concealed his men as before, in the woods. In a short time it began to rain and continued all the next day, a part of which time they lay in a barn. On the 12th it was fair, but their ammunition was all wet and he retired a little distance to a deserted house, built a fire, and dried their powder which occupied nearly all day, leaving the party, had they been attacked, entirely defenseless. That evening he approached nearer the works, concealed his men and commenced reconnoitering their condition. With one or two soldiers, who were familiar with the location, he continued his labor until near morning, creeping on his hands and knees to avoid detection by the sentries when very near the works. He ascertained the time of night by the aid of fire-flies, which are abundant at that season, and whose phosphorescent light enabled him to distinguish the hours on his watch. By the approach of early dawn, he had completed his observations and returned undiscovered to camp, on the 13th. The following day, a full and very intelligent report of the service was made to Gen. Washington; a copy of which is now among his manuscripts and no doubt contributed greatly to the success of the attack on Stony Point, which immediately followed. In relation to the statement made by Marshall, that *"two brigades under the command of Gen. McDougal, had been ordered to approach the enemy on the east side of the river, &c,"*—he doubts whether such an order was ever given, for the reason that McDougal commanded the post of West Point, and would not be allowed to leave so important a station. He further says that when he waited on Gen. Washington to make his report of the reconnaissance on the 14th, he told him that he had relinquished the plan of an actual attack on Verplank's simultaneously with that on Stony Point, but intended only to make a feint; and for that purpose had ordered Nixon's brigade to march that day, to Continental Village. He then instructed Col. Putnam to take as many men from the brigade as he thought proper, and make arrangements to be on the ground, ready to fire on the enemy at Verplank's, the moment he discovered that Wayne had begun his attack on Stony Point. At the same time, he told him that no one was aware of the intended attack, but those who were entrusted with its execution, and that but one of his own family was in the secret. From some error in the orders, Nixon's brigade did not march as expected; but on the evening of the 15th, Col. Putnam left Continental Village, with Lieut. Col. Smith, and a detachment of men for Verplank's and made the feigned attack by firing on the outer blockhouse and the guard stationed at the creek, which alarmed the garrison of Fort Fayette for their own safety and prevented their turning their guns on the Americans in their attack on Stony Point. This was all that was intended to be done on that night. On the morning of the 16th, he remained in full view of the enemy until eight or nine o'clock and then returned to Continental Village. In the course of that day, Nixon's and Patterson's Brigades arrived at the village but without field pieces, artillery men, axes, or tools. About ten o'clock at night, Gen. Howe arrived and took the command. He called on Col. Putnam for information, who told him of the need of artillery, &c, to attack the blockhouse in advance of the main works, and that they could not cross the creek without rebuilding the bridge which had been destroyed. On the 17th, two twelve pounders arrived; but before any attack was made, the approach of a numerous body of the enemy for the relief the post, caused the Americans to retreat and Fort Fayette remained in the hands of the British. Stony Point was also abandoned in a short time and fell into their possession; so that no advantage was gained, but the capture of six hundred prisoners and the glory of the victory. It infused fresh spirits into the country and convinced their enemies that no danger was too great or achievement too difficult for them to overcome.

In a short time after these events, Col. Putnam was appointed to the command of a regiment of light infantry in the brigade of Gen. Wayne, composed of four regiments. This body of men was the *elite* of the army and the officers selected by the advice of Gen. Wayne, composing as efficient a corps as the world ever saw. He continued in service this year, until the army had generally gone into winter quarters, and did not reach the station in the Highlands where his regiment was cantoned, until January, 1780; marching through the ice and snow from near Newark, in New Jersey, being a very tedious and fatiguing journey. During 1779, he was ordered on extra service to erect a battery on the ground of old Fort Montgomery, for the annoyance of the enemy's ships on the Hudson; and again, in December, by order of Gen. Wayne, he reconnoitered the position of a British fleet at South Amboy, accompanied by eight dragoons, to learn the time of their sailing. This was promptly performed amidst the cold and inclemency of December weather, and returned to camp by the way of New Brunswick. A number of letters from Gen. Wayne are on his file.

The latter part of the winter 1780, he had leave of absence to visit his family, and returned to camp in April. As early as the 6th of May he was on command with an advanced detachment on Croton River, watching the movements of the enemy. This was a fatiguing, hazardous duty, requiring the utmost vigilance in the commanding officer, and is only entrusted to men of tried courage and cautious watchfulness. It is considered an honorable post, and the officer selected by special appointment of the commanding general. During the early years of the war the Americans suffered severe losses in their detachments on this service, not only at Paoli, but at various other places, from the light dragoons under Tarlton and De Lancy, who acquired great honor by their surprises of our advanced posts, although it was not a little lessened by their cruelty. The constant watchfulness of Col. Putnam saved him from any disaster of this kind as may be seen in his correspondence with Gen. Howe, which is full, minute, and voluminous, and sometimes accompanied with plans and drafts, showing the positions of the different detachments of the enemy. The following letter will serve as a specimen of his style and manner in this line:

"Callaburg, July 1, 1780.

(This was a station on the cast of the Hudson, near the Highlands.)

Dear General:

By an officer returned from scout last evening, and other intelligence, I am informed that the enemy some day this week advanced in force by land from New York, and are now encamped, having their left on the North River, one mile above Phillips', and their right on the road from Stephen Wards to Elbert's. By this position their right and left wings are about five miles distant, and from the nature and situation of the country, their camps are detached or separated; their left division being on Phillips' Hill between North River and Sawmill River; their center division on Valentine's Hill, between Sawmill River and the Braux; and their right division between the Braux and East Chester. A sketch of the country which I sent you and what I have said, will give you a correct idea of their position. It is said, and I believe it to be a fact, that a number of wagons, with scythes for cutting forage, came out yesterday. I think if it be true that a French fleet is really in the way, Mr. Clinton has come out to give his troops an airing, after their fatigue and other sufferings in a southern climate; and at the same time, has a design to secure or destroy all the forage in his power, which might otherwise be of advantage to us; and I should not be surprised if he attempted a general ravage of the country as far as Salem or Danbury.

I am, Dear General, with respect, your humble servant,

Rufus Putnam.

To Gen. Howe."

During the campaign of 1780, no great battle was fought in the northern department. The events along the North River were mostly skirmishes. An invasion of New Jersey was made in June, by Gen. Knyphausen, in which he was so valiantly opposed by the American troops, that he retired without accomplishing much but the destruction of buildings and the murder of Mrs. Caldwell, the wife of a clergyman, which foul deed was done by some of the Tory troop's of Gov. Tryon, who was in the expedition. Early in July, Sir Henry Clinton returned with his army from the conquest of Charleston, S. C, and made demonstrations of an attack on West Point, but nothing was accomplished.

In September, the foul treason of Arnold took place, by which the enemy thought to obtain possession of this important post, in a more easy way than by hard fighting, but not half so honorable. A kind Providence, which overlooked and directed the American affairs, caused this wicked plan to be discovered in time to prevent its execution; and the country was thus saved from threatened ruin. Soon after this affair, Col. Putnam had leave of absence and returned to camp early in December. On the 6th of July, 1781, the French army, which had been sent to aid us, formed a junction with the Americans near Dobb's Ferry preparatory to marching for Virginia.

On the 21st of July, Col. Putnam was ordered by Gen. Heath to take the command of a detachment of three hundred light infantry, Col. Sheldon's Legionary Corps, with two companies of the New York Levies, and one piece of light artillery, with which to cover that part of the country. On this duty he was continued until the last of October, and thus did not witness the surrender of Cornwallis at Yorktown. While here employed, he received the following letter from Gen. Waterbury, of Connecticut:

"Horse Neck, September 13, 1781.

Sir:

After my compliments, I would inform you that I have received orders from his Excellency, Gov. Trumbull, to build some places of security for my troops to winter in, and, at the same time, to ask the favor of your assistance, in counseling with me where to build, &c"

This service he performed as requested. In November, he joined his regiment at West Point, and on the 14th of that month, received the following order from Gen. McDougal:

"Sir:

Gen. McDougal requests you to repair to Stony and Verplank's Points, and examine minutely into their state in every respect. The sentry boxes at those advanced works should be destroyed; every building within cannon range of either of those posts, and any cover that would afford a lodgment for the enemy, must be taken down, and removed before you leave the ground. You will please to have the garrisons paraded, and note every person, and the regiments they belong to, unfit for this service, &c"

This duty was faithfully performed, and was about the last of his military labors; as after this period, hostilities, in a manner, closed between the two nations, in the northern states. The capture of Lord Cornwallis, and the victories of Gen. Greene in South Carolina, discouraged Great Britain from further attempts at the subjugation of the United States. He was, however, still busily employed, as agent for his brother officers, in interceding with Congress and the Legislature of Massachusetts, for a redress of their grievances, which had become very serious. For this duty, his stern integrity, candor, honesty of purpose, and well known character for usefulness in the service of the country, eminently fitted him. His first employment of this kind was in 1778, and on the following occasion:

"At a meeting of the field and other officers of Gen. Nixon's brigade, September 9, 1778, Col. Rufus Putnam was unanimously chosen representative, to meet in a general convention of the army, to state our grievances to the honorable Continental Congress, and endeavor to obtain redress of the same.

Per order of the meeting:

Thos. Nixon, Col., Moderator."

In the winter of 1778-9, the sufferings of the officers and men had become so intolerable from the want of pay, clothing, and provisions, that the patience and patriotism of even the Massachusetts men was put to so severe a trial that they had well nigh failed under it. Gen. Nixon's Brigade, then in winter quarters in the Highlands, had formed articles of mutiny, by which, on a certain day, they were to march off in a body. A copy of those articles was somehow obtained by Col. Putnam, and transmitted to Mr. Davis, a member of the Legislature and an influential man in Boston. Finding his own personal efforts and those few who assisted him, unavailing in checking this disgraceful design, Col. Putnam made a confidential communication to Gen. McDougal of their intentions, and requested him to order the several regiments composing the brigade to separate, and occupy distant and distinct posts toward New York. This the general immediately complied with and thus put it out of their power to execute the plan they had formed, or at least not so readily as they could have done, when all in a body; and thus, by the integrity and faithfulness of this honest and upright man, was this sad calamity averted; and a foul blot on the fair escutcheon of his native state prevented.

In the winter of 1780, while on a furlough, the larger portion of his time was spent in Boston, soliciting the General Court, or Legislature of Massachusetts, for relief in aid of their troops, and especially for the officers who were prisoners on Long island. For the latter a small sum was obtained, for which he received their thanks in a letter of acknowledgment, through Col. Thompson, dated May 1st, 1780. While for the officers of the line no provision was made. For this reason, at the close of the year, a committee was appointed to repair to Boston and lay their claims before the Legislature, with the following instructions, which are given, in part, that posterity may judge of the justice of their cause.

After stating a number of their grievances, as to the manner of their pay, clothing, small stores, &c, under three distinct heads, they say, *"You will pointedly represent to the Legislature, the great inconveniences and losses, accrued and accruing to great part, nay almost the whole, of both officers and soldiers, from the notes we received the last year, not being negotiable in any manner for any kind of property, on which account many were, for want of almost every kind of clothing, obliged to sell their notes at a very great discount, from their nominal value when given; and by this representation you will endeavor to procure an act that will make the notes already, and those that shall be given, a tender for the confiscated estates when sold; or that will in some way be equally beneficial to the army and state — make them of such value that those who wish it may convert them into current money without loss."*

The whole of these instructions fill two or three pages, and seem to have been signed by all the officers of the Massachusetts line. It is dated West Point, January 1st, 1781. The names of the committee were as follows: Brig. Gen. Glover, Col. Putnam, Lieut. Col. E. Brooks, Col. H. Jackson, Col. J. Graton, Maj. Samuel Darbey, S. Larned and T. Edwards.

To fulfill this embassy the committee left West Point early in January and passed two or three months in Boston, prosecuting their claims. On their arrival, the recent alarm growing out of the mutiny of the Pennsylvania and Jersey lines had created such an alarm in the minds of the General Assembly that they listened favorably to the committee and actually sent on two months' pay in specie to their line of the army, which was about the result of their efforts. It relieved their most pressing wants and pacified the distressed soldiers for a time and the favorable prospects of a speedy termination of the war closed any further serious difficulties with the Massachusetts men.

In February, 1782, the state of New York having applied to Congress for remuneration for the forage consumed by the allied army in West Chester County, while encamped near Dobb's Ferry in 1781, he was appointed by Gen. Heath and Gov. Clinton one of the commissioners for settling the claim. It was a difficult and troublesome affair but was closed in July and shows the confidence of those eminent men in his character, for sound judgment and love of justice. After this, he obtained leave of absence for a short time, and while on furlough, heard of the intention of Congress to reduce the army.

Being tired and disgusted with much of the treatment he had received in regard to promotion in the Massachusetts line, which had not been made in accordance with common usage in such matters, especially as to the brigadiers, two of which were vacant and neither of them filled, viz: Gen. Learned's in 1777, and Nixon's in 1780, added to which the desire he felt to be with his family which greatly needed his presence, he concluded to quit the service, and made an arrangement with Lieut. Col. Brooks, the youngest commander of a regiment in the line, and would of course be deranged in the reduction, to remain, and let Col. Putnam retire, a mode of exchange heretofore practiced. Under these circumstances he did not return to the army until the receipt of the following letter from Gen. Washington, who had been informed of his intentions by some of his friends.

"Head Quarters, Newburg, Dec 2, 1782.

Sir:

I am informed you have had thoughts of retiring from service, upon the arrangement which is to take place on the 1st of January. But as there will be no opening for it, unless your reasons should be very urgent indeed; and as there are some prospects which may perhaps make your continuing more eligible than was expected, I have thought proper to mention the circumstances, in expectation they might have some influence in inducing you to remain in the army. Col. Shepherd having retired and Brig. Gen. Patterson being appointed to the command of the first brigade, you will of consequence be the second Colonel in the line and have the command of a brigade, while the troops continue brigaded as at present. Besides I consider it expedient you should be acquainted, that the question is yet before Congress, whether there shall be two brigadiers appointed in the Massachusetts line. Should you continue you will be a candidate for this promotion. The secretary at war is of opinion the promotion will soon take place—whether it will or not, I am not able to determine, and, therefore, I would not flatter you too much with expectations, which it is not in my power to gratify—but if upon a view of these circumstances and prospects, the state of your affairs will permit you to continue in the present arrangement, (which must be completed immediately,) it will be very agreeable to Sir, your most obedient servant,

G. Washington.

Col. Putnam."

On the receipt of this letter, and one from Gen. Potter, he repaired immediately to camp; but being determined not to remain in a situation approaching disgrace, as some of his senior officers had done, when Congress neglected to promote them to actual vacancies, on his arrival he wrote a very interesting letter to Gen. Washington, explaining all his views and thanking him for the interest he took in his welfare, but is too lengthy for insertion here. On the 8th of January following, he was commissioned as a Brigadier General in the army of the United States, and then left without any excuse to leave the service until the declaration of peace, which happily took place on the 9th of April, 1783.

In June the Massachusetts line was reduced to two regiments of which, Gen. Patterson or the oldest officer took the command, and the officers and soldiers retired on furlough, and were finally discharged in November.

During his continuance in the army, he shared largely in the confidence of Gen. Washington, who continued his friendship during his political life, appointing him to various posts of honor and profit, as will appear in the progress of this biography.

During this year he was consulted by Gen. Washington, as to the best plan of arranging "a military peace establishment," for the United States. Into this subject he entered quite largely, drafting a system embracing about thirty manuscript pages, giving in detail the whole arrangement, and must have been quite useful to the Commander-in-Chief, in forming his final report to Congress. In it is embraced, besides the regular troops, a plan for twenty-four regiments of continental militia, selected from the several states, officered and armed like the standing troops, and ready to be called into service when needed. Also a plan for a chain of military posts, or forts, for the defense of the frontiers, in the west, one of which is at the mouth of the Muskingum and was established in 1785. And, as in case of war with Great Britain, they would probably have the ascendancy on the northern lakes, he points out the most eligible routes for supplying the posts with provisions. It is an elaborate work and displays the genius of a great and calculating mind: the original draft of which is now among his manuscript papers.

In June, 1783, before the final reduction of the army took place at New Windsor, the officers of the army, to the number of two hundred and eighty-three belonging chiefly to the northern states, petitioned Congress for a grant of land in the western country, and Gen. Putnam, in their behalf, addressed a letter to Gen. Washington on the subject, requesting his influence with Congress in the matter. It explains the views and expectations of the officers, and the good results that would accrue to the United States, in a clear and masterly manner, and being now a rare document is given in full as justly due to his character and name.

Sir:

As it is very uncertain how long it may be before the honorable Congress may take the petition of the officers of the army, for lands between the Ohio River and Lake Erie, into consideration, or be in a situation to decide thereon, the going to Philadelphia to negotiate the business with any of its members, or committee to whom the petition may be referred, is a measure, none of the petitioners will think of undertaking. The part I have taken in promoting the petition is well known, and, therefore, needs no apology, when I inform you, that the signers expect that I will pursue measures to have it laid before Congress. Under these circumstances I beg leave to put the petition in your Excellency's hands, and ask with the greatest assurance your patronage of it. That Congress may not be wholly unacquainted with the motives of the petitioners, I beg your indulgence while I make a few observations on the policy and propriety of granting the prayer of it, and making such arrangements of garrisons in the western quarter, as shall give effectual protection to the settlers and encourage emigration to the new government, which, if they meet your approbation, and the favor not too great, I must request your Excellency will give them your support, and cause them to be forwarded with the petition, to the President of Congress, in order that when the petition is taken up, Congress or their committee, may be informed on what principles the petition is grounded. I am, sir, among those who consider the cession of so great a tract of territory to the United States, in the western world, as a very happy circumstance, and of great consequence to the American empire. Nor have I the least doubt but Congress will pay an early attention to securing the allegiance of the natives, as well as provide for the defense of the country, in case of a war with Great Britain or Spain. One great means of securing the allegiance of the natives I take to be, the furnishing them with such necessaries as they shall stand in need of and in exchange receiving their furs and skins. They have become so accustomed to the use of firearms, that I doubt if they could gain a subsistence without them, at least they will be very sorry to be reduced to the disagreeable necessity of using the bow and arrow as the only means for killing their game; and so habituated are they to the woolen blanket,

&c, &c, that absolute necessity alone will prevent their making use of them.

This consideration alone is I think, sufficient to prove the necessity of establishing such factories as may furnish an ample supply to these wretched creatures: for unless they are furnished by the subjects of the United States, they will undoubtedly seek elsewhere, and like all other people, form their attachment where they have their commerce; and then in case of war, will always be certain to aid our enemies. Therefore if there were no advantages in view but that of attaching them to our interest, I think good policy will dictate the measure of carrying on a commerce with these people; but when we add to this the consideration of the profit arising from the Indian trade in general, there cannot, I presume, be a doubt that it is the interest of the United States to make as early provision for the encouragement and protection of it as possible. For these, and many other obvious reasons, Congress will no doubt find it necessary to establish garrisons at Oswego, Niagara, Detroit, Michillimackinac, Illinois, and many other places in the western world.

The Illinois, and all the posts that shall be established on the Mississippi, may undoubtedly be furnished by way of the Ohio, with provisions at all times, and with goods whenever a war shall interrupt the trade with New Orleans. But in case of a war with Great Britain, unless a communication is open between the River Ohio and Lake Erie, Niagara, Detroit, and all the posts seated on the great lakes, will inevitably be lost without such communication; for a naval superiority on Lake Ontario, or the seizing on Niagara, will subject the whole country bordering on the lakes to the will of the enemy. Such a misfortune will put it out of the power of the United States to furnish the natives, and necessity will again oblige them to take an active part against us.

Where and how this communication is to be opened, shall next be considered. If Capt. Hutchins and a number of other mapmakers are not out of their calculations, provisions may be sent from the settlements on the south side of the Ohio, by the Muskingum or the Scioto, to Detroit, or even to Niagara, at a less expense than from Albany by the Mohawk, to those places. To secure such communication, (by the Scioto, all circumstances considered, will be the best,) let a chain of forts be established: these forts should be built on the bank of the river, if the ground will admit, and about twenty miles distant from each other: and on this plan the Scioto communication will require ten or eleven stockaded forts, flanked by block-houses; and one company of men will be a sufficient garrison for each, except the one at the portage, which will require more attention in the construction, and a larger number of men to garrison it. But besides the supplying the garrisons on the great lakes with provisions, &c, we ought to take into consideration the protection that such an arrangement will give to the frontiers of Virginia, Pennsylvania, and New York. I say New York, as we shall undoubtedly extend our settlements and garrisons from the Hudson to Oswego. This done, and a garrison posted at Niagara, whoever will inspect the map must be convinced that all the Indians living on the waters of the Mohawk, Oswego, Susquehanna, and Alleghany Rivers, and in all the country south of the lakes Ontario and Erie, will be encircled in such a manner as will effectually secure their allegiance, and keep them quiet, or oblige them to quit their country.

Nor will such an arrangement of posts, from the Ohio to Lake Erie, be any additional expense; for, unless this gap is shut, notwithstanding the garrisons on the lakes, and from Oswego to the Hudson, yet the frontier settlers on the Ohio, by Fort Pitt to the Susquehanna, and all the country south of the Mohawk, will be exposed to savage insult, unless protected by a chain of garrisons, which will be far more expensive than the arrangement proposed, and at the same time the protection given to these states, will be much less complete; besides, we should not confine our protection to the present settlements, but carry the idea of extending them at least as far as the Lakes Ontario and Erie.

These lakes form such a natural barrier, that when connected with the Hudson and Ohio by the garrisons proposed, settlements in every part of the state of New York and Pennsylvania, may be made with the utmost safety; so that these states must be deeply interested in the measure, as well as Virginia, who will, by the same arrangement, have a great part of its frontier secured, and the rest much strengthened; nor is there a state in the Union, but will be greatly benefited by the measure, considered in any other point of view; for, without any expense except a small allowance of purchase-money to the natives, the United States will have within their protection, seventeen million, five hundred thousand acres of very fine land, to dispose of as they may think proper. But I *hasten to mention some of the expectations which the petitioners have, respecting the conditions on which they hope to obtain the lands. This was not proper to mention in the body of the petition, especially as we pray for grants to all members of the army, who wish to take up lands in that quarter.*

The whole tract is supposed to contain about seventeen million, four hundred and eighteen thousand, two hundred and forty acres; and will admit of seven hundred and fifty six townships, of six miles square, allowing to each township, three thousand and forty acres, for the ministry, schools, waste lands, rivers, ponds, and highways; then each township will contain, of settlers' lands, twenty thousand acres, and in the whole, fifteen million, one hundred and twenty thousand acres. The land to which the army is entitled, by the resolves of Congress, referred to in the petition, according to my estimate, will amount to two million, one hundred and six thousand, eight hundred and fifty acres, which is about the eighth part of the whole. For the survey of this, the army expect to be at no expense; nor do they expect to be under any obligation to settle these lands, or do any duty to secure their title in them; but in order to induce the army to become actual settlers in the new government, the petitioners hope Congress will make a further grant of lands on condition of settlement; and have no doubt but that honorable body will be as liberal to all those who are not provided for, by their own states, as New York has been to the officers and soldiers that belong to that state; which, if they do, it will require about eight million of acres to complete the army, and about seven million acres will remain for sale. The petitioners, at least some of them, are much opposed to the monopoly of lands, and wish to guard against large patents being granted to individuals, as, in their opinion, such a mode is very injurious to a country, and greatly retards its settlement; and whenever such patents are tenanted, it throws too much power into the hands of a few. For these and many other obvious reasons, the petitioners hope no grant will be made but by townships of six miles square, or six by twelve, or six by eighteen miles, to be subdivided by the proprietors to six miles square, that being the standard on which they wish all calculations to be made; and that officers and soldiers, as well as those who petition for charters on purchase, may form their associations on one uniform principle, as to number of persons or rights to be contained in a township, with the exception only, that when the grant is made for reward of services already done, or on condition of settlement, if the officers petition, with the soldiers, for a particular township, the soldiers shall have one right only, to a Captain's three, and so in proportion with commissioned officers of every grade.

These, Sir, are the principles which gave rise to the petition under consideration; the petitioners, at least some of them, think that sound policy dictates the measure, and that Congress ought to lose no time in establishing some such chain of posts as has been hinted at, and in procuring the tract of country petitioned for, of the natives; for, the moment this is done, and agreeable terms offered to the settlers, many of the petitioners are determined, not only to become adventurers, but actually to remove themselves to this country; and there is not the least doubt, but other valuable citizens will follow their example; and the probability is, that the country between Lake Erie and the Ohio will be filled with inhabitants, and the faithful subjects of the United States so established on the waters of the Ohio and the lakes, as to banish forever the idea of our western territory falling under the dominion of any European power; the frontiers of the old states will be effectually secured from savage alarms, and the new will have little to fear from their insults.

I have the honor to be, sir, with every sentiment, your Excellency's most obedient and very humble servant,

Rufus Putnam.

Gen. Washington."

From the suggestions in this communication of Gen. Putnam, originated the system of laying out and surveying the public lands in townships of six miles square, continued in all the surveys of United States lands to this day. The townships of six miles square, and subdivided among the proprietors, about the average size of the New England farms, as well as the provision made for the support of schools and the ministry, could only have originated with a *Puritan mind;* although the latter was confined to the Ohio Company's and Symmes' Purchase, and not adopted by Congress.

Gen. Washington, in a letter addressed to the President of Congress, advocated the measure strongly, as advantageous to the United States as well as to the petitioners. Nothing, however, was done by them in the matter as to making any additional grant for United States securities, further than that of September, 1776, and this movement was finally the origin of the Ohio Company.

After his discharge from the army in 1783, he joined his family in Rutland, Mass., where they then lived, and resumed the occupations of farming and surveying.

In April, 1784, he addressed the following letter to Gen. Washington, on the subject of the projected settlement to be made by the officers and soldiers of the army in the Ohio country, which subject seems to have entered deeply into his heart, and occupied a prominent place in his attention; he may therefore well be called the projector and father of the settlements northwest of the Ohio River.

"Rutland, April 5th, 1784.

Dear Sir:

Being unavoidably prevented from attending the general meeting of the Cincinnati at Philadelphia, as I had intended, where I once more expected the opportunity in person of paying my respects to your Excellency, I cannot deny myself the honor of addressing you by letter, to acknowledge with gratitude the ten thousand obligations I feel myself under to your goodness, and most sincerely to congratulate you on your return to domestic happiness; to inquire after your health, and wish the best of Heaven's blessings may attend you and your dear lady.

The settlement of the Ohio country, sir, engrosses many of my thoughts; and much of my time, since I left the camp, has been employed in informing myself and others, with respect to the nature, situation, and circumstances of that country, and the practicability of removing ourselves there; and if I am to form an opinion on what I have seen and heard on the subject, there are thousands in. this quarter who will emigrate to that country, as soon as the honorable Congress make provisions for granting lands there, and locations and settlements can be made with safety, unless such provision is too long delayed; I mean till necessity turn their views another way, which is the case with some already, and must soon be the case with many more. You are sensible of the necessity, as well as the possibility of both officers and soldiers fixing themselves in business somewhere, as soon as possible, as many of them are unable to lie long on their oars waiting the decision of Congress, on our petition; and, therefore, must unavoidably settle themselves in some other quarter; which, when done, the idea of removing to the Ohio country will probably be at an end, with respect to most of them; besides, the Commonwealth of Massachusetts have come to a resolution to sell their eastern country for public securities; and should their plan be formed, and propositions be made public before we hear anything from Congress respecting our petition, and the terms on which the lands petitioned for are to be obtained, it will undoubtedly be much against us, by greatly lessening the number of Ohio associates.

Another reason why we wish to know, as soon as possible, what the intentions of Congress are respecting our petition, is the effect such knowledge will probably have, on the credit of the certificates we have received on settlement of accounts: those securities are now selling at no more than three shillings and six pence, or four shillings on the pound; which, in all probability, might double, if no more, the moment it was known that government would receive them for lands in the Ohio country. From these circumstances, and many others which might be mentioned, we are growing quite impatient; and the general inquiry now is, when are we going to the Ohio? Among others, Brig. Gen. Tupper, Lieut. Col. Oliver, and Maj. Ashley, have agreed to accompany me to that country, the moment the way is open for such an undertaking. I should have hinted these things to some member of Congress, but the delegates from Massachusetts, although exceeding worthy men, and, in general, would wish to promote the Ohio scheme, yet, if it should militate against the particular interest of this state, by draining her of inhabitants, especially when she is forming the plan of selling the eastern country, I thought they would not be very warm advocates in our favor; and I dare not trust myself with any of the New York delegates, with whom I was acquainted, because that government are wisely inviting the eastern people to settle in that state; and as to the delegates of other states, I have no acquaintance with any of them.

These circumstances must apologize for my troubling you on this subject, and requesting the favor of a line, to inform us in this quarter, what the prospects are with respect to our petition, and what measures have, or are likely to be taken, with respect to settling the Ohio country.

I shall take it as a very particular favor, sir, if you will be kind enough to recommend me to some character in Congress, acquainted with, and attached to the Ohio cause, with whom I may presume to open a correspondence.

I am, sir, with the highest respect,
your humble servant,

Rufus Putnam.

Gen. Washington."

In June, he received the following reply from Gen. Washington:

"Mount Vernon, June 2d, 1784.

Dear Sir:

I could not answer your favor of the 5th of April, from Philadelphia, because Gen. Knox, having mislaid, only presented the letter to me in the moment of my departure from that place. The sentiments of esteem and friendship which breathe in it are exceedingly pleasing and flattering to me, and you may rest assured they are reciprocal.

I wish it was in my power to give you a more favorable account of the officers' petition for lands on the Ohio, and its waters, than I am about to do. After this matter, and information respecting the establishment for peace, were my inquiries, as I went through Annapolis, solely directed; but I could not learn that anything decisive had been done in either.

On the latter, I hear Congress are differing about their powers; but as they have accepted of the cession from Virginia, and have resolved to lay off ten new states, bounded by latitudes and longitudes, it should be supposed that they would determine something respecting the former, before they adjourn; and yet I very much question it, as the latter is to happen on the 3d, that is to-morrow. As the Congress who are to meet in November next, by the adjournment will be composed from an entire new choice of delegates in each state, it is not in my power, at this time, to direct you to a proper correspondent in that body. I wish I could; for persuaded I am, that to some such cause as you have assigned, may be ascribed the delay the petition has encountered; for surely, if justice and gratitude to the army, and general policy of the Union were to govern in this case, there would not be the smallest interruption in granting its request. I really feel for those gentlemen, who, by these unaccountable delays, (by any other means than those you have suggested,) are held in such an awkward and disagreeable state of suspense; and wish my endeavors could remove the obstacles. At Princeton, before Congress left that place, I exerted every power I was master of, and dwelt upon the argument you have used, to show the propriety of a speedy decision. Every member, with whom I conversed, acquiesced in the reasonableness of the petition. All yielded, or seemed to yield to the policy of it, but plead the want of cession of the land, to act upon; this is made and accepted; and yet matters, as far as they have come to my knowledge, remain in status quo."

After speaking of his own lands on the Ohio and Kanawha, he closes with,

"I am, dear sir, with very sincere esteem and regard, your most obedient servant,

G. Washington."

The project of an immediate establishment in the wilderness, northwest of the River Ohio, having failed, he, on the 2d of August of this year, left his home once more, to survey a tract of land for the state of Massachusetts, bordering on the Bay of Passamaquoddy, and returned from that service in November.

In the course of this year, the Leicester Academy, one of the earliest and most respectable in the state, was incorporated, and Gen. Putnam became one of its principal friends and benefactors; giving, for its support, one hundred pounds, or three hundred and thirty-three dollars, and thirty-three cents, a liberal sum for one in his circumstances. He was appointed one of the trustees, in company with the Hon. Moses Gill, Hon. Levi Lincoln, Joseph Allen, Seth Washburn, Samuel Baker, and several respectable clergymen of the vicinity; thus showing his regard for such institutions as would benefit his country.

In 1785, the Legislature being well satisfied with his labor, and the correct, intelligent report, made to them, of his doings in the preceding year, appointed him on the committee for the sale of their eastern lands, and also superintendent of the surveys to be made this year. In June, while he was in Boston making preparations for the voyage, he received notice of his appointment, by Congress, as one of the surveyors of their lands, northwest of the River Ohio, recently ordered to be surveyed for sale, being seven ranges of townships, immediately west of the Pennsylvania line. As he could not honorably relinquish his engagement with Massachusetts, and also wished to accept the office, he wrote to the secretary an affirmative answer, and at the same time, a letter to the Massachusetts delegation, requesting them to get Congress to appoint Gen. Tupper temporarily, in his place, until his present contract was fulfilled. This object was accomplished, and Gen. Tupper proceeded on to Pittsburg, for this purpose, in 1785. On the 14th of June, he sailed, with his company of surveyors, from Beverly, and arrived at Blue Hill on the 20th. This season was occupied in surveying the coast, islands, and towns westward of Penobscot Bay, and laid the foundation for a correct chart of that stormy seaboard. He returned late in December, and spent the winter in protracting the results of his labors, for the use of the state.

In January, 1785, a treaty was made with the Indians claiming the lands now in Ohio, at Fort McIntosh, but with conditions so repugnant to the Delawares and Shawnees, who considered themselves as cheated and deceived by the commissioners on the part of the United States, that they threatened with death any who attempted to execute the surveys, and were so manifestly hostile, that it was deemed imprudent to make the attempt, and the work was abandoned for that year.

When Gen. Tupper returned in the winter, he made a very favorable report of the fertility and beauty of the country, and as there was no expectation of Congress doing anything more favorable for the officers and soldiers of the late army than was contained in their ordinance of the 20th of May, 1785, Gen. Putnam concluded to join with Gen. Tupper in proposing an association for the purchase of lands in the western country. Accordingly on the 10th of January, 1786, after nearly a whole night spent in conferring on this momentous subject, they issued a public notice addressed to the officers and soldiers, as well as other good citizens disposed to become adventurers in the Ohio country, to meet at Boston, by delegates chosen in the several counties, on the 1st day of March, for the purpose of forming an association by the name of "The Ohio Company." From that night's conference of these two men, who had long been close and firm friends, on the 9th of January, 1786, preceded the first germ of the present great State of Ohio. A full detail of the formation and progress of the Company, will be found in "The

History of the first Settlement of Washington County, and the Transactions of the Ohio Company," a work which precedes the volume of biographies.

In March, 1786, the United States surveyors were ordered to proceed west; and as Gen. Tupper had been at very serious expense in the last year's journey, without any profit, Gen. Putnam kindly continued him as his substitute, while he occupied the summer in closing the business of the Massachusetts lands. In addition to this, he was appointed by the state a commissioner, in conjunction with Gen. Lincoln, and Judge Paine, of Wiscasset, to treat with the Penobscot Indians, which was accomplished in August and September of that year. During the severe weather of January, 1787, he joined Gen. Lincoln at Worcester, as a volunteer aid to suppress the Shay insurrection, and continued to assist him with his advice and personal presence during this trying period, until the final dispersion of the insurgents at Petersham, in February. In April he was appointed a Justice of the Peace by Gov. Bowdoin, and in May chosen by the town of Rutland, a member in the General Assembly, and attended the spring and autumn sessions of that year.

In November, 1780, the directors of the Ohio Company appointed him Superintendent of all their affairs relating to the settlement of their lands northwest of the River Ohio. The first division of their pioneers left Danvers, in Massachusetts, under the direction of Maj. Haffield White, on the 1st day of December. The second assembled at Hartford, Conn., on the 1st of January, 1788, and were led by Col. Sproat; Gen. Putnam being obliged to go by the way of the city of New York, on the business of the company. On the 24th of that month he joined the division at Swatarra Creek, Pa., which they crossed with much difficulty, on account of the ice. On that night there fell a deep snow, which blocked up the roads, and with their utmost exertions they could get their wagons no further than Cooper's Tavern, now Strawsburg, at the foot of the Tuscarawas Mountain, on the 29th of January. Here they ascertained that no one had crossed the mountains since the last fall of snow, which, with that on the ground before, made about three feet. They therefore abandoned their wagons, built four stout sledges, to which they harnessed their horses in single file, preceded by the men on foot, who broke a track for the teams, and thus, after two weeks of incessant labor, they overcame the mountain ranges, and the numerous difficulties of the way, reaching Simrel's Ferry on the Youghiogheny on the 14th of February, where they found the party under Maj. White, who arrived the 23d of January.

By the 1st of April, having completed their boats and taken in their stores of provisions, they embarked on the western waters for the mouth of the Muskingum, which place they reached on the 7th of April, and landed at the upper point, where they pitched their camp among the trees. The next day Col. Sproat and John Mathews commenced the survey of the eight-acre lots and in a few days after the city lots and streets, of the town of Marietta. On his way out, Gen. Putnam procured copies of the several treaties heretofore made with the western Indians, from which he became impressed, that they would not long remain at peace, when they saw the whites taking actual possession of the country north of the Ohio River, which had for many years been considered the boundary line between their lands and those of the United States. For this reason he directly commenced the erection of a strong garrison on the margin of the plain, near the Muskingum River, for the protection of themselves and the emigrants soon expected to follow. This fort was called "Campus Martius," and is fully described in the preceding history. The pioneers that year planted about one hundred and thirty acres of corn, on the plain back of the garrison, after girdling the trees, and depositing the seed, in the loose earth with a hoe, there being no underbrush in the forests at this period. The season was propitious, and the yield about thirty bushels to the acre. He notes, *"We had no frost until winter; I had English beans blossomed in December."* Previous to taking possession of their lands, the directors and agents of the company had no correct knowledge of the face of the country, or the quality of the soil, on the Muskingum, at and near its confluence with the Ohio, where they had determined on locating their capital, to cover, including commons, four thousand acres; and contiguous to this, to lay off one thousand lots of eight acres each, for the convenience of the proprietors.

**Campus Martius, Marietta, Ohio
in 1791**

In June, Gen. Parsons and Gen. Varnum, two of the Directors, with a sufficient number of the Agents, arrived, to form a meeting, on the 2d day of July. On examining the location of the eight acre lots, they were much disappointed to find that no one of them had drawn a lot so near the town as to make it prudent to cultivate them. To remedy this evil, they voted to divide three thousand acres of the land reserved for city commons, into three acre lots; but this unwise division did not mend the difficulty: they were still as little accommodated as before. The project of laying out eight acre lots had been opposed from the first by Gen. Putnam and a few others, who advocated the plan of laying off small farms of sixty-four acres of the best lands, to each share bordering on the Ohio or Muskingum; of which the first actual settlers might take their choice; but they were overruled and the eight acre lots having been drawn, it was too late to adopt the other plan.

In July, Gov. St. Clair arrived, and a code of laws for the government of the territory promulgated. In September the Court of Common Pleas and Quarter Sessions held their *first* session. Of the latter Gen. Putnam was the presiding officer, and gave the charge to the Grand Jury, in a very appropriate and impressive manner. It was an august and ever-to-be-commemorated occasion — the first opening of the halls of civil justice in a region destined to be filled with millions of happy human beings. Much to the credit of the moral and peaceful habits of the first settlers of Ohio, no suit of a civil or criminal kind was entered on the docket of the session.

In the course of the year 1788, in addition to the first forty-eight who landed on the 7th of April, there arrived eighty-four men, with several women and children, embracing fifteen families, making at its close nearly two hundred souls; and let it be remembered that at the beginning of the year 1789, there was not a single white family within the present bounds of Ohio, but those in this settlement. Col. Harmar and many of his officers were proprietors in the Ohio Company. Judge Symmes passed down the Ohio during the summer, to his purchase, with a few families, but they spent the winter in Kentucky. The directors and agents early saw the necessity of providing some way to furnish actual settlers not proprietors, with lands, for the prosperity of the settlement. Emigrants were constantly passing down the Ohio River for Kentucky, many of whom were desirous of settling in the Ohio Company's purchase, if they could get lands. For this reason they resolved to donate one hundred acres from each share of land, to any actual settler who would take possession thereof; and a committee was appointed to reconnoiter the purchase, and select suitable spots for the settlements.

In 1789, the additions to the colony were one hundred and fifty-two men, and fifty-seven families, and settlements were commenced at Belpre, Waterford and Wolf Creek Mills. In this year Gen. Putnam was appointed, by the Governor, Judge of Probate, for the county of Washington. The insignia on his seal of office was a *balance;* an emblem of the exact justice that ever balanced his own mind.

In 1790, he was commissioned as a Judge of the United States Court, filling the place on the bench made vacant by the death of Gen. Parsons. In November of this year, he removed his family to Marietta, consisting of his wife, six daughters, two sons, and two grandchildren. During the autumn the French emigrants, nearly four hundred in number, arrived, and he was at a good deal of expense, on account of Mr. Duer, of New York, in erecting houses and supplying them with provisions, which was never repaid.

Wolf Creek Mills 1789

On the 2d of January, 1791, the Indians made their first hostile movements on the settlements of the company, sacking and destroying the station at Big Bottom, killing fourteen persons, and carrying five others into captivity. The troops had been withdrawn from Fort Harmar, in the unfortunate expedition into the country of the Shawnees, who were greatly exasperated, instead of humbled thereby; and now with the other tribes who sided with them, threatened the destruction of the new establishments on the Ohio and Muskingum. By the return of the muster rolls of the militia at the time, it appears that the whole force amounted to two hundred and fifty men, to which may be added thirty-seven old men and civil officers all that could be mustered for the defense of the three settlements. In this trying emergency, the wisdom and experience of Gen. Putnam were found to be of the utmost value. He, with the other old officers of the Revolution, devised the plan of erecting strong garrisons at Belpre and Waterford, while those at Marietta were strengthened with additional works; to all which the Ohio Company lent their ready assistance, and during the four years of the war expended above eleven thousand dollars of their money in provisions, pay, clothing, &c, for the militia, which was never repaid by the United States, although rightly and justly due them. The plan of appointing a company of Rangers to scour the woods in the vicinity of the stations, was the suggestion of Gen. Putnam, who had seen the wisdom of the system in the old French war, and was one of the principal causes of so little loss by the colonists. The principal events of the war are detailed in the History of Washington County, and will not be recapitulated here.

In May, 1792, while in Philadelphia, on business for the Ohio Company, he was appointed by the senate a Brigadier General in the army of the United States, at the suggestion of his old and firm friend, Gen. Washington. This appointment he accepted with great reluctance, as appears by his letter to the Secretary of War.

In a few days after, he received his instructions from the secretary; one of the first duties of which was *"to attempt to be present at the general counsel of the hostile Indians, about to be assembled on the Miami River of Lake Erie, in order to convince them of the humane disposition of the United States; and thereby to make a truce or peace with them."* He arrived at Pittsburg on his way home, the 2d of June, and on the 5th sent a speech to the hostile tribes, by two Munsee Indians who had been taken prisoners, and whom he released for that purpose.

The purport of the speech was to notify them of the object of his mission, and *"to request them to open a path to Fort Jefferson, where he expected to arrive in about twenty days; and that they should send some of their young men, with Capt. Hendricks, to conduct him with a few friends to the place they should name for their meeting."*

From unexpected delays, he, however, did not arrive at Fort Washington, or Cincinnati, until the 2d of July, where he learned that on the very day he had sent word to the Indians he should be at Fort Jefferson, a body of one hundred Indians, dressed in white shirts, and their leader with a scarlet coat, attacked a party of whites who were making hay in a meadow near the fort, and killed and carried into captivity sixteen men. From the extraordinary dress of these Indians, there is reason to suppose they were sent out, or at least furnished with their clothing, by the British agent at their post on the Miami, for the express purpose of decoying and taking off Gen. Putnam, which was further strengthened soon after by the murder of Col. Hardy and Col. Trueman, who had been sent out with flags of truce, and were to have accompanied him, but the providential delays of the journey prevented his being killed or captured with them. From these events and other circumstances, he became satisfied that the grand counsel were determined on war, and therefore it was useless to make any further efforts to induce them to treat of peace at present.

By a letter from Maj. Hamtramck, at Post Vincent, he was led to believe that the Wabash, and more western tribes, would listen to his proposals of peace. He, therefore, on the 24th, sent a speech to all the western tribes, inviting them to meet him in council, at Post Vincent, on the 20th of September; assuring them that he should bring their friends and relatives with him, now prisoners at Fort Washington. On the 16th of August, he left that post, in his twelve-oared barge, under the escort of Capt. Peters, with two Kentucky boats, the Indian prisoners, sixty in number, with goods, provisions, &c, intending to ascend the Wabash in pirogues. He reached the mouth of that stream in about eighteen days, being retarded by the low stage of the water. Here he met a guard of fifty-one men, and four pirogues, with each a French voyageur, to conduct him to Post Vincent, sent on by Maj. Hamtramck, the commander of the post, where they arrived on the 13th of September. At the time he left the falls of Ohio, a large drove of cattle was sent across the country, under an escort from Fort Steuben, which stood at the head of the falls, intended to supply food for the Indians at the treaty, who were expected to number seven or eight hundred. The commandant at Vincennes had sent the commissioner's speech, of the 24th of July, to all the tribes on the Wabash, of which, he received notice, by letter of the 31st of August; and the prospect of a full attendance at the treaty was very nattering. A regular correspondence was kept up with Gen. Wayne and Gen. Wilkerson, some of which letters are very interesting, detailing the progress of events on the frontiers. One from Wilkerson, of the last of September, gives an account of a reconnaissance, just made by him, to the outposts on the Miami and heads of the Wabash, across the battle ground of Gen. St. Clair, where he found two brass field pieces, left on the field by the Indians.

The treaty was opened on the 25th of September and concluded on the 27th; and was strictly a treaty of peace and amity, between eight of the Wabash tribes and the United States. It was signed by thirty-one of their kings, chiefs, and warriors. It contained seven articles; the purport of which was, that these tribes were taken into the protection of the United States, who warranted to them, the peaceable possession of their lands, and promised never to take them from them, without their consent and a just equivalent paid therefore. Perpetual peace was to be maintained between the contracting parties. All the white prisoners and

Negroes in their possession were to be delivered up at Fort Knox, or Vincennes, as soon as possible; and they promised to cease from stealing negroes and horses from the whites. It was witnessed by the officers of the post, and the interpreters William Wells, Rene Codine, and the Rev. John Heckewelder, who accompanied Gen. Putnam in his journey from Marietta, and was well known to many of the tribes.

In the journal of the proceedings, several of the speeches of the chiefs are given; some of which are quite sensible, but none of them equal to those made at the treaty of Greenville, in 1795, by the Shawnees, Pottawatomie, and Wyandots. Turkey, a Wyandot, said, *"I now tell you, that no one in particular can justly claim this ground; it belongs in common to us all; no earthly being has an exclusive right to it. The Great Spirit above is the true and only owner of this soil; and He has given us all an equal right to it."* He also said, *"We will offer our acknowledgments to the Great Spirit; for, it is Him alone who has brought us together, and caused us to agree in the good works which have been done,"* referring to the treaty. The New Corn, a Pottawatomie chief, and an old man, spoke at this treaty, and at the close, said, *"My friends, I am old but I shall never die. I shall always live in my children, and children's children."* A beautiful sentiment and worthy of the best days of Socrates. These few brief specimens of their speeches are given to show that they are not destitute of native genius, brilliant thoughts, and just sentiments.

The treaty accomplished by Gen. Putnam was of essential benefit to the country; as it neutralized, and detached a large body of warriors from the hostile tribes, who lived near to the borders of Kentucky, and thus lessened the strength of our enemies. There were in attendance at the treaty, six hundred and eighty-six men, women and children; two hundred and forty-seven of which were warriors. After its close, a large quantity of clothing and ornaments was distributed amongst them, which served to confirm their good intentions. On the 16th of September, nine days before the opening of the treaty, he issued a proclamation, reminding the inhabitants of Post Vincennes of the law prohibiting the sale of spirituous liquors to the Indians; and forbid any one, whether licensed or unlicensed, from selling any during the continuance of the treaty. This was a wise precaution; as when under the influence of its insane effects, no good could have been accomplished with the Indians.

On the 8th of October, the inhabitants of the town made a written address to Gen. Putnam, through Maj. Vanderburgh, in which they congratulate and thank him, for the happy manner in which he had accomplished the treaty of peace, with a part of the hostile tribes, and the benefits which would result to the inhabitants of that territory, from it. Amongst other things, they say, *"Your happy success in this arduous enterprise affords another proof, how much you merit the honors which government has conferred upon you, and will remain a memento of the justice of Congress, and of your integrity, to the latest times."* It was signed by Paul and Pierre Gamelin, and the principal French and English inhabitants of the place, and remains a memorial of their gratitude. To this, he returned a polite answer; and among other things, says, *"It must give a man of sensibility, peculiar pleasure, to find that his manner of treating the Indians meets the approbation of a people so long acquainted with their customs and manners;"* and closes with wishing them happiness and prosperity, *"under a wise administration and the blessings of peace."*

Amidst all this complication of business, he was suffering with severe illness, an attack of intermittent fever of the tertian type, on the 25th of September, the first day of the treaty. This continued to harass him until the 6th of October. On the 29th of September, ten of the Indian chiefs, who he had invited to visit their father, the President of the United States, left Post Vincent, under charge of Lieut. Prior and Mr. Heckewelder, who accompanied them as far as Marietta.

On the 10th of October, Gen. Putnam left the post, by water, being yet weak and feeble. From sickness and various delays, he did not reach his home until the 18th of December. On the way up, he encamped one night in company with some hunters, who had a full supply of bear and other wild meat. This was cooked in their camp-kettle, hunter fashion. Of this, he ate very freely, contrary to the advice of his physician, who had forbidden animal food; and ascribed his recovery to that night's repast, as from that hour, his health was rapidly restored, and ague subdued. As soon as he was able to travel on horseback, he set out for Philadelphia, to make his report to the Secretary of War, Henry Knox. Soon after this, he resigned his commission of Brigadier-General, he being unfit for actual service, and not wishing to retain an office, the duties of which he could not fulfill with benefit to the government. On the 15th of February, the Secretary of War addressed to him the following:

"War Department, Feb. 15th, 1793.

Sir:

Your letter of yesterday has been submitted to the President of the United States — while he accepts your resignation, he regrets that your ill health compels you to leave the army, as he had anticipated much good to the troops, from your experience as an officer. He has commanded me to tender you his thanks, for the zeal and judgment manifested in your negotiation with the Wabash Indians, and your further endeavors toward a general pacification. I am, sir, with great esteem, your obedient servant,

H. Knox,
Secretary of War.

Brig. Gen. Rufus Putnam."

In May, 1793, he was appointed by the directors of the Ohio Company, Superintendent of the surveys of one hundred thousand acres of land, donated by Congress to actual settlers, in the purchase, in lots of one hundred acres to each man, on the 21st of April, 1792. For the encouragement of settlers, the surveys were actually begun and carried on in certain allotments, on and near the Muskingum, in the midst of the war, and it was so ordered that no accident befell the surveyors from the Indians, although constantly liable to their attacks.

In 1794, a more safe and effectual mode of conducting the intelligence between the army assembling on the frontiers and the seat of government, than that by express through Kentucky and Carolina, or the chance and uncertain one by travelers up and down the river, had to be devised. Col. Pickering, the Post Master General, proposed that of sending the mails by water, in packet boats, which was submitted to Gen. Putnam, for his advice. He soon arranged a plan that was adopted, of light boats, manned with five men each, to run from Wheeling to Limestone, with regular relays, and stations of exchange, one of which was Marietta. This system was put under the superintendence of Gen. Putnam, and found on experience to be very useful, safe, and expeditious. A full account of which is given in the History of Washington County.

In 1795, he was appointed by Mr. Walcott, Secretary of the Treasury, to arrange the distribution and survey of the twenty-four thousand acres of land given by Congress to the French settlers at Gallipolis which tract is known by the name of the "French Grant." The President also, through Mr. Walcott, confided to him the superintendence of the laying out a national road, located by Ebenezer Zane, from Wheeling in Va., to Limestone in Ky.

In October, 1796, he was commissioned by the President Gen. Washington, Surveyor-General of the United States Lands — a post of great responsibility; requiring a thorough knowledge of the principles of surveying, and the higher branches of mathematics, astronomy, &c, to be able to detect any errors that might arise in the returns, of the field notes, plats, &c, of the subordinate surveyors. It also required great industry and constant vigilance, in attending to the duties of the office, which embraced large tracts of country in the Northwest Territory, now first ordered to be surveyed. The lands granted to the officers of the army for military services were surveyed under his direction, and platted by himself. In this map the width of the streams is given, as well as their direction. The tract contains one hundred and seventy-four townships or sections, of five miles square, in twenty ranges. The lands given to the Moravian Indians, at Schoenbrunn, Gnadenhutten and Salem, lie in this tract. This office he continued to hold, with great credit to himself, and entire satisfaction of the government, until September, 1803, when Mr. Mansfield was appointed to his place, by Mr. Jefferson.

Mr. Jefferson, in his reply to a remonstrance of the New Haven merchants, for some of his removals in that place, says, *"How are vacancies to be obtained? Those by death are few: by resignation none. Can any other mode than removal be proposed? I shall proceed with deliberation, that it may be thrown as much as possible on delinquency, oppression, intolerance, and anti-revolutionary adherence to our enemies."* And yet he was well known to have turned out some of the firmest Whigs of the Revolution. Gen. Putnam consoled himself under this mortifying act, by saying, *"I am happy in having my name enrolled with many others who have suffered the like political death, for adherence to those correct principles and measures, in the pursuance of which our country rose from a state of weakness, disgrace, and poverty, to strength, honor, and credit."*

In 1798, he devised a plan for erecting a building, by a company of proprietors, for the purposes of education, to be called the "Muskingum Academy," which is believed to have been the first in the state, for branches of learning higher than those taught in common schools. The stock amounted to one thousand dollars, of which he was one of the principal owners. A building was put up in front of the large Commons on the Muskingum, which continued to be occupied for the purposes of education for more than twenty years. It also served for a place of public worship until the year 1808, for the First Congregational Society, who were the principal owners.

In 1801, he was appointed by the Territorial Legislature, one of the Trustees of the Ohio University, established at Athens, and spent a great deal of time in bringing the lands for its support into available use; and in forming rules and regulations for the government of the college. It was a subject in which he felt the deepest interest, and had been one of the principal movers of the plan, appropriating two full townships of land for its support, in the purchase made by the Ohio Company from Congress in 1789. This land, be it remembered, *was not a gift of the United States,* but a part of the contract made in the bargain by the agents of the company with the Board of the Treasury. The endowment of this institution, and seeing it put in actual operation, were subjects which lay near his heart, and which he lived to see fulfilled, and a number of young men, now among the most eminent in the state, there educated and receive literary degrees.

In 1802, he was elected by the citizens of Washington County, then embracing a large territory, a member of the convention to form a constitution for the State of Ohio. It was an arduous and difficult labor, in which many conflicting views were to be harmonized, but was finally completed in the best manner the period and times would allow. A history of the parties, and the secret springs put in motion during the formation of this important document, which was to shape the destiny of future millions, for weal or woe, would now be a narrative of peculiar interest, and may be expected from the pen of one the few remaining living members of that convention, in an article for the Historical Society of Ohio.

In January, 1806, the Rev. Samuel Priuce Robbins was settled as pastor over the church and congregation of which he was a member. In 1807, he drafted the plan of a large frame building for a church, which was executed under his superintendence, the funds being raised by the more wealthy members of the society and his own liberal subscription, amounting to fifteen hundred dollars. It was finished and occupied in 1808, and yet remains a monument of his devotion and zeal to the cause of religion. Thirty of the pews were reserved by him, and in his will, the annual rents devoted to the support of the pastor, and a Sunday School equally divided between them. In his latter years, when he had retired from the active pursuits of life, his mind was much occupied in devising plans for the promotion of the gospel. In 1812, he was deeply engaged with several others in forming a Bible Society, the first that was organized west of the mountains, and subscribed very liberally for its support. It has continued to flourish until this day, and has been the means of spreading that blessed book amongst thousands of the destitute in this, and the adjacent counties.

A correspondence, by letters, was kept up with his old associates of the Revolutionary War, and in one of the letters from Gov. Strong of Massachusetts, in 1812, he writes, *"By your letter, I am convinced that your sentiments with regard to the present war are similar to my own. Your old acquaintances, Gen. Brooks, (afterward Gov. of Massachusetts,) and Gen. Cobb, are of the council. I read to them your letter, and they expressed in the warmest terms their friendship and respect for you."* Such manifestations of the regard and friendship of his early associates, served to animate and warm his heart, as old age approached, and console him for the great political changes which were continually going on.

In his religious character, he was equally faithful and energetic, as in his military and civil. In the year 1816, a gentleman removed to Marietta from Massachusetts, who had been engaged as a teacher in Sunday Schools, and well acquainted with conducting those seminaries of good principles, in which that state was ever foremost. At that period it was a new thing in the west, and none were in operation in the valley of the Ohio. Gen. Putnam was quite anxious to have one established in Marietta, and made many inquiries of the teacher as to the manner of conducting them. After one of these interviews, he sent for him one day, and related to him a dream he had the night before. He thought he was standing by a window in a large public building, and saw a procession of children neatly clad, approaching with music. He asked a bystander the meaning of the show who answered, *"These are the children of the Sabbath School."* After this relation he remarked to the teacher that he thought he should live to see the dream fulfilled. The following spring, a Sabbath School was commenced in the Muskingum Academy, and continued through the summer. The next year, or in 1818, three schools were opened in different parts of the town. In the autumn, when the time for closing them arrived, they then being laid aside in the winter, the three schools were assembled at the Academy, and a procession formed, which marched from that building on to the bank of the Muskingum, and thence to the Congregational Church. As the teacher before mentioned, they entered the house. Gen. Putnam was standing at the window from which he had viewed the approach of the procession and as the tears flowed from his eyes, exclaimed *"Here is the fulfillment of my dream!"*

In the spring of 1820, a revival of religion commenced in Marietta, and frequent evening meetings were held for prayer, but being very old and infirm, he was unable to attend them. A friend remarked to him that he supposed it was a source of regret to him, that he could not meet with them at this interesting period. *"I do meet with you,"* was his prompt reply; meaning by this, as was afterward ascertained, that he spent the whole time of the meeting in his closet, engaged in secret prayer.

About the year 1821, a company of missionaries from New England, arrived at Marietta, on their way to the Osage Indians. Two young ladies, who stayed with Mr. William Slocomb, expressed a strong desire of seeing Gen. Putnam, and he accompanied them to his house. After many inquiries as to the prospects of the mission, and expressing his ardent desire for its success, he abruptly asked them if they had any fresh meat on board their boat. Finding they had none, he turned to Mr. Slocomb and said, *"I now see through the whole mystery; I have an ox that has been fatting for more than a year, and for several months past have tried to sell him, but could not. I now understand the reason: the Lord has designed him for this mission family. I will have him killed and dressed by eight o'clock in the morning, and do you have barrels and salt ready at the boat, for packing what cannot be used fresh."* All was done as he directed.

For some time before his death, being unable to attend public worship, a duty he had never failed to perform, in all weather, while able to walk that distance, it was his weekly practice to rehearse in his own mind, the articles of the Assembly's Shorter Catechism, lest from not hearing the preached word, he might lose sight of the great principles and doctrines of the Christian religion; a practice well worthy the attention of modern professors. Many other examples might be given of his devotion to the cause of religion, but these will suffice to show his habitual feelings on this momentous subject.

He lost his excellent and faithful wife in the year 1820; but his last years were made comfortable and happy by the unremitting and affectionate attention of his pious maiden daughter, Elizabeth.

His final departure was like that of the righteous, and his last end full of hope and heavenly consolation. Although he was for many years the master of a lodge of Masons, to which he became attached during the war, yet he enjoined it upon his son, as one of his last orders, that his burial should be conducted without any of the forms and ceremonies common at the funerals of those the world calls great, but in the most simple manner ever practiced on these occasions; choosing rather to be buried as a humble follower of Christ, than with the showy forms of military or Masonic pageantry. He died in May, 1824, in the eighty-seventh year of his age.

In person, Gen. Putnam was tall, nearly six feet; stout and commanding: features strongly marked, with a calm, resolute expression of countenance, indicating firmness and decision, so peculiar to the men who figured in the American Revolution: eyes grey, and one of them disfigured by an injury in childhood, which gave it an outward, oblique cast, leaving the expression of his face strongly impressed on the mind of the beholder. His manner was abrupt, prompt, and decisive; a trait peculiar to the Putnam family, but, withal, kind and conciliating. In conversation, he was very interesting; possessing a rich fund of anecdote, and valuable facts in the history of men and things with which he had been familiar; delivered in a straightforward, impressive manner, very instructive and pleasant to the hearer. The impress of his character is strongly marked on the population of Marietta, in their buildings, institutions, and manners; so true it is, that new settlements, like children, continue to bear through life, more or less, the impressions and habits of their early childhood.

Chapter II
ABRAHAM WHIPPLE

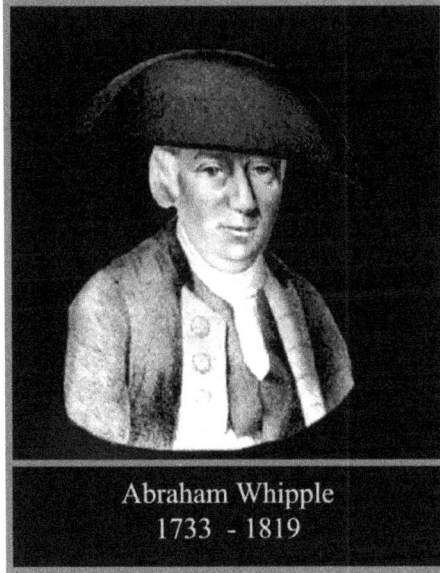

Abraham Whipple
1733 - 1819

Abraham Whipple was a descendant of John Whipple, one of the original proprietors of the Providence Plantations, and associate of Roger Williams, who is considered the founder of the colony. He was born in Providence, Rhode Island, in the year 1733.

His early education was very imperfect; but possessing a naturally strong mind, and great resolution of purpose, he acquired in the course of the sea-faring life which he followed at an early period, sufficient knowledge of navigation, and the keeping accounts, to conduct the command of vessels in the West India trade, with credit to himself and profit to his employers. The intercourse of the colonists was restricted by Mother Britain to that of her own possessions, with an exception in favor of the Dutch port of Surinam on the main, and the Danish island of St. Croix. This business he followed for many years previous to the war of the Revolution, and several letters from Nicholas Brown, one of the earliest merchants of Providence, and in whose employ he sailed, are on file amongst his papers, containing instructions for the conduct of the voyage. Toward the close, of the old French war, after the king of Spain had taken up arms against England, he was employed as the commander of a privateer called the "Game Cock".*

*The following notice of an early cruise of Com. Whipple was procured for me by my friend Dr. P. G. Robbins, of Roxbury, from an old file of the Boston Postboy and Advertiser, of February 4th, 1760, now in the Historical Society Room, at Boston.

"Last Tuesday returned to Providence, after a successful cruise, Capt. Abraham Whipple, of the Game Cock privateer; who sailed from this place on the 19th of July last, having taken in said cruise, twenty-three French prizes, many of which were valuable. Capt. W. on his passage home on the 26th of January spoke with Capt. Robert Brown, in a sloop from Monte Cristo, bound to New York, in lat. 39 deg. 30 min., and long. 72 deg. 40 min. in great distress for want of water and provisions, which he generously supplied him."

During the cruise he captured a valuable Spanish ship, by running alongside, and carried her by boarding without much resistance.

It was during this period of his early life that the following event took place, while in the southerly portion of the Gulf of Mexico, on his return from a West India voyage, in a large armed ship or letter of marque, the larger portion of whose guns, however, were of wood, technically called "Quakers". In a severe gale, he was obliged to throw overboard a part of his armament, especially a number of his metal guns, leaving him in quite a defenseless condition. Soon after this event a French privateer appeared in chase. She was full of men, as he ascertained by his telescope, and far outnumbered him in guns; although but for the late disaster, as his ship was much the largest, and pretty well manned, he might have made a stout defense, but under present circumstances his only chance for escape was by flight. Capt. Whipple, after sailing as close to the wind as possible, and trying the speed of the enemy on that course, found him constantly gaining on him, and that his hope of safety must rest on a *ruse de guerre*, in which he was always ready. He directed his sailors to set up a number of handspikes, with hats and caps on them, looking at a distance like men at their stations ready for action, which, in addition to his actual crew, appeared quite formidable. Being to the windward of the enemy, he directed the man at the wheel to put the ship about, and bear down directly upon him, showing his broadside of Quaker guns and deck full of men to great advantage. The privateer was taken all aback; and thinking the former attempt at flight only a stratagem to entice her within reach of her shot, instantly put about, and with all haste escaped from her cunning antagonist. Capt. Whipple kept on the chase until the privateer had run nearly out of sight, when, with a shrug of the shoulder, and a hearty laugh at the success of his stratagem, he ordered the steersman to up helm, and bear away on the proper course for his destined port.

His ready and prompt mind was never at a loss for expedients in all such emergencies, and generally succeeded in turning them to his own advantage, as will be seen in his afterlife. This exploit gained him a good deal of credit with his townsmen, and was doubtless the reason of his being selected a few years after to command the company of volunteers who captured and burnt the British schooner "Gaspe", the tender of a ship-of-war, stationed in Narragansett bay, to enforce the maritime laws. These restrictions had become very odious and unpopular to the inhabitants of Newport and Providence: the "Gaspe" especially, commanded by Lieut. Buddington, of the navy, with a crew of twenty-seven men, had become the terror of all the shipping entering these ports; not only by overhauling their cargoes, and confiscating the goods, but by pressing the men into the British service. At this time, the commerce of Newport and Providence together, exceeded that of New York, whose retail traders often visited the former town, to purchase dry goods and other merchandise of the importers, as the smaller cities now visit New York. Newport, next to Boston, owned a larger number of vessels than any other port on the coast. The attempts of the king and parliament of Great Britain to enforce the old navigation act, with the stamp act, duties on tea, and quartering large bodies of troops on the colonists, to tame them into obedience, only served to rouse their jealousy, and excite their disgust. While the inhabitants were filled with fears of coming evils, and the public mind roused up to resistance, an event took place in the waters of Rhode Island, which may be considered as the *"overt act,"* to the Revolution which soon followed.

On the 17th of June, 1772, a Providence packet, that plied between New York and Rhode Island, named the "Hannah", and commanded by Capt. Linsey, hove in sight of the man-of-war, in her passage up the bay. She was ordered to bring to, for examination; but Linsey refused to comply; and being favored with a fresh southerly breeze that was fast carrying him out of gunshot of the ship the tender was signaled to follow. In pursuing the chase, the "Gaspe" was led on to a shoal, which puts out from Nanquit Point, but which the lighter draught of the "Hannah" enabled her to pass in safety. The tender here stuck fast; and as the tide fell, she careened partly on to her side. The packet reached Providence before dark, and soon spread the news of the chase, and the helpless condition of the hated "Gaspe". A muster of the sailors and sea-faring people soon followed; who, after choosing Capt. Whipple for their leader, embarked, to the number of sixty, in eight row-boats. The men were without arms, excepting one musket, which was shipped without Whipple's consent, as he intended no harm to the crew, unless opposed by force, but only to board the vessel, land the crew, and then set her on fire. They, however, put into each boat a large quantity of pebble stones, intending them as articles of offense, if necessary. As they approached the schooner, about two o'clock in the morning, they were hailed by the sentinel, and asked, *"Who commands them boats?"* Whipple instantly answered, *"The Sheriff of the county of Kent; and, I come to arrest Capt. Buddington!"* The Captain was by this time on deck, and warned the boats not to approach; which they not heeding, he fired his pistol at them; at this moment, a boy who had possession of the musket, discharged it, and wounded the Captain in the thigh; a volley of pebbles followed the discharge, and Whipple, at the head of his men, boarded the schooner, driving the crew below. After securing them, they were taken on shore, and the "Gaspe" burnt. The party returned in triumph to Providence, and knowing that their conduct amounted to treason against the king, no one said anything about it; and, although the secret was confided to not less than sixty persons, so deep was the hatred and indignation of the people, that no one disclosed it, or let any hint drop that could be used as proof against their companions. This bold step naturally excited great indignation in the British officers, and all possible means were taken to discover the offenders. Wanton, the colonial Governor of Rhode Island, issued his proclamation, offering a reward of one hundred pounds sterling, for the discovery of any of those concerned. Soon after, the King's proclamation appeared, offering one thousand pounds for the man who called himself the High Sheriff, and five hundred pounds for any other of the party; with the promise of a pardon should the informer have been one of the party. But notwithstanding these tempting offers, so general was the dislike of the community to their oppressors, and their patriotism so true, that *"no evidence was ever obtained, sufficient to arraign a single individual; although a commission of inquiry, under the great seal of England, sat in*

Newport from January to June, during the year 1773." (Cooper's Naval History.) Capt. Whipple, however, soon after sailed on a trading voyage to the West Indies, and did not return until 1774, when the event was in a manner forgotten.

In the meantime, aggressions and restrictions were heaped on the colonists, until they became insupportable, and reaction began to take place. After the Boston Port Bill was passed, by which the commerce of that flourishing town was entirely destroyed, as an offset for the destruction of the tea chests of the East India Company, resistance became more open, especially subsequent to the passage of the act prohibiting the exportation of military stores from England to the colonies. Fully aware of the approaching contest, and the destitute condition of the inhabitants of the materials for resistance, they began, in many places, to seize upon the military stores of the Crown. Every garrison, fort and magazine, being in possession of the King's officers, and many of the inhabitants destitute of arms, and still more so of ammunition, it was absolutely necessary to resort to violence for the purpose of arming themselves. At Portsmouth, N. H., a quantity of powder was taken from the castle in the harbor, and the citizens of Providence seized on twenty-six guns at Fort Island, and carried them up to their town. It was to destroy a magazine of provisions and other stores, collected by the inhabitants for the coming contest, at Concord, Mass., that the British made their celebrated inroad on the 19th of April, 1775; and the war fairly opened by the slaughter of the militia at Lexington. From this point, the spirit of resistance flew, like an electric shock, from heart to heart, until it pervaded the land.

The little colony of Rhode Island, ever foremost in the cause of liberty, within one year and one month after the bloodshed at Lexington, renounced their allegiance to the King of Great Britain by a solemn act of their Legislature; thus preceding, by two months, the Declaration of Independence by the Congress of the assembled colonies. This simple, but resolute document ought to be preserved in letters of gold. It is styled, *"An Act of May, 1776, renouncing allegiance to the King of Great Britain;"* and thus proceeds:

"Whereas in all states existing by compact, protection and allegiance are reciprocal; the latter being only due in consequence of the former: and whereas George the Third, King of Great Britain, forgetting his

dignity, regardless of the compact most solemnly entered into, ratified and confirmed to the inhabitants of this colony, by his illustrious ancestors, and till of late, fully recognized by him; and entirely departing from the duties and character of a good king, instead of protecting, is endeavoring to destroy the good people of this colony, and of all the united colonies, by sending fleets and armies to America, to confiscate our property, and spread fire, sword, and desolation throughout our country, in order to compel us to submit to the most debasing and detestable tyranny; whereby we are obliged by necessity, and it becomes our highest duty, to use every means with which God and nature have furnished us, in support of our invaluable rights and privileges, to oppose the power which is exerted for our destruction."

They then go on to repeal a certain act of allegiance to the King, then in force, and to enact a law, whereby, in all commissions of a civil or military nature, the name of the King shall be omitted, and that of the Governor and company of the English colony of Rhode Island and Providence Plantations, substituted in its place; and in all oaths of office, the officers shall swear to be faithful and true to the colony.

Moved by the same feelings which produced this declaration in 1776, the Legislature, in June, 1775, two days before the Battle of Bunker hill, purchased and armed two sloops, one of twelve, and the other of eight guns, appointing Capt. Whipple to the command of the larger, and Capt. Grimes to the smaller, who was to act under the orders of Whipple. The larger vessel was named the "Providence". The object of this armament was to clear the bay of the British tenders to the frigate "Rose", under the command of Sir James Wallace, who blockaded the mouths of the harbors and rivers, preventing the getting to sea of numerous vessels, and the entry of such as were coming into port. On the 15th of June, Whipple sailed, with his command, down the bay of Narragansett, and attacked two of the enemy's tenders, which he disabled, and forced to retire under the guns of the frigate, and took one other a prize; while by the light draught of his own vessels he could keep out of the reach of the man-of-war. By this bold act the bay was cleared of these nuisances, and a large number of homeward-bound vessels entered the port.

Much has been said and written, as to whom was due the credit of firing the *first gun* on the sea, at the British, in the opening of the

Revolutionary War. After the above statement, which comes from the pen of Capt. Whipple himself, in a petition to Congress in the year 1786, little doubt need be felt as to the propriety of assigning to him that honor. It is true that an unauthorized attack was made on the British schooner "Margareta", by the Machias people in May, which for its spirit and bravery deserves great credit, but was a mere private transaction; while Whipple fired the first gun under any legal or colonial authority. This daring deed was performed at a time, when no other man in the colony would undertake the hazardous employment, lest he might be destined to the halter by Capt. Wallace, who threatened to apply it to all who should be taken in arms against His Majesty. The people were not yet ready for open resistance to the King, but expected that Parliament would finally relent from their rigorous measures, and love and friendship be again restored between their revered parent and her undutiful children.

Since the prospect of an open rupture daily increased, the old affair of the "Gaspe" was no longer kept in the dark, but the name of the leader in that daring exploit, came to the ears of Capt. Wallace, who sent him the following plain, if not very polite note:

"You, Abraham Whipple, on the 17th of June, 1772, burned his majesty's vessel, the Gaspe, and I will hang you at the yard-arm.
James Wallace."

To which the Captain returned this laconic and Spartan answer:

"To Sir James Wallace:
Sir: Always catch a man before you hang him.
Abraham Whipple."

Notwithstanding these threats, he continued to cruise in the Narragansett Bay until the 12th of September; during which period he fought several actions with vessels of superior force, beating them off, and protecting the commerce of the state. These spirited combats infused new courage into the inhabitants of the neighboring colonies, as well as his own, and demonstrated that the British were not invincible on the water. Maritime events like these, with those conducted by Capt. Manly, led Congress to the consideration of defending themselves and the country on the ocean, as well as on the land; and in October, 1775, a Marine Committee was appointed to superintend the naval affairs.

About the 20th of September, he was ordered by the Governor of Rhode Island, to proceed, with the sloop "Providence", to the island of Bermuda, and seize upon the powder in the magazine of that place; this article being greatly needed by the country, which depended altogether on foreign supplies, not yet having learned to manufacture for themselves. This order was obeyed with due diligence and bravery, but was unsuccessful, from the circumstance of the powder having been removed before his arrival. While on this service, he narrowly escaped capture by two of the enemy's ships of war, which were on that station. He, however, by his daring and nautical skill, escaped; and arrived at Rhode Island on the 9th of December, and resumed his former employment of cruising in the bay, until the 19th of that month.

While absent on the voyage to Bermuda, Congress directed the Marine Committee to purchase two swift sailing vessels; the one of ten and the other of twelve guns. Under this order the "Providence" was purchased. Still later in the month, the Marine Committee were directed to purchase two additional ships, one of thirty-six guns, and the other of twenty. In pursuance of this order, the "Alfred" and "Columbus" were bought at Philadelphia, both of them merchant ships. To these were added two brigs, the "Cabot", and the "Andrea Doria", making a naval force of six vessels, belonging to the United States; of which the little "Providence" was the only one that had been in active service.

At this period of the contest, no regular warships had been built, and the government had to select such vessels as the mercantile service afforded, until ships of war could be constructed. In the month of December, 1775, Congress directed thirteen warlike vessels to be built, and the Marine Committee increased to thirteen, or one for each state. In 1776, two Navy Boards, consisting of three persons each, one for the eastern district, and one for the middle district, were established, subordinate to the Marine Committee; by which arrangement a large portion of the executive business was accomplished. Several letters from these boards will be referred to in the course of this biography.

On the 19th of December, Capt. Whipple received orders from the Marine Committee, to proceed with the "Providence" sloop, now under their direction, to Philadelphia. On his way out, he captured one of the enemy's vessels, and sent her into Providence.

On the 22d of the month, by a resolution of Congress, Dudley Saltonstall was appointed Captain of the "Alfred" frigate, Abraham Whipple of the "Columbus", Nicholas Biddle of the "Andrea Doria", and John B. Hopkins of the "Cabot". Haysted Hacker, Lieutenant of the "Providence" was promoted to her command. The celebrated John Paul Jones was First Lieutenant of the "Alfred", and Jonathan Pitcher, of the "Columbus"; Esek Hopkins, an old man, Commander-in-Chief, as they chose to style the leader of their squadron. During the winter, the young flotilla, while fitting for a cruise, was frozen up in the Delaware River. Com. Hopkins, however, got to sea on the 17th of February, 1776, with seven armed vessels under his command, the largest of which was the "Alfred" of twenty-four guns instead of thirty-six, and bore away southerly, in quest of a small squadron under Lord Dunmore; but not falling in with him, concluded to make a descent on the island of New Providence, for the purpose of capturing military stores. This service was performed under the conduct of Capt. Nichols, the senior officer of the Marines, at the head of three hundred men, whose landing from the boats of the squadron was covered in gallant style, by Capt. Hacker, of the "Providence", and the sloop "Wasp". The attack was entirely successful, and possession was taken of the fortifications and the town. The main object of the attempt, a magazine of gunpowder, was in part secreted by the Governor; but they brought away four hundred and fifty tons of cannon and other military stores, with the Governor and some others as prisoners. Having accomplished this victory, they sailed on the 17th of March, for the United States. At one o'clock in the morning of the 6th of April, the squadron fell in with the "Glasgow", British man-of-war of twenty guns, off the easterly end of Long Island. The little "Cabot" of fourteen guns, Capt. Hopkins, being the nearest to the enemy, ranged manfully along side, discharging her broadsides with great spirit, but was soon obliged to haul off from the superior fire of the "Glasgow". The "Alfred" now came up to the rescue, but after a short running fight, had her wheel ropes cut away and became unmanageable. The "Providence", by this time, had passed under her stern and fired a number of broadsides with great effect. Capt. Whipple, in the "Columbus", could not get into action for want of wind, which was light and baffling; sufficiently near to afford much aid or the "Glasgow" would have been captured. The darkness of night still continued, when seeing the approach of another antagonist, she spread all sail in flight, with the "Columbus" in pursuit, but was soon signaled by the Commodore to give up the chase; as they were approaching so near the harbor of Newport, where lay a large fleet, that the report of the cannonade would call them out to the rescue and thus perhaps the whole American force might fall into their hands; as they were so deeply laden with the captured military stores as to make them all dull sailers. On his way back, Capt. Whipple fell in with, and made prize of the bomb ship of the British fleet, which had long been a terror to the people of Newport. The fleet arrived safely into the harbor of New London but were soon after removed to Providence by the Commodore, the British having left the Bay of Narragansett.

The escape of the "Glasgow" from so superior a force caused no small sensation, with a good deal of censure from the public As Whipple commanded the second largest ship, and was not actually engaged with the enemy, he was accused of cowardice. This aroused the spirit of the veteran, and he demanded a court martial to inquire into his conduct. It was held in Providence; and after a full examination he was honorably acquitted; it appearing in evidence, that his vessel, from the lightness of the wind and her leeward position, could not be brought into contact with the Glasgow, until after her flight, when he pursued her with all the speed in his power, until called off by Com. Hopkins.

After the close of the trial, he was ordered to take command of the "Columbus" again; while Com. Hopkins, on the 16th of October, was formally censured by a vote of Congress and on the 20th of March, 1777, dismissed from the service for disobeying their orders. Capt. Hacker, of the "Providence", was removed from her command, and the vessel given to John Paul Jones,* who, in the course of the summer, captured no less than sixteen sail of the enemy's ships. In the fall of that year, he was transferred to the "Alfred", and sailed, in company with the "Providence", on a cruise to the eastward, along the coast. Here they fell in with and captured a number of prizes; amongst them a transport for Burgoyne's army, with ten thousand suits of soldiers' uniforms.

* The history of the last years of the Providence sloop, is taken from Cooper's Naval History.

The "Providence" was now commanded by Capt. Rathbone and in 1778, again visited New Providence, unaccompanied by any other vessel, and took possession of the place and six ships lying in the harbor, one of which was a privateer of sixteen guns. On his landing, he was joined by about thirty American prisoners, making with his own crew, eighty men. He kept possession two days, and brought away many valuable stores and four of the prizes. In 1779, the little "Providence" was restored to her former master, Capt. Hacker, who took the enemy's ship "Delinquent", of equal force, after a severe action. In July, with other vessels, she was ordered to convey a body of militia, under Gen. Lowell, to the Penobscot River, where the British had formed a military station. The expedition proved disastrous; and the "Providence", with the other ships, was lost, by the superior naval force of the enemy, the 15th of August. Capt. Hacker, to keep her from the hands of the enemy, after landing the crew, ordered her to be blown up. Thus perished, in a blaze of light, the favorite vessel and first love of Capt. Whipple. She had been one of the most successful cruisers that floated on the ocean, and made more prizes than any other vessel in the service; hurling defiance at Great Britain in many a well fought action, from June, 1775, to August, 1779. Her name was perpetuated in the navy, by the frigate "Providence". In October, 1776, Capt. Whipple was recommended by the Marine Committee, to the command of the frigate "Providence", of twenty-eight guns, then building in Rhode Island, which was confirmed by Congress.

In November of the same year, Congress *"Resolved that a bounty of twenty dollars be paid to the Commanders, Officers and men of such Continental ships, or vessels of war, as shall make prize of any British ship, or vessel of war; for every cannon mounted on board each prize at the time of capture; and eight dollars per head for every man then on* board, and belonging to such prize." This was a wise and salutary provision, for the encouragement of our sailors; but as it relates to Capt. Whipple, he says he never received any compensation for guns and munitions of war captured by himself.

At the same time they passed the following order, regulating the comparative rank of officers in the navy with the land service; viz. *"An admiral as a General; Vice-Admiral, as a Lieutenant-General; Rear-Admiral, as a Major General; Commodore, as a Brigadier-General; the Captain of a ship of forty guns and upward, as a Colonel; from ten to twenty guns, as a Major; a Lieutenant in the navy, as a Captain."* This arrangement was not only for etiquette in their intercourse, but was also intended to apply in exchanges of prisoners.

The pay of the officers and men in the American navy, *"under the free and independent states of America,"* was established as follows. *"The Captain of a ship of twenty guns and upward, received sixty dollars a month; that of a ship of ten to twenty guns, forty-eight dollars a month; a Lieutenant of the larger vessel, thirty dollars a month — the smaller, twenty-four dollars; a surgeon twenty-five dollars, and the surgeon's mate, fifteen dollars, and so on in the descending scale to the common seamen whose pay was eight dollars a month."*

When we look back on those times of trial and adversity, we admire the prudence and economy, which pervaded every branch of the government: when we consider the poor apology for money in which they were paid, the officers might be said *"to serve for nothing and find themselves"*. But if we reflect on the deep poverty of the country, and that all the expenses were paid by a direct tax on the people, we arrive at the secret of this seeming parsimony. It was the prudent expenditure of the public money which enabled Congress to carry on the war at all; and as it was, they were often bankrupt and on the verge of ruin. In these days when the public expenses are raised by a tariff on commerce and money is plenty, the pay of naval officers is very different; some of the older Captains get three hundred and seventy five dollars a month, and the younger Captains of frigates, three hundred dollars—being just five times as much as they received in the Revolutionary War.

On the 10th of August, 1776, he received orders from the Navy Board to sail on a cruise to the eastward with the "Columbus" frigate, for the purpose of intercepting the homeward-bound Jamaica fleet. , In his passage out of the bay from Newport, he had to "run the gauntlet" through a number of British ships of war, which he fortunately escaped. Off the coast of Newfoundland he fell in with the object of his search and took five large ships laden with sugar. Two of his prizes reached ports while the other three were retaken, as was the fate of more than half of all the American prizes, which they attempted to run into their own ports, the coast being closely guarded by the enemy's ships.

In October, Capt. Whipple returned, with the "Columbus" to Providence, at which place Congress had directed two frigates to be built; the "Warren", of thirty-two guns, and the "Providence" of twenty-eight gum. On the 10th of that month, he was recommended by the Marine Committee, and appointed, by Congress, to the command of the "Providence" and directed to superintend the fitting out of both frigates. While occupied in this employment, with his own ship nearly ready for sea, so rapidly had the work been prosecuted, on the 7th of December, the enemy's fleet took possession of the harbor of Newport, where the "Providence" had been lying, and landed a large army. To preserve his ship from capture, Capt. Whipple run her up the river to Providence Harbor, where several other vessels had retreated, protected by the batteries and the army of Gen. Spencer then assembled on the adjacent main, to guard the country from the inroads of the British troops. In this mortifying durance the new frigates were confined during the whole of the year 1777. During this period, several plans were arranged for getting to sea as appears by the letters of the eastern Navy Board, composed of James Warren and John Deshon, of September 11th and October 28th. In March preceding, there was a plan for burning some of the British vessels by means of fire-ships, in which Capt. Whipple was engaged; as by letter of Esek Hopkins, who was in command at Providence, as late as the 9th of that month. From some cause, it was not successful, although Congress offered large bounties to effect it. In October, under the order of Gov. Cook, he dismantled and saved the guns and stores of the enemy's frigate "Syren" which ran on shore at Point Judith, R. I. and had been abandoned. While at this employment he fell over the side of the frigate, amongst the guns and other matters, receiving a serious injury, which caused lameness all his life. On the 20th of March, 1778, orders arrived to fit the Providence for sea with all dispatch, being assigned to carry important dispatches from Congress to our ministers in France.

Capt. Whipple made up his crew from the men of the "Warren", in addition to his own ship, selecting such as were known to be of tried courage as the passage out to sea was blockaded by a numerous fleet, as well as the outlets of each of the three passages from Providence River, as the long, deep, narrow inlet was called, which connects Narragansett Bay with the harbor of the town. They were guarded by frigates and a sixty-four gun ship, expressly stationed to watch these channels, for the American ships. All movements of any importance, about to be made by either of the belligerent parties, were certain to be known to the other within a short time after their concoction, by means of spies and secret intercourse constantly kept up by men employed for this purpose. The order for the sailing of the "Providence" was soon known to the British Naval Commander at Newport, and every preparation made for her capture. Capt. Whipple was perfectly familiar with all the channels, head lands, shoals, and windings of the outlets from his earliest youth; so that no man could be better fitted to conduct this hazardous enterprise. His well known character for courage and love of daring exploits gave additional hope to his prospect of success. It could only be attempted in the night, and that night must be a dark and stormy one, adding still more to the grandeur of the exploit. After every preparation was made for sea he had to wait until the 30th of April for one of those gloomy, windy nights, attended with sleet and rain so common on the New England coast at this season of the year. At length, on the last day of the month, such a night set in, with rain and wind from the northeast, cheerless and dispiriting on all ordinary occasions but now more prized than the brightest starlight, and entirely favorable to his wishes. In making his choice of the three outlets, he selected the westerly one, which passes down between the island of Conanicut and the Narragansett shore, which was guarded by the frigate "Lark", rated as a thirty-six, but actually mounting forty guns. This vessel was moored in the channel against the island with her stern up stream and springs on her cables, ready to get under way at a moment's notice. Some distance below her, and nearer the outlet, was moored in the same manner, the "Renown", a ship of sixty-four guns; while in the bay beyond, lay ten or twelve ships and sloops of war ready to fire upon the Providence should she, by possibility, escape the two ships above. The middle passage led through the harbor of Newport, occupied by the ships of the line, and the easterly one was crooked, and not passable in the night. William Jones, subsequently the Governor of Rhode Island, was Captain of Marines under Whipple. He was a very gentlemanly, noble-looking and brave man. To him was consigned the charge of the dispatches. As the gallant little frigate, under close reefed topsails, so stiff was the breeze, approached the "Lark", every light on deck was extinguished and the utmost silence maintained by the crew who were stationed at their guns with lighted matches, while the lanterns in the rigging of the enemy served to show exactly her position. Instead of sailing wide of his enemy and avoiding a conflict, he ran within half pistol shot and delivered his broadside, firing his bow guns when against the stern of the ship, determined that she should feel her enemy if she could not see her. At the same moment Capt. Jones, with his musketry, poured in a destructive fire on her quarter and main deck, killing and wounding a number of the crew. So sudden and unexpected was the attack that before the "Lark" could make any return of the broadside, the "Providence" was out of sight, having by this well directed fire dismounted several of her guns and killed some of the men. The report of Whipple's cannon awakened the sleeping crew of the sixty-four, who, hurrying to their quarters, filled the rigging with lights, ready for the coming conflict. As the gallant ship came rushing on the wings of the wind enveloped in the mist and darkness of the storm, Whipple, as he neared the "Renown" to put his enemy well on their guard, bellowed forth with his speaking trumpet in a voice louder than the winds, as if addressing the man at the helm, "Pass her on the Narragansett side:" at the same time, as he stood close to the steersman, he bid him luff ship and pass her on the larboard or Conanicut side of the vessel thus throwing his antagonist entirely off his guard, on the point he really meant to steer. The order was promptly obeyed, and while the crew were mustered on the Narragansett side of the sixty-four, ready for a discharge of their heavy guns, his starboard broadside was fired into her as he rapidly passed, with great effect; several shot passing through the cabin, and one directly under the Captain's head, as he lay in his berth, knocking his pillow out of place. Another shot unshipped the rudder, and before the "Renown" was ready to discharge her larboard guns, the "Providence" was out of reach and out of sight. This very vessel was the leading, or Admiral's ship, at the capture of Charleston and the officers related the effects of his fire in a familiar conversation with Capt.

Whipple, after the surrender of the place, and he was their prisoner. These two broadsides aroused the crews of the fleet in the bay below, and put them on the lookout for the rebel frigate, and the "Providence" received more or less of the fire from eleven different ships of war, before she reached the open sea. Like the king-bird surrounded by a flock of vultures, she glided swiftly among her enemies, veering now to the larboard, and now to the starboard, as fresh ships opposed her way; returning their fire with occasional shots, but anxious mainly to escape too close a contact with any of her foes; the object being to run, and not to fight.

The day following this perilous night, when he had gained the open ocean and thought all present danger past, he narrowly escaped capture by a seventy-four gun ship, which came directly across his course, but by superior management in sailing, luckily escaped. The damages to the rigging of the "Providence", although considerable, were soon repaired, and the little frigate, with a flowing sheet, sped on her way to the port of Nantz, where she arrived in twenty-six days, being on the 26th of May, 1778.

On the voyage out, Capt. Whipple captured a British brig, laden with one hundred and twenty-five pipes of wine, nine tons of cork and various other articles, which arrived safe in port, near the same time.

The names of the officers who so nobly aided in sailing and fighting the "Providence" through that host of enemies, and may well be ranked among the most remarkable feats of bravery and daring, as well as nautical skill that took place during the war of the Revolution, were as follows: Thomas Simpson, First Lieutenant, and soon after promoted to the command of the "Boston" frigate of twenty-four guns. Silas Devol, Second Lieutenant. He was the brother of Capt. Jonathan Devol, and the personification of bravery. In a year or two after, he was taken at sea and perished miserably in the old Jersey prison ship, that den of wholesale murder to the Americans. Jonathan Pitcher, Third Lieutenant, George Goodwin, Sailing Master, William Jones, Captain of Marines, and Seth Chapin, First Lieutenant.

On the third day of their voyage out, the Lieutenants and other Officers presented a petition to Capt. Whipple, asking him to allow them to draw money for the purpose of purchasing proper uniform dresses as without them they could not maintain the dignity of their stations, and as they say, *"That all may appear alike, as brothers united in one cause."* From this circumstance it would seem that no regular uniform for the Navy had yet been established by Congress.

The appearance of the "Providence" in the harbor of Nantz, excited a great deal of curiosity as few if any American frigates had visited that port. On landing, Capt. Jones was charged with the dispatches to the American ministers at the Court of Versailles and proceeded on his way to Paris. Dr. Franklin introduced him to the King and the principal courtiers who received him with great politeness. His noble personal appearance, gentlemanly manners, and rich, showy uniform made him appear to great advantage and highly creditable to the American nation. Owing to unforeseen delays and the cautious policy of the French Court, it was as late as August before a cargo was provided and the return dispatches of the American ministers ready for Congress. Strange as it may appear, the "Providence" frigate was loaded with clothing, arms and ammunition like a merchantman. Capt. Whipple, although as brave as Caesar, was not too proud to engage in any honest service which would be useful to his country. He had spent years in the merchant line and felt not that repugnance to turning his ship into a transport so often expressed by the haughty Britons. The cargo was of immense value and more safe in a frigate than a common ship. On the 13th of July, he received notice from the American Commissioners, B. Franklin, Arthur Lee, and John Adams, that they had ordered Capt. Tucker, of the "Boston" frigate, to join him on his return voyage. On the 16th, he received the following letter and order.

"Passy, July 16th, 1778.
Capt. Whipple:
Sir: We have ordered Lieut. Simpson, to whom the command of the Ranger devolves, by the destination of Capt. Jones, (John Paul,) to another service, to join you and obey your orders respecting his future cruises and voyage to America. We wish you to use all possible dispatch in getting to sea, with the Boston, Providence, and Ranger.

You are to use your utmost endeavors to take, burn, sink, and destroy all privateers of Jersey and Guernsey, and all other British cruisers within the command of your force, as you may have opportunity.

We are, sir, your most humble servants,

B. Franklin,
Arthur Lee,
John Adams.
P. S. You are to leave all the prisoners in such place and in the custody of such persons as Mr. Shwinghauser shall advise."

Mr. Shwinghauser was the Naval Agent for the United States, making purchases, &c; a number of his letters are on file among Com. Whipple's manuscripts. From the time of the date of this letter, giving him the command of three public armed ships, he may fairly take the rank of Commodore; although he was, in fact, entitled to that distinction while cruising in the Narragansett Bay, in June, 1775, with the two armed sloops under his orders. On the 26th of August, having loaded the "Providence" with arms, ammunition, clothing, and copper, on account of the United States, and taken on board a number of passengers, ordered by the commissioners, he sailed for America, touching at the harbor of Brest, where he was joined by the "Boston" and "Ranger". On their voyage out, they took six prizes, but how many got into port, is not ascertained.

While on the banks of Newfoundland, in a dense fog, so common to that misty part of the ocean, he had a very narrow escape from capture. The "Providence" being the leading ship, for the purpose of notifying her consorts of her position every five or ten minutes, a few blows were struck on the ship's bell. A British seventy-four gun ship, hearing the signal, bore up in the direction of the sound and before the crew of the "Providence" had any notice of her approach, she was close along side. The first appearance of the frigate with her ports all closed and lying deep in the water, was that of a large merchant ship. On hailing the stranger, the Captain, in the usual style of British naval officers, ordered the *"d----d rebel to strike his colors, drop under his stern, and send the boat aboard."*

It so happened, that his colors were not up at the time. Capt. Whipple at once saw his danger and knew that nothing but a bold maneuver could save him. He, therefore, answered the hail, as if intending no opposition, *"Aye, aye, sir."*

With a readiness of thought which none but a mastermind can call to his aid, in emergencies which admit of no delay, his plan was instantly formed and sending some men aloft to busy themselves with the sails and prepare for striking the colors, as if about to comply with the order, he, at the same time, passed the word below to make all ready for a broadside as he passed under the stem of the seventy-four. As he was rather slow in complying with the order to strike, it was repeated by the Briton in a still more commanding tone, threatening to fire into him. Whipple answered, rather peevishly, that *"he could not haul down his colors, until he had run them up,"* at the same time swearing at the sailor for his bungling manner of performing the duty, having ordered him, when they were up, not to haul them down again, on pain of death.

By the time the stars and stripes were fluttering in the breeze, the gunners were at their posts, the frigate had fallen off under the stern of the enemy, when, with a stamp of his foot on the quarter deck, the ports flew open, and a full broadside was fired into her cabin, the tompions of the guns going in with the shot, there being no time to remove them. When relating the incident in after life, the Commodore used to say, he *"heard a terrible smashing among the crockery ware in the cabin."* The Briton suspecting no resistance, and being entirely unprepared for such an event, was utterly astonished, provoked, and confounded; but before he could make any preparation to avenge this "*Yankee trick,*" the "Providence" was enveloped in the fog and out of sight on another tack. Whipple took good care not to tinkle his bell again for some time while his consorts, being warned of their danger by his broadside, escaped discovery and all reached the harbor of Boston in safety. This, however, was accomplished in almost a miraculous manner, having to pass through a squadron of the enemy's ships which were blockading that port. The cargo thus saved by the presence of mind, and bold stratagem of Com. Whipple was of immense advantage to the country; furnishing the army with several thousand stands of arms, ammunition, and clothing; articles of more value to the United States, at that time, than a ship-load of gold.

Soon after his arrival, which was the 13th of October, Capt. Jones went on to Congress with the dispatches which were highly gratifying to that body. In November he received the following congratulatory letter from his Excellency, Gen. Washington:

"Head Quarters, Fredericksburg, Nov. 25th, 1778.

Sir:

Maj. Nicholas handed me your favor of the 12th inst. I am greatly pleased with the gallant circumstance of your passage through the blockaded harbor, and much obliged to you for the detail of your voyage. It was agreeable to hear of your safe arrival with the valuable articles of your invoice. With my best wishes for your future success, I am, sir, your most humble servant,

Geo. Washington.

To Capt. Abraham Whipple, Esq., Commander of the Continental frigate Providence at Boston."

During this year the influence of the American Commissioners at the court of France was so great, especially with the queen, who had taken so deep an interest in the welfare of the young republic and especially in Dr. Franklin, whom, on all occasions she treated with as much respect as she could her own father, that the king finally came out openly on the side of the United States, sending a fleet of men-of-war to the American coast, which entered the harbor of Newport, and forced the enemy from

Narragansett Bay. Before their departure they sunk several of their ships to keep them from the hands of the French. Among them was Whipple's old antagonist, the "Lark". Near the close of the war some of these frigates were raised by the ingenuity of Griffin Greene, Esq.

The winter following this never-to-be-forgotten cruise, was passed in refitting his vessel for sea and in visiting his family. On the 9th of March, 1779, he received orders from James Warren and William Vernon, the Navy Board in the eastern department, to cruise with the "Providence" in Boston Bay, for the protection of the navigation, and in quest of the enemy's cruisers, which were now numerous on the coast. On the 4th of April he returned to port and remained until the 23d of June, when he again proceeded on a cruise with the "Ranger" and "Queen of France" under his command. On this occasion the following letter was addressed to him, giving the outlines of the cruise, and the general orders to be observed while at sea:

"Navy Board, Eastern Department,
Boston, June 12th, 1779.

To Abraham Whipple, Esq., Commander of the ship Providence:

Your ship being ready for the sea, you are to proceed with the ships Queen of France and Ranger, if the last be ready, on a cruise against the enemy. You being the superior officer, will, of course, command the whole: and ours will be that they obey yours accordingly. You are to proceed with these ships immediately, to the southerly parts of the banks of Newfoundland, and there to cruise; and to the southward of said banks, as the most likely cruising ground to effect the double purpose of intercepting the enemy's outward-bound transports for New York, &c, and the homeward-bound West India ships. You will keep that ground steadily, so long as is consistent with your security: taking care to alter your station, when you have reason to suppose, from your long continuance on that ground, or other circumstances, that the enemy may have gained intelligence of you; in which case you will proceed to such places as you and the commanders of the other ships shall judge most likely to answer the purposes of the cruise: taking care, also, at proper times, to be on the banks, so that any ships we may hereafter send to join you, may be able to find you. During your cruise you are to take, burn, sink, or destroy as many of the enemy's ships as may fall in your way, directing to the Continental Agent of any port, such prizes as you may think proper to send in. You are to take proper care of your ship and her stores, and to cause proper returns of the expenditures of all provisions and stores, to be made on your return. You will observe the greatest frugality and strict discipline on board, taking care at the same time to use your officers and men well and your prisoners with humanity. You are to continue your cruise as long as your provisions and other circumstances will admit, and then return into this, or some other convenient port of the United States, leaving you at liberty, nevertheless, if on consulting the other commanders, it shall be judged practicable to intercept the homeward-bound ships from Hudson's Bay, to proceed for that purpose toward the end of your cruise; and if you meet with little success and your ships should remain well manned, you may, when your provisions are near expended, proceed and cruise in the West Indies during the winter: Mr. Stephen Caronia at Cape Francois, or Mr. William Bingham at Martinico, Continental Agent, will supply you with the necessaries. On your way out you are to see this coast clear of the enemy's cruisers, and particularly range down the eastern shore, and if the Ranger do not sail with you, rendezvous at for a few days, where she will join you. You are to return lists of your men and stores on board, and at the end of the cruise cause proper returns to be made of the expenditure. We wish you a successful cruise.

And are your servants, &c,

J. Warren,
Wm. Vernon. "

In pursuance of the above orders he proceeded on to the eastern coast, to look for the enemy's cruisers, and spending nearly four weeks in cruising on and off the coast of Newfoundland. He, on the 24th of July, fell in with the homeward-bound Jamaica fleet of nearly one hundred and fifty sail, convoyed by a seventy-four gun ship and some smaller vessels. He continued with them for two days under British colors, pretending to be ships from Halifax, joining the convoy. From the first prize captured by boarding in the night, he got possession of the signals of the Commodore, and made use of them to keep up the deception. Some of the prizes were taken possession of by inviting the Captain of the Jamaica ship on board the Halifax vessels, and while he was below, sending his boat with their own well manned to secure the balance of the crew, and man the ship with his own men, which was accomplished without making so much noise as to attract the notice of the convoy. During the night each captured ship slackened sail and altered her course so much as to be out of sight of the fleet in the morning. At night the seventy four carried a light at her mizzen-top, as a guide to the course to be pursued by the fleet. Whipple, taking advantage of this, hoisted one at his own mizzen, and thus decoyed several ships so far out of their course as to be beyond the reach of aid in the morning, and then took possession of them. This could easily be done amongst one hundred and fifty sail without their number being missed from the fleet. By these devices he managed to gain possession of ten large Jamaica ships, which were as many as he could man with American crews. Had he attempted their capture in an open manner, by daylight, he might have lost some of his own squadron and taken less prizes, as he was unable to contend with the seventy-four gun ship with all his force. The merchant ships also carried a number of guns and could have afforded considerable aid in beating him off. His object ever was, like a sensible man, to annoy the enemy as much as he could with the least possible loss to himself and gain by ingenuity what he could not do by open force. Eight of his prizes were brought safely into Boston Harbor, while two were recaptured. They had on board six thousand hogsheads of sugar, besides ginger, pimento, and cotton, being valued at more than a million of dollars. The eight prizes were armed with an average of fourteen guns each, or one hundred and thirteen in the whole. Could these prizes have been sold at their real value, Com. Whipple's share would have been one-twentieth of this sum; the rules adopted by Congress in the distribution of prize money, allowing this portion to the commander of a squadron, and two-twentieths to the Captains of single ships, of those captured by them when on a cruise. Yet, from the impoverished condition of the country, and the scarcity of money, it is not probable he actually realized more than a moiety of the amount. He, however, received sufficient to greatly improve his present condition, which was actually that of a poor man. With the avails of this cruise he bought a handsome house and lot in Providence, and a fine farm in the neighboring town of Cranston.

On the 20th of November, he received the following order from the Navy Board:

"Navy Board, Eastern Department,
Boston, November 20, 1779.

To Abraham Whipple, Esq., commander of the ship Providence:

Your ship being now ready for the sea, you are, as commanding officer, to take under your command the ships Boston, Queen of France, and Ranger; and with them you are to embrace the first fair wind, and without any kind of delay, proceed to sea; and when the fleet under your command are five leagues to the southward of the light-house, you are to open the orders enclosed, and follow the directions therein given. If by any misfortune to you, the command of the Providence should devolve on Capt. Hacker, now acting as first Lieutenant, he will, as the eldest Captain, take command of the fleet, and is to obey the orders given you. We wish you success, and are your servants, &c,

Wm. Vernon,
J. Warren."

What those sealed orders were, does not appear on record; but doubtless were for him to proceed with all expedition to Charleston, S. C, and place himself and fleet under the command of Gen. Lincoln, who was charged with the defense of that place. On the 23d of that month, he sailed, with the ships under his command, and when united with those at Charleston, formed the largest American squadron, under the command of one officer, ever assembled during the war. The voyage out was rough and tempestuous, and his ships received considerable damage; nevertheless, he reached the destined port on the 19th of December.

On the 20th of January, being weary of inactivity, he applied to Gen. Lincoln for liberty to make a cruise of observation, and ascertain the position of the enemy's fleet, which had been looked for, a considerable time, on its way from New York, with the army of Gen. Clinton, to invest Charleston. On the second or third day out, he fell in with the British fleet, and took four of their transports, laden with troops, provisions, &c, but was himself chased back into port, by four ships of war; and in a short time after, the enemy commenced their preparations for a regular siege of the city. This was his last feat on the ocean; the brilliant sunshine of success, which had so long brightened his course, now set in clouds and gloomy disaster. Neptune, the ruler of the sea, had befriended him all his life, and when he forsook his service, and entered into battle on the solid land, his good fortune departed, and his beloved ships perished, or fell into the hands of the enemy. Amidst all his exposures and hairbreadth escapes in his numerous sea-fights, he was never wounded; but, like Washington, bore a charmed life, not to be destroyed by his enemies.

The defense of Charleston was the first attempt of the Americans to maintain a town against a besieging army and its disastrous termination taught them, when too late, that their un-walled, open cities, were poorly calculated for defense. The winter of 1780 proved to be one of great severity, even at the south, and the cold nearly as great as that common to the middle states. The sailors in Com. Whipple's fleet had been shipped for a six months' cruise in a southern latitude and not knowing their final destination, were entirely un-provided with clothing for the severe winter which followed. There was no clothing for them in the vessels, and no other resource to relieve their wants but from his own funds. The generosity of their commander toward sailors was unbounded and to alleviate their sufferings, he advanced several thousand dollars from his own funds to cover their shivering bodies in garments suited to the season. These supplies were delivered to the pursers of the several ships under his command, and the amounts deducted from their wages, as is customary in such cases; and yet, from the subsequent loss of the fleet, and perhaps, also, the books of the pursers, he had not, in 1786, received a single dollar for this noble and generous expenditure in the cause of his country, nor did he ever obtain a tithe of the amount justly due him.

During the siege an almost daily correspondence was carried on with Gen. Lincoln, who constantly consulted him in the disposition of the ships for the defense of the city, and the annoyance of the enemy. A large number of these letters are on the files of his naval manuscripts, preserved with much care; but as they relate to no very interesting or particular events, they will not be quoted, but the history of the siege given, as related by Dr. Ramsey. From the beginning to the end of this disastrous affair, Com. Whipple, with his officers and men, exerted themselves with untiring assiduity and the greatest gallantry, in defending the place, as well after the destruction of their ships as before. The batteries erected from the ship's guns on the banks of the Cooper River, and manned by their crews, were very annoying to the besiegers, and prolonged the investment until the expenditure of their provisions threatened them with starvation, and did full as much toward their final surrender as the guns of the enemy.

"The British fleet, with their troops on board, six thousand in number, under the command of Sir Henry Clinton, sailed from New York on the 26th of December, 1779.Their outward course was boisterous and disastrous, losing nearly all their cavalry horses, and it was as late as the 11th of February, 1780, before they landed at the distance of thirty miles from Charleston. On the 29th of March, Clinton passed over Ashley River, and commenced erecting batteries for the siege of the town. Gen. Lincoln constructed lines of defense across Charleston neck, from Cooper to Ashley River. On the 12th of April the British batteries were opened. Their fleet under Admiral Arbuthnot, of eight ships, one a sixty-four, crossed the bar on the 20th of March, and anchored in 'five fathom hole;' while the fleet under Com. Whipple, composed of smaller vessels, being unable to prevent their crossing the bar at the mouth of the harbor, retreated up to Charleston, where his ships were disarmed, and the crews and guns of all the fleet but one, were put on shore to reinforce the batteries." Although sailors are the bravest of men, whether fighting on the land or the water; yet when on shore they are deprived of their favorite element, and lose that esprit de corps so peculiar to them on ship board. The commodore felt the want of sea room, and the fresh breezes of the ocean, by which to maneuver his ships, and to point his guns. When he reluctantly abandoned his vessels and stepped on to terra firma, he was like an eagle with his wings clipped, unable to soar aloft, or pounce upon his prey; nevertheless, his men behaved bravely, and did all they could for the defense of the town. The fire of the British was much superior to that of the Americans; the former having twenty-one mortars and royals, and the latter only two; while their battering cannon were much larger and more numerous, with three times as many men. During the siege Sir Henry Clinton received a reinforcement of three thousand men, making in all nine thousand land forces to oppose, while Gen. Lincoln had less than three thousand. By the 6th of May the provisions of the besieged were nearly exhausted, and the inhabitants of the town became clamorous with the American commander for a surrender of the place, as they could sustain the siege no longer. On the 11th of May the town was surrendered, and the brave defenders became prisoners of war to a man who proved to be a very ungenerous enemy, and treated his captives with all the rigor so prevalent at that period, when the Americans were considered as rebels, and not as common enemies, and, therefore, not entitled to the usages of the laws of nations." On the final results of the siege, he remarks, *"I faithfully exerted myself to promote the interest and honor of my country; and although the town was surrendered, American honor was triumphant."*

After the capitulation, he made an arrangement with Admiral Arbuthnot, into whose charge the seamen luckily fell instead of Sir H. Clinton, for their parole; agreeing that the seamen and marines should be exchanged, when an opportunity offered. But none such occurred, as the British Government decided on keeping in prison all the American seamen which fell into their hands until the close of the war. Their depredations had been so severe on their commerce, that they considered this the only effectual mode of restraining them. While their seamen amounted to eighty-five thousand, the Americans could at no time muster, probably, more than five thousand. The loss of so large a number of the continental ships, at the fall of Charleston, nearly ruined the American navy, and put a stop to any further effective operations by sea. The presence of the French fleet on our coast, supplied in some degree the loss of our own, and caused Congress to think there was not so much need of a navy as in the early years of the war, when they had to contend singlehanded with the most powerful marine in the world. Admiral Arbuthnot was doubtless acquainted with the name and character of Com. Whipple, and felt more respect for a brave man in misfortune than many of the enemy's commanders in the land service, who were generally notorious for their cruelty and ungenerous conduct to their American prisoners. Some delay must have taken place in carrying out the capitulation, as he did not reach Chester in Pennsylvania, the place of destination for the seamen, until the last of June. Disease prevailed extensively amongst his men, as is almost universally the case in besieged towns, especially the small-pox, which continued to be the scourge of the American troops, from the beginning to the end of the war. At Chester, no regular hospitals were provided for the sick, and with his characteristic generosity, Com. Whipple, hired a suitable house for their accommodation at his own expense, furnishing them with all needed supplies for their comfort, whereby he says, *"Many useful lives were preserved to their country."*

At this place he remained two years and seven months, a prisoner, the most dreary of his life, until at the close of the war, he was exchanged for Capt. Gayton, of the Romulus, a forty-four gun frigate. During all this period, he was deprived of the means of earning subsistence; and himself and family were to be supported out of his former stores, so that at the declaration of peace, he was left in a destitute condition, at the age of fifty years, a period when the energies and ambition of most men begin to fail.

In 1786, he petitioned Congress for a redress of his grievances; and that they would do him justice, by repaying the amount they justly owed him. At the close of the petition, after stating his services in the cause of liberty, (a paper which has afforded dates for all the interesting events of his life,) he says, *"Thus having exhausted the means of supporting myself and family, I was reduced to the sad necessity of mortgaging my little farm, the remnant I had left, to obtain money for a temporary support. This farm is now gone; and having been sued out of possession, I am turned into the world at an advanced age, feeble and valetudinary, with my wife and children, destitute of a house, or a home that I can call my own, or have the means of hiring. This calamity has arisen from two causes; viz.: First, from my disbursing large sums in France and Charleston. In the former, I expended for the service of the United States, to the amount of three hundred and sixty French guineas; a large part of that sum was appropriated to the pay of a company of marines; the other part for sea stores to accommodate a number of gentleman passengers, sent on board by the commissioners, to take passage for America, for which I have never been recompensed. And secondly, my having served the United States from the 15th of June, 1775, to December, 1782, without receiving a farthing of wages, or subsistence from them, since December, 1776. My advances in France and Charleston amount, in the whole, to nearly seven thousand dollars in specie, exclusive of interest. The repayment of this, or a part of it, might be the happy means of regaining the farm I have been obliged to give up, and snatch my family from misery and ruin."*

This sum with the interest would, in 1786, amount to at least ten thousand dollars; add to this, six years' pay and subsistence, at one thousand dollars a year, and there was sixteen thousand dollars due him for time and money, expended in the service of the United States. On the 10th of October, 1786, the Commissioner of Accounts in the Marine Department, to whom was referred the petition, reported in its favor, when Congress directed him to refund the money advanced in France, but say nothing about the disbursements at Charleston. What the sum allowed to him was, is not stated, but in an application which he made in 1811, for a pension, he says he was paid in "final settlements", or United States securities, which, owing to his indigent circumstances at that time, he was obliged to sell for two shillings and sixpence in the pound, or a discount of more than eighty per cent. He had but two choices; either to do this, or to let his family suffer for the necessaries of life. Thus, the government, instead of paying him in specie, or money equivalent to that which he had advanced for them, paid him in their worthless paper, which, purporting to be valuable for its face, was little better to him than so many rags. Owing to the low credit of the country, it fell into the hands of greedy speculators, who finally realized, and put into their own pockets, the very money due to Com. Whipple. But he, generous man, was not the only one who suffered from his country's poverty; hundreds of others, both of the army and navy, who had spent years in the service of the republic, received nothing in return but these *"final certificates"* the mere shadow of a reality. Soon after his exchange, he received permission from Robert Morris, one of the Board of Admiralty, to leave the service of the United States. It is as follows:

"Marine Office, Philadelphia, April 23d, 1782.

Leave of absence is hereby granted to Capt. Abraham Whipple, of the American navy, to go into private service, until called upon.
Robert Morris."

He now resided, like Cincinnatus, on his little farm in Cranston, and guided a plow instead of a ship. After the peace was fully established in

1784, the merchants of Providence resumed their foreign navigation; and one of the first ships sent to Great Britain, was built and owned by John Brown of Providence. She was called the "General Washington," and a fine figure of his noble person graced her bows. The command of this vessel was given to Com. Whipple, and he had the honor of first unfurling the American flag on the river Thames. Her fine model and attractive name excited the notice of the cockneys, and hundreds of persons daily visited her, as a rare sight from the new republic. This notice was not a little flattering to the pride of the commodore, who fully sustained the dignity of his country, and answered their numerous questions with propriety and kindness.

After his return from this voyage, he continued to live on his farm, and during the stormy period of the paper-money war in Rhode Island, was elected a Representative to the Legislature from the town of Cranston, in 1786. The advocates of the paper-money system were then in power, and chose Othniel Gorton, a clumsy old man, for speaker. Mr. John Howland, who narrates the following anecdote, says, *"It was the habit of Gorton to keep a large quid of tobacco in one side of his mouth, which pressed out one of his cheeks. The most of the debaters were on the opposite side of the hall from that on which the commodore sat, and the speaker's face was generally turned that way. Once in the course of the debate, Whipple had cogitated a speech, which he waited for a chance to deliver. At last, out of patience, he rose and called, 'Mr. Speaker!' The speaker, whose face was the other way, did not hear him. He then raised his voice to its utmost limit, 'Mr. Speaker!' The speaker started, and turning to the commodore said, 'I hear you, sir,' rather audibly. Whipple then began as follows: 'I wish, Mr. Speaker, you would shift your quid of tobacco from your starboard to your larboard jaw, that it might give your head a cant this way, so that you could sometimes hear something from this side of the house! He then commenced his speech, which was not a long one, and when through, sat down."* This anecdote is in character with the man, who often spoke in nautical phrases, and sometimes in language rough as the ocean's winds, amidst whose waves he had been cradled.

On the formation of the Ohio Company, he emigrated with his wife and son to Marietta, in company with the family of Col. Sproat, who had married his daughter Catharine. He was now fifty-five years old, when he left the land of his forefathers, to seek a new home in the valley of the Ohio. The fertility of the new world had been so much lauded by its advocates that it conveyed to the mind the idea of a second Paradise. The first settlers, however, found that the "briers and thorns" of the curse were there, ii not in reality, yet under the semblance of the tomahawk and knife of the Indian. The first six years of his residence here, were passed in constant danger from the savage foe, although, from his age, he was not exposed so much to their attacks as younger men. He, however, once had a little taste of the feeling which attends the too near approach of the hostile Indian. Col. Sproat, with whom he constantly resided, during the war, had built a log house about midway between the garrison at the Point and Campus Martius, and cleared a piece of ground for a garden. On this land Com. Whipple had a fine patch of melons, which somebody stole and carried away for several nights. Supposing the boys of the garrison were the depredators, he one moonlight night concluded to watch for the rogues, by standing sentry in the log house, a few yards only from the melons. With his old musket well charged, he took his stand by one of the loop holes in the logs. About midnight three Indians stepped over the fence and commenced searching for ripe melons. Not expecting depredators of this kind, he looked quietly on, in silence. He could have easily killed one or more of them, with his well loaded musket; but he felt no enmity toward them; they had never injured him or any of his kindred; but on the contrary, himself and countrymen were intruding on them, and taking the land of their fathers and themselves from them. And as to the melons they were not worth the life of a man, even of a savage. He resolved thus with himself. *"If they do not attack me, I will not attack them."* Had they been his old oppressors, the redcoats, and in time of war, as it then was with the Indians, his conduct would have been very different. He did not refrain from any fear of the result, for the report of his shot would have brought instant aid from the garrison not one hundred rods distant, and the Indians would have fled without any attempt on the house, as they would at once conclude it contained more than one man. When they had selected such melons as suited them, they retired; and the commodore rested quietly the remainder of the night. At sunrise he returned to the garrison, but did not watch the melons again.

After the peace in 1796, he moved with his wife on to a small farm of twelve acres, on the bank of the Muskingum River, two miles from its mouth. He was now in his sixty-third year, and had no other means of support than the produce of this land, cultivated with his own hands. On this scanty plantation he continued to live and to labor for fifteen years, raising barely sufficient of the most common necessaries of life to support him and his aged partner in a very frugal manner, but lacking the most of its comforts, especially comfortable clothing, which was scarce and dear in the new settlements. He thus manfully struggled on, without murmuring or complaining, respected and honored by his acquaintance for his perseverance and industry.

At length in 1811, when he was seventy-eight years old and the powers of nature has so far failed that he could no longer follow the plow, or delve the earth, he applied to Congress, urged thereto by his friends, for a pension. They granted him half-pay of a Captain in the navy, or thirty dollars a month. This relieved him from any further anxiety as to a support in the last days of his life, and rendered the remaining years easy and free from care.

Once during this agricultural period, he was allowed to visit the sea, snuff its saline breezes, and again be lulled to sleep in his cot by the dash of the ocean's waves, strangely calling to mind the scenes of his early manhood.

In the year 1800, some of the enterprising men of Marietta, formed a company for building a small vessel, and actually built, rigged, and loaded with produce, a brig of one hundred and four tons, named the "St. Clair", in honor of the Governor of the Northwest Territory. Her cargo was made up of pork and flour, and she cleared from Marietta in May, 1801, that town having been made a port of clearance. She crossed the falls of the Ohio in safety, and early in July was at New Orleans, then in the occupancy of the Spaniards, where the brig lay some days anchored in the stream, from the extravagance of the port charges, while she took on board some stores for the voyage. In July he sailed for the town of Havana, with a crew composed chiefly of landsmen. His First Mate was a good seaman, but entirely ignorant of navigation, not being able to take an observation, or ascertain the latitude, so that if any accident had happened to Com. Whipple, no one on board could navigate the vessel. The Second Mate was Bennet Cook, a young, active man, and a good sailor, but ignorant of navigation. The "St. Clair" however, reached her destined port in safety. Provisions of all kinds were scarce and dear, affording a fine market for her load. The flour sold for forty dollars a barrel, but was subject to a duty of twenty dollars. This port has always been noted for its high duties, which served to enrich the government, but to impoverish the people. With the proceeds of the cargo, he bought a load of sugar. It was late in August before the brig left the port of Havana on her voyage to Philadelphia, where she was consigned and finally sold. In the meantime the yellow fever broke out in the place and attacked several of the crew, some of them several days after leaving the island. Fortunately for Com. Whipple, he found his son John, who had been several years on the sea, and a finished sailor, at this port, and engaged him for the voyage as his mate. His health remained firm, and with his aid the brig reached Philadelphia, in distress, from sickness and death amongst the crew. The voyage was a productive one to the owners and encouraged the inhabitants of Marietta to continue the business. Com. Whipple returned to his home by land, but did not navigate any more vessels to the sea. The St. Clair was the first rigged vessel ever built on the Ohio River and he had the honor of conducting her to the ocean. In after life he used to claim the distinction of firing the first gun at the British in the Revolutionary war on the ocean, and the navigating the first vessel built on the Ohio River, to the sea. On the latter occasion Capt. Jonathan Devol, who possessed all the imagination of a poet, if he lacked the harmony of measure, wrote the following lines.

The scene is laid at the mouth of the Mississippi, and as Com. Whipple entered the ocean with the "St. Clair", Neptune and his Tritons are supposed to welcome him with military honors.

"The Triton crieth,
"Who cometh now from shore?"
Neptune replieth,
"Tis the old Commodore."
Long has it been since I saw him before,

In the year seventy-five from Columbia he came,
The pride of the Briton on ocean to tame:

And often, too, with his gallant crew,
Hath he crossed the belt of ocean blue.
On the Gallic coast,
I have seen him tost,
While his thundering cannon lulled my wares,
And roused my nymphs from their coral cares;
When he fought for freedom with all his braves,
In the war of the Revolution.
But now he comes from the western woods,
Descending slow with gentle floods,
The pioneer of a mighty train,
Which commerce brings to my domain.
Up, sons of the wave,
Greet the noble and brave!
Present your arms unto him.
His gray hair shows,
Life nears its close:
Let's pay the honors due him.
Sea-maids attend with lute and lyre,
And bring your conchs, my Triton sons;
In chorus blow to the aged sire,
A welcome to my dominions."

For several years after this period, shipbuilding was carried on with great spirit at Marietta; but Com. Whipple, having opened the way to the ocean, left the future guidance of the navigation to younger men. Not less than twenty ships, brigs and schooners, from one hundred and fifty to four hundred and fifty tons burthen, were built up to the year 1808, besides some of Mr. Jefferson's gunboats. Two or three of their number were lost in attempting to pass the rapids at Louisville, when the water was too low, but at a proper stage no difficulty was experienced. Several of them took in cotton from the plantations on the Mississippi, for Liverpool, in addition to their other lading, as the cotton bales were so loosely packed at that time that a ship could not be fully loaded with that article. Owing to its bulky nature, ten cents a pound was charged for the freight.

As has been observed, in 1811, Com. Whipple received from Congress the half-pay of a Captain in the service, or thirty dollars a month; which enabled him to cease from laboring with his own hands for the support of himself and wife, which he had been obliged to do for the last twenty-three years.

In early life he married Miss Sarah Hopkins, the sister of Gov. Hopkins, of Rhode Island, a woman every way worthy of him and with whom he lived to enjoy the smiles, or to bear the frowns, of fortune, for more than fifty years. The fruits of this marriage were two daughters and one son. The oldest daughter was married to Col. Ebenezer Sproat, and the younger to Dr. Comstock, of Smithfield, R. I., where she resided after her father's removal to Ohio. John, his only son, continued to follow the sea after leaving Marietta and never married, so that the family name perished at the death of its illustrious founder. Several descendants of the female branches are living in the states of Michigan, Rhode Island and Massachusetts under the names of Sibley, Comstock, and Fisher.

In person Com. Whipple was rather short, thick-set and stout, with great muscular strength in the days of his manhood: eyes dark grey, with manly, strongly marked features, indicating firmness and intrepidity. He was fond of daring exploits, and the more hazardous they were, with so much the greater alacrity he entered into them. For stern, rigid discipline, no man in the American Navy exceeded him; and yet from numerous letters on his files addressed to him by his subordinates, he appears to have been loved and highly respected by those under his command. It was often noticed by the sailors, that in fair, pleasant weather, with a smooth sea, he was irritable and surly; but as soon as a severe gale or storm arose, and there was actual danger, his countenance brightened, while the most cheerful, animated air, took possession of the man, diffusing life and courage into all around him, so that no crew could be cowardly with such a leader. When in the greatest danger, he was the most at his ease. His benevolence and kind feelings for those under his charge were often put to severe trials, and always shone with brilliant luster. Thousands of dollars were expended by him to relieve their wants, which were never repaid by the government and for which he suffered years of privation and labor, at a period of his life when want bears most heavily on the mind of man. It is presumed that no other one amongst the military or naval commanders of the Revolution expended as much for the men under their care, with the exception of that extraordinary and good man, the Marquis Lafayette. His success on the ocean was not exceeded by that of any other in the Navy; and, although exposed to the greatest dangers and hazards, was never captured or wounded by his enemies, while at sea; but when he stepped on to dry land, his good fortune forsook him and at the surrender of Charleston, he became a captive for more than two years. His exploits and character will long be remembered by the inhabitants of Rhode Island and Marietta; while his name and portrait ought to occupy a distinguished place, instead of being passed by in silence, in The American Portrait Gallery, amongst the celebrated men of the Revolution.

He died after a short illness, on the 29th of May, in the year 1819, aged eighty-five years, at a small farm, three miles from Marietta where he had resided for several years, near his widowed daughter, Mrs. Catharine Sproat, whose soothing cares and tender assiduities smoothed her parent's progress to the grave. His wife, Mrs. Sarah Whipple, died in October, 1818, preceding him but a few months, aged seventy-nine years. They lie buried side by side, in the beautiful mound square at Marietta, and his tombstone bears the following inscription, written by the Hon. Paul Fearing, his warm friend and admirer:

SACRED TO THE MEMORY OF
(Commodore Abraham Whipple)
WHOSE NAME, SKILL, AND COURAGE,
WILL EVER REMAIN THE PRIDE AND BOAST OF HIS
COUNTRY.
IN THE LATE REVOLUTION, HE WAS THE
FIRST ON THE SEAS TO HURL DEFIANCE AT PROUD BRITAIN;
GALLANTLY LEADING THE WAY TO ARREST FROM
THE MISTRESS OF THE OCEAN, HER SCEPTER,
AND THERE TO WAVE THE STAR-SPANGLED BANNER.
HE ALSO CONDUCTED TO SEA,
THE FIRST SQUARE-RIGGED VESSEL EVER BUILT ON THE
OHIO,
OPENING TO COMMERCE
RESOURCES BEYOND CALCULATION.

Chapter III
HON. JAMES MITCHELL VARNUM*

James Mitchell Varnum

*The following sketch is chiefly extracted from a full and well written biography of Gen. Varnum, by Wilkins Updike, Esq., of Kingston, R. I., and published in the Memoirs of the Bar of Rhode Island, in 1842.

"Two brothers of the name of Varnum, emigrated from Wales to Boston, just prior to the year 1660 and from thence to Ipswich, where one died without issue. Samuel, the survivor, purchased a large tract of land of the Indians, in the town of Dracut, County of Middlesex, Mass., and settled on it in 1664. He had issue—five sons: John, Thomas, and Joseph, and two who were shot in a boat while crossing the Merrimack with their father. The descendants of John and Thomas reside in Dracut and elsewhere. Joseph was Colonel of the militia, and wounded in the Indian War of 1676. He erected a garrison house, which is still standing as the family mansion, in a good state of preservation. Joseph Varnum left two sons, Joseph and Samuel, who inherited a large estate from their father. Joseph had issue, and several families have descended from him. Samuel had four sons: Samuel, James Mitchell, Joseph Bradley, and Daniel Varnum. Samuel died in Maine, about twenty years since; Joseph

B. in 1821; and Daniel in 1822, on the patrimonial estate, which has remained in the family since the first purchase from the natives.

Most of the brothers held prominent official stations in Massachusetts. Joseph B. was elected a member of Congress from his native district in 1795, and successively re-elected till 1811, and then elected senator one term, making his whole service in Congress twenty-two years. From 1807 to 1811, comprising two Congressional terms, he was elected speaker of the House of Representatives.

The subject of this memoir, James Mitchell Varnum, was born in Dracut, the residence of his ancestors, in 1749. He entered Rhode Island College, now Brown University, then established in Warren, and was in the first class that graduated from that institution, in 1769, at the age of twenty. He received the first honors of his class, and in a forensic discussion, vindicated the rights of the colonists in their resistance to British taxation, with signal ability. He kept a classical school for a short period after he graduated, and always spoke highly of its benefit to a student, to plant deeply in the mind those elements acquired in the college hall; and his whole life demonstrated that he had profited by it. He was deeply attached to mathematical science, and delighted in its pursuits. His whole life was in evidence that he was naturally a mathematician. His habits were those of intense study and boisterous relaxation. He was fond of exhibiting his skill in gymnastics, and ever ready to exercise in that ancient art with anyone who would engage with him, noble or ignoble. Strong and active in frame, and ardently attached to such exercises, he gave his inclination for such sports, the fullest range, to a late period of his life.

Soon after his college course he entered the office of Oliver Arnold, in Providence, then attorney-general of the colony. William Channing, Thomas Arnold, John S. Dexter and himself, were students together, at the time of Mr. Arnold's death, in 1770; and in the succeeding year, Varnum was admitted to the bar. He settled at East Greenwich, where his talents acquired for him an extensive practice; and he traveled the circuits of the state, reaping the honors and the rewards of his profession.

Mr. Varnum had a great taste for military life, and early joined the Kentish Guards, and was appointed Commander of that company in 1774; a company which, from their acquirements in military tactics, became the nursery of so many distinguished officers during the

Revolutionary War: Gen. Greene, Gen. Varnum, Col. Greene, Col. Crary, Maj. Whitemarsh, and others, making thirty-two in all, who entered the Revolutionary army as commissioned officers from this company alone. The prominent part Mr. Varnum had taken in the colonial controversy inspired an ambition to enter the military service of his country. The venerable John Howland, president of the Historical Society of this state, in a communication, states, that "When the news of the Lexington Battle reached East Greenwich, Varnum's company mustered, and marched to Providence, on their way to the scene of action. I recollect seeing them on their arrival; Nathaniel Greene, of Coventry, afterward the General, was a Private, with a musket on his shoulder; and Christopher Greene, afterward Col. Greene, who defended Red Bank, was also there, a Private in the same company. They marched beyond Pawtucket, and hearing that the enemy had retired to Boston, they returned. The next week, the General Assembly convened, and resolved to raise three regiments of infantry and a company of artillery. Mr. Nathaniel Greene, then a member of the House of Representatives, was appointed Brigadier-General, and Varnum, Colonel of the regiment to be raised in the counties of Kent and King's; Daniel Hitchcock to be Colonel of the regiment to be raised in Providence, and Church to be Colonel of the regiment to be raised in the counties of Newport and Bristol. Varnum took rank over Hitchcock and Church, from having commanded in the Kentish Guards, with the rank of Colonel. The time for which these troops were called out, expired December 31st, 1775. The state raised two regiments for the year 1776. Varnum commanded the first, and Hitchcock the second. The officers of these troops afterward received commissions from the President of Congress, when Washington was appointed Commander-in-Chief. They were then styled Continental Troops. In January, 1776, the state raised a regiment called State Troops, to be stationed in Newport. They remained there until the disastrous battle on Long island. This regiment, commanded by Col. Lippitt, was taken into the Continental service, and ordered to join Gen. Washington at New York; they arrived at Harlem after the evacuation of the city. This regiment composed part of the brigade commanded by Gen. John Nixon, which consisted of five regiments, commanded by Cols. Nixon and Little, of Massachusetts; Varnum, Hitchcock, and Lippitt, of Rhode Island. Toward the close of the year, Gen. Nixon was dispatched, by the Commander-in-Chief, on furlough, to Massachusetts, to urge the raising of new recruits for the army, to supply the place of those whose term of service would expire on the 31st of December; as without reinforcements, Gen. Washington would be left without an army at the commencement of the succeeding year. Gen. Varnum then succeeded to the command of the brigade. But the necessity of the case, and the perilous situation of the country, induced Gen. Washington soon after to send Gen. Varnum to the Assembly of Rhode Island, for the same purpose; selecting, for this all-important mission, those officers, for their known influence with their respective legislatures. The command of this brigade of five regiments then devolved on Col. Hitchcock, as the senior officer. He commanded it at a period the most important in our Revolutionary history, and led his brigade with courage and ability, in the memorable battles of Trenton and Princeton; and for his signal gallantry, received the special thanks of Gen. Washington, in front of the college at Princeton, and which he was requested to present to the brigade he had so ably commanded.

In February, 1777, Col. Varnum was promoted by Congress to the rank of Brigadier-General. The appointment was announced to him by Gen. Washington, by letter, under date of March 3d, of that year, which contains ample evidence that his military bearing had met the full approbation of the Commander-in-Chief. The General Assembly of this state in their December session, 1776, having appointed Gen. Varnum, Commander of the state forces, at their March session, 1777, entered the following honorable testimonial of approbation on their journal: *"Whereas, the appointment and commission of Brig. Gen. James M. Varnum, in the service of this state, has been suspended by his being appointed by the honorable continental Congress, to the same rank in the continental army: this assembly do, therefore, in grateful remembrance of his services, vote and resolve, that he is dismissed from his said appointment, and that he be paid to the time his pay commenced in the continental service."*

"Under the latter appointment," continues Mr. Howland, "Gen. Varnum commanded all that body of troops on the Jersey side of the Delaware, when the British and Hessians took possession of Philadelphia. Gen. Washington's purpose was to prevent the passage of the enemy's shipping up the river, and for this purpose a strong fort was

erected on Red Bank, and a regiment of Marylanders on Mud Island. Col. Christopher Greene commanded the two Rhode Island regiments: Lieut. Col. Samuel Smith, on Mud Island, and Varnum the whole line of the coast of New Jersey. In October the enemy made a determined attack; but the battery and fort were so valiantly defended, that the invaders were defeated and compelled to withdraw, and temporarily abandon the enterprise. The gallant defense of Fort Mifflin, or Mud Island, and the defeat of the Hessians at Fort Mercer on Red Bank, drew from Congress, then sitting at Yorktown, a resolution of thanks, and votes of elegant swords to Col. Greene, Lieut. Col. Smith, and Com. Hazelwood, for their intrepid defense of these two forts."

"But the British, resolved on the capture of these posts, so important in their position, renewed the attack in November. They brought up their shipping, the Somerset, of sixty-four guns, and a number of floating batteries, to break up the chevaux de frise, which extended across the river, and our forts opened their fire to prevent it. Col. Smith was wounded on the 11th of November, and the command devolved on Lieut. Col. Russell, of the Connecticut line, who, exhausted by fatigue, and destitute of health, requested to be recalled. The moment was critical. The Commander-in-Chief, Gen. Washington, had no idea of defending the place through the campaign, but wished to retard the operations of the enemy, until the main army should be reinforced by the Massachusetts brigade, marching from the conquest of Saratoga, when he would be in sufficient force to cover the country, or to meet the enemy's whole force in the field. Upon the 12th, he signified his wish to Gen. Varnum, to defend the island as long as possible, without sacrificing the garrison. Gen. Varnum, considering the imminent danger of the post, immediately convened the field officers of Red Bank Fort, with a request that one of them would volunteer, as Gen. Washington desired the island to be defended as long as possible, and take command of it in lieu of Smith, who had left. At this momentous crisis, Maj. Simon Thayer immediately offered himself, to the inexpressible satisfaction of Gen. Varnum. In the defense, to an officer knowing all the circumstances, nothing presented itself but death, or an improbable escape, without the possibility of contending on even terms. But Maj. Thayer gallantly defended it day and night from the 12th, to twelve o'clock at night on the 16th of November, when the breastworks were beaten down, and no cover left for his men, when the general ordered him to abandon it. By those unacquainted with the transaction, all the glory has been ascribed to Col. Smith. If heroic valor was to be rewarded, who should have had the sword? When the swords which were wrought in France, arrived, and were to be presented, Gen. Varnum published a letter, dated at East Greenwich, August 3d, 1786, narrating all the circumstances attending the heroic defense of Mud Island by Maj. Thayer. It is written in a natural, straightforward style, and in justice to the memory of this intrepid soldier of Rhode Island, and of his country, ought to be preserved in some durable form. Gen. Varnum continued in active service during the year 1778, and commanded a brigade in Sullivan's Expedition on Rhode Island.

In 1779 he resigned his commission in the army, there being at that time more general officers in the service than were needful, in proportion to the men, and his talents being more congenial with political life than the duties of the camp; although he was respected and esteemed as a good and gallant officer. The legislature of this state, in consideration of his national services, and effectually to secure them in defense of the state, in May, 1779, elected him Major-General of the Militia, to which office he was unanimously re-elected during the remainder of his life. In April, 1780, the people of the state, in grateful recollection of his eminent services in the cause of public liberty, and desirous to throw into the national councils, those distinguished talents which could be spared from the field, elected him their delegate to the confederated Congress of that year. As that body sat with closed doors, his voice could not be heard by the public, but his name appears oftener in the published journals, than many others of that body.

Mr. Howland continues to observe, "The old Congress under the confederation, had no power to raise money to carry on the war, either by taxes or imposts, and the states had enough to do, to furnish their own treasuries. Congress, on the 3d of February, 1781, requested the several states to grant them power to levy an impost of five per cent., *ad valorem*, on all imported goods; and all prizes and prize goods, to be appropriated to the discharge of principal and interest of debts contracted, or to be contracted, on the faith of the United States, for the support of the war. This was thought necessary to the salvation of the country, and to maintain our independence."

The granting of this power to Congress, to raise revenue, was a new question, and divided the politicians in its discussion. To place the case, in its urgent necessity, before the respective legislatures of the states, several of the best speakers in Congress requested, or thought proper to return home, and persuade the people to grant the power. Rufus King advocated it in Massachusetts; Dayton left his seat to advocate the cause in New Jersey; and Varnum came to Rhode Island for the same purpose. The states which had little or no maritime commerce, readily granted the power. This question brought a new man into the field in Rhode Island. David Howell, knowing the importers would generally oppose the power, and that the people at large would unwillingly be deprived of a rich source of state revenue, at a crisis so distressing, came out in the Providence Gazette, and in all public places, with violent declamation against the five per cent, as it was called. He argued, if you once grant them five, they will soon take ten, then twenty, &c Gen. Varnum vindicated the grant, in the same paper, over the signature of "Citizen Howell", over that of "Farmer," knowing the Majority of every state were farmers. At length the question came before the General Assembly; Varnum's speech occupied the forenoon, and, in strength of argument and eloquence, had not been equalled since the settlement of the state. Howell occupied the afternoon; the question was then taken, and decided in the negative. It was afterward ascertained, that a Majority had predetermined and agreed not to grant the power. Eleven of the states granted the five per cent. New York, headed by George Clinton, never decided one way or the other; and Rhode Island refused. So Congress was defeated in the necessary source of revenue; all the states not concurring in the measure.

After the war, Gen. Varnum recommenced the practice of law at East Greenwich, with increased reputation, and was promptly engaged in all the important causes in the state. At that period great and important cases arose, growing out of the new position in which the state and nation were placed. The great case of Trevett vs. Weeden was one which stirred the community to its very foundations. Upon its issue was involved the destiny of thousands. Public feeling and anxiety were intense upon its result. The period succeeding the Revolution was the most eventful in our history. The crisis arose, and the experiment was on trial, whether the people were capable of self-government; and upon its issue depended the fate of the nation. The country was exhausted by a protracted contest; and disappointed in the expectation of sufficient national resources, to meet the embarrassments produced by it; insubordination and misrule showed themselves everywhere. The army returned unpaid and discontented, with certificates upon a bankrupt treasury, instead of money, amidst a state population as impoverished as themselves. The state itself was insolvent, and wholly unable to pay the bills of credit against it. The stock of the farmer was selling at the auction posts, for the payment of taxes. The old Congress was as embarrassed as the states for pecuniary means to discharge their engagements. They made requisitions in conformity to the powers delegated to them under the confederation: owing to inability the states rejected them. The bills which Congress had negotiated in Holland for the payment of the army, were unpaid at maturity, and returned protested: the damages alone amounting to the startling sum of six hundred and thirty-six thousand dollars. At this act of sovereign dishonor and disgrace of the new republic, our ambassadors, Franklin, Jay, and Adams, were in despair. Prompted by exorbitant profit, the merchants shipped to Europe, all the remaining specie that could be obtained to supply the country with fabrics, which the war had exhausted. Massachusetts alone exported three millions of specie from the commencement of peace, to July, 1785; and we can only judge, by estimation, of the vast amount exported from other seaports for the same purposes: so that in a short period, all the gold brought by the French, and the silver imported from the Spanish West Indies, was drained from the country. The avaricious course pursued by the merchants compelled the borrower to pay *twenty* per cent, per annum, and some *four* per cent, per month. Such was the posture of affairs at this momentous crisis. The confederation was powerless. The veteran soldiers, who had exposed themselves to tempests and battles through the whole contest, and whom peace had dismissed with laurels, returned to their families, penniless and clamorous. Necessity and distress showed themselves by insurrections and commotions in every quarter. If Shays had possessed courage equal to his address and ability, he might have marched in triumph through the nation, gathering to his standard, spirits enough to have insured him victory; such was the perilous condition of the republic The state threw itself upon its reserved rights; and the demagogues, who could best live and nourish in turbulent political waters, seizing upon the agitated occasion, roused the distressed of every class into a frenzy, and made them believe, that Midas-like, they could touch paper, and convert it to gold. The paper money party obtained an overwhelming Majority, and expressly instructed their representatives for the purpose; and in May, 1786, emitted the enormous sum of one hundred thousand pounds in paper bills. It was further enacted, that said bills' should, *"be a good and lawful tender for the complete payment and final discharge of all fines, forfeitures, judgments, and executions, that had become due and recovered, of every kind and nature whatsoever."* There was no time fixed when said bills were to be redeemed, nor was their ultimate payment charged upon any fund, nor was it designated how they were to be paid. They were to be loaned for fourteen years upon mortgage, pro rata, to all the people, at four per cent, interest for the first seven years, and to be repaid in the next seven years, in seven equal installments, without interest, and then they were *"to be consumed by fire;"* thus intending to annihilate the merchants, then fancied opponents, at a blow. These bills fell into immediate discredit, and those who had property chose rather to retain, than exchange it. They further enacted that if any one refused to take it in place of specie, he should be fined one hundred pounds, and stand disfranchised. Every citizen was also to swear that he would use his endeavors to give it currency equal to gold and silver, and sell their property at the same prices for one, as the other. Trials under the law could be had at a called court, and the culprit was denied the privilege of a jury. These curious movements of the public mind go to prove that "the Inquisition" may exist in a republic, in civil affairs, as well as in a Roman Catholic country, in matters of religion.

The paper-money system gave rise to a celebrated lawsuit, in which Gen. Varnum was engaged, and where he displayed his eloquence and law knowledge in a masterly manner. John Trevett, of Newport, bought meat of John Weeden, a butcher, in the market, and tendered to him bills of the emission of May preceding in payment, which Weeden refused. From thence arose this trial, before a special court, in September, 1786. If the complaint was sustained by the judgment of the court, all the commerce and business of the state would be destroyed and all previous obligations canceled by this irredeemable trash. The whole population was deeply interested, and gathered, in vast numbers, at the courthouse. Here Gen. Varnum displayed his vast powers, as an orator, in a manner never developed before, and came fully up to Patrick Henry's famous tobacco case, in exciting the applause and approbation of the people. The court adjudged the amended acts of the legislature, unconstitutional, and so void. The fearless independence of the bench overthrew the tyranny of the demagogues, and the state was saved. But it was eulogium enough on Varnum, that the power of these speeches wrought such a triumphant victory over public opinion, that the dominant party, to save themselves from political prostration, were compelled to repeal their arbitrary and unconstitutional acts, within sixty days from the time of their passage. Gen. Varnum was not cold and phlegmatic in his eloquence; his temperament was naturally ardent; and when excited or roused by the circumstances or events of his cause, was vehement. None can impart warmth or zeal, that have none of their own; and to impress an assembly with the truth or sanctity of our cause, we must ourselves be convinced that it is true.

In 1786, Gen. Varnum was again elected a representative to the old Congress, and was an efficient member. At the same session, the distinguished William Samuel Johnson was also a representative from Connecticut; an intimacy was contracted between them, which continued during their lives. This circumstance is mentioned to show why Dr. Johnson spoke of Gen. Varnum, in the case of Smith, of Connecticut, against John Brown, of Providence, in such favorable terms. It was a prize cause, of magnitude, and from the parties concerned, and the eminence of the counsel engaged, it excited unusual interest. It was tried before Judge Foster, Judge of the State Admiralty Court at Kingstown. Jesse Root, afterward chief Justice of the Supreme Court of Connecticut, and compiler of Root's reports, opened the case in behalf of Smith, and William Channing, Attorney-General of Rhode Island, and Gen. Varnum conducted the defense in behalf of Brown, and the distinguished jurist and Christian, Dr. Johnson, of Stratford, closed for the claimant. From the splendor of the talents of counsel, unusual attention was attracted to the scene. The neat, concise, and clear openings by Root and Channing, the brilliant language and thundering eloquence of Varnum, and the calm, placid, unostentatious and classical oratory of Johnson, furnished a legal and intellectual banquet, such as was never seen before, and probably never since, in Rhode Island. To sustain himself against such power, was victory enough; but Varnum did more; he not only sustained the high expectations of his friends, and the reputation of the Rhode Island bar, but drove his adversaries finally to a non-suit. Dr. Johnson, whose heart was too magnanimous for envy, beside paying to Gen. Varnum, merited compliments in the close, stated, at a party in the evening, That he knew Gen. Varnum in Congress, and that he was a man of uncommon talents, and of the most brilliant eloquence. We feel assured that he was justly entitled to this eulogium, or Dr. Johnson would not have given it. The following is a description of the person and dress of Gen. Varnum at the bar: It was the fashion of that day to be very well, or rather elegantly dressed.

"Gen. Varnum appeared with a brick-colored coat, trimmed with gold lace; buckskin small clothes, with gold lace bands; silk stockings, and boots; a high, delicate, and white forehead; eyes prominent, and of a dark hue; his complexion rather florid; somewhat corpulent; well proportioned, and finely formed for strength and agility; large eyebrows; nose straight, and rather broad; teeth perfectly white; a profuse head of hair, short on the forehead, turned up some, and deeply powdered and clubbed. When he took off his cocked hat, he would lightly brush up his hair forward and with a fascinating smile lighting up his countenance, take his seat in court."

This was the last great effort of Gen. Varnum in Rhode Island. At what precise time this trial took place, cannot now be ascertained, as no record of that court can be found. That it was after the confederated Congress of 1787, is presumable; because he spoke of their intimacy while in Congress together; and Dr. Johnson and Gen. Varnum were not both members of the same Congress before that period.

Gen. Varnum was a warm and unwavering advocate for a federal constitution; he knew the inefficiency of the confederation, and also the selfish considerations that governed the states. If an instrument cementing the Union was not speedily adopted, he felt that future efforts would be unavailing. The legal profession, with Gen. Varnum at their head, the mercantile, and the sound portion of the agricultural interests, urged the Legislature of Rhode Island, at their June session, 1787, in the strongest terms, to send delegates to the federal convention, assembled at Philadelphia. But the advocates of the paper-money system, and the revenue accruing to the state from imposts, Rhode Island being then the second or third importing state, defeated the measure. The minority in the Legislature, and those friendly to the federal constitution, addressed the convention on the subject, and enclosed it to Gen. Varnum, to be delivered to that body.

Early in the year 1787, the Ohio Land Company was organized in Boston; it was originated by the disbanded officers of the late army, many of whom were stockholders, while the larger portion was made up from the citizens at large. The Ordinance of Congress, establishing the Northwest Territory, was passed the 13th of July, 1787; in August of that year, Gen. Varnum was appointed one of the Directors of the Ohio Company. In September, Gen. Arthur St. Clair was appointed Governor of the new territory, and, in October following, Gen. Varnum, Samuel H. Parsons, and John Cleves Symmes, Judges of the Supreme Court. He left his home in Rhode Island in the spring of 1788, on his route to the Northwest Territory, by the way of Baltimore, and arrived at Marietta early in June. Gen. Parsons was there on the 26th of May; Gov. St. Clair arrived on the 9th of July, at Fort Harmar, under the escort of Maj. Doughty, who went up with the garrison barge and a party of soldiers to meet him at Fort McIntosh. On the 4th of July, the American Independence was celebrated at Marietta, by the citizens, and the officers of Fort Harmar, in a long bowery built near the upper point at the mouth of the Muskingum. Gen. Varnum was invited to deliver an oration, which was done with his usual eloquence. *"The oration is short, but contains many beauties both in sentiment and language."* It was published at Newport in the same year, by order of the directors and agents of the Ohio Land Company, to which is annexed the speech of Gov. St. Clair, and proceedings of the inhabitants. A copy of the speeches is attached to the appendix of this volume.

His health was poor when he arrived at Marietta, having for some time been threatened with a lung complaint. The long journey and change of climate, no doubt led him to expect would effect a favorable change in his disease; but his health gradually declined after his arrival, so that by the setting in of cold weather, he was quite feeble, and evidently in a deep consumption. During the summer and autumn he was able to attend to the duties of a director in the meetings of that board, and no doubt his fine taste for the beautiful was exerted in promoting the resolution for the preservation of those ancient remains erected on the present site of Marietta, as memorials of that departed race of men who once inhabited the valley of the Ohio. He also had made preparation for opening a farm; and a clearing of several acres, made by him, a mile or two east of the town, was, for many years, known by the name of Varnum's Clearing, and now occupies the center of one of the finest farms in this vicinity. He assisted Gov. St. Clair and Gen. Parsons in forming a code of laws for the government of the Northwest Territory, twenty-six of which were promulgated during his life; the last of them being signed on the 21st of December. About this time he addressed the following letter to his wife. It is written with that entire truth, honesty, and deep sensibility, which all more or less feel at the approach of death; but which few have the ability to express in such fervent and beautiful language. It was published in 1791, in the American Magazine, as a fine specimen of elegant composition; but is now copied from his life, as a memorial of the heart and soul of Gen. Varnum.

"My Dearest And Most Estimable Friend:

I now address you from my sick chamber, and perhaps it will be the last letter that you will receive from me. My lungs are so far affected that it is impossible for me to recover, but by exchange of air and a warm climate. I expect to leave this place on Sunday or Monday next for the falls of Ohio. If I feel myself mend by the tour, I shall go no farther; but if not, and my strength should continue, I expect to proceed to New Orleans, and from thence, by the West Indies, to Rhode Island. My physicians, most of them, think the chances of recovery in my favor; however, I am neither elevated nor depressed by the force of opinion, but shall meet my fate with humility and fortitude. I cannot, however, but indulge the hope that I shall again embrace my lovely friend in this world; and that we may glide smoothly down the tide of time for a few years, and enjoy together the more substantial happiness and satisfaction, as we have already the desirable pleasures of life. It is now almost nineteen years, since Heaven connected us by the tenderest and the most sacred of ties; and it is the same length of time that our friendship hath been increased by every rational and endearing motive; it is now stronger than death, and I am firmly persuaded will follow us into an existence of never-ending felicity. But my lovely friend, the gloomy moment will arrive when we must part; and should it arrive during our present separation, my last and only reluctant thoughts will be employed about my dearest Martha. Life, my dearest friend, is but a bubble; it soon bursts, and is remitted to eternity. When we look back to the earliest recollections of our youthful hours, it seems but the last period of our rest, and we appear to emerge from a night of slumbers, to look forward to real existence. When we look forward, time appears as indeterminate as eternity, and we have no idea of its termination, but by the period of our dissolution. What particular relation it bears to a future state, our general notions of religion cannot point out; we feel something constantly active within us, that is evidently beyond the reach of mortality; but whether it is a part of ourselves, or an emanation from the pure Source of existence, or re-absorbed when death shall have finished his work, human wisdom cannot determine. Whether the demolition of the body introduces only a change in the manner of our being, or leaves it to progress infinitely, alternately elevated and depressed, according to the propriety of our conduct, or whether we return to the common mass of unthinking matter, philosophy hesitates to decide. I know, therefore, but one source from whence can be derived complete consolation in a dying hour and that is the divine system contained in the gospel of Jesus Christ. There, life and immortality are brought to light; there, we are taught our existence is to be eternal, and, secure in an interest in the atoning merits of a bleeding Savior, that we shall be inconceivably happy. A firm and unshaken faith in this doctrine, must raise us above the doubts and fears that hang upon every other system, and enable us to view with a calm serenity, the approach of the king of terrors, and to behold him as a kind and indulgent friend, speeding his shafts only to carry us, the sooner, to our everlasting home. But should there be a more extensive religion beyond the Vail, and without the reach of mortal observation, the Christian religion is by no means shaken thereby, as it is not opposed to any principle that admits of the perfect benevolence of the Deity. My only doubt is, whether the punishment threatened in the New Testament, is annexed to a state of unbelief, which may be removed hereafter, and so a restoration take place; or whether the state of the mind at death, irretrievably fixes its doom forever. I hope and pray that the Divine Spirit will give me such assurances of an acceptance with God, through the merits and sufferings of his Son, as to brighten the way to immediate happiness. Dry up your tears, my charming mourner, nor suffer this letter to give too much inquietude. Consider the facts at present as in theory; but the sentiments such as will apply whenever the change shall come. I know that humanity must and will be indulged in its keenest grief, but there is no advantage in too deeply anticipating our inevitable sorrows. If I did not persuade myself that you would conduct with becoming prudence and fortitude, upon this occasion, my own unhappiness would be greatly increased, and perhaps my disorder too; but I have so much confidence in your discretion, as to un-bosom my inmost soul. You must not expect to hear from me again, until the coming spring, as the river will soon be shut up with ice, and there will be no communication from below; and if in a situation for the purpose, I will return as soon as practicable. Give my sincerest love to all those you hold dear; I hope to see them again, and love them more than ever. Adieu, my dearest friend; and while I fervently devote, in one undivided prayer, our immortal souls to the care, forgiveness, mercy, and all-prevailing grace of Heaven in time, and through eternity, I must bid you a long, long, long farewell.

James M. Varnum."

His fast declining health, and the rapid approach of winter, prevented his making the attempt to remove to a warmer climate. It was fortunate he did not, as he would have died amongst strangers, with no one on whom he could lean in his last moments; while in Marietta he was surrounded with warm and devoted friends who did all in their power to alleviate his sufferings and make his final passage as easy as mortality will allow. He died on the 10th of January, 1789, the day after the signing of the treaty with the Indians at Fort Harmar, which accounts for the attendance of the chiefs at his burial, and in less than eight months after his arrival. The funeral took place on the 13th, and was attended with all the ceremony and respect due to so distinguished a person. On this occasion Dr. Drowne from Rhode Island, delivered a funeral oration, a copy of which is attached to the appendix.

The following order of procession is copied from the original manuscript, in the handwriting of Winthrop Sargeant, Secretary of the Territory, and found among the papers of Griffin Greene, in 1846.

"Early in life Gen. Varnum married Martha, the eldest daughter of Cromwell Childe, of Warren, in Rhode Island, a family of very considerable distinction. Mrs. Varnum was an amiable, virtuous, and high minded lady, and one of the most cheerful, sociable, and best of wives. She survived her husband forty-eight years, and died at Bristol, without issue, October 10th, 1837, at the advanced age of eighty-eight years.

The career of Gen. Varnum was active, but brief. He graduated at *twenty;* was admitted to the bar at *twenty-two;* entered the army at *twenty-seven;* resigned his commission at *thirty-one;* was member of Congress the same year; resumed practice at *thirty-three,* and continued four years, was elected to Congress again at *thirty-seven;* emigrated to the west at *thirty-nine,* and died at the early age of *forty.* From what researches have been made, it conscientiously can be stated that he was a man of boundless zeal, of warm feelings, of great honesty, of singular disinterestedness; and, as to talents, of prodigal imagination, a dexterous reasoner, and a splendid orator. He was a man made on a gigantic scale; his very defects were masculine and powerful, and, we shall not soon look upon his like again.

ORDER OF PROCESSION.

THE MILITARY.

MARSHALS.   MARSHALS.

Mr. WHEATON, bearing the sword and   Mr. LORD, bearing the civil commission
military commission of the deceased on   on a mourning cushion.
a mourning cushion.   Mr. FEARING, bearing the insignia of
Mr. MAYO, with the diploma and order   masonry on a mourning cushion.
of Cincinnati on a mourning cushion.

PALL-HOLDERS.   CORPSE.   PALL-HOLDERS.
GRIFFIN GREEN, Esq.,   Judge CRARY,
Judge TUPPER,   Judge PUTNAM.
THE SECRETARY.   Judge PARSONS.

PRIVATE MOURNERS.
CHARLES GREENE and RICHARD GREENE.
FREDERICK CRARY and PHILIP GREENE.
Doctor SCOTT and Doctor FARLEY.
DEACON STORY and DOCTOR DROWNE.
Private citizens, two and two.
Indian chiefs, two and two.
The militia officers.
Officers of the garrison at Fort Harmer.
The civil officers.
The Cincinnati.
The Masons.

Messrs. Clark and Leech, Mr. Stratton and Mr. Balch, were requested to superintend the order of the procession. In returning from the grave the order was the same, preceded by the military under Capt. Zeigler.

Chapter IV
SAMUEL HOLDEN PARSONS
BY HIS GRANDSON, S. H. PARSONS, ESQ., OF HARTFORD, CONN.

Maj. Gen. Samuel Holden Parsons was bom at Lyme, in the county of New London, and state of Connecticut, May 14th, 1737, and was the third son of the Rev. Jonathan Parsons, a distinguished clergyman, who removed from Lyme to Newburyport, Mass., in 1746. His mother was the sister of Gov. Matthew Griswold, of Lyme, lineally descended from Henry Wolcot, of Windsor, the ancestor of all of that eminent name in Connecticut.

He graduated at Harvard College, in 1756; and after completing his professional studies in the office of his uncle, Gov. Matthew Griswold, he was admitted to the Bar of New London County, in February, 1759, and settled at Lyme in the practice of law. [Note A.] In September, 1761, he married the daughter of Richard Mather, of Lyme, a lineal descendant of the Rev. Richard Mather, who was born in Lawton, Lancaster County, England, 1596, and settled as the first clergyman of Dorchester, Mass., Aug. 23, 1636, where he died, April 22d, 1669. In 1762, at the age of twenty-five, he was elected a member of the General Assembly of the colony of Connecticut, and was successively re-elected until his removal to New London in 1774. During this period he received repeated proofs of public confidence in various appointments of honor and trust.

In May, 1768, he was appointed by the General Assembly, Auditor, *"to settle and adjust the colony accounts with the treasurer and all others who have received any of the moneys that belong to the colony."* In 1769, the same appointment was continued, with *"further powers to renew, and better secure the moneys and estate due on mortgages, bonds, or other securities, belonging to this colony, which are in danger of being lost."*

In October, 1773, under an act of the General Court, *"concerning the western lands, so-called, lying westward of Delaware River, within the boundaries of this colony,"* he was appointed and associated with the Hon. Matthew Griswold, Eliphalet Dyer, Roger Sherman, Wm. Samuel Johnson, Silas Dean, Wm. Williams, and Jedediah Strong, Esqrs., a Committee with full power to assist his honor, Gov. Trumbull, in *"stating and taking proper steps to pursue the claim of the colony of Connecticut to said western lands; and any three of said committee were authorized and directed to proceed to Philadelphia to wait on his honor, Gov. Penn, in the subject, and to treat with Gov. Penn and the agent or agents of the proprietaries of Pennsylvania, respecting an amicable agreement between the colony and the aforesaid proprietaries concerning the boundaries of this colony and the province of Pennsylvania, to agree upon and ascertain the boundaries between this colony, and the claim of said proprietaries, and such agreement to lay before the General Assembly for confirmation: but if said proprietaries shall prefer joining in an application to his majesty for commissioners to settle said line, then the said Committee are directed to join in behalf of the colony in such application. The Committee were likewise empowered to treat with said Gov. Penn with respect to the peace of the inhabitants who are settled upon said lands, and to agree upon such measures as shall tend to preserve good order, and to prevent mutual violence and contention while the boundaries between this colony and the said province shall remain undisturbed."*

In January, 1774, the same Committee were *"appointed and empowered to assist his honor, Gov. Trumbull, in collecting and preparing all exhibits and documents necessary to pursue and prosecute the claim and title of the colony to the lands lying within the boundaries of the grant and charter of the colony west of the Delaware River, at the court of Great Britain, and to make a proper statement of said cause, to be transmitted to Great Britain for that purpose; and to report to the General Assembly, from time to time, of their proceedings thereon."* Mr. Parsons was an active member of this Committee, and contributed materially by his abilities and unwearied diligence in promoting the important object of the appointment. In May, 1773, he was appointed by the House of Representatives of the Connecticut Colony, one of the *"Standing Committee of Correspondence and Inquiry,* to obtain all such intelligence, and to take up and maintain a correspondence with our sister colonies respecting the important considerations mentioned and expressed in certain resolutions of the patriotic House of Burgesses of Virginia in March last. [Note B.] Mr. Parsons was an energetic member of this Committee, and entered zealously into the cause of the colonies. He had previously corresponded on these subjects with the prominent leaders of the sister colony of Massachusetts. Among the number was the eminent patriot, Samuel Adams, who, says his biographer, (American Quarterly Register, February, 1841, p. 2,) originated the suggestion of assembling the first Congress, which subsequently met at New York—an act which led, at a later period, to the Continental Congress, to the Confederation, and that great chain of events connected with the War of Independence.

The writer of the preceding paragraph was not probably aware that among the manuscripts of Samuel Adams, (in the possession of Hon. Mr. Bancroft,) an original letter exists, written March 3d, 1773, by Samuel Holden Parsons to Mr. Adams, *originating* the suggestion above stated, the honor of which has been heretofore attributed to Mr. Adams---a letter so full of fervent patriotism it may not be amiss to insert entire, as follows:

"Sir:

When the spirit of patriotism seems expiring in America in general, it must afford a very sensible pleasure to the friends of American liberty to see the noble efforts of our Boston friends in the support of the rights of America, as well as their unshaken resolution in opposing any, the least invasion of their charter privileges. I was called to my father's on a very melancholy occasion, and designed to have seen you before my return, but some unforeseen difficulties prevented. I therefore take the liberty to propose to your consideration whether it would not be advisable in the present critical situation of the colonies, to revive an institution which had formerly a very salutary effect— I mean an annual meeting of commissioners from the colonies to consult on their general welfare. You may recollect this took place about the year 1636, and was continued to 1684, between the united colonies of New England. Although they had no decisive authority of themselves, yet here everything was concerted which will be easily suggested to your mind. If we were to take our connection with Great Britain into consideration, it would render the measure convenient, as at present our state of independence on one another is attended with very manifest inconvenience. I have time only to suggest the thought to you, who I know can improve more on the subject than is in my power, had I time. The idea of inalienable allegiance to any prince or state, is an idea to me inadmissible; and I cannot see but that our ancestors, when they first landed in America, were as independent of the crown or king of Great Britain, as if they never had been his subjects; and the only rightful authority derived to him over this people, was by explicit covenant contained in the first charters. These are but broken hints of sentiments I wish I was at liberty more fully to explain. I am, sir, in haste, with esteem,

    Your most obedient servant,

Sam. H. Parsons.

    To Mr. Samuel Adams, in Boston.
Forwarded by Mr. Howe."

In November, 1773, he was appointed "King's Attorney for New London County," and in May, 1774, was also appointed by the General Assembly, " Agent for the *Governor and Company of the Colony,* to receive, sue for, and recover, all such debts or demands as were due to the Governor and Company of the colony, on bonds, notes of hand, or mortgages, deeds, from persons residing in the County of New London; as also to sue for and recover the possession of all such lands within said County of New London, that belonged to said Governor and Company and detained from them, with full power to appear before any court or courts of judicature, and represent said Governor and company for the purpose aforesaid. All these duties were faithfully and satisfactorily performed. The limits of this brief sketch will just permit a detailed view of his arduous labors as a member of the Committee of Correspondence.

The following letter, addressed to the Committee of Boston, on the 17th of May, 1774, (original among the manuscripts of Samuel Adams,) evinces an eagle-eyed vigilance, and a fixed, determined spirit of resistance to oppression, and a bold, daring patriotism, peculiar to the times that tried men's souls.

"Hartford, May 17, 1774.

Gentlemen:

This moment a post from New York arrived here, on his road to Boston, with intelligence of the spirit and firmness with which the inhabitants of that city concur with the friends of America, in support of the cause of our country: we cannot suffer him to pass, without informing you, who immediately feel the effects of ministerial despotism, that the American cause, the state of the town of Boston in particular, and the effect and operation of the late detestable act of an abandoned venal Parliament, were this day brought before our House of Assembly for consideration; and, on discussing the matter, there is no reason to doubt a hearty, spirited concurrence of our Assembly in every proper measure for redress of our wrongs. A committee is appointed to report proper measures to be pursued, and make drafts for the declaration of our rights, &c, which will probably be reported and passed this week; a copy of which will be transmitted as soon as possible. We consider the cause the common cause of all the colonies, and doubt not the concurrence of all to defend and support you. Let us play the man for the cause of our country, and trust the event to Him who orders all events for the best good of his people. We should not have written you at this time, and when no more of our committee are present, but that your distressed condition requires the aid of every friend for your relief. We cannot be warranted in having this made public, as from our committee, there not being a quorum present, but you are at liberty to use it, as from us personally, if it can, in the least, tend to strengthen the hands and encourage the hearts of those in distress.

We are, gentlemen, (the post waiting,) your friends and countrymen, the Committee of Correspondence at Hartford.

Samuel H. Parsons.
Nathaniel Walis, Jr.

To the Committee of Correspondence, at Boston."
[Superscribed to Samuel Adams, Boston.]

By a resolution of the House of Representatives of the Colony of Connecticut, passed June 3d, 1774, the Committee of Correspondence were empowered, on application to them made, or from time to time, as might be found necessary, to appoint a suitable number to attend a congress, or convention of commissioners, or committee of the several colonies, in Boston, America, to consult and advise on proper measures for advancing the best good of the colonies; and such conferences, from time to time, to report to the House of Representatives. [Note C] In pursuance of the above resolution, the Committee of Correspondence met on the 13th of July, 1774, at New London, and nominated the Hon. Eliphalet Dyer, the Hon. Wm. Samuel Johnson, Erastus Wolcot, Silas Dean, and Richard Law, Esq., either three of whom were authorized and empowered, in behalf of the colony, to attend the General Congress of the colonies, proposed to be held at Philadelphia, the first day of September. Three of the above-named gentlemen, viz.: Messrs. Johnson, Wolcot, and Law, by reason of previous engagements and the state of their health, declined the nomination. The committee met at Hartford, the ensuing month of August, [Note D,] and nominated, in their place, the Hon. Roger Sherman and Joseph Trumbull. The first-named gentleman, with the Hon. Eliphalet Dyer, and Silas Dean, Esq., represented the colony of Connecticut in the first Congress, assembled at Carpenter's Hall, Philadelphia on September 5th, 1775.

The passing of the above resolution was immediately communicated, by the Committee of Correspondence, to the Committee at Boston and the House of Representatives of Massachusetts; they, therefore, on the 17th of June, adopted a similar resolution, upon the motion of Samuel Adams. [Note E.] To the colony of Connecticut, therefore, belongs the honor, (heretofore claimed by Massachusetts,) of *first suggesting, and first acting* upon the important subject of the first National Congress of the American Colonies. The first suggestion having been made by Mr.

Parsons, in his letter to Mr. Samuel Adams, March, 1773, and the first action taken by the Connecticut Legislature, June 3d, 1774, of which Legislature Mr. Parsons was a prominent member.

Believing that the possession of Ticonderoga and Crown Point, and the consequent command of Lakes George and Champlain, were objects of essential importance in the approaching conflict, Mr. Parsons, with a few Connecticut gentlemen, formed the bold design of seizing the fortress by surprise. Accordingly, soon after the Battle of Lexington, they borrowed on their *individual credit* the requisite funds from the colonial treasurer to enable them to carry on the enterprise. As success depended upon secrecy and dispatch, and it would be difficult to march any number of men through the country without discovering their plans, they determined to proceed with a small body of volunteers, whom they dispatched immediately on the 27th of April, under Edward Mott, of Preston, a Captain in Col. Parsons' regiment. He proceeded to Bennington, where he met Col. Ethan Allen, a *native of Connecticut,* who readily entered into their views, and agreed to conduct the enterprise. After having assembled at Castleton about two hundred and seventy men, Col. Allen assumed the command, and successfully completed the whole plan; capturing the forts, and making prisoners of the garrison without the loss of a single man. This was the first blow— the first *offensive* blow struck by the colonies. At Concord and Lexington the Americans acted on the *defensive,* but this was the *first* act in which our countrymen were the assailants—the first attack planned and successfully executed — an enterprise highly important in its glorious results, and tending to inspire the Americans with additional confidence in themselves. It was planned by Connecticut, executed under her instructions, and paid for and maintained by her men and treasury. [Note F.]

In 1770 Mr. Parsons was appointed Major of the Fourteenth Regiment of Militia; and on the 26th of April, 1775, was commissioned by the colony of Connecticut as Colonel of the Sixth Regiment, raised *"for the special defense and safety of the colony,"* and soon after marched to and continued at Roxbury, until the British evacuated Boston, when he was ordered to New York. He was actively engaged at the Battle of Long Island, August, 1776. In describing this battle, the historian Botta says, *"Lord Percy came up with his corps, and the entire* columns descended by the village of Bedford from the heights into the plain which lay between the hills and the camp of the Americans. During this time, Gen. Grant, in order to amuse the enemy and direct his attention from the events which took place upon the route of Flatland, endeavored to disquiet him upon his right: accordingly as if he intended to force the defile which led to it, put himself in motion at midnight, and attacked the militia of New York and of Pennsylvania who guarded it. They at first gave way, but Gen. Parsons being arrived, and having occupied an eminence; he renewed the combat and maintained his position until Brig. Gen. Lord Sterling came to his assistance with fifteen hundred men. The action became extremely animated, and fortune favored neither the one side nor the other. The Hessians, on their part, had attacked the center at break of day, and the Americans commanded by Gen. Sullivan, valiantly sustained their efforts. At the same time, the English ships, after having made several movements, opened a very brisk cannonade against a battery established in the little island of Red Hook, upon the right flank of the Americans, who combated against Gen. Grant. This, also, was a diversion, the object of which was to prevent them from attending to what passed in the center and on the left. The Americans defended themselves with extreme gallantry, ignorant that so much valor was exerted in vain, since victory was already in the hands of the enemy."

In Mrs. Williams' *"Life of Olney"*, she says, *"The militia of New York and Pennsylvania were attacked by Percy, and about giving way, when Parsons arrived to their relief, and renewed the combat, maintaining his position against fearful odds until Sterling came to his relief."*

"President Stiles, in his diary, says *"It was said that Grant, (British Colonel,) was slain by our Gen. Parsons."*

In August, 1776, he was appointed by Congress Brigadier-General, and was with the army at Harlem Heights, Kingsbridge, and in the Battle of White Plains. He was subsequently stationed at Peekskill with a portion of the army to protect the important posts upon the North River, and from thence was frequently detached on various expeditions.

In 1777, about the middle of May, returning to Peekskill from Connecticut with a body of recruits, and learning while passing through New Haven that the enemy had collected a large quantity of forage and provisions at Sagg Harbor, for the supply of their army at New York, Gen. Parsons determined to seize the same, and with that view dispatched Lieut. Col. Meigs with about one hundred and sixty men, who completely effected the object of the expedition, and also burnt one of the enemy's armed vessels, took ninety prisoners, and re-crossed the sound without the loss of a single man. This was the most important operation of the campaign of 1777, and proves, by its successful results, great wisdom and judgment in its design, and consummate skill and valor in its execution. It was specially noticed by Congress and by Washington in a very complimentary manner, and is particularly described by Marshall, in his "*Life of Washington*", vol. iii, p. 96, as well as in the following letter from Gen. Parsons to Gov. Trumbull, dated New Haven, May 30th, 1777:

"*I sincerely congratulate your honor on the success of our arms at Long Island. Col. Meigs left Sachem's Head on Tuesday, at one o'clock, P. M., with a detachment of one hundred and sixty men, officers included, and landed within three miles of Sagg Harbor, about one at night; and having made the proper arrangements for attacking the enemy in five different places, proceeded in the greatest order and silence within twenty rods of the enemy, when they rushed on with fixed bayonets upon the different barracks, guards and quarters, while Capt. Troop, with a party under his command, at the same time took possession of the wharves, and vessels lying there. The alarm soon became general, and an incessant fire of grape and round shot was kept up from an armed schooner of twelve guns, which lay within one hundred and fifty yards of the wharves, for an hour; notwithstanding which, the party burnt all the vessels at the wharf, killed and captured all the men who belonged to them, destroyed about one hundred tons of hay, large quantities of grain, ten hogsheads of rum, and other West India goods, and secured all the soldiers who were stationed there. The prisoners are about ninety, among whom are Mr. Chew and Mr. Bell. I have the satisfaction of being informed that the officers and men, without exception, behaved with the greatest order and bravery, and not a man on our side either killed or wounded. Eleven vessels, great and small, were destroyed in the above affair, and the prisoners taken were about* one-third seamen; the others, generally American recruits, are sent to Hartford."

See letter to Gen. Washington, May 25, 1777. [Note C]

In June, 1777, we find him in New Jersey, reinforcing the army of Gen. Washington, encamped at Middlebrook, anticipating an attack from Gen. Howe, who, it was supposed, had designs on Philadelphia. The following letter, written June 22, 1777, by Gen. Parsons, to his wife, describing the *locality of a marching army* watching the movements of his enemy, may not be uninteresting:

"I have no way to tell you where I am, but by describing the place which has no name. Our camp is about two miles advanced in front of the mountain where the army is posted, on the road to Quibbletown, about one and a half miles north of that town, about two and a half miles northwest of Samptown, about three miles west of Browsetown, and about ten miles northwest of Spanktown, about eight miles northeast from Brunswick, six miles from Middlebrook, about one mile from the stream called Bonn's Brook, eastward, but further distant from the village of that name. If you can find me by this description, I shall rejoice to hear from you. I expect to remove from this place very soon. Our neighborhood with the enemy gives us frequent skirmishes, though nothing very material has occurred since the rascals retreated in so scandalous a manner from Somerset Courthouse to Brunswick. Their grand encampment seems now to be extended from Brunswick to Amboy. We are induced to believe they are embarking for some other place, and this state will soon be clear of them; however, this is at present not certain. I think their retreat must have an exceeding good effect in every point of view. If they advance to Millstone or Somerset to try the credit they may give their friends, and see what number will join them, they must be greatly mortified to find almost every man who had received his majesty's protection and most gracious pardon in arms against them. Not the militia only of this state, but almost every man in it able to bear arms, have voluntarily flown to arms on this occasion. If they designed to penetrate the country to Philadelphia, they are convinced it is impracticable. If they designed to turn the flank of our army, and draw us from our strong grounds, they are disappointed.

The effect this maneuver will have on their army and our forces, and on the minds of the disaffected in the country, will probably be of great advantage to us. Our army is now respectable, but not such as that we incline to attack them in their strongholds at present; especially as delay is considered as fatal to them, if we prevent their penetrating the country. The general is very well, and in good spirits; and our affairs have a more promising aspect, than since the war began. Where their next movement will be, is yet uncertain; perhaps, if I live, I may see you sooner than I expected, when I left home. About one thousand of my brigade have joined us; more are expected every hour. Col. Butler and Maj. Sill are at Morristown; I expect they will soon have orders to join their brigades. Every necessary of life is exceedingly dear; salt is from ten to twenty dollars per bushel, and other things very extravagant. I am in very comfortable circumstances myself, though not very well.

Since writing the above, the enemy has evacuated Brunswick, with great precipitation and evident signs of fear, and are fled to Amboy. They left Brunswick at ten o'clock, and Gen. Gaines took possession by the time they were out. They left a considerable quantity of flour and other things, but I have not seen the return yet. We pursued them, and attacked their rear and flank, to Amboy, where they are going on board their ships. This state is once more delivered from those pests of society; who will next be infested with them, is uncertain, but we are in high spirits, and ready to march to any part of the country. I expect orders to march, very soon, perhaps to the North River again, where I shall write you.

I am, my dear, with love to children,
Your affectionate husband,

Samuel H. Parsons."

After the retreat of Gen. Howe from New Jersey, the brigades of Parsons and Varnum were detached from Middlebrook to Peekskill; and those Continental Troops at Peekskill, which had been ordered by Gen. Washington to join him in New Jersey, and had proceeded as far as Pompton Plains, now returned to their former station, with directions to hold themselves in readiness to move on the shortest notice. (Marshall, Vol. iii, p. 119.) It was conjectured that the British Gens. Burgoyne and Howe would endeavor to effect a junction of their two armies at Albany.

Orders were therefore given to Gen. Putnam, who commanded at Peekskill, to prepare for such an event, by concentrating at that post the militia of the country, and to guard against any sudden attempt from New York. The importance of defending the Highlands, and the necessity of large reinforcements, was strongly urged by Gen. Parsons, in a letter to Gen. Washington, July 30, 1777. [Note H.] The result shows the wisdom and foresight which prompted the suggestion. Large requisitions were made on the militia of the adjoining states, but before effectual measures were consummated, Gen. Clinton, with a large force, advanced up the North River, captured Forts Montgomery and Clinton, and proceeding above the Highlands, compelled Gen. Putnam to evacuate the post at Peekskill, and Forts Independence and Constitution, and return to Fishkill. In the meantime, he visited Connecticut, to urge upon his countrymen the importance of prompt and energetic action. The appeal was not in vain. Always ready in the hour of trial, that patriotic state had not forgotten that on the day succeeding the Battle of Long Island, eighty- four companies of her volunteers had marched to the relief of Boston: that she had struck the most offensive and effectual blow for liberty, and had sent one thousand of her brave sons to maintain the conquest of Ticonderoga and Crown Point, planned by her wisdom, and achieved by her valor: that more than fourteen thousand of her brave and hardy yeomanry composed the army of Washington at New York, in 1776; yet she was ready, ever ready, with her accustomed energy and undaunted spirit, to shed her best blood in defense of the rights of a bleeding country. A general levy was made, and two thousand men obeyed the call, marched to meet the enemy, and again planted the standard of liberty upon the summit of the Highlands.

Among the several military expeditions during the year 1777, allusion is made by Gen. Parsons in a letter to Gen. Washington, dated December 29,1777, to a descent on Long Island for the purpose of destroying the timber and boards prepared at the east end of the island, for barracks in New York—to decoy the fleet at Southold from Rhode Island, loaded with wood, attack a regiment stationed about eight miles eastward of Jamaica, and remove or destroy whatever public stores should be found on the island at Shetucket. With this view Col. Meigs was to have landed at Hempstead harbor, to attack the regiment near Jamaica—Col. Webb near Huntington to sustain Meigs, and afford such aid to the division eastward as should be wanted, and destroy whatever was collected in that part of the county of Suffolk for the use of the enemy. The easternmost division under Gen. Parsons landed at a place called Huckaback, about forty miles from the east end of the island. The fleet, (except the Swan and Harlem sloops of war and four other vessels,) had sailed: one sloop had taken in her cargo of timber and boards; the other three had taken none, but being light, hauled into the bay under cover of the armed vessels.

The loaded sloop was captured, and all the timber and boards prepared for New York; also a large quantity of wood cut for another fleet expected from New York. The boats commanded by Capt. Ascough, of the ship "Swan", were attacked within twenty yards of the shore; two of the officers, with their commander, badly wounded, as well as several soldiers, and eight killed. The enemy's ships kept a constant fire, but without execution. The eastern division under Gen. Parsons, after accomplishing their designs, returned to the main again with about twenty prisoners. Col. Meigs, who was to have crossed from Sawpits, through the roughness of the water, was unable to pass over in his boats. The other two divisions under Col. Webb, sailed from Norwalk the evening of the 9th instant, with fair prospects, but unfortunately the next morning, just before light, the sloop in which Col. Webb embarked, fell in with the British frigate "Falcon" on her passage from New York to Newport, was forced on shore near a spot called the Old Man's, and captured.

This expedition was well planned, and would have been fully and most successfully accomplished, but for the adverse elements which prevented the embarkation of Col. Meigs, and the unfortunate capture of Col. Webb by the frigate Falcon, circumstances which could not have been anticipated nor avoided.

In November, 1777, Gen. Parsons learning that the enemy was practicing a system of warfare inconsistent with the common principles of humanity, by burning the dwellings and imprisoning the persons of peaceful and unoffending citizens, with many outrageous acts, addressed to Gov. Tryon a letter remonstrating against such savage barbarity. It is written with energy, and that fervent patriotism peculiar to the author, containing sentiments bold, dignified, and unanswerable, while the reply of Gov. Tryon evinces a mind puerile, ignoble, base and cowardly.

Sir:

Adding to the natural horrors of war the most wanton destruction of property, is an act of cruelty unknown to civilized nations, and unaccustomed in war until the servants of the king of Great Britain have convinced the impartial world, that no act of inhumanity, no stretch of despotism, are too great to exercise toward those they term rebels. Had any apparent advantage been derived from burning the houses in Phillips' Manor last Monday, there would have been some reason to justify the measure; but when no benefit whatever can be proposed by burning those buildings and stripping the women and children of apparel necessary to cover them from the severity of a cold night, and when captivating and leading in triumph to your lines, in the most ignominious manner, the heads of those families, I know not what justifiable cause to assign for those acts of cruelty, nor can I conceive a necessity for your further orders to destroy Tarrytown. You cannot be insensible it is every day in my power to destroy the houses and buildings of Col. Phillips and those belonging to the family of Delancey, each as near your lines as those buildings were to my guards; and notwithstanding your utmost vigilance, you cannot prevent the destruction of every house this side of Kingsbridge. It is not fear—it is not a want of opportunity has preserved those buildings; but a sense of the injustice and savageness of such a line of conduct has hitherto saved them; and nothing but necessity will induce me to copy the examples of this sort, frequently set by your troops. It is not my inclination, sir, to war in this manner, against the inhabitants within your lines, who suppose themselves within your king's protection. But necessity will oblige me to retaliate in kind upon your friends, to procure the exercise of that justice which humanity used to dictate, unless your explicit disavowal of the conduct of your two Captains Emmerick and Barns shall convince me that those houses were burned without your knowledge, and against your orders.

I am, sir, your humble servant,

Samuel H. Parsons."

Gov. Tryon.

The following is Gov. Tryon's reply to the foregoing:

"Kingsbridge, November 23, 1777.

Sir:

Could I possibly conceive myself accountable to a revolted subject of the King of Great Britain, I might answer your letter, received by the flag of truce yesterday, respecting the conduct of the party under Capt. Emmerick command, upon the taking of Peter and Cornelius Van Tassell. I have, however, candor enough to assure you, as much as I abhor every principle of inhumanity or ungenerous conduct, I should, were I in more authority, burn every committee-man's house within my reach, as I deem those agents the wicked instruments of the continued calamities of this country; and in order the sooner to purge this colony of them, I am willing to give twenty-five silver dollars for every active committee-man who shall be delivered up to the King's troops. I guess, before the end of the next campaign, they will be torn in pieces by their own countrymen, whom they have forcibly dragged, in opposition to their principles and duty, (after fining them to the extent of their property) to take up arms against their lawful sovereign, and compelled them to exchange their happy constitution for paper-rags, anarchy, and distress. The ruins from the conflagration of New York, by the emissaries of your party last year, remain a memorial of their tender regard for their fellow beings, exposed to the severity of a cold night. This is the first correspondence I have held with the King's enemies, on my part, in America; and as I am immediately under the command of Sir Henry Clinton, your future letters, dictated with decency, would be more properly directed to his Excellency.

I am, sir, your most obedient servant,

William Tryon, Major-General.

To Gen. Parsons."

Gen. Parsons to the Hon. Mr. Laurens, President of Congress:

"Sir:

On the 18th ult., Gen. Tryon sent about one hundred men, under the command of Capt. Emmerick, to burn some houses within about four miles of my guards, which, under cover of a dark night, he effected, with circumstances of most savage barbarity, stripping the clothing from the women and children, and turning them, almost naked, into the street, in a most severe night: the men were made prisoners, and led, with halters around their necks, with no other clothes than their shirts and breeches, in triumph to the enemy's lines. This conduct induced me to write to Gen. Tryon upon the subject; a copy of my letter and his answer I have herewith sent you. As the practice of desolating villages, burning houses, and every species of unnecessary distress to the inhabitants, ought to be avoided, I would not wish to retaliate in any instance, but where, in its consequences, the enemy may be injured, or one of our people saved by it. I am aware, if, in any instance, this shall be done, I shall subject myself to censure, unless it is in consequence of some general orders of Congress, by which I may be warranted. As these instances may be frequently repeated by the enemy, I wish to know in what, or whether in any instance, Congress will direct retaliation.

I am, sir, your obedient humble servant,

Samuel H. Parsons."

Gen. Parsons answer to Gen. Tryon's letter of 23d of November, 1777:

"Fishkill, January 1st, 1778.

Sir:

Since I received yours of the 23d of November, I have till now been employed in matters of importance, which have not left me at liberty to acknowledge the receipt of your letter before, and lest you should think me wanting in respect due to your character, I beg your acceptance of this letter, which closes our epistolary correspondence. It will ever be my design to "dictate with decency" any letters I may send; however remote it may be from my intention to copy the examples of the persons my duty compels me to correspond with. As propriety and decency ought to be observed in every transaction, even with the most infamous characters, I never wish so nearly to assimilate myself to them, as to be found destitute of that respect which is due to my fellow beings in every station in life. I should not have entertained a thought that you had been deficient in the duty you owe your king in every part of the globe, or that you did not inherit the spirit of his ministry, which has precipitated the present crisis, even if you had omitted to assure me this had been the first correspondence you had held with the king's enemies in America. The conflagration of New York you are pleased to charge to American troops, under the decent name of a "party". This deserves no other answer than to assure you it has not the least foundation in truth, and that we are assured it gains no credit with officers whose rank and candor gives opportunity to know and believe the truth. This, like many other occurrences, is charged to the account of those who were never believed guilty, to excite to rage, and direct the resentment of the ignorant and misruled against very improper objects. Perhaps I might with equal propriety and more truth suggest this unhappy event was brought about by your own party, from the same motives which induced them in August, 1776, to mangle the dead bodies of some of the foreign troops, in a most shocking and inhuman manner, and place them in the most conspicuous parts of the road through which their brethren were to pass.

A justifiable resistance against unwarrantable invasions of the natural and social rights of mankind, if unsuccessful according to the fashion of the world, will be termed rebellion, but if successful, will be deemed a noble struggle for the defense of everything valuable in life. Whether I am considered as a revolted subject of the king of Great Britain, or in any other light by his subjects, is very immaterial and gives me little concern. Future ages, I hope, will do justice to my intentions, and the present to the humanity of my conduct. Few men are of talents so very inconsiderable as to be unalterably excluded from every degree of fame. A Nero and Caligula have perpetuated their memories. Perhaps "twenty silver dollars" may be motives with those you employ to do great honor to your Machiavellian maxims, especially that which advises never to commit crimes to the halves, and leave lasting monuments of your principles and conduct, which will hand your memory down to the latest posterity in indelible characters. We act on a different scale, and hold ourselves indispensably bound never to commit crimes, but to execute whatever is necessary for our welfare, uninfluenced by sordid, mercenary motives. In the field of conjecture I shall not attempt to follow you. You may have a better talent of "'guessing" than I can boast of. This satisfaction at least you may enjoy, that if you find yourself mistaken in one conjecture, you have an undoubted right to guess again. I shall content myself to wait until the event verifies your prediction, or shows you are mistaken, assuring you I shall never pursue your measures for restoring peace, whether my authority is "greater or less", further than necessity shall compel me to retort the injuries the peaceable inhabitants of this country may receive from the hand of violence and oppression.

I am, sir, your obedient servant,

Samuel H. Parsons.

Gov. Tryon."

During the winter of 1777, Gen. Parsons, suffering under feeble health, and a constitution broken down in the service of his country, expressed to the Commander-in-Chief a desire to retire temporarily from the active duties of the army, but in consequence of the urgent solicitation of Gen. Washington, he relinquished the desire, as may appear by the following letter, dated:

"Highlands, On Hudson River, February 18th, 1778.
Dear General:

I had the honor of receiving yours of the 10th of January about eight days since, at this place, where I have returned to take charge of my brigade. In the present state of the army, I shall continue in my command, lest a different conduct may prove injurious to the cause of my country, at this critical conjuncture of affairs. However my inclination may induce me to retire to the enjoyment of domestic happiness, I cannot think myself warranted to indulge my wishes at a time when so many officers under my command are desirous of leaving the toils of war for the pleasures of private life."

About this time Gen. Putnam went to Connecticut and left West Point, and all the troops stationed at the Highlands, under the command of Gen. Parsons, with the additional *duty of constructing military works at West Point,* which had been delayed in consequence of misapprehension in regard to the several resolves of Congress upon the subject. It seems that on the 5th of November, 1777, Congress appointed Gen. Gates to command in the Highlands, connecting that post with the Northern Department, and empowered him to make obstructions in and fortifications on the banks of the Hudson River, but as he was made President of the Board of War, he never entered upon these duties.

Again, on the 18th of February, Gov. Clinton was requested to take the superintendence of the works, but the multiplicity of his civil employments made it necessary for him to decline the undertaking. Meantime, Gen. Putnam went to Connecticut, and left the post in charge of Gen. Parsons, who entered promptly upon the discharge of his arduous and perplexing duty.

In a letter of 18th of February, to Gen. Washington, he remarks, *"Almost every obstacle within the circle of possibility has happened, to retard the progress of the obstructions in and fortifications on the banks of Hudson River. Preparations for completing them are now in a state which will afford a good prospect of completing them in April, and unless some difficulties yet unforeseen should prevent, I think we cannot fail, by the forepart of that month, to have them in a good degree of forwardness. Nothing on my part shall be wanting to put them in a state of forwardness to answer the reasonable expectations of the country, as early as possible."*

Again, in a letter to Gen. Washington, dated 7th of March, 1778, explaining the perplexities arising under the resolves of Congress of the 5th of November, and 18th of February, in regard to Gen. Gates and Gov. Clinton, whose powers were deemed strictly *personal*, he remarks, *"I shall exert myself to have the works in a state of defense as early as possible, by the due exercise of such directions as your Excellency shall please to give me. Col. Radiere, finding it impossible to complete the fort and other defenses intended at this post, in such manner as to effectually withstand the attempts of the enemy to pass up the river early in the spring, and not choosing to hazard his reputation on works erected on a different scale, calculated for a short duration only, has desired leave to wait on your Excellency and Congress, which I have granted him. In justice to Col. Radiere, I ought to say he appears to be a gentleman of science and knowledge in his profession, and disposed to render us every service he is able to do. I shall expedite the building of such works as are most necessary for immediate defense."*

Again, in another letter, dated:

"Camp West Point". March 16th, 1778.

On the 14th instant I had the honor of receiving your letter of the 7th of March, and also one of the 8th, containing a copy of the 5th of March. I shall pay particular attention to forwarding the work of the boats designed for transporting over, as well as to those which are to be employed for defense on Hudson River. I have ordered all the boats and other crafts on the river to be collected in different places, and put in the best possible state immediately. When I was last at Poughkeepsie the gunboats were in such a state as to give hopes of their being fit for use within a few weeks; and as Gov. Clinton has been kind enough to take upon himself the direction of them, I think we may hope to see them completed soon. I will send to Albany, and know the state of the boats there, and as the river will be soon clear of ice, I will order down such boats and other crafts as can be had there, fit for transportation over the river. If the chain is complete, we shall be ready to stretch it over the river next week. A sufficient number of chevaux de frise to fill those parts left open last year, are ready to sink as soon as the weather and the state of the river will admit it to be done. I hope to have two sides and one bastion of the fort in some state of defense in about a fortnight. The other sides need very little to secure them. There is a prospect of having five or six cannon mounted in one of our batteries this week. I think the works are going on as fast as could be expected from our small number of men, total want of materials provided, and of money to purchase them. We have borrowed, and begged, and hired money to this time. I have several times advanced my last shilling toward purchasing materials, &c; and I believe this has been the case with almost every officer here. As we still live, I hope we shall accomplish the works in the river in season, if the enemy moves with their accustomed caution and tardiness; when I hope Congress will repay what has been advanced, and cannot think us blamable if we have been compelled to save the public credit, and forward the business entrusted to our care."

From the above correspondence it appears that the fortifications at *West Point*, and upon the Highlands, were built under the *superintendence of Gen. Parsons*, where he was stationed the principal part of the years 1778 and 1779, but was frequently detached upon expeditions to protect the seacoast of his native state, near Horseneck, Greenwich, New Haven and New London. Time and space, however, will not permit a full statement of his services. It appears also from his *numerous opinions,* recorded and preserved among the manuscripts of Gen. Washington, that he was frequently consulted in questions of great moment, and in critical times of public danger.

On the 23d of June, 1779, Gen. Washington removed his headquarters in consequence of the enemy having taken possession of Verplank's Point and Stony Point, from Smith's Clove to New Windsor, where he might be contiguous to the forts, and better situated to attend to different parts of the army on both sides of the Hudson River. The main body of the army was left at Smith's Clove, under the command of Gen. Putnam. The object now in view was to guard against an attack upon West Point. Gen. McDougall was transferred to the command of West Point. Three brigades were stationed on the east side of the river; Nixon's at Constitution Island, *Parsons'* opposite *West Point, with instructions to assist in constructing the works,* [Note K,] and Huntington on the principal road leading to Fishkill. These three brigades were put under the command of Gen. Heath, who had been recently ordered to repair from Boston to headquarters.

In July, 1779, Gen. Washington, understanding that Gen. Tryon had invaded Connecticut with twenty-six hundred British troops, immediately directed Gen. Parsons, (then stationed near the Highlands,) to hasten to the scene of action, with a view of giving confidence to his countrymen, and guiding their efforts. [Note L.] Placing himself at the head of one hundred and fifty continental troops who were supported by the militia under Gen. Erastus Wolcot, he attacked the British in the morning of the 12th, so soon as they had landed at Norwalk; and, although too weak to prevent the destruction of that fort, he harassed and annoyed the enemy throughout the day in such a manner that they re-embarked and returned to Huntington Bay for fresh supplies of artillery and reinforcements of men; and soon after abandoned the undertaking of penetrating the Connecticut territory, returned to New York. [Note M.] Before invading Connecticut, Gen. Tryon addressed to Gens. Putnam and Parsons the following letter:

"New York, June 18th, 1779.

Sir:

By one of His Majesty's ships of war, which arrived here last night from Georgia, we have intelligence that the British forces were in possession of Fort Johnstone, near Charlestown, the first of June. Surely it is time for rational Americans to wish for a reunion with the parent state, and to adopt such measures as will most speedily effect it.

I am your very humble, obedient servant,

Wm. Tryon, Major-General.

To Gen. Putnam, or in his absence, to Gen. Parsons."

The following is Gen. Parson's reply:

"Camp, Highlands, September 7th, 1779.

Sir:

I should have paid an earlier attention to your polite letter of the 18th of June, had I not entertained some hope of a personal interview with you, in your descents upon the defenseless towns of Connecticut, to execute your master's vengeance upon rebellious women and formidable hosts of boys and girls, who were induced, by insidious proclamations, to remain in those hapless places, and who, if they had been suffered to continue in the enjoyment of that peace their age and sex entitled them to expect from civilized nations, you undoubtedly supposed would prove the scourge of Britain's veteran troops, and pluck from you those laurels with which that fiery expedition so plentifully crowned you. But your sudden departure from Norwalk, and the particular attention you paid to your personal safety, when at that place, and the prudent resolution you took, to suffer the town of Stamford to escape the conflagration to which you had devoted Fairfield and Norwalk, prevented my wishes on that head. This will, I hope, sufficiently apologize for my delay in answering your last letter. By letters from France, we have intelligence that his Catholic Majesty declared war against Great Britain in June last; that the combined fleets of France and Spain, amounting to more than sixty sail of the line, having formed a junction with twenty-five thousand land forces, are now meditating a blow on the British dominions in Europe; and that the grand fleet of old England find it very inconvenient to venture far from their harbors. In the West Indies, Admiral Byron, having greatly suffered in a naval engagement, escaped, with his ships in a very shattered condition, to St. Christopher's, and covered his fleet under the batteries on the shores, and has suffered himself to be insulted in the road of that island by the French Admiral; and Count de Estaing, after reducing the islands of St. Vincent and Grenada to the obedience of France, defeating and disabling the British fleet, has sailed for Hispaniola, where it is expected he will be joined by the Spanish fleet in those seas, and attack Jamaica.

The storming your strong works at Stony Point, and capturing the garrison, by our brave troops; the brilliant successes of Gen. Sullivan against your faithful friends and allies, the savages; the surprise of Paulus Hook, by Maj. Lee; the flight of Gen. Provost from Carolina; and your shamefully shutting yourselves up in Now York and the neighboring islands, are so fully within your knowledge, as scarcely to need repetition.

Surely it is time for Britons to rouse from their delusive dreams of conquest, and pursue such systems of future conduct as will save their tottering empire from total destruction.

I am, sir, your obedient servant,

        Samuel H. Parsons.

To Maj. Gen. Tryon."

On the 29th of October, 1780, he was appointed, by Gen. Washington, one of the Board of General Officers at West Point, for the trial of Maj. Gen. Andre, of the British army, as a spy.

In the same month he received from Congress, a commission as Major-General, and succeeded Gen. Putnam in the command of the Connecticut Line of the Continental Army.

The defenseless inhabitants between Greenwich and New York, having been much annoyed, and suffered great losses by the frequent incursions of Col. Delancey's Corps at Morrisania, Gen. Parsons determined to destroy the enemy's barracks, which could not be rebuilt during the winter; and thus afford some protection to the inhabitants in that vicinity. For this purpose, he advanced, with rapid marches, to West Chester and Morrisania, with a few continentals, attacked the British troops, and effectually accomplished his object.

Gen. Washington, in a letter addressed to the President of Congress, January 31st, 1781, thus alludes to this expedition: *"Enclosed are two reports of Maj. Gen. Parsons and Lieut. Col. Hull, respecting our enterprise against Delancey's Corps at West Chester; in which, with a small loss on our side, the barracks of the corps, and a large quantity of forage were destroyed, fifty-two prisoners and a considerable number of horses and cattle brought off, and a bridge across Harlem River, under one of the enemy's redoubts, burnt. Gen. Parsons' arrangements were judicious; and the conduct of the officers and men employed on the occasion, is entitled to the highest praise. The position of the Corps, two or three miles within some of the enemy's redoubts, required address and courage in the execution of the enterprise."*

Congress passed a resolution directing Gen. Washington to present to Gen. Parsons and the officers under his command, the thanks of Congress for his judicious arrangements, and for the courage displayed by the officers and men.

In the year 1781, he was appointed by the Governor and Council of Connecticut to command the state troops and coast guards, raised for the protection of the state, and to dispose them in such manner as he should judge expedient to protect the inhabitants from the incursions of the enemy on the seacoast.

At the close of the war he resumed the practice of law in Middletown; whither his family had been removed during the Revolution, and frequently represented that town in the Legislature.

In the prosecution of measures for the formation of Middlesex County, he was more engaged and more influential than any other man. He was an active and influential member of the State Convention which assembled at Hartford, January, 1781, and adopted the Constitution of the United States. He was a member and for some time President of the Society of Cincinnatus in Connecticut.

In the latter part of the year 1785, he was appointed by Congress, a Commissioner, in connection with Gens. Richard Butler, of Pittsburg, and George Rogers Clarke, of Kentucky, to treat with the Shawnee Indians, near the falls of Ohio, for extinguishing the aboriginal title to certain lands within the Northwestern Territory. This treaty was held on the northwestern bank of the Ohio, near the mouth of the Great Miami, January 31st, 1786, and the Indians then ceded to the United States a large and valuable tract upon which the flourishing city of Cincinnati now stands.

Under the ordinance of Congress of 1787, he was appointed Judge in and over the territory of the United States northwest of the river Ohio. The commission is dated October 23d, 1787, and signed by Arthur St. Clair, President, and Charles Thomson, Secretary of Congress. In 1789 he was nominated by Gen. Washington, by and with the consent of the Senate, Chief Judge in and over the same territory, then embracing the present states of Ohio, Indiana, Illinois and Michigan, which office he held until his death. His associates were Gen. James Varnum, of Rhode Island, and the Hon. John Cleves Symmes, of New Jersey. In 1789 he was appointed by the state of Connecticut a Commissioner with Gov. Oliver Wolcot, of Litchfield, and Hon. James Davenport, of Stamford, to hold a treaty with the Wyandots and other tribes of Indians, for extinguishing their claim, (the aboriginal title to the lands called the Connecticut Western Reserve, and in the fall of 1789 he visited that country with a view to preliminary arrangements for holding a treaty with them. While returning to his residence at Marietta, he was drowned in descending the rapids of the Big Beaver River, the 17th of November, 1789, aged fifty-two years.

Among the manuscripts of Gen. Parsons in the possession of his grandson, Samuel H. Parsons, of Hartford, are a journal of observations and occurrences when he first visited the western country; a communication to the American Academy of Arts and Sciences in October, 1786, describing the western mounds, manners and customs of the aborigines; original address to the Shawnee tribes; besides a voluminous correspondence before, during, and after the Revolutionary War, with the distinguished men of that period.

Chapter V
GEN. BENJAMIN TUPPER

The Battle of Monmouth

The sketch of the life of Gen. Benjamin Tupper
was written by his grandson, Anselm Tupper Nye, of Marietta.

Gen. Benjamin Tupper was born at Stoughton, Mass., in that part now called Sharon, in 1738, but the precise time is unknown to his descendants in this state. He was the youngest of eight children of his parents, seven sons and one daughter. His brothers' names were Mayhew, Levi, Seth, Simeon, Reuben and Judah. His sister, Joanna, was married to Benjamin Este, of Stoughton. His brothers emigrated to different parts of the country. Mayhew went to New York; Simeon lived in Vermont, and with two of his sons, served in the Revolutionary army. Reuben died at Sharon; Judah came to Marietta with Gen. Tupper, where he died in 1793. Gen. Tupper's father died when he was quite young, and he was apprenticed to a tanner in Dorchester by the name of Witherton, with whom he lived until he was sixteen years of age. After leaving Dorchester, he worked on the farm of Joshua Howard, of Easton, with whom he continued to reside the most of his time until he was married.

At the commencement of the French War, he engaged as a private soldier in the army, and was connected with it the most of the time for two or three years, though absent from it during the winter, except in the winter of 1756-7, when he acted as Clerk of a company in the eastern army. Whether he was in any engagement during that war is not known. He kept a district school in Easton two or three winters during the war or soon after.

He was married at Easton, November 18th, 1762, to Huldah White, who resided in the same town, and with whom he had long been acquainted. She was a woman of no ordinary talents, and was eminently fitted for the trials and difficulties through which they were called to pass in the latter period of their lives. She died at Springfield, now Putnam, Ohio, on the 21st of February, 1812. She was well known to many of the now oldest inhabitants of Marietta, having survived her husband more than twenty years.

They resided at Easton for a short time after their marriage, when they removed to Chesterfield, in Hampshire County, Mass., which continued to be the residence of his family until they removed to Marietta.

At the commencement of our Revolutionary War, Gen. Tupper was a Lieutenant of the Militia, in Chesterfield. His first military duty during that war was in stopping the Supreme Court acting under the authority of the crown, at Springfield. Under the command of Maj. Halley, of Northampton, a body of men prevented the sitting of the court, thus manifesting the determination of the people of that state to resist the authority of the British Government.

In 1775 he held the rank of Major of a regiment of six months men, serving near Boston. While there he collected a number of boats and men for an expedition to Castle Island, in Boston harbor. They passed with muffled oars close to the British fleet then in the harbor, to the castle, burnt the lighthouse, brought off considerable property in light articles, and returned safe to the main land without any loss of men, or perhaps with the loss of one man. The enemy repaired the lighthouse, and Maj. Tupper in another expedition with boats, burnt it the second time. After his return from one of these expeditions, he wrote the following letter to Gen. Ward:

"Chelsea, Wednesday, 10 o'clock, P. M.

Sir:

By Lieut. Shepherd you will receive two horses and eleven head of cattle taken from the Governor's island. I obeyed my orders in burning the boat. If it should seem that I went too much beyond in burning the house, hope your honor will suspend hard thoughts until I am so happy as to see you. I was not so lucky as to find any of liberty; was so unhappy as to leave a number of horses on the island, which I humbly conceive I can give a sufficient reason for. My party is all well, in good spirits: the wind very high: shall return to camp as soon as possible: must humbly beg the favor of the sorrel horse, if you judge in your known candor that I deserve him. As the cattle too were not taken in the enemy's camp, I conceive they will belong to the party.

I am, with the highest esteem, your honor's most obedient, humble servant,

Benj. Tupper.

To the Hon. Gen. Ward."

In Washington's Letters, vol. ii, page 20, the following account of one of these expeditions will be found:

"August 4th, 1775.

The other happened at the lighthouse. A number of workmen having been sent down to repair it, with a guard of twenty-two marines and a subaltern, Maj. Tupper, last Monday morning, about two o'clock, landed there with about three hundred men, attacked them, killed the officer and four privates; but being detained by the tide on his return, he was attacked by several boats; but he happily got through, with the loss of one man killed, and another wounded. The remainder of the ministerial troops (three of whom are badly wounded) he brought off prisoners with ten Tories, all of whom are on their way to Springfield jail. The riflemen, in these skirmishes, lost one man, who (we hear) is a prisoner in Boston jail."

In the following winter, an incident occurred, which serves to illustrate the character of Gen. Tupper, for cool, deliberate courage, which he possessed in an eminent degree. Three men in a boat had been out fishing; while out, the wind shifted, and blew the ice toward the shore, where they must land. The men attempted to return, but found their way completely blocked up with floating ice. Their situation was one of great danger. All their efforts to get their boat through the ice were unavailing; nor were they able to turn back. The wind blew severely cold, and they were in a situation in which they must soon have perished, in view of thousands of spectators, full of consternation, but making no effort to relieve these perishing men. Maj. Tupper learning their condition, instantly contrived a plan for their relief. Procuring three pair of *rackets,* or snow shoes, he repaired immediately to the shore, putting one pair on his own feet, and with a pair under each arm, made his way for the boat, over the floating ice. Fixing a pair of rackets to the feet of two of the men, and encouraging the other that he should be relieved in his turn, he succeeded in bringing them all to shore.

In 1776, Gen., then Col., Tupper, commanded a regiment of six months men. With the other troops, they repaired to New York before the battle on Long Island. Tupper's and Nixon's Regiments from Massachusetts, and Sage's from Connecticut, were placed on Governor's Island in the harbor. The next morning after the battle, the "Roebuck" man-of-war was ordered up to summon the garrison on Governor's Island, to surrender. An officer, with a flag of truce from the ship, landed from a boat, and held up his flag. An officer from the fort, Maj. Coburn, was dispatched to answer, that *"the fort would not be surrendered at any rate."* When these officers met, they found themselves to be old acquaintances, having served together during the French War. After shaking hands heartily, and some little conversation, the British officer made known his errand; Coburn told him the fort would not be surrendered, and they parted. The ship soon opened her fire upon the American fort, which was returned by the fort, but to little purpose; their work was not capable of being defended against the fire of the ship; hence all were in alarm. During the previous night, the American troops on Long Island had been taken off with boats, with all their baggage, light artillery, and entrenching tools. Under the superintendence of Col. Rufus Putnam, acting then as Chief Engineer of the Army, or of Gen. Israel Putnam, boats were sent to Governor's Island, and Tupper's and Nixon's Regiments were brought to the city of New York, but Sage's Regiment was left behind. While the troops were thus landing in the city, the officer in command hoisted his flag to surrender; upon which the firing ceased. The boats were hurried from the city back to the island, and brought off Sage's Regiment, with the loss of one killed and one wounded.

The next military event, in which Gen. Tupper is known to have been engaged, was in August, 1776, when he was sent in command of a number of gun-boats, or galleys, up the North River. Near Fort Washington an engagement took place between these boats and several ships of war belonging to the enemy. Gen. Washington makes honorable mention of this engagement, in his letter dated August 5th, 1776, as follows:

"The enclosed copy of a letter from Col. Tupper, who had the general command of the galleys, will inform Congress of the engagement between them and the ships of war up the North River on Saturday evening, and of the damage we sustained. What injury was done to the ships I cannot ascertain. It is said they were hulled several times by our shot. All accounts agree that our officers and men, during the whole of this affair behaved with great spirit and bravery. The damage done to the galleys shows beyond question, that they had a warm time of it.

See Washington's letter, vol. ii, p. 176. In this engagement his eldest son, then thirteen years of age, was with him.

In the campaign of 1777, Col. Tupper served with his regiment in the Northern Army under Gen. Gates. What part he took in the Battle of Bemis' Heights is not known; but he is mentioned by Wilkinson, in his memoir, as attending a council with Gen. Lamed, Col. Wilkinson, Col. Brooks, and others, the day after that battle, in regard to a retreat of the left wing of the American Army, which had been precipitated on the enemy when they held a strong position across the Fishkill. The left wing, according to the suggestion of Wilkinson, fell back half a mile, which position was held until the surrender of Burgoyne.

In 1778, Col. Tupper served under Gen. Washington, and was in the Battle of Monmouth, June 28th, on which occasion he had his horse killed under him.

In 1780, he had charge of the work of preparing and stretching a chain across the Hudson at West Point. The work was completed in April, and placed in the river under his direction.

In May, 1781, Col. Tupper returned to his family on furlough. While at home he took an important part in dispersing a mob arising out of the arrest and trial of one Samuel Eli, for high treason, at Northampton.

During the campaign of 1781, the Indian and Tory refugees threatened the northern frontier of New York, on the Mohawk and Lake George. A regiment from Massachusetts was sent up into that quarter. In September or October an action took place between these troops and some Tories and Indians, in which the Major of the regiment was killed. After the action, Gen. Stark, who commanded on the northern frontier, sent out a scout to Lake George. The officers reported that they had discovered the camp of a large force, by their fire. Stark immediately sent off an express to headquarters for a reinforcement and Col. Tupper's regiment, with Col. Kinston's, of New York, went up. While they were waiting for the enemy, the news from the main army reached them that Cornwallis had surrendered at Yorktown. With this event the war was in effect closed. Col. Tupper's Regiment, however, remained at the north. About the close of the war he was promoted to the rank of Brigadier-General by brevet. After the close of the war he returned to his family at Chesterfield, and soon after was elected by his town as their representative in the Legislature of Massachusetts.

During the darkest period of the Revolutionary War, Gen. Washington had turned the attention of officers and soldiers to the valley of the Ohio, as a place of refuge to which they might retire, should the British army be successful against them. The result of that war rendered such a retreat unnecessary; notwithstanding, many of the officers and soldiers of the army looked to the west as a retiring place for themselves and their families, after a war of eight years. Among the most prominent of this class was Gen. Tupper. Indeed, in the foresight of Gen. Rufus Putnam and himself, the enterprise of the settlement at Marietta had its origin.

Fort Harmar in 1790
Drawing by Hon. Joseph Gilman

The ordinance of 1785 provided for a survey of a portion of the lands northwest of the river Ohio. In the summer of that year the first regiment of United States Troops, or one battalion of them, had taken post at the mouth of the Muskingum, under the command of Maj. Doughty, and erected a fort, which received the name of Fort Harmar. In that year Gen. Rufus Putnam had been appointed to command the survey of a portion of the lands in Ohio, but being otherwise engaged, Gen. Tupper was appointed in his place. In the summer of that year he came as far west as Pittsburg. The condition of the Indian tribes prevented the execution of that work until the treaty made by Gen. Parsons, and others, on the Miami, in January, 1786. Gen. Tupper returned to Massachusetts in the winter of 1785-6, but left again for the west in June, 1786, with his eldest son, Maj. Anselm Tupper. That season the survey of the seven ranges was completed, under his direction. During that season he visited Maj. Doughty, at Fort Harmar.

(Addendum by Badgley Publishing Company. Fort Harmar was named after the Commanding Officer of the U.S. Army in the Ohio Country. Josiah Harmar was a Brigadier General during the American Revolution and was appointed to this post by Congress after the Treaty of Paris was signed. In Ohio, Harmar faced rising tensions with the Native Americans. The influx of thousands of white settlers into Ohio upset the Indians. In October 1785, Harmar ordered Major John Doughty to construct a fort along the Ohio River. Doughty chose to build Fort Harmar along the western bank of the Muskingum River, near the river's mouth. Harmar also ordered the construction of Fort Steuben the following year at modern-day Steubenville. The main purpose of these forts was to prevent additional squatters from flooding into Ohio. Instead of stopping settlement, the fortifications actually encouraged it, as the whites believed the soldiers manning the forts were there to protect the settlers.)

Josiah Harmar
1753 -1813

On Gen. Tupper's return from his first visit to the west, he visited his friend, Gen. Rufus Putnam, then residing at Rutland. In the language of another, *"A night of friendly offices and conference between them, gave at the dawn a development to the cherished hope and purpose of Gen. Tupper. They united in a publication which appeared in the public papers of New England, on the 25th of January, 1786, headed "Information", dated January 10th, 1786, signed Rufus Putnam, Benjamin Tupper."*

As the result of this conference and address, the Ohio Company was formed. Dr. M. Cutter, in connection with Winthrop Sargent, was appointed to negotiate a contract with Congress for land. At the third meeting of the company at Boston, August 29th, 1787, Dr. Cutter reported that the contract had been completed.

The spirit of disorganization which had manifested itself in Massachusetts in 1781 was not entirely eradicated; on the contrary, it made its appearance in a more formidable and extensive manner in 1786-7, in what is termed as Shays' Insurrection. The only officers of the Revolutionary Army engaged in this affair were Shays, who had been a Captain in Gen. Putnam's Regiment, Capt. Wiley, and Ensign Day. Each of them had a party, and their aggregate force amounted to about two thousand men. When Gen. Tupper returned from the west, after completing the survey of the seven ranges, this insurrection had assumed a formidable aspect. Immediately on his return he took an active part in putting it down. The duty of calling out the militia to suppress this rebellion, devolved on Gen. Shepard, who acted under the orders of the Governor. Gen. Tupper offered his services to him, and acted in the capacity of voluntary aid. By his advice, and through his influence, the plan of calling out the militia by drafts or in mass was abandoned, and that of calling for volunteers adopted. This was a measure of the first importance, as it served to distinguish between the friends of the government and those who were secretly infected with the spirit of rebellion. Under this plan, out of a company in Chesterfield, fifteen to eighteen offered their services. In the northern part of Hampshire County, an entire regiment was organized for this service, to meet at Chesterfield. Gen. Tupper had been appointed a Justice of the Peace about two years previous. His efforts, in connection with an address to the people, which he had made a short time before, combined with the presence of the volunteers, had made a favorable impression on many persons of good standing. While the regiment raised in the northern part of the county was being assembled at Chesterfield, Gen. Tupper, as Magistrate, administered the Oath of Allegiance, as prescribed by the laws of the state, to many of the people. This was also a measure which served to distinguish the friends of law from the mob.

The immediate object of Shays and his party was to get possession of the arms and public stores at Springfield. At that point, therefore, the troops raised by the state were concentrated. Gen. Tupper, after his arrival at Springfield, acting under the orders of Gen. Shepard, took charge of the organization of the different companies as they arrived. He ordered the different fragments of companies into regular order, and officered them out of the best officers on the ground. He also organized a small troop of horse, under Capt. Buffington; and selected all who were in any manner acquainted with artillery duty, adding others to them, and had them all regularly trained every day. The men were all armed from the arsenal, the arms being there in good order, and all things were put in the best possible order for defense. Shays was not, however, in any hurry to make an attack, as he wished to increase his force. Gen. Shepard's orders from the Governor were simply to defend the stores; however, he made no effort to disturb any of Shays' men. The consequence was that Shays' different parties collected around Gen, Shepard's camp, and cut off his supplies from the country. In the meantime, Gen. Lincoln had collected a body of men at Bristol to aid Gen. Shepard. Two weeks elapsed before any movement was made by Gen. Lincoln. An express was sent to him, to inform him of the situation of Gen. Shepard. When the express reached Gen. Lincoln, only a part of his troops were ready to march, but he immediately pushed on one division, by forced marches; but before they reached Springfield, Shays had made his attack, and been defeated. By some means Capt. Buffington had intercepted a letter from Shays to some of his subordinates, directing the manner of attack. On obtaining this letter, Gen. Tupper took immediate measures to fortify the camp by log forts, commenced like blockhouses, at each point of attack, and three brush forts as outworks. This was done with great promptness and dispatch. In the meantime, the troops were supplied with provisions by the people of Springfield.

Shays finally advanced to attack Gen. Shepard. He was repeatedly warned not to approach any nearer; but he treated all these messages not only with neglect, but contempt. Cannon were first fired over his column, but this was disregarded. At last, a fieldpiece was brought to bear upon Shays' advance, and the first shot killed four of his men. This was a more effectual hint. They immediately recoiled, broke their ranks, and fled. They were rallied by Shays, at Pelham, where he remained for awhile. In consequence of the interception of the letter from Shays to some of his officers, which fell into the hands of Capt. Buffington, Wiley and Day, of Shays' party, were not engaged in the affair at Springfield. Gen. Lincoln arrived from Bristol on the second day after the defeat of Shays, and took immediate measures to dislodge Day from West Springfield, and Wiley from Chicopee Bridge; but before the movement could be made, they had fallen back, and joined Shays at Pelham. Some of their men were taken prisoners at West Springfield. Such of them as would take the oath of allegiance, were sent home, and the rest detained as prisoners. Shays retreated to Petersham, where his adherents were finally dispersed by Gen. Lincoln. Before this, however, Gen. Putnam made an ineffectual attempt to withdraw Shays from his party, but failed to accomplish his object. Shays himself appeared disposed to listen to the advice of Gen. Putnam, but he informed the general that his friends would not suffer him to leave them.

Within a day or two after the defeat of Shays at Springfield, Gen. Tupper was discharged, and returned at Northampton, where he was visited by many of his old friends. Known also as having visited the

Ohio country, many persons called upon him to inquire about the lands, rivers, &c, of the valley of the Ohio. In the spring he went to Worcester to see Gen. Putnam, and concert measures to set forward the proposed emigration to Ohio. Dr. Cutler having completed the contract for lands, the first thing to be done was to raise the money necessary for their object. Many formidable difficulties which attended the organization of the company were overcome, and Gen. Tupper began his own arrangements for moving to the Ohio in the summer of 1787. At that period wagon makers were not common, even in New England. One, however, was obtained, and two wagons were built, one for the family, the other for their baggage With his own family, including that of Ichabod Nye, his son-in-law, that of Col. Nathaniel Cushing, and Maj. Goodale, they made their way to the Ohio River, which they reached at Wellsburg, then Buffalo, where they were joined by the family of Maj. Coburn and his son-in-law, Andrew Webster. These families formed, in fact, the first settlers of Ohio, and arrived at Marietta on the 9th of August, 1788. The men who came on with Gen. Putnam, had none of them families with them, and had been previously discharged.

After his arrival at Marietta, Gen. Tupper was actively engaged in promoting the plans and interests of the Ohio Company, being intimately associated with Gen. Putnam in the management of its affairs.

On the 9th of September, 1788, the first civil court in the Northwestern Territory was held at Col. Battelle's, in *Campus Martius.* This was the Court of Quarter Sessions. *Rufus Putnam* and *Benjamin Tupper* were Justices of the Quorum, assisted by justices of the bar.

Judge Putnam gave the charge to the Grand Jury. After one or two sessions Judge Tupper presided, until his death, in June, 1792.

At an early period in his life, Gen. Tupper made a public profession of the Christian religion, by uniting with the Congregational Church at Easton. After his arrival at Marietta, he did not forget his obligation. His efforts were directed to preserve to his family and associates the benefits of public and social worship of God. Before the arrival of the Rev. Daniel Story, the first minister, meetings for social worship were held on the Sabbath. The usual place of worship was the same room in which the first court was held, near the west corner of the stockade.

Gen. Tupper had seven children, three sons and four daughters. His sons were Anselm, Edward White, and Benjamin Tupper.

Maj. Anselm Tupper died at Marietta on the 25th of December, 1808. Col. Benjamin Tupper died at Putnam in February, 1815. Gen. Edward W. Tupper died at Gallipolis, in 1823. His daughter, Miss *Rosoma*, who married Gov. Winthrop Sargeant, died at Marietta, in 1790. *Sophia*, who married *Nathaniel Willys, Esq.,* now of Conn., then of Mass., died in October, 1789. Minerva married Col. Ichabod Nye, and died at Marietta in April, 1836. The other daughter died young, before the family emigrated to Ohio. The only representative of the family bearing the family name is Edward W. Tupper, of Putnam, son of Benjamin Tupper, Jr.

Chapter VI
COL. EBENEZER SPROAT

Colonel Ebenezer Sproat

Col. Ebenezer Sproat was born in Middleborough, Mass., in the year 1752. He was the son of Col. Ebenezer Sproat, a respectable yeoman, who owned one of the finest farms in that vicinity, with a large, commodious dwelling-house, which, for many years before, and during the Revolutionary war, was occupied as a tavern. Like his son, he was an uncommonly tall and portly man. He was a Colonel in the militia; and the venerable John Howland, from whom many of these facts were derived, says, that when the British took possession of Newport and a part of Rhode Island, he performed a tour of duty with his regiment in Providence. A brother of Ebenezer was a lawyer, and settled in Taunton.

His early education must have been the best the schools afforded at that day, as he was familiar with the principles and practice of surveying. During his boyhood and youth, he assisted his father in cultivating the farm; and when the war of Independence commenced, it found him in the prime of manhood, with a frame invigorated by the toils of agriculture, and fitted, by labor, to undergo all the perils and hardships of a soldier's life. He entered the service as Captain of a company, and soon rose to the post of Major, in the Tenth Regiment of the Massachusetts

Line, commanded by Col. Shepherd. In 1778, Glover's Brigade of four regiments was stationed at Providence, at which time he was a Lieutenant-Colonel, and said to be the tallest man in the brigade, being six feet and four inches high, with limbs formed in nature's most perfect model. In the duties of his station, he excelled as much as in size, being the most complete disciplinarian in the brigade. His social habits, pleasant, agreeable manners, and cheerful disposition, rendered him a general favorite with the officers, as well as with the private soldiers, who always followed with alacrity, wherever he led. Of the dangers and perils of the war, he partook largely, being engaged in the Battles of Trenton, Princeton, Monmouth, and many others. His superior tact and excellence in discipline attracted the notice of Gen. Steuben, who appointed him inspector of the brigade, which office he filled with great credit to himself, and the entire satisfaction of the Baron.

Near the close of the war, he was engaged in the following affair, which is thus related by Dr. Thatcher, in his journal of military events: "In the mutiny which broke out in January, 1781, in the New Jersey Line, stationed at Pompton, in New Jersey, a detachment of five hundred men was ordered out to suppress it. In this detachment Col. Sproat was second in command, and Maj. Oliver one of the field officers. The distance from the main encampment was thirty or forty miles, and the snow two feet deep; it took nearly four days to accomplish the march. When they came in sight of the insurgents, Gen. Robert Howe, the Commander, ordered his men to load their arms; and as some of the officers distrusted the faithfulness of their own men, so prevalent was disaffection in the army, that, before making the attack, he harangued the troops on the heinousness of the crime of mutiny, and the absolute necessity of military subordination; that the mutineers must be brought to an unconditional submission. The men entered fully into the patriotic spirit of their officers, and marching with the greatest alacrity, surrounded the huts so as to admit of no escape. Gen. Howe ordered his Aid-de-Camp to command the mutineers to parade in front of their huts, unarmed, in live minutes. Observing them to hesitate, a second message was sent, when they instantly obeyed, and paraded in a line, unarmed, two or three hundred in number. The General then ordered three of the ringleaders to be selected for condign punishment. These unfortunate men were tried on the spot, Col. Sproat being President of the court-martial, standing on the snow, and they were sentenced to be shot immediately. Twelve of the most active mutineers were selected for their executioners. This was a most painful task, and some of them, when ordered to load their guns, shed tears. Two of them suffered death on the spot; the third one was pardoned, as being less guilty, on the representation of their officers. Never were men more completely humbled and penitent. Tears of sorrow and of joy streamed from their eyes, and each one seemed to congratulate himself that his forfeited life had been spared. The General then addressed the men in a very pathetic and impressive manner: showing the enormity of their crime, and the inevitable ruin to the cause of the country, to which it would lead. They remained true and faithful soldiers to the end of the war.

This was a sorrowful and heart-rending duty to Col. Sproat: with his tender feelings and love for all engaged in the cause of freedom, the effect must have been great. The time made it still more impressive: the depth of winter, the white snow, an emblem of innocence, crimsoned with the blood of his fellow soldiers, shed by their own comrades, and not in battle, rendered the sight one not to be forgotten while life should last. But order and military subordination demanded this sacrifice to duty and he could not retreat. These men had served their country faithfully, probably for three or four years; had suffered hunger, and cold, and nakedness; had sometimes been without any food, and for weeks lived on a half or a third of a ration of the poorest kind of meat. Their wages were often withheld, and when paid at all, were in a depreciated government paper, thirty dollars of which, at this time, were worth only one in specie, and there was little prospect of its being any better. Some of them had families at home suffering like themselves. That men should become desperate under such circumstances is human nature; the greatest wonder was that the whole army had not revolted and turned their arms against Congress until they had redressed their grievances.

It is greatly to the credit of New England that no revolts or mutinies took place amongst her troops. The strict principles of obedience impressed in early childhood on her sons by their Puritan fathers, gave them a Spartan cast of character, while the intelligence imparted to their minds by their common schools, gave the whole population a decided superiority of intellect over the common soldiers of the middle and southern states. Nearly every man was a patriot, and they suffered little or nothing compared with these states, from the effects of Tory principles, which were productive of more real suffering to the inhabitants, where they prevailed, than all the ravages of the British armies. Well might Washington exclaim, on those trying occasions, "God bless the New England troops!" A mighty debt of gratitude is still owing to the memory of these patriotic men, who stood firm under all these trials, and accomplished the work of independence in spite of foes without and foes within. Their contests with poverty and want were five times more severe than all their battles with the enemy.

Having served through the war with credit to himself and the regiment to which he belonged, and witnessed the acknowledgment of the freedom of his country by the British, and the reception of the United States as an independent sovereignty amongst the nations of the earth, he retired satisfied, to the pursuits of private life. As a proof of his attachment to the common soldiers, and all who were or had been engaged in fighting the enemies of his country, the following anecdote is related.

Col. Sproat was, all his life, fond of keen repartee, and a good joke, whenever an opportunity to exercise it occurred. At an early period of the war, while he was a Captain, he was at home on a short furlough. His father, as has been before noticed, kept a house of entertainment, more especially for eating than drinking. While there three private soldiers on their way home from the army, called for a cold luncheon. His mother set on the table some bread and cheese, with the remains of the family dinner, which Ebenezer thought rather scanty fare for hungry men, and especially as the bones were already pretty bare. He felt a little vexed, that the defenders of the country were not more bountifully supplied. After satisfying their appetites, they inquired of him, how much was to pay? He replied he did not know, but would ask his mother; so, going to the kitchen door, where she was busy with her domestic concerns, he inquired, *"Mother, how much is it worth to pick those bones?"* She replied, *"About a shilling, I suppose."* He returned to the room, and taking from the drawer in the bar, three shillings, with a smiling face, handed each man one, wishing them a good day and pleasant journey home. The soldiers departed, much gratified with their kind usage. Soon after they had gone, his mother came in, and asked Ebenezer what he had done with the money for their dinners? In apparent amazement he exclaimed, "*Money! Did I not ask you what it was worth to pick those bones; and you replied, a shilling? I thought it little enough for such a job, and handed them the money from the till, and they are gone.*" It was such a good joke, and so characteristic of her favorite son, that she bore it without complaining.

After the close of the war, he lived, for some time, in Providence, employing himself occasionally at surveying.

Here he became acquainted with Miss Catharine Whipple, the daughter of Com. Abraham Whipple, and was united with her in marriage. Her father presented her, as a marriage portion, his own dwelling-house and lot, on Westminster Street, Providence, and retired to his farm in Cranston, a few miles distant.

Soon after this marriage, he entered into merchandise; purchasing a large store of goods from Nightingale and Clark, a noted importing house of that day. Being entirely unacquainted with mercantile affairs, fond of company and generous living, with the liberal habits of a soldier, in the full vigor of life, it is not to be wondered at, if he did not excel in trade, as he had done in military matters. Nothing can be more unlike than the two callings; and out of hundreds who tried it, scarcely one succeeded. He had no taste for his new business, and in a short time he failed; swallowing up his wife's patrimony, as well as his own resources.

About this time, 1786, Congress ordered the first surveys of their lands, west of the Ohio River, to be executed. Seven ranges of townships, beginning on the Ohio, at the western boundary line of Pennsylvania, were directed to be prepared for market. Col. Sproat was appointed the surveyor for the state of Rhode Island, and commenced operations in the fall of that year. The hostility of the Indians prevented the completion of the work, and his range was not finished until the following season.

In 1789, the Ohio Company was formed, and he was appointed one of the surveyors of their new purchases, for which his hardy frame and great resolution eminently fitted him. In the autumn of 1789, they resolved to send on a company of boat-builders and artificers to the head waters of the Ohio at Simrel's Ferry, for the purpose of preparing boats for the transportation of the provision and men, to commence the colony in the spring. Col. Sproat led one of these detachments. On their way out the following incident occurred, to lighten the tediousness of the way:

The party arrived at the house of a thrifty German farmer, near the foot of the mountains, on Saturday night. He received them with the greatest hospitality, supplying all their wants with cheerfulness, and when Monday morning arrived, wished them a favorable journey; and so pleased was he with his wayfaring acquaintance, that he refused any pay. Col. Sproat not only returned him his sincere thanks, but felt grateful for his kindness. The hospitable German had a beautiful little dog, to which he was much attached and greatly valued. One of the laboring hands, named Danton, had the baseness to put him into the wagon, unknown to anyone. When they stopped again for the night, a messenger placed in the hands of the Colonel the following note from his German friend: "Meeshter Col. Sproat, I dinks I use you vell; den for what you steal my little tog?" The Colonel was much mortified and greatly enraged when the dog was found, but met with an opportunity of sending him back the following morning, with a polite, explanatory note, to his master. Danton never outgrew the infamy of this nefarious act, but had it often cast at him in his future life. The detachment, after great fatigue, reached their destination, and spent the remainder of the winter in building a large boat called the Mayflower, in remembrance of the vessel that transported their forefathers to a new home, as this was to convey the pilgrims of the west to their home in the wilderness. The party arrived at the mouth of the Muskingum on the 7th of April, 1788. Col. Sproat immediately commenced his labors as surveyor for the company, and continued them until the breaking out of the war in January, 1791, when all further operations in the woods were suspended. Many of the savages visited the new settlement to see the Bostonians, as they were called, and to exchange their meat, skins, and peltry, for goods with the traders at Marietta and Fort Harmar. The tall, commanding person of Col. Sproat, soon attracted their attention, and they gave him the name of Hetuck, or Big Buckeye. From this, no doubt, originated the name of Buckeye, now applied to the natives of Ohio, as the phrase was familiar to all the early settlers of Marietta.

On the arrival of Gov. St. Clair and the organization of the county of Washington, he commissioned him as sheriff, which post he held for fourteen years, or until the formation of the state government, when a change in the political measures of the administration threw him out of office. He was also, at the same time, commissioned as Colonel of the militia. In the fall of 1790, just before the commencement of the attack on the settlements, he was authorized by Gen. Knox, secretary of war, to enlist a company of soldiers for the defense of the colony, appoint Rangers, and superintend the military affairs of the United States in Washington county, with the pay of a Major, which post he filled with fidelity, to the satisfaction of the settlers and the government. His experience in military matters, was of great advantage to the inhabitants, while his bold, undaunted manner, inspired them with courage in times of greatest danger.

His family arrived here, with Com. Whipple, in 1789. It consisted of his wife and one daughter. After the close of the war she married Solomon Sibley, Esq., of Detroit, who commenced the practice of law in Marietta.

As Sheriff of the county, he opened the first court ever held in the territory, now Ohio, marching with his drawn sword and wand of office, at the head of the Judges, Governor, Secretary, &c, preceded by a military escort, from the Point to the northwest blockhouse of Campus Martius, on the 2d day of September, 1788. It was an august spectacle, conducted with great dignity and decorum, making a deep impression on the red men of the forest, many of whom witnessed the ceremonies, and at this time bestowed on him the Indian name, by which they ever after designated him.

During the whole period of the war he performed his duties as Superintendent of the military posts at Belpre, Waterford, and Marietta, and Paymaster to the Rangers and Colonial troops. These certificates of dues for services rendered the Ohio Company—for they too kept up a military band at their own expense—as well as the United States, served in place of money, and formed nearly all the currency afloat during the five years of the war. They were generally for small sums, and taken in payment for goods at the stores, who received their cash for them in Philadelphia, and also passed as a tender between the inhabitants. Had it not been for these assignats, the sufferings of the settlers would have been much greater. It is said by Col. Convers, who resided at Waterford, that he did not believe that settlement, in 1792, could have raised ten dollars in specie amongst them. They had little or nothing to sell, and experienced the greatest difficulty in producing the common necessaries of life. The Ohio Company expended more than eleven thousand dollars of their funds in defending the settlements, which was never repaid them by the United States, as it in justice ought to have been.

In disposition and temperament, Col. Sproat was cheerful and animated; exceedingly fond of company and jovial entertainments; much attached to horses and dogs; always riding in his long journeys over the country, then embracing half the State of Ohio, some of the finest horses the country afforded, and generally accompanied by two or three large dogs, who, next to horses, shared largely in his favors. In executing the sterner requisitions of the law among the poorer classes of society, he has been often known to furnish the money himself for the payment of the debt, rather than distress an indigent family. His heart, although full of merriment and playfulness, overflowed with kindness. He had no enemies but those of a political kind. In personal appearance, he was remarkable for his tall, majestic figure, and exact proportions; towering like a Saul, a full head above the height of other men.

The office of Sheriff was filled with great dignity and propriety, commanding by his noble presence and military bearing the strictest silence and decorum from the audience, while the court were sitting; and when on duty, wearing his sword as an emblem of justice, as well as of execution in fulfilling the requirements of law. This badge of office was very appropriate, and was kept up in several of the states for many years after the war, but, like many other good and wholesome usages, has given way under the prevalence of ultra democratic principles.

He was a Federalist of the old school, warmly attached to his country and to the precepts taught by his venerated commander, Gen. Washington, in the times which tried men's souls.

For several years of the latter part of his life he devoted his leisure time to cultivating the earth, for which he ever retained a strong predilection, formed in early youth. He was fond of the rougher kinds of labor, such as driving a team of young oxen, and in ascending a hill with a load beyond the strength of his team, delighted in applying his shoulder to the wheel, and helping them out of the difficulty. Gardening was another favorite pursuit. The Bank of Marietta now occupies one corner of his garden, which covered nearly an acre. It was laid out in squares and spacious walks, very tastefully, embracing ornamental shrubs, and all the varieties of fruits cultivated in the middle states. An ancient pear tree is still standing, planted by his hand.

The garden was kept in nice order by an old black woman named Suke, who outlived him many years, but always spoke of her kind, old Master Sproat, in terms of exalted admiration.

The dwelling house is now owned by Capt. Daniel Green, and is a specimen of New England architecture very creditable to the period in which it was built, nearly fifty years ago.

He died suddenly, in the full vigor of health, in February, 1805, having his oft-repeated wish of a sudden exit fully answered. His memory is held in grateful remembrance by all who knew him.

Chapter VII
CAPT. JONATHAN DEVOL

Jonothan Devol
1756 - 1824

From the earliest ages, and even from the first invention of letters, it has been one of the most pleasing duties of the historian to record the lives and actions of distinguished and useful men. In this way a kind of immortality is given to their names, and they live again amidst the descendants of future generations; their good deeds stimulating others to imitate their virtuous and praiseworthy examples. Abounding, as the first colony of the Ohio Company settlers did, with excellent men, in numbers and qualifications far exceeding those of any other settlement in the valley of the Ohio, yet few of them were more deserving than the subject of the following memoir.

Jonathan Devol was born at Tiverton, in the colony of Rhode Island, in the year 1756. His ancestors were of French descent. His father settled in Rhode Island, and was a dealer in West India produce. The mother belonged to the sect called Quakers, who in that day composed a large portion of the inhabitants; the mild sway of Roger Williams encouraging perfect freedom of conscience, and good-will to all mankind. The family was quite numerous, he being the youngest of seven sons.

Schools of learning, before the Revolutionary War, were of rare occurrence, and his whole education was embraced in one year's schooling. It fortunately happened that his father possessed a small library of choice books, from the perusal of which he reaped valuable instruction, and acquired a taste for reading that never forsook him in afterlife. When quite young he learned the trade of a ship carpenter, and in manhood became quite noted for his skill in constructing boats of beautiful model and rapid sailing. One of his boats took a purse of fifty guineas, in a race between some gentlemen amateurs of Newport and Providence, where this manly sport was brought to great perfection.

When the War for Independence broke out between Great Britain and the colonies, he took the side of his country, and before he was twenty years old, received a commission as Ensign. In October, 1775, on the first call for troops for the interior defense of the colony, he marched with a part of a company of men, and joined the regiment to which he belonged, on the heights back of the town of Newport. In December following, he was appointed to the same rank, in a regiment enlisted for a year. In June, 1776, he was commissioned as a Lieutenant in the Continental Service. In December following, he was promoted to the Adjutancy of the First Regiment in a brigade raised to repel the British, who had invaded Rhode Island.

In July, 1777, he resigned that post, in consequence of being superseded in the promotion of the Adjutant of the Second Regiment, to the vacancy of Brigade-Major, to his wrong, and retired to private life, as any spirited man would have done, in a similar case. This disregard to the military rates of promotion, in the early years of the war, was a source of heart burnings and of serious injury to the cause, until corrected by more just views of this important spring in the service.

In September of the same year, he acted as a volunteer in the badly conducted expedition of Gen. Spencer, against the British in Rhode Island. After the evacuation of the island, in January, 1780, he retired to Tiverton, and was appointed to a Captaincy in the Militia. While occupied in the busy scenes of that eventful period, he was often selected to conduct hazardous expeditions above his rank, and for several services of this kind, received the thanks of the Commanding General of the troops on this station. Amongst other dangerous exploits was the following, of cutting out a British brig from under the stern of a twenty gun ship, in the outer harbor of Newport.

On the evening of the 11th of April, 1776, there arrived in the roadstead of Newport, a sloop-of-war of twenty guns, a transport-ship of eighteen guns, with a brig and sloop as tenders; the latter were moored directly under their sterns. A plan was soon arranged for making an attack on them with the row galleys then in port. To effect this, it was necessary to procure a party of volunteers from the brigade, then quartered in the town of Newport. Lieut. Devol was at that time sick in bed, with an attack of the mumps; and nothing but the certain failure of the measure, from the want of his assistance, could have induced him to leave his room. In a short time he procured twenty volunteers to accompany him in the hazardous attempt. They embarked on board the galley of Capt. Grimes, the Commodore of the station, about eleven o'clock, in a dark, rainy night. She was worked with oars, and carried one long eighteen pounder. The Captain attempted to lay the galley alongside the brig, intending to carry her by boarding; but the force of the tide, and the imperfection of the human vision in the darkness of the night, caused the galley to fall upon her quarter. Lieut. Devol, at the head of his boarders, who stood ready to spring up the side of the enemy, as soon as the vessels came in contact, now mounted over her quarter, followed by only five of his men, the others being prevented by the falling off of the galley, before they could get on board. While in the act of climbing over the quarter, the sentinel on deck hailed, and fired his musket down among the assailants; the ball passed very near the head of Mr. Devol who instantly returned the salute with one of his pistols. Followed by his five brave men, he was soon on the deck of the brig, and, cutlass in hand, drove the midshipman who had command, with ten men, below, and instantly fastened the hatches down upon them. The next act was to cut loose the cable and get their prize under way. In performing this service, they had a tedious time; for the axe and the carpenter were both left in the galley, with the residue of the boarders. In this dilemma, recourse was had to a cutlass, and by repeated and strenuous hacks in the dark, they, at length, after thirty minutes, divided the fourteen inch cable by which she was moored, and the tide soon put her in motion. In the meantime, the twenty gun ship had got under way, and came down on her larboard side, to the rescue of the tender. The galley had now recovered her lost ground by the aid of her sweeps, and came up on the starboard side, just as the cable gave way, so that as the prize swung round she fell afoul of the galley. The ship all this time kept firing into her, both with cannon and musketry, but from the darkness and confusion of the night, did but little damage, except to her rigging and spars, with the loss of one man mortally wounded. As soon as the galley was free, she opened her fire on the ship with her long gun. The enemy soon gave up the pursuit, and the brig, with her crew, was brought in and moored at the wharf in Newport.

This was as brave and gallant an exploit as was enacted during the war. Had the whole twenty men succeeded in boarding the brig, it would have been a bold achievement, considering how near she lay to the twenty gun ship. But when the number is reduced to five, to oppose ten men on their own deck, it deserves all our praise. And then to stand for twenty or thirty minutes, hacking at the cable with such an inefficient tool, exposed to the constant fire of the enemy, required the utmost coolness and intrepidity. The effects of this night's exposure to the rain and cold, confined Mr. Devol to his bed for a long time, and laid the foundation of a disease from which he severely suffered for the last twenty years of his life.

On the 1st of May, 1777, a party of British and Hessians were seen from the American lookout, at Battery Hill, on the main land, about a mile and a half from their lines on the island, in search of deserters that had come off the night before. Lieut. Devol, with twenty men, was ordered over across the inlet, near Rowland's Ferry, to attack them. He landed his party undiscovered. Two men were left in charge of the boats, and one sent to an adjacent eminence to give notice of any other body of their foes that might be in sight. With seventeen men he charged at full speed on the enemy. They immediately fled, and their commander, a Lieutenant in the Twenty-Second Regiment, fell a prisoner into their hands. The party under his orders consisted of twenty-five men, as confessed by himself. They were hotly pursued as near to the lines as was prudent. Soon after the British took possession of Newport, a number of the disaffected inhabitants of Rhode Island, called Tories, joined them. These renegades from their country's cause, felt a greater inveteracy to the Whigs than the British themselves, and sought every opportunity to distress and destroy them. One dark night they fitted out a marauding party from Newport, in a swift sail-boat, manned with tea or twelve men, who were well acquainted with the adjacent country along the shores and inlets of the bay which embosom the island. In this expedition they attacked and plundered the house of Job Amy, an old but very respectable citizen, robbing him of a part of his furniture, and considerable valuable plate, taking the old man also with them, hoping to extort money from him by way of ransom. His son Job, an active young man, was so fortunate as to escape by jumping out of a chamber window, and half-dressed as he was, hastened with all speed to Howland's Ferry, where Mr. Devol then lived, knowing that he commanded a party of men and one of the swiftest boats, for the purpose of rescuing the inhabitants and harassing the enemy. The distance he had to run was about ten miles, which he performed in an incredibly short time, along the sandy beach of the shores. He reached the ferry about midnight, across which he had to swim, and awakening Mr. Devol, related the disasters of the night. He directed him to go and arouse the boat's crew, while he procured a keg of water and some provisions. In a few minutes all were ready, and Job entered with them as a volunteer in the cruise. Knowing the course which the robber boat must pursue in her return to Newport, they concluded that if they could reach Sckonet Point, a noted headland, which she must pass, they could overtake them before they arrived within reach of the protection of the British shipping, and recover the plunder, as well as make prisoners of the crew, and release their own friends whom they had forced away with them. By great exertion in rowing and the utmost skill in sailing, they hove in sight of the point just as the day dawned, and made out the robber boat a short mile distant. Bill Crowson, the commander of the Tory crew, a violent villain and robber, espied his pursuers at the same time; expecting that he might, possibly, be intercepted from the escape of Job Amy; and yet the distance was so great that he did not believe he could travel that far in so short a space of time as to bring Devol down upon him by daylight. One of Crowson's prisoners, an active, bold man, as soon as he saw the pursuing boat jumped upon the thwarts, and swinging his hat, shouted with all his might, saying he knew it was Devol's boat, one of the swiftest in all those waters, and they should surely be retaken. Bill d----d him for an impudent rebel, and with a terrible oath, swore if he did not seat himself quietly in the boat, as the motion disturbed her sailing, he would shoot him on the spot. He boldly answered that he dare not do it, for his friends would shortly be up with him and revenge his death. His prediction was soon verified. Devol's crew, by great exertions with their oars, as well as the nicely adjusted sails under his own care, soon ran alongside, and on being ordered to surrender in a tone that meant to be obeyed, they gave up without firing a shot, although manned by a more numerous crew. Knowing their cause to be a dastardly one, they could not defend it with the courage of men who have right and justice on their side. After the surrender, the young man who had been ill-treated and abused by Crowson, sprang at him with a sword which he snatched from the hand of one of the men, and would have put him to death but for the interference of Mr. Devol, who could not suffer a prisoner to be injured, however mean and villainous he might be. The boat returned in triumph with her prize, although the British fleet lay at anchor within gunshot of the spot. Crowson was such a notorious rascal, that the inhabitants of Tiverton were with difficulty restrained from hanging him up without trial. He was, however, sent off under a guard to Taunton jail, and confined as a British prisoner. Job Amy, the young man who gave the alarm, never recovered from the exertions of that night, but died of a consumption before the end of a year.

In 1776, Capt. Devol married Miss Nancy Barker, the daughter of Capt. Isaac Barker, for many years a noted ship-master of Newport. Her father was lost at sea some years before the war, and she, with her widowed mother and several sisters, now resided on a farm, near the center of the island, on the road from Howland's ferry to Newport. When the British troops took possession of the place, many of the inhabitants were suffered to remain quietly in their houses. Mrs. Barker was one of this number, and three or four of the officers were quartered the winter following at her house. They, however, treated her and the young ladies very politely and paid her honorably for their board. The fiery and patriotic spirit of the young Lieutenant could not brook the thought of his betrothed remaining in the society of the enemies of his country, lest their fascinating manners and rich dresses should lessen her devotion to the Whig cause. He accordingly, after giving her timely notice, planned an expedition on to the island with a party of men, and one dark wintry night, at the imminent hazard of his life from the sentries, brought off his intended wife in safety. Shortly after this event, they were married at the house of an elder sister, near Fairhaven. This union proved to be a very happy one, though checkered with many vicissitudes. She was the mother of thirteen children, and shared with him the dangers and privations of settling a new country in the wilderness, amidst the horrors of an Indian war.

After the close of the Revolution, and he had witnessed the triumph of his country over her enemies, he settled down in quiet at Howland's Ferry. Here he carried on the boatbuilding, and kept a small store of groceries.

When the Ohio Company was formed in 1789, he became one of the associates. In the autumn of that year, he joined the little band of pioneers who preceded the actual settlers with their families, and spent the winter on the Youghiogheny River, at Simrel's Ferry. Here he was employed by Gen. Putnam to superintend the building of a large boat for the transport of the advance guard of the Ohio Company and their provisions to the mouth of the Muskingum. She was named by the adventurers, the "Mayflower". This is said to have been the first decked boat that ever floated on the Ohio. She was built with stout timbers and knees like a galley with the bottom raking fore and aft, and decked over with planks. The deck was sufficiently high for a man to walk upright under the beams, and the sides so thick as to resist a rifle bullet. The steersman and rowers were thus safely sheltered from the attack of enemies on the banks. She was forty-five feet in length and twelve in breadth. Subsequently, gang boards were added on the outside, so that she could be pushed against the current with poles, like a keelboat; and was used in transporting a number of the colonial families from Buffalo, above Wheeling, to Marietta, in the summer of 1788. It was at first supposed she could be worked up stream with sail, but the variable nature and uncertainty of the winds on the Ohio River, frustrated their arrangement.

After the pioneer corps had established themselves at the mouth of the Muskingum, he was actively engaged in the erection of the stockaded garrison, called Campus Martius. This imposing structure answered the double purpose of a fort and for dwelling-houses. Within these walls the colonists were safe from the attack of Indians. The blockhouses, as well as the dwellings which formed the curtains between, were built of planks four inches thick, and eighteen or twenty inches wide, sawed by hand from the huge poplar trees which grew near the ground occupied by the garrison. These were dovetailed together at the corners, and with the smooth surface left by the whip-saw, gave to the exterior a finished and beautiful aspect. The fort, as it may well be called, was a square of one hundred and eighty feet on each side, as figured in the preceding volume. The settlers were allowed to build a part of the dwelling-houses in the curtains for themselves, after the plan laid down by Gen Putnam. Capt. Devol built one on his own account, forty feet long by eighteen wide, and two stories high, furnished with neat brick chimneys, a kiln being made and burned the first season.

Mrs. Devol, with five children, came on and joined him in December. The following winter his house sheltered seventy persons, young and old, so few were the finished dwellings. The summer of 1789 was spent in completing the works at Campus Martius, and in the winter he was employed with two others in exploring the lands of the company for suitable spots for mills, and to commence farming settlements. In February, 1790, he moved his family to Belpre, and settled on a small farm, in company with other associates, united together for mutual assistance and protection, as the western tribes, notwithstanding the treaty with Gov. St. Clair, appeared to be hostile, and on the eve of a rupture. During the first six months of the year the settlers suffered very much from a want of food, as more fully noticed in the history of Belpre.

Early in January, 1791, the Indian War broke out, and the inhabitants were compelled to leave their improvements and go into garrison. The news of the massacre at Big Bottom reached Belpre the day after that event, at a time when nearly all the men, especially the heads of families, were at Marietta, attending the Court of Quarter Sessions. Most wretched was the night following this news, to the women and children, as they watched with trembling hearts in the slender log-cabins in which they dwelt, the approach of the Indians, expecting every hour to hear their terrific yells. Mrs. Devol directed her children to lie down with their clothes on, ready to rush into the woods at the first alarm. The court was soon adjourned, and Capt. Devol, with the others, returned with all speed to their homes, expecting to see their houses in flames, and their wives and children slaughtered or taken captives by the savages. A council of the leading men was promptly called, and it was decided to build a strong garrison three miles below the Little Kanawha, against the center of the island, since known as the island of Blennerhassett. This garrison contained thirteen large block-houses, ranged in two lines, about six rods apart, near the bank of the Ohio, and was very appropriately called Farmers' Castle. The whole was enclosed with stout palisades, and made a formidable defense against the attack of Indians. It was forty rods long by eight rods wide. Two large gates were placed at the east and west ends, while two smaller ones led down to the river. This work was chiefly planned and built under the direction of Capt. Devol, aided by the council of several old and experienced officers of the settlement, in an incredibly short space of time, and sheltered thirty or forty families, besides single men, during the war. When we consider the labor of cutting and hauling such a multitude of trees, to afford pickets fifteen feet long, with all the timber for eleven large block-houses, two stories high and twenty feet square, we are struck with admiration at the resolution and enterprise of this handful of pioneers, about twenty-five or thirty in number. A considerable portion of this timber was dragged on to the ground by men (as they had but few ox teams, and no horses,) on sledges, the snow fortunately being a foot or more deep. All this was accomplished in about six weeks' time, and was acting over again the labors of the Pilgrim Fathers at Plymouth Rock. While at this work they had the protection of the two block-houses built on this ground the year before by Col. Battelle and Griffin Greene, and was the probable cause of their selecting this spot for their main garrison.

During the first two years of the settlement, their meal was all ground on hand-mills, with great labor and fatigue. Soon after they were settled in the new castle, the active mind of Mr. Devol suggested a remedy for this inconvenience. Some time previous, in conversation with Mr. Greene, he learned that he had seen floating mills in Holland. He directly proposed a project for a grist-mill, to be built on boats, and anchored in the Ohio, at some ripple, within sight of the castle, where it would be safe from their savage foes. A few of the intelligent men joined, and a company was formed for executing the work, and in the course of the year 1791, a mill was completed and put in operation, which ground the meal used by the inhabitants during the war.

The First Floating Mill on the Ohio River
1791

It was built on two boats: one a large pirogue, formed out of an immense hollow sycamore tree: the other a large flatboat, made of planks fifty feet long and ten wide. This sustained the mill-stones, gearing, hopper, &c, while the other boat supported the outer end of the water-wheel shaft. The boats were connected by stout timbers, to keep them steady against the wind and current of the river, planked over so as to make a floor between the bow and stern of each. The open space was ten feet square, in which the water-wheel worked, and was similar in structure to those of a steamboat. The main boat was secured by a chain cable attached to a rock anchor; the other by a grape vine. The mill was stationed about thirty yards from the shore of the island, nearly half a mile above the castle, as seen in the annexed plate. In a favorable state of the river, she could grind forty bushels in twenty four hours. A small frame house stood in the main boat, and protected the machinery and grain, as well as the miller, from the rain. During winter it was taken nearer the shore, under some point for protection against the ice. Floating trees sometimes broke it loose from the moorings, but as there was usually someone on board, timely notice was given, and the inmates of the castle turned out and towed it back again. Finally, near the close of the war, it broke loose in the night, and floated down the Ohio seventy miles, when the chain cable got entangled in a rock, and brought it up.

The distance was too great for towing back again, and it was sold to the French settlers at Gallipolis. This mill not only did the grinding for Belpre, but many canoe loads of grain were brought from Point Pleasant, Graham's Station, and Bellville.

During the period of the war the small-pox and scarlet fever both visited the inhabitants. By the latter disease he lost his oldest son, a lad of fourteen years, and two other children. It was of a malignant type, carrying off from fifteen to twenty children, beside several with the small-pox.

About this time he executed the work of a complicated piece of machinery, for Esq. Greene, who thought he had discovered the true principle of perpetual motion. The discriminating mind of Capt. Devol saw, at once, the fallacy of the principle, and so expressed himself to the inventor; nevertheless, he was willing to assist him in the experiment. It proved a failure, like all other attempts of the kind.

The inhabitants, feeling the want of saccharine matter in their food, being cut off from their former supplies from the sugar maple, by the watchfulness of their savage foes, he constructed a mill, with wooden rollers worked with oxen, for grinding and pressing out the juice of the stalks of Indian corn, in the manner lately proposed by the secretary of the patent office. Many gallons of syrup were in this way made, that supplied the place of a better article not within their reach. The rich juice of the pumpkin was subjected to the same process, and afforded good sweetening for many uses.

In 1792, he built a twelve-oared barge, of about twenty-five tons burthen, for Gen. Putnam, of the wood of the red cedar. The materials were collected on the Little Kanawha a few miles above the mouth, at the hazard of his life, in the midst of the Indian War. For beauty of model and workmanship, she was said to excel any boat ever seen on the Ohio.

After Wayne's treaty in 1795, he moved his family to Marietta, and cultivated the lands of Paul Fearing, Esq., who boarded in his family. Here he remained until 1797, when he purchased lands at Wiseman's bottom, five miles above, on the Muskingum River. At this place there was a ripple, or slight fall, which he thought a suitable site for a mill; his mind always running on some mechanical operation that would be useful to the destitute colonists. In 1798 he built a floating mill at his new home, which for many years did nearly all the grinding for the inhabitants on the Ohio and Muskingum Rivers for fifty miles above and below the mill; the travel being in canoes and larger boats. In 1803 he built a larger mill, which ground a hundred bushels in twenty-four hours, and made fine flour. In 1801 he built a ship of four hundred tons, for B. I. Gilman, a merchant of Marietta. The timbers of this vessel were wholly made from the wood of the black walnut, which grew with great luxuriance in the rich bottoms of the Muskingum, after which stream the ship was named. In 1802 he built two brigs of two hundred tons each; one called the "Eliza Green", the other, "Ohio". In 1804 the schooner "Nonpareil" was built, In 1807 he built a large frame flouring mill on the spot where the floating mill was moored. The water-wheel was forty feet in diameter, the largest ever seen in that day west of the mountains. During all these busy operations he was improving his farm, planting fruit trees, and making his home comfortable and pleasant. In 1809 he purchased and put in operation machinery for carding sheep's wool, which article had now become so abundant as to need something more than hand cards for its domestic manufacture; some farmers owning flocks of several hundred sheep. Still further to aid in the domestic manufactures, he, in 1808, erected works for dressing cloth and fulling, both of which operations are believed to have been the first ever carried on in this part of Ohio, if not in the state. The machinery for cloth-dressing was procured at McConnellsville, on the Youghiogheny River; these articles were not then manufactured in Ohio.

Amidst the latter period of these operations, when about fifty years of age, he began the study of the French language; and solely by the aid of Boyer's Dictionary, he in a short time learned to read, and translate as he read, with ease and fluency, any book in that tongue, especially works of history. When master of this subject, he commenced, in 1811 or 1812, the study of astronomy, and became quite familiar with this sublime branch of science. He had always a relish for the mathematics, and entered readily into the elements of this deeply interesting study. With the aid of a celestial globe, he constructed a plan of the path and course of the great comet of 1812, and sent it to Josiah Meigs, Esq., then at the head of the United States Land Office, for his examination. It excited his admiration at the genius and skill of Capt. Devol, in a branch of science so little understood by a great portion of mankind. His knowledge of geography was complete, and superior to that of any other man known to the writer of this memoir. For this he was partly indebted to his extensive reading, which was always accompanied by a map of the region treated of in the book or newspaper before him. Many years before steam had come into general use as a moving power, he directed a letter to the Secretary of the Navy, on the advantages to be derived from steamships of war. Nevertheless, he was a man of peace; and often at the celebration of the Fourth of July was accustomed to say that the reading of certain portions of the Declaration of Independence ought to be omitted on that day, as it served to keep up the old ill-will and hatred, which, as the nations are at peace, ought to be forgotten.

His house was open to all his friends and acquaintances; while the hospitality of himself and good wife were proverbial. So affable and kind were the manners of this worthy couple, that all visitors were made to feel how very welcome they were, and that their company was a favor bestowed on them, instead of a trouble.

For many years preceding his death, he suffered greatly from a disease of the hip joint, the origin of which he traced to the night of his hazardous enterprise in the harbor of Newport.

His powers of conversation on nearly all subjects, were unbounded, as well as his magazine of ideas and facts; of course, when he visited Marietta, as he often did on business matters, he was frequently delayed until long after bedtime, in conversations at the firesides of his friends; nevertheless, he could seldom be persuaded to tarry all night, but climbing, with much effort, into his little one-horse wagon, would jog cheerfully along, solitary and alone, the distance of five miles, all the while, if the night was clear, delighting his imagination with studying out the names, and classing the constellations of the heavenly hosts.

He had six brothers, several of whom settled in Ohio. An early example of his kindness may be seen in his treatment of the children of his brother Silas. This brother was a trader, and lived in Boston at the beginning of the War of Independence. He joined the infant navy of the country, and acted as Captain of Marines, under Abraham Whipple, during the first year of the war. He was at length taken prisoner, and died in the murderous British prison ships at New York, with thousands of his countrymen. His wife and three children were left destitute at Boston. Capt. Devol, although then poor, and supporting his own family with his labor, brought the three children to his house, and fed and clothed them as his own, till the daughter was married, and the two sons old enough to take care of themselves.

He used sometimes to try his skill in poetry, a small sample of which is given in the life of Com. Whipple. The ideas and imagination of the poet were not wanting, but he lacked one necessary qualification, harmony of verse.

In person Capt. Devol was of a medium size and height, muscular, and well-proportioned; quick and rapid in his motions like the movements of his mind; a well formed head; light complexion; reddish colored hair; blue, transparent eyes, sparkling with good humor and intelligence; a well-proportioned nose, of a Roman cast; broad, positive chin, indicative of decision and firmness. In his youthful days, in the full, showy dress of the period of the Revolution, he was said to have been, by one who knew him well, the most perfect figure of a man to be seen amongst a thousand.

Mrs. Devol died in 1823, during the great epidemic fever which pervaded all the valley of the Ohio.

He died in 1824, aged sixty-eight years, greatly lamented by all who knew him.

Chapter VIII
COL. RETURN JONATHAN MEIGS

Return Jonathon Meigs

This excellent man was one of the choice spirits brought out by the stirring times of the American Revolution, a season which tried men's souls and purified their patriotism in the furnace of affliction. Some of the best blood of the Puritans warmed his heart, and inspired him at an early day to resist the oppressions of the mother country, and to preserve for himself and his posterity the civil and religious liberty purchased at so dear a rate by his forefathers, who had left their country and homes across the Atlantic to enjoy these rights in the wilderness of North America.

The subject of this sketch was born at Middletown, Conn., in December, 1740. His early education was such as the public schools of that day afforded. He was a neat penman; specimens of his writing are seen in the early records of the Court of Common Pleas of Washington County, Ohio, of which he was Prothonotary. His knowledge of mathematics must have been considerable, as he was one of the surveyors of the Ohio Company. The larger portion of the active and prominent men at the period of the Revolution, were bred to farming, or some useful mechanical occupation, which gave them healthy, muscular frames, and vigorous, thinking minds. Col. Meigs was bred to that of a hatter; and the old shop may now be seen in a plan of the ancient town, attached to Barber's History of Connecticut.

At the breaking out of the war, he was thirty-five years old, a period in the life of man, when his physical and mental powers are fully developed. For one or two years preceding, the people of Middletown had noticed the gathering storm and like others of their New England brethren, prepared themselves for its coming by forming volunteer military companies, and rolls of minute men, who had for many months been trained in martial exercises. One of these was organized in this town, well armed and uniformed, which made choice of Mr. Meigs for their Captain. At the first news of the bloodshed at Lexington, he marched his company of light infantry to Cambridge, and offered his services for the defense of the country. Soon after this he was appointed a Major by the state of Connecticut. Encouraged by the successes of Allen and Arnold, in their attacks on the British Canadian posts, and believing they had many friends amongst the French inhabitants, who had never become fully reconciled to the sovereignty of the English since their conquest by Gen. Wolfe, it was thought advisable by Gen. Washington and a Committee of Congress, who visited the camp at Cambridge, to send a body of troops into Canada by the way of the Kennebec and Chaudière Rivers, to act in concert with the army of Gen. Montgomery, already in the vicinity of Montreal. Benedict Arnold, born in Norwich, Conn., in the same year with Col. Meigs, a bold, active man, was selected to lead the expedition, and commissioned by the Commander-in-Chief, as a Colonel. About eleven hundred men were detached from the main army, composed of ten companies of infantry from the New England states, and three companies of riflemen from Pennsylvania and Virginia, under Capt. Daniel Morgan. The field officers of the infantry were Lieut. Col. Christopher Green, of Rhode Island, Lieut. Col. Enos, and Majors Bigelow and Meigs.

The troops left the camp near Cambridge, on the 11th of September, 1775, in high spirits, looking forward to a glorious result with hope and confidence, and arrived at Newburyport, where they were to embark the following day. On the 18th they entered on board ten transports, and sailed that evening with a fair wind for the mouth of the Kennebec, which place they reached the next day, without any accident, or meeting any of the enemy's ships. The vessel proceeded up the river to Coburn's ship-yard, opposite the present town of Gardiner, where the troops embarked with their baggage in two hundred bateaux, already prepared by carpenters, sent on from Cambridge, and proceeded up the river to Fort Western, opposite to the present town of Augusta. Before leaving this place, Arnold dispatched a party of eight men, with two guides, under Lieut. Steel, an intelligent, faithful man, in birch-bark canoes, to mark out the carrying places and water-courses, to be pursued by the army. This was an arduous duty, but promptly executed, and the route marked out over to the head-waters of the Chaudière, by the 8th of October, or in seventeen days, as appears from the journal of Judge Henry, of Pennsylvania, who was one of the exploring party. The main army did not reach this point in their march, until the 30th, a difference of twenty-two days. Although every exertion was made, their progress was slow, not averaging more than ten or twelve miles a day. The constant recurrence of ripples, falls, and carrying places, across which it required the aid of all the men to carry their heavy bateaux, barrels of pork and flour, with their own arms and baggage. One of these carrying places across a bend, from the Kennebec to the Dead River, a westerly tributary, up which the most direct course led, was fifteen miles, with two or three small ponds, which aided a little. Some of the carrying places were so boggy and deep, that causeways of logs had to be made; while others were rocky and full of bushes and fallen trees. In these Herculean labors the officers were as deeply engaged as the men; as where they led, the soldiers would follow. It was the most arduous and laborious enterprise performed during the war, where the men suffered not only from cold and fatigue for nearly forty days, but for the last ten days from actual starvation. As they approached the heads of Dead River, the elevation of the country rendered the nights cold even in summer, and by the 29th of October, so cold as to cover the calm, shallow water, with a thin coat of ice. In proof of the elevation of this region, by referring to a map, it will be seen that the Connecticut, the Androscoggin, the Kennebec, and the Chaudière Rivers all take their rise in this vicinity.

Near the head of the Dead River lived the remnants of an ancient tribe of Indians. The leading warrior was named Natanis. For some reason Col. Arnold concluded they were hostile to the Americans, and directed Lieut. Steel to capture or kill him. He visited his cabin, a neat, small structure near the bank of the river, but he had received notice of the intention, and fled. A few miles above his hut, a large westerly branch puts in, which the exploring party were about to ascend as the right course to pursue, when one of the men noticed a stake driven into the water's edge, on top of which was a piece of folded birch bark, secured in a split; on examining this, it proved to be a map of the route over to Chaudière, rudely marked on the bark, no doubt left there by Natanis for the benefit of the Americans, as he subsequently proved himself to be friendly, and several of the St. Francis Indians joined Arnold's troops.

The progress of the troops and their laborious march is fully described in the letters of their leader to Gen. Washington and others, as published in the American archives, extracts from which follow. Fort Western was supposed to be only one hundred and eighty miles from Quebec, but subsequently proved to be over three hundred. At this place, for the greater convenience of marching, the troops were separated into five divisions, with the distance of one day's travel between each. The first division was composed of three companies of riflemen, under Capt. Morgan, and was in advance; second division, three companies of infantry, under Col. Christopher Green; third division, of four companies, under Maj. Meigs; fourth division, of two companies, under Maj. Bigelow; fifth, of three companies, under Col. Enos, formed the rear-guard. Norridgewock falls are fifty miles above Fort Western: a little below these falls, was once the seat of a Catholic mission to the Indians, under Father Ralle, so basely murdered in the old French war by a party of colonists.

The river being so full of rapids and falls, together with the leakage, and throwing the water over the sides of the boats, caused great damage, and loss of provisions. Near the heads of the Dead River were many small ponds, abounding in salmon trout. The men caught large quantities for food. They were so abundant that one person could take with a hook eight or ten dozen in an hour. In size, they averaged about half a pound, while in some of the ponds they were much larger. This region has within a few years past become a noted resort for sportsmen in trout-fishing.

On the table lands, between the Kennebec and Chaudière, there was considerable flat land, very wet and miry, the men sinking six or eight inches deep at every step. Dead River is described by Arnold as a fine, deep stream, with a current hardly perceptible, between the falls and ripples. Two or three log-huts were built on the way for the accommodation of the sick men, ten or twelve in number. Although they were constantly wet and the labors of the march excessive, yet very few of them fell sick. No doubt the excitement and novelty of their pursuits in this wild, desolate region, gave a stimulus to their minds which rendered them in a manner insensible to bodily ailment. The moose-deer were quite plenty here, and numbers were killed by Morgan's riflemen.

The weather, to the middle of October, was very fine, which aided the army in its progress very much. On this river a few Indians were found at their fall hunt, and one of them, named Evans, was sent by the Commander with a letter to his friends in Quebec, notifying them of his approach, of which the enemy had yet no suspicion. This Indian betrayed his trust, delivering the letter to a British officer. By the 20th of the month heavy rains set in, and raised the river so high as greatly to impede their progress. On the 24th they were thirty miles from Chaudière, with a stock of provisions only sufficient for fifteen days. From this point he sent back all the sick and feeble men. About this period a party of twenty men was sent forward to clear the four mile portage from the head of Dead River over to Chaudière, and make it easier to pass by the army. It lies across a mountain or high hill. Over this elevation Morgan's men carried all their bateaux; while the other troops took only one for each company, for the transport of their baggage. Provisions they had none, or only five pounds of flour to each man, which was baked into cakes in the ashes of their campfires.

The distance to Quebec from this portage, was one hundred miles. The Chaudière, or Boiling Cauldron as named by the French, was too rapid and full of falls for navigation, and nearly all the boats were stove and sunk in the first day's voyage, to the great peril of the men and loss of baggage. The first night passed on the Chaudière, being the 31st of October, there fell four inches of snow, so that the men in their bivouac were covered with it, when they awoke in the morning. From this time food became more and more scarce. Previous to this, the rear division had advanced fifty miles up Dead River, where Enos overtook Col.

Green's men, entirely out of provisions. Arnold had gone forth to seek an interview with the French inhabitants, and get them to furnish supplies for his men. Under these disheartening circumstances, it was concluded by the officers that Col. Enos' men should deliver all their provisions but rations for three days, to Col. Green's Division, and return back to the settlements, as they must certainly starve if all went forward. Those who returned suffered much from want of food; but those who went on, far more. Several died on the way, from starvation and fatigue, while others barely preserved life, by eating leather, bones, bark of trees, and soup made of the flesh of their dogs. Had not the commander gone on in advance, and purchased provisions of the French, who were very friendly, and got them to carry them up the river to meet the troops, many more would have died.

In a letter to Gen. Schuyler, dated 8th of November, at St. Marie, two and a half leagues, from Point Levi, he says, *"I was not then apprised, or indeed apprehensive of one half the difficulties we had to encounter—of which I cannot at present give you a particular detail — can only say, we have hauled our bateaux up over falls, up rapid streams, over carrying places, and marched through morasses, thick woods, and over mountains, about three hundred and twenty miles; many of which we had to pass several times to bring over our baggage. These difficulties the soldiers have, with the greatest fortitude, surmounted; and about two-thirds of the detachment are happily arrived here, and within two days' march, most of them in good health and high spirits. The other part, with Col. Enos, returned from Dead River, contrary to my expectation, he having orders to send back only the sick, and those that could not be furnished with provisions. The Chaudière was amazingly rapid and rocky for about twenty miles, where we had the misfortune to stave three of our bateaux and lose their provisions, &c, but happily no lives. I then divided the little stock left, and proceeded on with the two remaining boats and six men, and very fortunately reached the French inhabitants the 30th of October, at night, who received us in the most hospitable manner, and sent off early the next morning a supply of fresh provisions, flour, &c, to the detachment."* This timely aid, which saved many lives and encouraged the men to proceed, reached them on the 3d of November.

In all these privations and hardships, Maj. Meigs bore a conspicuous part, suffering equally with his men. Several females, wives of the soldiers, bore the fatigues of this dreary march, wading through bogs and ponds of water coated with ice. Aaron Burr was a volunteer in this heroic, but calamitous expedition. On the 14th of November, in a letter to Gen. Montgomery, he says he crossed the St. Lawrence with about five hundred and fifty men, between the hours of nine at night and four in the morning, without being discovered until they were nearly all over. This was effected in twenty birch-bark canoes, although the river was guarded by two vessels of war. About one hundred and twenty-five more men subsequently crossed, increasing his little army to six hundred and seventy-five. Nearly three hundred had returned with Col. Enos, leaving one hundred and twenty-five as the number lost and left on the way by sickness and death, as the troops at Fort Western amounted to eleven hundred men.

With this small force of resolute soldiers, he immediately invested the walls of Quebec, hoping by cutting off the supplies to force them to capitulate. One of the officers from his camp wrote as follows: *"The difficulties that our detachment underwent in the woods are beyond description. For forty days I waded in the water, more or less; my feet constantly wet, except nights; the most of the time freezing weather. We were at an allowance of half a pint of flour a man for a fortnight, and half that time no meat; passing through morasses, cedar swamps and drowned lands, wading creeks and rivers at the same time. The number that we lost was small, not exceeding three or four, and these with hunger."*

The result of the attack on the city is well known. Maj. Meigs, with his battalion, was attached to that portion of the army which penetrated within the town, where, with Morgan, Dearborn, and others, he was taken prisoner. *"The prisoners within the city were kindly treated by Gov. Carlton. He sent out Maj. Meigs for their clothes and baggage, allowed them to be supplied with money and other conveniences by their friends; and after they were released, they bore a unanimous testimony to the humanity and good usage of the British commander."* (Spark's Life of Arnold.)

During the long and dreary winter which followed their captivity, Mr. Meigs did all he could to alleviate the sufferings of the men, which arose more from the lack of warm clothing than of food. To relieve their necessities, he, with Col. Christopher Green, advanced money to the amount of two hundred dollars. This was justly chargeable to the American Congress, but was not repaid until three years after the cessation of hostilities, or nearly ten from the time of advancement, when we find on their journals the following resolution:

"September 28th, 1785; on the memorial of R. J. Meigs and Job Green, son and heir of Christopher Green, deceased.

Resolved, That the Board of Treasury take order for paying to R. J. Meigs, late a Colonel in the service of the United States, and to the legal representative of Christopher Green, deceased, late a Colonel in said service, the sum of two hundred dollars, the same having been expended for the use and comfort of the unfortunate prisoners in Quebec, in the year 1776."

In the course of this year he was duly exchanged, and returned home; soon after which he received from Congress the commission of Colonel, and was authorized to raise a regiment of choice men, which was afterward known in Connecticut as the Leather Cap Regiment. *"Col. Meigs, having enlisted a part of his regiment, marched to New Haven, to carry into execution a plan projected for the surprisal of a party of the enemy at Sagg Harbor, on Long Island, where a large amount of stores and forage had been collected for the army in New York."*

The following account of this transaction is from "Marshall's Life of Washington":

"Gen. Parsons entrusted the execution of this plan to Col. Meigs, a very gallant officer, who had accompanied Arnold in his memorable march to Quebec, and had been taken prisoner in the unsuccessful attempt made on that place by Montgomery. He embarked with about two hundred and thirty men, on board thirteen whale-boats, and proceeded along the coast to Guilford, from whence he was to cross the sound. Here he was detained some time by high winds and a rough sea; but on the 23d of May, about one o'clock in the afternoon, he re-embarked one hundred and seventy of his detachment, and proceeded, under convoy of two armed sloops, across the sound to the north division of the island, near Southold. The east end of Long Island is deeply intersected by a bay, on the north side of which had been a small foraging party, against which the expedition was in part directed; but

they had marched to New York two days before. Here, however, information was received that the stores had not been removed from Sagg Harbor, which lies in the northern division of the island, and that a small guard still remained there for their defense. The boats were immediately conveyed across the land, a distance of about fifteen miles, into the bay, where the troops re-embarked, and crossing the bay, landed within four miles of Sagg harbor, at two o'clock in the morning; which place they completely surprised, and carried with fixed bayonets. At the same time, a division of the detachment secured the armed schooner and the vessels, with the forage which had been collected for the supply of the army at New York. These brigs and sloops, twelve in number, were set on fire and entirely consumed. Six of the enemy were killed, and ninety taken prisoners. A very few escaped under cover of the night. Col. Meigs returned to Guilford with his prisoners, having thus completely effected the object of the expedition, without the loss of a single man, and having moved with such uncommon celerity as to have transported his men by land and water ninety miles in twenty-five hours."

Shortly after this brilliant affair, Congress passed the following resolution:

"July 25th, 1777—Resolved, That Congress have a just sense of the merit of Lieut. Col. Meigs, and the officers and men under his command, who distinguished their prudence, activity, enterprise, and valor, in the late expedition to Long Island, and that an elegant sword be provided by the commissary-general of military stores, and presented to Lieut. Col. Meigs." (Jour. Congress.)

Col. Meigs continued to sustain an active part in all the privations and sufferings of the American army, during the period of 1778 and 1779; and in the latter year was engaged in one of the most brilliant events in the course of the war — the capture of Stony Point. In this heroic adventure, Col. Meigs acted a conspicuous part, his regiment being attached to the right column of the attacking forces.

The following description of the locality, and events connected therewith, is from Marshall's Life of Washington:

"Some miles below West Point, about the termination of the Highlands, is King's Ferry, where the great road between the middle and eastern states crosses the North River. The ferry is completely commanded by the two opposite points of land; the one on the west side, which is a rough elevated piece of ground, is denominated Stony Point; and the other on the east side, which is a flat neck of land, projecting far into the water, is called Verplank's Point. The command of this ferry was important to either army: to the British, as it gave them the control of an extensive district of country in which to forage, and also the advantage of a strong post, which communicated with New York by water: to the Americans it was important, as it afforded a ready and safe intercourse with the stations on both sides of the river, and the loss of it would oblige them to seek a longer and higher route, through a rough and broken country. The last of May, Sir Henry Clinton, strengthened by a large body of British troops from Virginia, under Gen. Vaughan, embarked his army from New York, on the river, and on the 31st landed a numerous division on the east side of the Hudson, eight miles below Verplank's Point, while the remainder landed on the west side, three miles below Stony Point. The works at this place being unfinished, were abandoned. The British, under Gen. Patterson, immediately took possession, and erecting a battery of heavy cannon and mortars, were ready next morning to open a fire on Fort Fayette at Verplank's Point. The river between the two points is about one thousand yards in width. The troops landed below, invested it by land, and some galleys stationed above, prevented the escape of the American garrison by water. Capt. Armstrong, being unable to defend himself against this superior force, surrendered the post. They immediately proceeded to fortify their acquisitions, and especially Stony Point, in the strongest manner. When fully completed, Sir H. Clinton left strong garrisons in each, and returned to New York. The importance of these posts to the Americans induced Gen. Washington to attempt their recovery. He also wished to achieve some important action to stimulate the courage of the army, and arouse the dormant energies of the country, sinking under a long course of disaster, from the depredations of the British in Connecticut. After carefully reconnoitering these posts, and getting all the information possible, he was satisfied they could only be taken by surprise. His first plan was to attack both posts simultaneously; but as such operations are very difficult of attainment, he decided to turn all his attention to the attack of Stony Point. As the capture of this, from its elevated position, would give it command over the fort at Verplank's Point. To Gen. Wayne, the commander of the

American light infantry, was entrusted the conduct of the enterprise. Twelve o'clock on the night of the 15th of July was chosen for the assault. Stony Point is a commanding hill, projecting far into the Hudson, which washes three-fourths of its base; the remaining fourth is, in a great measure, covered by a deep marsh, over which there is only one crossing place; but at its junction with the river is a sandy beach passable at low-tide. On the summit of this hill was erected the fort, furnished with an abundance of heavy ordinance. Several breast-works and strong batteries were advanced in front of the principal works; and about half way down the hill were two rows of abatis. The batteries commanded the beach and the crossing place of the marsh, and could rake and enfilade any column approaching the fort from either of those points. Several vessels of war were also stationed in the river, so as to command the ground at the foot of the hill. The fort was garrisoned by six hundred men, under Lieut. Col. Johnson. At noon of the day preceding the night of attack, the Light Infantry commenced their march from Sandy beach, distant fourteen miles from Stony Point, and passing over an exceeding rugged and mountainous country, arrived about eight o'clock P. M., at Steel's Spring, one and a half miles from the fort, where the dispositions for the assault were made. It was intended to attack the works on the right and left flanks at the same instant. The regiments of Fibiger and Meigs, with Maj. Hull's detachment, formed the right column; and Butler's Regiment, with the companies under Maj. Murfree, formed the left; one hundred and fifty volunteers led by Lieut. Col. Fleary and Maj. Posey, constituted the van of the right; and one hundred under Maj. Stewart, composed the van of the left. At half past eleven, the two columns moved on to the charge, the van of each with unloaded muskets and fixed bayonets. They were each preceded by a forlorn hope of twenty men, commanded by Lieuts. Gibbons and Knox, whose duty it was to remove the abatis and other obstructions, to open a passage for the columns which followed close in the rear. Proper measures having been taken to prevent notice of their approach, the Americans reached the marsh undiscovered. Here some unexpected difficulties arose, and the assault did not commence until twenty minutes after twelve. Both columns then rushed forward under a tremendous fire of musketry and grape shot; surmounting every obstacle, they entered the works at the point of the bayonet, without discharging a single piece, and obtained complete possession of the fort.

The humanity of the conquerors was not less conspicuous, nor less honorable, than their bravery; not a single individual suffered after resistance ceased. All the troops displayed the greatest courage, and all distinguished themselves whose situation enabled them to do so. Out of the forlorn hope, led by Lieut. Gibbons, seventeen were killed or wounded. The loss of the Americans was not in proportion to the apparent danger and amounted to only about one hundred in killed and wounded. That of the British was one hundred and thirty-one, of whom sixty-three were killed. It was intended to make an attack on Verplank's as soon as Gen. Wayne got possession of Stony Point, but from some mistake that plan failed. Gen. Washington examined the position of Stony Point, and thought it not advisable to maintain it, as it would require at least fifteen hundred men to garrison it, more than he could spare from the army without weakening his means of defense in the Highlands. It was, therefore, reluctantly abandoned. Sir H. Clinton directly took it in possession and fortified it stronger than before.

The success of this enterprise infused new courage into the country, and revived the drooping spirits of the American people. It was a proof that the bravery and enterprise of their soldiers was fully equal to that of their enemies, a fact which the British always stoutly denied, but were now obliged to confess. Col. Meigs shared largely in the honors and dangers of the assault, mounting the breast-work at the head of his men, and with his hand clasped in theirs, assisted many to gain the top of this formidable obstruction, who with fixed bayonets, leaped down into the fort amidst their enemies. Every man engaged in it, through life, was noticed by his countrymen as one of the Heroes of Stony Point.

From this period to the close of the war, he continued to serve his country with fidelity, and at the close shared in the honors and blessings of civil liberty, so dearly bought with the blood and toil of his countrymen. After the war he still lived at Middletown.

On the formation of the Ohio Company, in which many soldiers of the Revolution engaged, he was appointed one of their surveyors, and in the spring of the year 1788 he landed at Marietta, and entered on the duties of his office. A government for the Northwestern Territory had been prepared by an ordinance of Congress, in 1787. Gov. St. Clair and the Judges of the territory had not arrived. The emigrants were without civil laws or civil authority. Col. Meigs drew up a concise system of regulations, which were considered by the emigrants as the rule of conduct and preservation, until the proper authorities should arrive. To give these regulations publicity, a large oak, standing near the confluence of the rivers, was selected, from which the bark was cut off, of sufficient space to attach the sheet on which the regulations were written; and they were beneficially adhered to until the civil authorities arrived in July. This venerable oak was to the emigrants more useful, and as frequently consulted, as the oracle of ancient Delphos, by its votaries."*

* Obituary notice of Col. Meigs, by his son, the Postmaster-General.

Soon after the arrival of Gov. St. Clair, he was appointed a justice of the peace, and one of the Judges of the Court of Quarter Sessions. He was also commissioned as the clerk of this court, and Prothonotary of the Court of Common Pleas. The first session of the latter was held on Tuesday, the 2d of September, 1788. This being the earliest court ever assembled in the Northwestern Territory, it was honored with all the ceremony due to so important an occasion. A procession was formed at the Point, composed of the inhabitants, with the United States officers from Fort Harmar, who escorted the judges of the Court of Common Pleas, with the Governor and Supreme Judges of the territory, to the hall in the northwest blockhouse of Campus Martius, distant about half a mile. The procession was headed by the Sheriff, Col. E. Sproat, a man six feet and four inches high, and large in proportion, with a drawn sword in his right hand, and wand of office in the left; the whole making quite an imposing appearance, and exciting the admiration of the friendly savages, a number of whom were loitering about the new city. When all were assembled within the hall, the services of the day were opened with prayer by the Rev. Manasseh Cutler, one of the directors of the Ohio Company. The court was then organized by reading the commissions of the judges, the clerk and the sheriff, after which the latter opened it for business, by proclamation. The duties of Clerk were executed by Col. Meigs, with accuracy and fidelity, for a number of years.

In 1789, he was engaged a part of the summer in surveying the meanders of the Ohio River, from the Muskingum down to the mouth of the Big Sandy, which was supposed to be near the line of the western boundary of the purchase. While on this trip by water, in a large flatboat, then in use for traveling up as well as downstream, the Indians made an attack on John Matthews, who was surveying the western range of townships, and killed seven men of his company. He fled to Col. Meigs, who received him on board, and crossed over the Ohio River. A little below Twelve Pole Creek he erected a small blockhouse, for the security of his men, until another party of surveyors, under Mr. Backus, could come in. This they did in a day or two; and having completed his survey of the river, they all returned to Marietta. During the period of the Indian War, the labors of the surveyors were suspended: and for several years he suffered all the privations and dangers of that distressing time.

During the treaty with the Indians at Greenville, in 1795, Col. Meigs was appointed a commissary of the clothing department; issuing the goods furnished to the Indians as well as the troops. Here he exercised his benevolent feelings in behalf of the whites who were prisoners with the Indians, to see that all were delivered up, as stipulated in one of the articles. Amongst those who were known to have been captured, was Joseph Kelly, a lad taken from Bellville, Va., in 1791, and whose widowed mother now lived in Marietta, her husband being killed at the same time. In the autumn of 1795, the Indians had brought in and given up all their prisoners; yet no account could be had of young Kelly and it was quite uncertain whether he was dead or alive, as no news had ever been received of him since his captivity. But as the Indians seldom or never put boys to death, after they were prisoners, it was probable he was yet living, and kept back by some family who had become greatly attached to him. Although nearly all hope had ceased of his recovery, yet Mr. Meigs continued to inquire of every new Indian face he saw at the store. At length two Indians said they knew of two white boys on the heads of the Auglaize River, who were kept back by their owners. Hoping that one of these boys might be the widow's son, he immediately applied to Gen. Wayne for a messenger to be sent for them. One of these Indians, as a guide, and a white man were sent out. Joseph had been adopted into the family of an old warrior, named Mishalena, who had lost five sons in the wars with the whites, and had now no child left but a daughter; and yet he adopted this boy, the son of his mortal enemies, as his own, and ever treated him as such. What a lesson for the professors of Christianity! Mr. Kelly says that the old warrior was one of the most kind and benevolent men that he ever met with in his life, as well as of a noble and commanding appearance. He was now too old for war, but in great favor with the tribe, as one of their most able counselors. His adopted mother's name was Patepsa. She never accepted him with the hearty goodwill and affection of Mishalena, but always gave him plenty to eat, when she had it. Joseph was only six years old when adopted, but he was now eleven. He parted with his Indian parents and the boys of the tribe, with nearly as much regret as he had formerly done with his white ones. He had lived with them so long, in the wild freedom of the forest, that he had forgotten his native language, and almost his former name; for his Indian parents had given him a new one, Lalaque, but for brevity, spoken Lala. They accompanied him to Greenville, parting with him very reluctantly, and poor Mishalena was now left in his old age, like a deadened forest tree, around whose roots no green shoot appears. As a parting gift he presented his son with a beautiful bow and arrows, made with his own hands. The boy who accompanied him was named Bill, from Kentucky, whose family was all killed at the time of his capture. He had forgotten the family name, but had been adopted by a widow woman, who had no children. She loved him with all the tenderness of a natural mother, and parted with him in deep sorrow. On the arrival of the two boys at the fort, Col. Meigs sent for the tailor and had them fitted out with new warm woolen dresses, after the fashion of the whites, and the blanket and leggins of the Indians laid aside. A short time before, he had written to Mrs. Meigs, that no discovery could yet be made of the widow's son, and that he greatly feared he was dead; cautioning her not to let the afflicted woman know the worst of his fears. Joseph's mother had described his hair, eyes, and looks, so accurately, that at the first glimpse of the two boys, he picked him out. The Indian interpreter soon confirmed his opinion, by talking with him in the Shawnee dialect. On being questioned, he remembered the names of his brothers and sisters and that his own name was Joseph Kelly. This satisfied him that he was the lost son of the sorrowing widow, who, for the whole period of his absence, had never omitted him in her daily prayers, or sat down to the table with her other children, without mentioning his name. So anxious was this good and kind-hearted man to restore him to the bereaved mother that he started, in February, across the swamps and pathless forests for Marietta. A young, active Shawnee Indian, named Thorn, guided the party, which consisted of six soldiers and six or eight horses, through the wilderness, without deviation, and struck the Muskingum

River at Big Rock, a noted Indian landmark, twenty-four miles above Marietta.

While on their journey, an incident occurred that places in a strong light the acuteness of their observation and tact in tracing their way through the woods. During a cloudy and snowy day, the party got bewildered in a thick beech swamp. Col. Meigs took out his pocket compass, and after examination, said the course lay east. Indian Thom pointed to the southeast. The Colonel still insisting on the authority of the compass, and the known general direction of the route, the Indian became vexed, and shouldering his rifle, muttered in broken English, *"D—n compass,"* and pursued his own course. In a few minutes travel, Thorn's judgment proved to be right and the Colonel and the compass wrong.

The party reached Marietta early in March, and the fervent, oft-repeated prayer of the widow for the restoration of her lost son, was at length answered, to the great joy and thankfulness of Col. Meigs, by whose unwearied exertions and perseverance it had been accomplished, as well as to the delight of the mother.

In 1798, he, with Col. Robert Oliver, was elected by the people of Washington County, to represent them in the territorial Legislature, then assembled for the first time. In this body were several able and talented men. Col. Meigs was not excelled by any of them for sound sense or integrity, and performed his duties with credit to himself and to the people who had elected him.

In 1801, he was appointed by President Jefferson, Indian Agent amongst the Cherokees, where he resided until the time of his death, in January, 1823. The inhabitants of Marietta parted with him very reluctantly, holding his person and virtues in the highest estimation. His upright, manly conduct, dignified manners and kind heart, had enlisted all in his favor. *"During a long life of activity and usefulness, no man ever sustained a character more irreproachable than Col. Meigs. He was a pattern of excellence as a patriot, a philanthropist, and a Christian. In all the vicissitudes of fortune, the duties of religion were strictly observed, and its precepts strikingly exemplified. In the discharge of his duties among the Cherokees, he acquired their highest confidence. They loved and revered him as a father, denominating him, for his integrity and uprightness, the White Path."*

The family of Col. Meigs was not numerous. By his first wife he had two eons, Return Jonathan and John. The former was one of the Governors of Ohio. Timothy was the son of a second wife, and accompanied his father to Georgia.

In person Mr. Meigs was thin and spare, of a medium height, with a highly intelligent countenance; nose Grecian, with a lofty, bold forehead; eyes keen and black, sparkling with benevolence, but striking with awe the boldest heart, when bent in anger on the guilty or undeserving; active and graceful in all his motions, even in old age practicing the athletic sports of the young Indians with the buoyancy of youth. He died suddenly, at the age of eighty-three, full of the Christian's hope, surrounded by the sorrowing Cherokees, who mourned his death with deep and heart-felt grief.

Chapter IX
GRIFFIN GREENE, ESQ.

Griffin Greene
1749 - 1804

The little state of Rhode Island, so fruitful in eminent and brave men, was the birthplace of Mr. Greene, being born on the 20th of February, 1749, in the town of Warwick. His ancestors were from England, and settled in Rhode Island at an early day. Education, at that period, was a minor concern, and he received no other than such as was afforded by the common or public schools. At an early age he was bred to the smith and anchor-making business; few men of that day being able to live without the aid of some handicraft or agricultural pursuit. It was the age of honest industry. Of his youth and childhood, little has been preserved.

At a suitable time of life, he married Miss Sarah Greene, of the same town, but of a family not connected by blood with his own. There were many of this name in the state, who were all wealthy in lands, and ranked high amongst the first citizens of the colony, one of them holding the office of Governor. His wife was a sister of Col. Christopher Greene, who commanded the noted black regiment, which was one of the most efficient and brave in the service. The commissioned officers were white men, and the privates Negroes. By this marriage he had four children, who lived to manhood, viz.: Richard, Philip, Griffin, and Susan. The descendants of Richard are several of them living in Ohio: the others left no issue.

Previous to the commencement of hostilities between the colonists and the mother country, Jacob Greene, a cousin, and himself erected a forge for the manufacture of iron. Before the discovery of steam-power, a stream of water was necessary to work the machinery, and for this purpose a spot was selected on the Pawtuxet, distant about five miles from the head of Greenwich Bay, the nearest point where pigs could be landed from vessels. In addition to the expense of wagoning them over a rough road to the forge, they had to be transported from the North River, and when manufactured into bar iron, returned to the village for sale. It was carried on during the war, and furnished cannon balls and wrought iron for the use of the country, at a period when such articles were scarce in the colony. The site of the old works is now occupied by cotton factories.

At the breaking out of hostilities, he acted with his countrymen in throwing off the yoke of Great Britain, for which praiseworthy deed he was cast out of the synagogue of the Quakers, to which sect he belonged, at the same time with his cousin, Gen. Nathaniel Greene, and never returned to them again. During the war he became acquainted with many leading men of that day, with whom intercourse was kept up in after life. In 1775 he commenced his military career, by serving as commissary to the Rhode Island troops, although, in the previous year, he had been trained to military exercises, as a volunteer in the company to which Christopher and Nathaniel belonged, with many of the most active and prominent young men in the colony. In 1777 he was Paymaster to the regiment commanded by Christopher Greene, and during the attack on the fort at Red bank, was exposed to the shot of the enemy, in taking a supply of powder to his countrymen. This act he performed with great intrepidity, although not in the line of his duty.

In 1778, his cousin, Gen. Nathaniel Greene, with whom he had been brought up and lived in the closest intimacy, working with him at the same forge in the manufacture of anchors, and also engaged with him in various mercantile pursuits connected with the iron business, was appointed, by Gen. Washington, Quartermaster-General of the army. He found the affairs of that department in the greatest disorder, and needing several deputies, his cousin Griffin Greene was selected as one of them.

Under their efficient control, in a few months that branch of the public service, so important to the welfare of an army, was placed in complete order, greatly to the relief and satisfaction of the Commander-in-Chief. He was employed in this business until near the time of Gen. Greene's appointment to the command of the Southern Army. Connected with his purchases of provisions, he also entered into that of merchandise: many goods being needed for the use of the troops, large quantities were bought from Clark and Nightingale, a celebrated firm of that day.

During the whole period of the war, a correspondence was kept up between him and the general: a number of the letters having been preserved among the family papers, extracts will be given, as interesting specimens of the thoughts of the master minds of that trying era. In them are many sensible remarks on men and measures, especially that troublesome one of the currency, which, in 1779, had fallen to its lowest ebb, and had well nigh destroyed the country. In April of that year, one specie dollar was worth twenty dollars of the paper-money of Congress. This depreciation of the currency, with the heart-burnings of the soldiery and people thereon, was one of the main reliances of the King and his counselors, for the subjugation of the colonies. Money and credit are the sinews of war, and of both these Congress was destitute. Had it not been for the timely aid of France, it is more than probable that the independence of America would not, at that time, have been achieved.

The policy of Congress in their finances is thus commented on, in one of his letters, dated at camp, May 18th, 1779:

"The Congress should appoint a Board for this purpose; but they are very fond of reserving all their powers within their own body. It has been clear to me, for a long time, that the business of that House is too complex and multifarious to be digested into method and order. They are always in a hurry, and never bring anything to perfection, until its advantages are lost. I mean not to arraign their intentions, but I am sure their policy is bad. Two things are essential to the interests of these states; one is that the proceedings of Congress be more generally known; and the other is that their authority be more generally acknowledged by the states."

In a short time after this, a Board of Treasury was established, and by the aid of that eminent financier, and most excellent man, Robert Morris, their monetary affairs were placed in a more propitious train. In the January preceding, Gen. Greene was in Philadelphia, and thus writes to Griffin:

"The luxuries and extravagance of this city exceed anything you ever saw. There has been nothing going on here, but entertainments, assemblies, and balls. His Excellency, Gen. Washington, has been here about a month, and the citizens have exerted themselves to make him as happy as possible. But I can truly say I feel serious amidst festivity, and gloomy amongst the most joyous. The extravagance of the times is very unfriendly to a republican government, and greatly enervates the national strength."

How just and true, this sentiment; and not less true now, than then. The thoughts of Gen. Washington and this excellent man were too much occupied with their country's cares, to enter, with satisfaction, into the amusements of the careless and the gay.

In April of this year, the French Minister visited the American Army in their camp at Middlebrook, and was received with great respect. He is represented as one of the most polite men of the age, and says, *"The alliance with France is a most happy affair, and alleviates a thousand of our distresses."*

In September, 1779, Mr. Greene engaged as a partner in a company for fitting out two brigantines as privateers, the coast at that time being pretty clear of British ships of war. They were called the "Black" and the "Rattle Snake"; but before the one had time to erect its head, and the other to shake its rattles, in defiance of the British lion, they were driven on shore at Sandy Hook, in April, 1780, by the enemy's cruisers, and lost. This was the fate of many American privateers, and in the ultimate, it is probable, as much was lost as won, by the colonists, in this nefarious business. It is certain that the loss of these vessels was seriously felt.

In the spring of 1780, he writes:

"Our public affairs are tinder great embarrassments. The treasury is entirely without money, and the public offices without credit. Our stock

of provisions is next to nothing, and the troops frequently upon half allowance for a third part, of the time, and many times entirely without. In a word, we are on the high road to starvation, when there is plenty of everything in the country, and only want ways and means to draw it out. Our prospects at the south are in a disagreeable train, and I set down the certain loss of Charleston, unless some very providential intervention occurs, which we have no reason to expect in favor of a people not remarkable for religion or piety." This prognostic proved correct, as the place surrendered a short time after. *"Upon the whole, our situation in political life is not very eligible; neither will it be soon, unless there is more energy, consistency, and good policy pursued by our civil rulers. We want men of liberality, sound judgment, and attention to business, to conduct our public affairs. Happy is that nation, which has wise and honest men to manage national matters."*

In July, the Marquis de Lafayette visited Rhode Island. The general wrote to his cousin Griffin and brother Jacob, to pay him every attention due to his rank and merit. *"I hope the inhabitants of the state will exert themselves a little to convince the French officers that we give them a most cordial reception. But such is the state of human nature and the caprices of mankind that it is ten to one if ever we part with the same good-will toward each other, that we came together."*

Although the treason of Arnold has been written by a hundred hands, here is a fresh account of it, not before published.

"Camp Tappan, September 29th, 1780.

Treason, Treason! Of the blackest kind, has been most providentially discovered. Gen. Arnold, who commanded at West Point, was in contract with the British Adjutant-General for delivering into the enemy's hands, all the forts and fortifications of that place. The plan was laid, the conditions settled, and the time fixed for the execution. Happily for the cause of America, the whole was discovered before the thing was ripe for execution. The Adjutant-General had been up to King's Ferry to see Gen. Arnold, and on his return to New York, near the White Plains, was taken up by three militia-men, who carried him prisoner to Maj. Jameson, of Sheldon's Light-Horse; and on his being searched, plans of the works, the strength of the garrison, and a hundred other observations necessary to be known in order to favor an attack, were all made out in Arnold's own handwriting. They were immediately sent to Gen. Washington, who was then on his return from Hartford. But unfortunately, Jameson, from a false delicacy, reported to Gen. Arnold, that he had taken prisoner one Anderson, which gave him time to just make his escape before Gen. Washington got to the Point. The Adjutant-General and one Mr. Joseph Smith, are now both prisoners in this camp, and doubtless will be hung tomorrow. We have only to lament that Arnold is not to grace the gallows with them. It appears, from an inquiry into Arnold's conduct, that he is the most accomplished villain in the world: nothing can exceed his meanness. I am called upon to attend a court martial, and, therefore, cannot go further into this dark and wicked business. The militia lads that took him, (Mr. Andre,) deserve immortal honor, and will be most liberally rewarded."

Treason! Treason! The sound of this most odious word and hateful act of Arnold, as it pealed through the nation, turned pale the cheeks of every true friend to his country. It was more dangerous to the cause of freedom than the loss of several battles. Washington knew not whom to trust in this alarming crisis, ignorant as he was of the extent of the conspiracy. But a few days reassured him, and with such men as Greene, Putnam, and a host of others to rally around him, in whose patriotism he could safely trust, his confidence was restored, and the affairs of the army resumed their regular train.

In a letter of October 20th, 1780, on occasion of some losses in Mr. Greene's mercantile business, he says, *"We have one consolation, that good men are not always fortune's greatest favorites. If we are not rich, we will be honest; and if we are not respected for our wealth, we will be for our industry. Your judgment is good in business; your industry and attention unquestionable. Nothing is wanting but the smiles of fortune: without this all our endeavors are in vain:"* another name for a superintending providence that rules the affairs of men, and not the blind goddess of the Romans. *"I am appointed to the command of the southern army, and am now just setting forward on the journey. It is a most difficult command, and hitherto has proved a disgraceful one to all who have gone that way. I wish it may not be my lot. One thing I shall avoid if possible: that is, giving the public just grounds for censuring me. If I am unfortunate, that I cannot help."* The result proved how justly he estimated the difficulties of that weighty affair, and how nobly he conducted the southern campaigns, for his own and his country's glory.

In July, 1781, from the high hills of Santee, he writes, *"Thus far I am safe and in good health, though I have had several very narrow escapes. If I can get off with whole bones and a decent reputation, it is more than I expect. New England should rejoice that she has really felt nothing of the war. It rages here like a fire at large, and destroys everything before it. Such destruction and waste, such misery and distress as this country affords, have not been seen in America. The burning of a town, or the plunder of a few farms, are nothing to the cruelties practiced here. But enough of this disagreeable subject."*

In one of his last letters, dated at Charleston, in May, 1783, he writes, *"I beg leave to congratulate you upon the happy issue of the war. It affords me the highest satisfaction to find my judgment and opinions confirmed by experience. The Revolution has been important and successful, although not very promising in the beginning. It has more than once been in doubt, but I always trusted for success in the general prejudices of human nature. It would have aggravated my own misfortunes, to have led my friends into ruin and disgrace, in the same manner as it now affords me pleasure in having contributed to their happy deliverance."* At the close, he says, *"Remember me affectionately to all at Potowamut:"* the place where he worked at anchor-making before the war. *"Don't forget my old friend, Master Maxwell, and ask him what he thinks of the mighty power of Britain now?"*

The handwriting of Gen. Greene was strong, nervous, and bold; greatly resembling that of Gen. Washington, whom he more nearly imitated in vigor of mind and excellence of character, than any other of his Generals.

During the time of the war, while the British fleet was lying in the harbor of Newport, they *were* obliged to put suddenly to sea, on account of the French fleet threatening to blockade them. Some transport ships and a small frigate called the "Flora", were sunk, to keep them from the enemy. They lay in rather shoal water, and at low ebb tides a part of their hulls was above the surface. In 1780, before the close of the war, the fertile mind of Mr. Griffin Greene devised a plan for raising them from their oozy bed, in which his cousin Jacob assisted him. By the aid of a diving-bell, a man went down and closed up the holes by which they were scuttled. A powerful forcing pump, discharging twenty-five hundred hogsheads an hour, worked by horses in a flatboat alongside, enabled him so effectually to heave the water from their holds, that with the assistance of lighters, they rose to the surface, and once more floated on the ocean. After the close of the war, the commerce of the new republic being at low ebb, and no demand for ships, he took the "Flora" to France for sale. This transaction detained him about two years, in which time he visited Holland and the adjacent countries.

Soon after his return, the project for settling a New England colony on the banks of the Ohio was matured by some of the officers of the Revolution, amongst whom were many of his acquaintance, especially Gen. Varnum, a leading man in carrying out the enterprise. After closing his partnership concerns, and selling out to his cousin Jacob, he joined the company, and invested a part of his money in their lands. In 1788 he moved his family to Marietta, loading three large wagons with his household goods, and all kinds of mechanical and agricultural implements. Amongst other items, was a large library of valuable books; knowing that the mind needed food, as well as the body, even when surrounded by a wilderness. The first anchors made on the Ohio River, for the brig "St. Clair", in the year 1800, were made under his direction. Soon after his arrival at Marietta, Gov. St. Clair commissioned him as a Justice of the Peace, and one of the Judges of the Court of Quarter Sessions. In 1789 he was appointed, by the agents of the Ohio Company, a Director, in the place of Gen. Varnum deceased, which post he continued to occupy until the close of their affairs. In 1790 he joined the colony at Belpre, and was a leading man in that settlement, solemnizing marriages, and settling civil disputes amongst the pioneers.

In January, 1791, the Indian War commenced, by the destruction of the settlement at Big Bottom, the news of which arrived while he was at Marietta, attending court, It was directly adjourned, and each man hurried home as fast as he could, expecting to meet the enemy on the way, and find their cabins and families destroyed. But fortunately the Indians retreated without further mischief. In the erection of Farmers' Castle, he took an active part, and lived there with his family five years during the war. For the whole of this period, he regularly attended the sitting of the courts, making his journeys up and down by water, in a canoe, exposed to the rifles of the Indians.

His active mind could not be idle while confined to the castle, but was busily occupied in studying out useful and curious machinery. He assisted Capt. Devol in planning the model of a floating mill, from the recollection of one he had seen in Holland; probably moved by the tidal currents. He also spent more than a year in planning a self moving machine, for perpetual motion, thinking it might be applied to the propulsion of boats on the Ohio River. "When built, it moved with the accuracy and steadiness of a nice timepiece, but after running a few hours, would finally come to a stand-still, in spite of the efforts of its inventor, being bound by the laws of gravitation, which it had not power to resist. It was reluctantly abandoned, and the curious wheels and levers with which it was made, were in being a few years since, lying in the garret of the old Mansion House in Marietta, amidst the dust and rubbish of by-gone days.

In 1794, when salt was worth six or eight dollars a bushel, he projected an expedition into the Indian country, near the Scioto River, for the discovery of the salt springs, said to be worked by the savages, near the present town of Jackson. At the hazard of his own life and all those with him, ten or twelve in number, he succeeded in finding the saline water, and boiled some of it down on the spot, in their camp kettle, making about a table spoonful of salt. While here he narrowly escaped death from the rifle of an Indian, who discovered them unseen by the party, and after the peace related the circumstance of his raising his rifle twice to fire at a tall man who had a tin cup strung to his girdle on the loins, and who was known to be Mr. Greene. As he might miss his object, being a long shot, and be killed himself, he desisted and hurried back to the Indian village, below the present town of Chillicothe, for aid. A party of twenty warriors turned out in pursuit, and came on to the bank of the Ohio, at Leading Creek, a few minutes after the whites had left it with their boat, and were in the middle of the river. They were seen by the men in the boat, who felt how narrowly and providentially they had escaped.

The right of this discovery was sold to a merchant in Philadelphia for fifteen hundred dollars, and divided with his partners.

In 1795, after the perpetual motion had become an acknowledged failure, he turned his attention to the feasibility of applying steam to the moving of boats on the western waters, and invented an engine so perfect in its model as to attract the confidence of Mr. Elijah Backus, a man of discernment, and owner of the island opposite to Farmers' Castle, and since known as Blennerhassett's. He became jointly concerned in the project, and about the year 1796, they visited Philadelphia and employed an ingenious mechanic to build a steam engine. In this enterprise they expended about a thousand dollars. The man proved to be unskillful or unfaithful, and the work was dropped without being finally put to the test.

In January, 1802, he was appointed Postmaster at Marietta, where he had previously moved his family, in place of David Putnam, Esq., removed by G. Granger. This office he held until his death. In July, 1802, he was appointed Collector for the District of Marietta, under the revenue laws of the United States, by Thomas Jefferson. He was also inspector for the port of Marietta, ships being built and cleared from that place. After his decease, his son Philip held the post-office to the period of his death, in 1806, when it was given to Griffin Greene, Jr.

He died in June, 1804, aged fifty-five years, after a lingering illness which he bore with patience and fortitude, fully persuaded of a happy immortality.

Mr. Greene was a man of intelligent aspect, quick apprehension, and a ready, vigorous application of his mind to any subject before him. In person he was tall, of genteel and accomplished manners, having seen and associated with much refined company and men of talents. His dress was that of the fashionable days of the Revolution, and very becoming to one of his stature. As a man of genius and intellect, he ranked with the first of the Ohio Company's settlers, abounding as it did with able men.

Chapter X
HON. PAUL FEARING

Mr. Fearing was born in Wareham, county of Plymouth, Mass., the 28th of February, 1762, and was the son of Noah and Mary Fearing. His parents were industrious, honest people, with no pretensions to distinction above the class of common farmers, who formed the glory and the strength of the country, before and at the time of the struggle for independence. He had one brother older than himself, and one sister younger. Lucy married Mr. Wyllis, an eminent attorney of Massachusetts.

Of his early childhood but little is known; but as the boy is said to be the father of the man, he was doubtless an upright, open-hearted youth. The Minister of the parish prepared him for college, as was common in that day, which he must have entered before the close of the war, as he graduated in 1785, at a time when the resources of the country were at the lowest ebb. From some reverses in the fortune of his father, about the period of his graduation, he was unable to assist his son in the payment of the customary fee on that occasion, and young Fearing was in danger of missing the honors of the university, for the want of a small sum of money. At this unpleasant crisis, Joseph Barrel, a gentleman of Boston, heard accidentally of the circumstance, and kindly proffered the loan of the requisite sum, which was gratefully accepted. Having decided on law, for a profession, he commenced the study in May, 1780, in the office of Esq. Swift, of Windham, Conn., where he remained nearly two years, and was admitted as an Attorney in the courts of law of that state, on the 19th of September, 1787, by Richard Law, Judge of the Supreme Court.

In July he was enabled to refund the money to Mr. Barrel, and notes in a brief journal of passing events, *"I shall feel under obligation to Mr. Barrel, and am to pay the interest by forgiving fees to some poor client."* This act still further elucidates the benevolent heart of his friend, and proves that he felt good-will toward all mankind.

During this year the Ohio Company was matured, for establishing a colony in the Northwest Territory, and was a general topic of conversation in New England. The glowing descriptions of the country and climate in the valley of the Ohio, caught the fancy of many young men, as well as older persons, and he decided on visiting that distant region. On the 1st of May, 1788, he bid adieu to his friends, and embarked at Boston in a vessel, by the way of Baltimore, for Muskingum, where he arrived on the 16th of that month. Here he put his trunk into a wagon and commenced the journey across the mountains on foot. When he reached the little village of Fannetsburgh, at the foot of the first ranges, he was inoculated with the small-pox, having been exposed to the disease in Baltimore. The eruption came out while he was on the journey, but it does not appear that he laid by, on account of it, although detained two or three days by the breaking down of the wagon. He reached Pittsburg the 10th of June, and embarked the same day, in a boat for Marietta, where he arrived on the 16th. On the 4th of July, he says, Gen. Varnum delivered an oration, and a public dinner was given in honor of the day. At this feast was served up a famous fish, called the Pike that weighed a hundred pounds. The dinner was spread under a long bowery at the mouth of the Muskingum. Many patriotic toasts were given and guns fired from Fort Harmar. About twenty families came on from New England, in the course of the summer and autumn. In May and June, Judges Parsons and Varnum, with Col. Sargent, Secretary of the Territory, arrived, and on the 9th, Gov. St. Clair. The 15th of that month he delivered his inaugural address, in presence of the Judges, officers of the fort, and the assembled citizens of the territory. It was responded to, on the part of the people, by Gen. Rufus Putnam. On the 20th of July he listened to the first sermon ever preached in the English tongue northwest of the Ohio, by the Rev. Mr. Breck from Massachusetts. The Moravian missionaries had preached in the Delaware tongue, at Schoenbrunn and their mission stations on the Tuscarawas River, as early as twenty years before this time. On the 2d of September, 1788, the first Court of Common Pleas was held in the northwest blockhouse of Campus Martius, when he was admitted as an Attorney, and on the 9th of that month, received the following certificate from two of the United States Judges:

"The undersigned, Judges of the territory of the United States, northwest of the river Ohio, make known that they have admitted Paul Fearing, Esq., an attorney at law of said court, and have given unto him permission to appear before, and practice in, any and all the Courts of Record, and others that are or shall be erected in the said territory.

Samuel H. Parsons,
James M. Varnum.
Marietta, September 9th, 1788."

On the 9th of this month the Court of Quarter Sessions sat for the first time, and he was appointed Attorney, or Counsel, in behalf of the United States, for the County of Washington, which was the first organized in the territory. But little law business was done this year, the attention of the settlers, as well as that of Mr. Fearing, being given to the clearing of lands, and making preparations for a permanent home in the wilderness.

In December the Indians of several tribes came in to Fort Harmar, to make a treaty of amity with the United States, under the superintendence of Gov. St. Clair, who is styled Commissioner Plenipotentiary. It was a slow affair, the Indians being much divided as to the policy of the measure, some declining to treat at all, unless the Ohio River was made the boundary between their possessions and the whites; although, at former treaties, they had ceded to the United States a large portion of the present State of Ohio. They saw with feelings of anger and regret, the gradual encroachments of the whites on their country, and that in a few years they would be driven beyond the Mississippi. They finally made a treaty, agreed to by a portion, only, of the tribes, and these did not adhere to it long. In the following year their country on the Miami was invaded by Gen. Harmar and the war actually commenced by the Americans. It was a disastrous campaign, and terminated in favor of the Indians.

The last of January, 1789, Mr. Fearing set out on a journey to New England, in company with several persons, amongst who was Gen. Parsons. They went up the Ohio in a boat, but when about half way to

Wheeling, the floating ice became so troublesome that they left the river and went up by land. The travel over the mountains was accomplished on horseback, in twenty-six days, from Wheeling to Middleborough, in Massachusetts, when at this time it can be done in three or four days, so great are the improvements in travel. He returned in August, by way of Alexandria, and being a fine pedestrian, again crossed the mountains on foot. He reached Red Stone, a famous port for boats, on the Monongahela, on the 14th of that month, and from the low stage of water, had to wait until the 26th of November, for a rise in the river, whereas it was usually navigable as early as September. There was no road through the wilderness, nor any inhabitants, the larger portion of the way. While waiting here in daily expectation of rain, Com. Whipple came on with his family and that of his son-in-law, Col. Sproat. With them he embarked in a small boat, and reached Marietta in four days, on the 30th of the month.

The following year was passed in attending to his law business, which began to increase some, as the emigration this season was very great, being the year before the war began on the Ohio Company settlements. In November he was appointed a deputy contractor for supplying the troops at Fort Harmar with fresh meat, at the low rate of thirteen dollars and thirty-three cents a month, and rations. Labor of all kinds was at a depressed state, a common hand on a farm getting only four dollars, and a private soldier three dollars. Money was very scarce. This post he held until the close of the war, and the avails of it aided much in his support, at a time when all were suffering under the pressure of want.

From his first arrival in the country he kept a journal of the weather, freshets in the Ohio, &c, which are valuable in comparing our present seasons with those of the first settlement of the country. From his notes it is ascertained that the weather, previous to the assault on the blockhouse at Big Bottom, was very cold, and the Muskingum was crossed on the ice from the 22d of December to the 11th of January, which gave the Indians every facility for making the attack. In the course of the summer of 1791, Gen. St. Clair invaded the Indian country, and was defeated on the 4th of November, the news of which did not reach Marietta until the 4th of December, when it was brought by Maj. Denny, on his way with dispatches to Philadelphia, so difficult and slow was the intercourse between the settlements in the wilderness. There were no mails until 1794, when packet-boats were established from Wheeling to Cincinnati.

The Indians had full command of all the country between the lakes and the river, and no dispatch could be sent that way.

Mr. Fearing's first attempt as an advocate before the Court of Quarter Sessions was rather discouraging to his hopes as an orator. He rose with great diffidence, being naturally modest, and was only able to say, *"May it please your honors—may it please your honors"* — another long pause, when he said, *"I have forgotten what I intended to speak,"* and took his seat. This embarrassment vanished in his next trial, and he was able to deliver himself with fluency and fine effect. His frank, manly civility, and sound discriminating mind, soon made him a favorite with the people, as well as the courts, and he had at his command much of the law business of the county. The Hon. R. J. Meigs was his first competitor at the bar, and for the favor of the public. Many well contested battles were fought, and many knotty cases unraveled by these early combatants for fame. Mr. Meigs was the most prompt and witty, with a ready flow of language, and Mr. Fearing the most industrious and patient in investigation, so that, in final results, they were very well matched. They were the only attorneys until 1791.

The following is a list of the lawyers who practiced at the courts of Washington County, with the time of their admission, until the close of the territorial government, taken from the Records of the Courts: Paul Fearing, September, 1788; R. J. Meigs, 1789; Dudley Odlin, March, 1791; Matthew Backus, June, 1793; William Littel, June, 1797; Solomon Sibley, September, 1797; David Putnam, autumn, 1798; Edwin Putnam, 1799; Wyllis Silliman, June, 1801; Philemon Beecher, March, 1802; Lewis Cass, March, 1803; William Woodbridge, 1804; Charles Hammond, 1804. The names of several of these early attorneys are identified with the history of the country, holding public posts of the first importance.

The Courts of Quarter Session and Common Pleas were held each four times in a year. The United States Court also held four sessions in a year, but at wide and distant places, viz.: at Detroit, the first Tuesday in May; at Port Vincent, the second Tuesday in June; at Cincinnati, the first Tuesday in October; and at Marietta, the second Tuesday in November. Mr. Fearing attended regularly in this court at Marietta, and sometimes at

Cincinnati, but the distance was so great, and the mode of travel so slow, that it was a tedious labor.

In 1792, he was admitted an Advocate in the Court of Probate. The following is the form of the oath, preserved amongst his papers, in his own handwriting:

"I swear that I will do no falsehood, nor consent to the doing of any, in the courts of justice; and if I know of any intention to commit any, I will give knowledge thereof to the justices of said courts, or some of them, that it may be prevented. I will not willingly or wittingly, promote or sue any false, groundless, or unlawful suit, nor give aid or consent to the same, and I will conduct myself in the office of an attorney within the said courts, according to the best of my knowledge and discretion, and with all good fidelity, as well to the courts as my clients. So help me, God."

Paul Fearing,

Washington County, ss."

"Sworn to in the General Court of Quarter Session, March 12th, 1793, before

Joseph Gilman, Commissioner."

The spirit and letter of the above oath were always kept in good faith while he was an attorney, as well as in all his transactions of private life. Honesty, candor and fair dealing were cardinal virtues which he never violated.

When the troops left Fort Harmar, Maj. Doughty, an intimate friend, made him a present of his dwelling-house, a well finished log building, standing in the southwest angle of the fort. To this was also added the contents of his garden, planted with fruit trees; amongst them was a fine peach, still cultivated in Marietta, and called to this day, the Doughty peach. During the war, Mr. Fearing and his father occupied this house, which afforded a safe retreat from the attacks of Indians, who frequently appeared on the hill back of the garrison, where they had a view of the cleared fields in the bottoms, and watch for anyone who might be out at work, a distance from the walls. Several were shot at, and one or two killed, within a quarter of a mile. Peace was established in August, 1795.

Late in November of this year, Mr. Fearing had a narrow escape from drowning. He was coming up from the settlement at Belpre in a canoe, which was the usual mode of travel for many years. Although a pretty skillful canoeman, yet, having with him in the boat his future wife and her sister, his attention was taken up with them, or from some other cause, in passing by a fallen tree top which projected several rods into the river, the canoe upset, and threw them all into the water. None of them could swim but his boy, Tousant Shoeman, then about fourteen years old, who soon reached the land. In their attempts to hold on to the canoe, it would roll from their grasp. Miss Betsy Rouse, the sister of his intended wife, an active, courageous girl, exerted herself so effectually, that she soon reached the shore, after having been at the bottom once or twice. Cynthia being clad with a large camlet cloak, was more buoyant, and kept upon the surface, sometimes clinging to the canoe, and at others floating near it. After struggling along in this way for several rods, Mr. Fearing encouraging her with his voice, and retaining fully his presence of mind, although unable to assist her in any other way, they both reached so near the shore as to be able to get hold of the willow bushes, and were helped to the dry land by the boy, nearly famished with the cold, and exhausted with their struggles, as there was considerable ice in the river at the time. Fortunately, a large flatboat, laden with goods, came in sight, and at their request landed and took them on board. By wrapping them in warm blankets, and giving them hot drinks, they were soon restored to comfort. The boat landed them at Farmers' Castle; and their next attempt to reach Marietta proved more fortunate, taking with them an experienced canoeman. When we consider the rare occurrence of flatboats, and especially one at this particular juncture, with everything on board necessary to the comfort of the shipwrecked company, and that there was no house between Belpre and Marietta, where they could receive aid, and the fact of their being enabled to escape from the watery element under such hopeless circumstances, the whole affair may be viewed as one of those plain and manifest interpositions of Providence, in overruling and guiding the destinies of man, while a sojourner in this ever-changing world.

Flatboat on the Ohio River

On the 28th of this month Mr. Fearing was married to Miss Cynthia Rouse, at his own house at Marietta. The ordinance was performed by the Hon. Joseph Gilman, one of the judges of the territory. The fruits of this marriage were a daughter and two sons.

In the year 1797 he received the appointment of Judge of Probate, for Washington County, under the seal and commission of Winthrop Sargent, then acting as Governor of the Territory. After the close of the war the country filled up rapidly, and in 1799 the first legislature held its session in Cincinnati. In 1800 the second session was held, and in this he was a member. During this period he was chosen a delegate, to represent the territory in Congress, which post he filled for 1801 and 1802, with credit to himself and the entire satisfaction of the people. About this time, the two great political parties of Federalist and Republican were organized all over the United States, and even in this remote wilderness the voice of political strife was loud and boisterous. He was attached to the Federal party, which at this time, was the most numerous.

After his return to private life he resumed the practice of the law, with increased reputation. His manly, open countenance, with his well known character for uprightness and honesty, gave his pleadings great and deserved weight with a jury; and he was often spoken of and named in a familiar manner, by the country people, as "Honest Paul," a phrase which gave more weight and popularity to his opinions, than any high sounding title.

On his farm, a little below the mouth of the Muskingum, he erected a neat dwelling-house, and planted an extensive orchard of the choicest fruits, of which he was an intelligent and successful cultivator. The garden was arranged with neatness and taste, and ornamented with shrubbery, flowers, &c, showing a relish for the beautiful as well as the useful.

He was one of the first in Ohio who paid attention to the raising of Merino sheep. His flocks embraced several hundreds of these valuable animals, propagated from a few individuals, bought at enormous prices, a single buck commanding from six to eight hundred dollars, and a ewe from two to three hundred, and sometimes much more. He engaged in the sheep culture as early as 1808, and during the yeaning season, passed many weary and sleepless nights during the cold winter weather, in watching and protecting the young lambs from the effects of frost, so fatal to them if long exposed to its chilling influence. By his knowledge of their maladies, and discretion in feeding and studying their habits, he became one of the most successful growers of merinos, an animal difficult to rear, and requiring a different management from that applied to the common sheep of the country. His practical knowledge, acquired by actual experiment, was freely imparted to others, and was of great use to the farmers of this county. The growth of this valuable animal was for many years extensively conducted in this part of the state, and was profitable so long as the government, by protecting duties, encouraged the woolen factories to work up the wool of the country, thereby not only making the nation independent, but the people rich.

In 1810, he was appointed an Associate Judge of the Court of Common Pleas. The commission is signed by Samuel Huntington, then Governor of Ohio. In this office he served seven years, with much credit as a sound jurist and impartial judge. At the expiration of that period, the leaders in political affairs placed the office in other hands, more congenial to their views. In 1814, he received the appointment of Master Commissioner in Chancery.

From the first entering of the lands of the Ohio Company for taxation by the state, he acted very extensively as an agent for the shareholders in the eastern states, paying their taxes, examining and preparing their lands for sale. In this way, a large portion of his time, not devoted to the care of his farm, was occupied.

In his disposition, Mr. Fearing was remarkably cheerful and pleasant, much attached to children, and never happier than when in their company. He had great sympathy for the poor and the oppressed, and was ever ready to stretch forth his hand, and open his purse for their relief.

He died the 21st of August, 1822, after a few days illness, victim to the fatal epidemic fever, which ravaged the country for two or three years, in the sixtieth year of his life. His wife died the same day, a few hours after, in the forty-sixth year of her age.

Chapter XI

HON. JOSEPH GILMAN AND MRS. REBECCA GILMAN

Joseph Gilman was born in Exeter, New Hampshire, A. D., 1736, and was the third generation of the descendants of John Gilman, who emigrated from Norfolk, England, in 1637. He married Rebecca Ives, granddaughter of the Hon. Robert Hale, of Beverly, Massachusetts, one of the provincial council, and an intimate friend of Gov Hutchinson.

When the struggle for liberty commenced, he took an early and decided part on the side of the colonists. His high standing for integrity, and honorable, upright character, soon attracted the notice and favor of the Whigs, and he was appointed Chairman of the Committee of Safety for New Hampshire, a post which none but the most able and influential men were selected to fill. This station brought him into immediate intercourse with a number of the leading men in the adjacent states, especially Massachusetts. In the early periods of the Revolution, these Committees of Safety were the most important public bodies in the country, transacting much of the business afterward done by the legislatures, in collecting and purchasing arms, ammunitions, and clothing for the state troops. Mr. Gilman, as Chairman of this Committee, made large advances from his own private purse, at a very pressing period, for the purchase of blankets for the New Hampshire Line, which was repaid in continental paper, and became a dead loss, entirely ruining his family estate. In proof of the intense feeling and ardor infused into the minds of the leading men of the period, and the deep interest they took in the welfare of the country, it is stated that at the period of the disastrous events which followed the retreat of the American Army from New Jersey, when it seemed as if the cause of liberty was hopeless, Samuel Adams had occasion to visit Mr. Gilman at Exeter, for consultation on the best course to pursue, and to devise ways and means to raise supplies for the starving and naked soldiers. It so happened that Mr. Gilman was abroad, and Mr. Adams was received by his wife. After a few minutes conversation, observing the abstracted manner and downcast looks of her guest, she ceased any further attempt to engage his attention, and applied herself quietly to her needle, an occupation then followed by females of the first families. Mr. Adams continued to walk rapidly up and down the room, too uneasy to sit quietly in a chair. After a few moments her attention was called to her visitor, by a deep sigh, amounting nearer to a groan. Casting her eyes on hit, face, the tears were rolling down his cheeks, and wringing his hands in agony, he uttered with a broken voice the deep thoughts within him, *"O, my God, must we give it up!"* How intense must have been the feeling of that great mind, when the physical man thus bowed beneath its sway. Happily for us, the friends of freedom were not long permitted to live in darkness, but the brilliant events which soon followed at Princeton and Trenton, revived their desponding spirits, and covered Washington and his few brave followers with a mantle of glory.

When the Ohio Company was formed, Mr. Gilman became an associate, and moved his family, consisting of a wife and one son, B. Ives Gilman, to Marietta, in 1789. The country was then a wilderness, and those who entered it had to partake of the hardships, privations, and dangers which attend the forming of a new settlement several hundred miles beyond the borders of civilization. The journey was performed in safety, and the family settled down in their new home, established on the lower Point, near Fort Harmar, determined to be contented, and do their best for the good of the country.

In 1790 Mr. Gilman was commissioned Judge of Probate, in place of Gen. Putnam, resigned. He also received commissions from Gov. St. Clair, as judge of the Court of Quarter Sessions, and also of the Court of Common Pleas, which posts he continued to fill during the territorial period. In 1796 he was appointed by Congress one of the United States Judges for the Northwest Territory, and attended the sittings of this court at Post Vincent, Detroit, Cincinnati, and Marietta. The journeys to these remote points were made through the wilderness on horseback, attended with pack-horses to carry the baggage, in company with the other judges and lawyers, so that the ride through the woods, although tiresome and tedious, was not without many things to make it interesting. The trip to and from Cincinnati was usually made in a canoe or large pirogue, and occupied eight or ten days. They slept at night under a hut on the shore, and cooked their food in the woods, there being few cabins at convenient points, for a number of years after the war.

He was a man whom everybody respected and esteemed, for his candor, honesty, good sense, and social qualities. As a jurist his reputation stood deservedly high. He was a careful student of the laws of nature, as well as those of his country, and kept a meteorological journal, which for that day was rather rare. He died in 1806, aged seventy years. Mrs. Gilman was Rebecca Ives, the daughter of Benjamin Ives and Elizabeth Hale. Her education was far superior to that of most females of her time, being chiefly acquired under the direction of her grandfather, the Hon. Robert Hale. By him her literary taste was highly cultivated, and a habit acquired for books and useful reading, that attended her late in life. She was familiar with the best British classics of the days of Queens Ann and Elizabeth; could read French authors with facility and ease, and her acuteness was such in polite literature, that when any disputed point arose amongst the learned visitors and circles at her fireside, she was often appealed to as umpire, and her decisions were usually decisive of the question, and seldom appealed from. This was often done by men of classical education, few of whom, in matters of history, pure English literature, poetry, or *belles-lettres*, excelled her in general knowledge, or critical acumen. Her early and youthful associates were generally men of superior minds and talents; amongst whom a favorite one was Timothy Pickering, a resident of an adjacent town, and a frequent visitor in the family. These acquirements gave a tone and cast to her conversation, very fascinating and engaging to such cultivated minds as came within the sphere of her influence, and her society was much sought, and highly valued by all her acquaintances. In person she was tall and commanding, with the most graceful and dignified manners: her countenance open, prepossessing, and intelligent. Children were much attached to her, as she was fond of giving them useful instruction and advice, in such a pleasant and agreeable manner, as to win their attention, and impress it deeply on their minds. One of the early citizens of Marietta, whose parents lived the next door to her in 1796, says, that he received, when a boy, more valuable advice from her, than he ever did from his own mother, and she was a woman of no ordinary capacity. In her domestic concerns she was a pattern to all good housewives, for industry, frugality, order, and promptness of execution; practices rather rare in literary females. Her dress was always neat, but plain; indicating good taste, and purity of principle. After the death of her husband, she lived in her own house at Marietta, surrounded by her grandchildren, until 1812, when she moved with her son to Philadelphia, and died in the year 1820, full of peace, and joyful expectation of a blessed immortality.

Chapter XII
BENJAMIN IVES GILMAN AND MRS. HANNAH GILMAN

Mr. Gilman was born in Exeter, New Hampshire, in the year 1765. His early education was strictly attended to, and he had the advantages of the academy established in that place by Mr. Phillips. As his father was engaged in mercantile pursuits, he was brought up to the same employment. When a small boy, he received the instruction and advice of a very intelligent and highly educated mother, who, having but one son on whom to bestow her care, his moral and intellectual culture were highly finished, and his whole after life showed the training of this early period. Richly was she rewarded for her labor of love, for no son ever more venerated and respected a mother than did Mr. Gilman. That *"the boy is the father of the man,"* is an old, but very true axiom; and nothing is more certain than that the impressions, whether for good or evil, made on the mind of youth, retain their hold during the remainder of life. Blessed is that son who has an educated, moral, and religious mother: his happiness for time and eternity depends very much on the instruction received while he is more immediately under her care.

In 1789 he moved with his parents to Marietta. In 1790 he returned to New England, and married Hannah Robbins, the second daughter of the Rev. Chandler Robbins, D. D., pastor of the first church in Plymouth, Mass., the ceremony being performed by her father. Soon after, in company with his young bride, they returned across the mountains on horseback. At that early period, it was a serious and laborious journey, occupying from twenty-five to thirty days. The roads were very poor over the Alleghenies, and the accommodations for travelers scanty and coarse. From Red Stone, or Pittsburg, the passage was usually by water, in a flat, or Kentucky boat.

About the year 1792 he commenced the sale of merchandise, in a store at Fort Harmar. From small beginnings his business was gradually enlarged to the most extensive in Marietta.

During the war Mr. Gilman several times narrowly escaped the rifle and tomahawk of the Indians. About eighty rods from the fort, he had commenced a new clearing for agricultural purposes. One day, in the spring of the year 1794, he was out in this lot at work with a hired man named Robert Warth. Robert had just cut off a log for rail timber, and was still standing on it, with the axe resting at his feet, when he spoke to Mr. Gilman, who was thirty or forty yards distant, but more out of sight, inquiring further about the work. Before he had time to answer, the sharp crack of a rifle caused him to turn quickly in the direction of the shot, when he saw poor Robert falling dead from the log, and two Indians in the act of jumping over a brush fence, close by, where they had lain concealed. Being unarmed, he instantly ran for the fort, with one of the Indians in close chase, while the other was occupied in taking the scalp of Robert. An intervening fence gave his pursuer some hope of overtaking him, but he cleared it at a single leap. The Indian now stopped and fired at his flying foe, but happily missed his mark. The field was so near the blockhouse where he resided, that his wife and mother both heard the shots and the yell of the savages. Knowing the exposure of Mr. Gilman, they hastened to the window of the house to ascertain his situation, and as he came running up, eagerly inquired who was killed. The young wife of the backwoodsman was standing by the side of Mrs. Gilman, as he answered, *"Robert,"* and thus suddenly heard the fall of her husband. The Indians were instantly pursued and fired at by the Rangers, as they ascended the side of the hill which overlooks the alluvions on which the fort stood, but they escaped, although it was thought one of them was wounded.

In traversing the woods for strayed cattle, and in looking at the quality and boundaries of adjacent lands which he wished to purchase, he had many narrow escapes, but would never *send a man* where he was afraid to *venture himself.* In walking and running, few men could excel him; and unless fired at from a hidden enemy, he did not fear a surprise, as he could escape by his own activity.

After the close of the war he dealt largely in peltries, especially bear skins, having small trading stations on the Big Sandy and Guyandotte Rivers, where this animal abounded, and the chief employment of the inhabitants was hunting them for their skins, and the digging of ginseng, a plant which grew in wonderful abundance and great luxuriance on the rich hillsides of this broken country. Both of these articles, from 1798 to 1808, were in great demand for exportation, and many large fortunes realized by persons who dealt in them.

Mr. Gilman was appointed Clerk of the Court of Common Pleas of Washington County in the year 1796, and continued in office until the territory became a state. In 1802, he was one of the delegates at the convention for forming a constitution, and was a very active and useful man in completing that instrument.

In 1801, he commenced the business of ship-building, employing Capt. Devol for the master-builder, and subsequently James Whitney. This was continued from that year to 1808, when the embargo put a stop to all mercantile operations, and ruined a number of the merchants of Marietta, who had embarked in this business. The ships when built were exchanged for merchandise in the Atlantic cities, and were the most profitable returns they could make; and, although the country was thinly peopled, yet the vessels were always loaded with flour, pork, and other produce, in their downward voyage, thus yielding a double profit on the investment. But the wisdom of Mr. Jefferson put a stop to all the enterprising efforts of these western men, and overwhelmed several of them with ruin, especially such as had ships on hand, unsold in 1808. One man, who had a ship in New Orleans at the time of the embargo, sunk over ten thousand dollars on her and the cargo. No town in the United States suffered so much as this, according to its capital, by this unwise measure. Mr. Gilman escaped any serious loss, but all his plans were deranged, and the place where from four to six vessels were built in a year, giving employment to a large number of men, and increasing rapidly in population, was entirely paralyzed. Three extensive rope-walks, working up large quantities of hemp raised in the country, and furnishing rigging for the ships, were put out of employ, and in a few years fell into ruins. The business of the town did not revive for many years; and in 1813, Mr. Gilman moved his family to Philadelphia and entered into merchandise, as a wholesale dealer. For this business his clear, calculating mind, enlarged views and industrious habits, eminently fitted him, and for a number of years it was prosecuted with great success. His business operations often called him to visit the valley of Ohio, for which he always felt a warm regard; two of his sons having settled at Alton, Ill and when on a visit to that place in 1833, he was attacked with a fever and died at the age of sixty-eight years.

In person, Mr. Gilman was rather above the medium size, very erect, graceful and quick in his motions, with the manners and address of the most polished gentleman; eyes black, brilliant and expressive; nose slightly aquiline; forehead broad and high; face full and without, a fault. The impression made on a stranger, who saw him for the first time, would be, that he was in the presence of a man of more than ordinary capacity and intellect. His powers of conversation were great and varied, and no one left his company without adding something to his stock of useful information.

Mrs. Hannah Gilman was the second daughter of the Rev. Chandler Robbins, D. D., for many years the pastor of the first church in Plymouth, Mass. She was brought up with great care and tenderness by her venerable father, and received as good an education as was customary to bestow on females of the first families in that day. She was a girl of great sprightliness and vivacity; always cheerful and abounding in kindness to her associates, as well as to her own family. A joyful, kind spirit animated her frame through the whole course of her life.

In February, 1790, she was married to B. I. Gilman, a man every way worthy the hand and the heart of so excellent a woman. Nothing marred the joy of this festive occasion, but the circumstance of her being removed to so great a distance from her parents; the location of her future home being on the banks of the Ohio, far toward the setting sun. The New Englanders at this time were an untraveled people; they had not then learnt to roam into all parts of the earth, but a journey of a hundred miles was a great event in the life of that primitive people, and seldom undertaken by the pious, without the public prayers of the church for its success. How formidable then must have seemed to the old people, this journey of eight hundred miles; so far, that the expectation of seeing her again in this world, was almost hopeless, and the final adieu was affecting and solemn marks in a letter, sent by Capt. Smith to Jamestown, while a prisoner in his dominions.

The ancestors of the Robbins family were amongst the first settlers of Massachusetts; their blood unmixed, and strictly Puritan.

On their arrival at Marietta, she found many intelligent and kind friends, to greet her with a warm and hearty welcome, while the society of her husband's mother, in whose family they lived, was itself sufficient to make her home very pleasant, and the loneliness of the wilderness forgotten. From her she received all that love and tenderness she could have expected from her own mother and which the affection of the female heart only knows how to bestow on a beloved daughter. Before many years, the cares of a growing family in some measure divided her regards between her own household and that of her dear father and mother at Plymouth, so that the separation was more easily borne than at first. A frequent intercourse by letters also solaced her uneasy mind, so that she had often occasion to bless the happy inventor of this divine mode of an interchange of thoughts, so wonderful in itself, and which struck with admiration, the savage and untaught mind of Powhattan, when he first saw the effects of these mysterious

Many of her early letters to her brother, the Rev. Samuel Prince Robbins, while he was a boy, and when in college, also after his settlement as a pastor over the first Congregational church in Marietta, have been preserved by his family. Some extracts from these will be given, to show her talents as a writer, and the amiable and pious feelings which pervaded her heart, and made her worthy of the parentage of so excellent and noble a stock. The first is written in an easy, playful style, suitable to the subject, when her first child was about six months old, to her brother, then aged ten or twelve years, and dated Marietta, 16th of September, 1791. It was in answer to one he had sent to his sister, with a specimen of his drawing:

"I received the picture you sent me, and was much astonished to see how much you had improved in drawing. Did you do it all yourself? I

can hardly believe it. I suppose by the time I visit Plymouth with your little niece, you will be able to take her picture. If so, and it is a likeness, it will be the prettiest picture you ever saw."

To her parents she wrote regularly once a month, when there was an opportunity of sending a letter, which, until 1794, was only by private conveyance. In 1798 her brother Samuel graduated at Cambridge University. Her younger brother, Peter Gilman Robbins, was then a freshman.

In writing to Samuel, she speaks of the rapid passage of time in reference to Peter, who, she did not think, could be old enough to enter college, as she had been absent only seven years, and he was then a very small boy. *"How fast time flies. The further you advance in life, the faster time will appear to fly. How important it is, that we improve it to the best purpose."* In the same letter she sends a message to Peter, who was rather disposed to be a little wild; charging him to refrain from *"going to the theater, as it would be injurious to his morals."* At that period it was a fashionable amusement, and practiced by nearly all classes of society. Her nice sense of propriety saw its hidden evils, and her voice was raised against it.

After her brother had completed his college course, he studied Divinity, under the care of the Rev. M. Hyde, of Stockbridge, in Connecticut. In the spring of 1805, at the urgent request of Mrs. Gilman, he visited Marietta, with an ulterior expectation that he might be settled in the ministry there, over the first Congregational church in this place. The Rev. Daniel Story, who had been their pastor for a number of years, from feebleness, and other infirmities, had resigned his charge, and they were now without a teacher. When he arrived, the society was so small, and the prospect of an adequate support so doubtful, that after preaching a few times he returned to Norfolk, Conn., where he was itinerating. At that day there was no home missionary society, to aid feeble and newly formed churches, but they had to struggle into existence in the best manner they could.

In August, 1805, she wrote to him a very feeling letter, urging it upon him as a duty to return. *"For my own part, I feel as if I could not receive a negative answer from you. It was so long since I had been favored with such preaching as I once lived under, that when you were here I got roused up in some manner; but now we are all asleep, and myself among the rest. However, I desire not to trust too much in an arm of flesh: a sovereign God, who orders all events, will provide."* After mentioning the names of several of his acquaintances who had called to inquire after him, amongst whom were Gen. Putnam and Dr. True, she says, *"I hope, my dear brother, you will write as often as possible, and O that you may be directed to the path of duty."* This prayer was soon answered, for the trustees of the society directly after sent him *a call* to be their pastor, to which he returned a consenting answer, and the following January he was ordained over the first Congregational Church and Society of Marietta. Under his faithful and apostolic ministry it was soon enlarged, embracing many from the adjacent towns of Belpre and Adams, where he preached about one-third of the time. In 1807, chiefly through the efforts of Gen. Rufus Putnam, aided by the liberality of several other citizens, especially Mr. Gilman, a large and handsome church was erected, at a cost of about seven thousand dollars: a vast effort for so small a society; and it yet remains a monument to their praise. This was the first house erected specially for public worship; the Muskingum academy having been occupied for this purpose since the year 1799. No man was ever more diligent and faithful in his Master's service than Mr. Robbins, and his sister now felt an addition to her happiness of a spiritual nature, not before experienced. Earthly comforts had been showered upon her in rich abundance. A most excellent husband, children *"like olive plants sprung up around her table,"* with all the wealth she could desire, made her rich in this world's goods; but the longings of the immortal spirit could only be satisfied with the bread of everlasting life. During a revival in 1811, she united herself with the church, under her brother's care, and while she remained in Marietta, was one of its chief ornaments and supports. In 1890, her soul was tried with one of the sorest afflictions that can befall poor humanity, in the loss of her first-born child, the wife of Mr. D. Woodbridge. This bereavement was sustained with Christian resignation, and by it her spiritual graces were greatly quickened and refined. The sympathy and prayers of her dear brother were now doubly consoling, and from him she learned that uncomplaining submission to the divine will, so hard to he practiced by the natural heart.

In 1813, Mr. Gilman moved his family to Philadelphia, where he could enlarge the sphere of his mercantile operations, more in accordance with his capacious mind, so highly fitted for extensive and wide-spread operations. Nevertheless, he quitted the scenes of his early manhood with regret; the spot where his life had been often endangered, and the place where the foundations of his early wealth were laid. It was still more trying to his wife, who now bid adieu to the home where she had lived twenty-three years, amidst many dear and excellent female friends; but, above all, to that brother beloved, whom she cherished with an ardor only known to those who, to a naturally warm temperament, feel the impulses of the Christian's love, in addition to that of the natural heart. This is the love which abides and endures when life itself vanishes away. The first letter after her arrival, is dated October 20th, 1813, and addressed to Mr. Robbins and his wife, who was a granddaughter of Gen. Putnam, and explains the references to persons in Marietta.

"We arrived here the 25th of September, all well. The dear children were never so hearty. 0, what shall I render to the Lord for all his goodness? The city was so healthy; we thought it best to come immediately in. But O, what noise — what confusion. That evening they had received the intelligence of the victory gained on the lakes: the whole city was illuminated, and every mark of joy and mirth. I was ready to say, 'God is not in this place.' But surely he is, for the heaven, and heaven of heavens, cannot contain him; and I think I can say from sweet experience, since my arrival, 'I have found Him whom my soul loveth,' and I have seen his stately goings in the sanctuary." After describing the public institutions of the city, Bible Society, Sunday School for the poor children, &.c, she says, *"So you see there must be some good people here, but 1 have not been introduced to many as yet. I have not found your good grandmother, your aunt Betsy, your mother, and many others with whom I used to hold sweet converse. I feel at times exceedingly at a loss what to do about joining the church; I am much attached to our customs at Marietta, and feel unwilling to be dismissed from them. But there is no Congregational church here, and I feel alone: what shall I do?"*

It would seem that her brother advised her to unite with Mr. Skinner's church, which she did, and sat for many years under his teaching with great profit to her soul.

In November following she writes, "I have received yours of October 20th, which was a cordial to me." Speaking of a dear Christian uncle who was on his death-bed, she says, *"0, that it were possible I could see him; he could teach me how to live, and show me how to die. O, that my last end may be like his. Surely never were religious privileges so great as those which I now enjoy."*

From this time to 1820, a regular correspondence was kept up with her brother Samuel. Her letters are filled with the reflections of a Christian and pious heart, and the most affectionate expressions for her brother Samuel and his family. In May, 1820, after a visit from one of her Marietta acquaintances, she writes: *"Mr. Cram tells me that you have taken a few scholars. Does it not interfere with your studies? It appears to me that clergymen in general, ought to devote more of their time to the cause of Christ: else how can they expect that their preaching will be blessed to the souls committed to their charge?"* He, good man, would have been very happy to have given all his time to the work of the gospel; but the smallness of his salary, a mere pittance, and the increasing wants of a growing family, compelled him to this extra labor, for their support.

But his time was short, and in about three years after that period he received a summons from his divine Master, to enter into the joy of his Lord.

From 1820 to 1823 the correspondence is continued, and would fill a small volume. They contain evidences of a constant growth in grace, increasing love for her family and all around her, and anxiety for their salvation. During this time many interesting events took place, such as the marriage of a beloved daughter, the arrival of her sons to manhood, and entry into business, in wide and distant parts of the country. *"We are all scattered, my dear brother; but, O, if we can all, through grace in the dear Redeemer, meet at last in heaven, what a mercy! When I think of the separation between yourself, Isaac, and myself, it is a comfort to me that we do meet at a throne of grace."*

The epidemic fever which prevailed along the waters of the Ohio in 1822, again visited that region in 1823, with fatal severity. By this visitation Mrs. Gilman lost one of her sons, and also her dearly beloved and venerated brother Samuel, who died in August. Her letter to his widow is full of ardent piety and heavenly consolation, and breathes a depth of affection for the departed and calm resignation to the divine will, which only the Christian can feel. Its perusal cannot fail to soften the heart of the most obdurate unbeliever, and soothe the sorrows of the desponding mourner. It is dated at Cincinnati, November 3d, 1823, where she then was, to attend on her husband in a dangerous illness.

"With a heart filled with anguish, my dear sister, do I now address you. My tears had not ceased to flow for the best of sons, when I was called in Providence to weep afresh for the dearest and best of brothers. And is my beloved brother Samuel gone forever? Shall I never more hear his pleasant voice? Never more hear him pray? Never more see him break the bread, bless the cup, and give us all to drink? O, no! He has gone forever from our view, and the places which knew him shall know him no more, forever. The loss to me is great; but to you my beloved sister, and the dear fatherless children, is irreparable. Permit me then to tell you, how much we all sympathize with you, on this sorrowful occasion. But for your comfort, remember, that although the affliction is great, your heavenly Father is able to support you, and has said, He would never leave you, nor ever forsake you. He has promised to be the widows' God, and a father to the fatherless. Be grateful to Heaven, that you were blest with his society, comforted with his advice, and consoled by his prayers so many years. You have now, my dear sister, a double part to act, that of a father and mother, to the children committed to your care. For their sakes, sink not under this deep affliction. Spread all your wants and trials before your heavenly Father, who will never lay upon you more than you can bear, and will work all things for good to those who put their trust in him. The Lord will not forsake his dear children, and though He cause grief, yet will He have compassion according to the multitude of his mercies; for whom the Lord loveth, He chasteneth. 'The mountains shall depart, and the hills be removed, but my kindness shall not depart from thee, neither shall the covenant of my peace be removed, saith the Lord of hosts.' Take these precious words of your God, my dear sister, to yourself. They belong to you. Live upon them; and may our blessed Redeemer comfort you with the consolations of his Holy Spirit. I am extremely anxious to hear the particulars of my dear brother's sickness and death. I want to know every word that passed from his lips. What were his views in the near approach of the king of terrors? Was his mind clear, or did he sink down under the weight of his disease, without feeling his situation and sufferings?"

In February following, she writes,

"I received your communication, my dear sister, and thank you kindly for it. But O, my dear Patty, it was not half so particular as I wished. I wanted you to write just as if you were talking with me. I feel very anxious about you, but desire to commend you to that merciful Being, who is husband of the widow, and father of the orphan. Look daily to Him, my dear, for comfort under this severe and trying affliction. I wish you would begin a letter to me soon; and if you recollect anything of my brother which you have not told me, add it to the letter from time to time, until you have filled it. Kiss the dear children for their aunt, and tell them never to forget the advice, the prayers, and dying words of their loving father.

From your ever affectionate sister,

H. Gilman."

Mrs. Robbins was herself sick at the time of her husband's death, and, therefore, could not be so particular in her account of his last moments as Mrs. G. desired.

The foregoing extracts are sufficient to show the religious and social character of this excellent woman.

Before her own death, which took place at New York, in 1836, she was called to mourn the loss of her dear husband and several of her children; but that God whom she had so faithfully served and trusted in all her life, did not leave her in these trying moments, but was with her and supported her, according to his promise. Like gold tried in a furnace, her Christian graces were purified, and shone brighter and brighter under every new affliction; and she has gone to inherit that crown prepared for all those who love and obey him.

In person, Mrs. Gilman was of a medium height, with a handsome, well-formed frame; her manners graceful and very attractive, combined with a dignity that always commanded respect; face full and round; features of the exactest proportions, with a naturally sweet expression; hair black; eyes dark, and full of intelligence. When engaged in animated conversation, her face and eyes were radiant with meaning, giving an interest to her expressions very striking and pleasing to the beholder. Her voice was full of harmony, while her powers of conversation were unrivaled; having a volubility and flow of language which few could equal, whether male or female. Her love and care for her husband and children were unbounded, and no sacrifice of personal comfort too great for their happiness. Her memory is still dear to many who knew her in Marietta, and the history of her life and Christian character, are the rightful heritage of that place.

Chapter XIII
MRS. MARY LAKE

Amongst the early pioneers of Marietta, were many excellent women. The times of the Revolution tried the temper and spirit of females, as well as the men, and they, by their example and encouragement in the common cause, often accomplished much good for the country. Some showed their patriotic spirit by manufacturing garments for the half naked soldiers, while others nursed the sick and wounded, soothing the last moments of the dying by their merciful ministrations. The names of deserving females should be preserved with as much care and veneration as those of the men who fought their country's battles. The scripture biographical sketches of Sarah, Deborah, Miriam, Susannah, and many others, may be ranked amongst the most interesting of that species of writing.

Mrs. Mary Lake was a native of Bristol, England. Her father was a silk-weaver, and her maiden name Mary Bird. She was born in 1742, and about the year 1762 married Archibald Lake, a sea-faring man, and moved to St. Johns, in Newfoundland. Here he followed fishing on the Grand Bank, which, at that day, was a profitable calling, as the strict observance of lent in Catholic Europe caused a great demand for fish. When that place came into the possession of the French, he moved his family to New York, and worked in the ship-yards.

At the period of the American Revolution, he was living in the city, and embraced the cause of liberty. After the disasters of Long Island, when Gen. Washington evacuated the city, the family followed the army into their cantonments up the North River. The general hospitals being established, first at Fishkill, and then at New Windsor, she was employed as matron, to superintend the nursing of the sick, and see that they were provided with suitable nourishment, beds, &c, and the apartments kept clean. Here, under the direction of the surgeons, she became familiar with all the details of treating the diseased in fevers, smallpox, and various other ailments, acquiring a tact and confidence that remained with her the rest of her life, and was of great use to the poor and destitute sick on the frontiers. The more poverty-stricken was the sick family, the greater was her obligation to wait upon them.

Her meek, quiet spirit was once a little tried by a man in the garrison at Marietta, whose wife had sickened and died, notwithstanding her unremitting care of her. The family had just moved into the country, and was excessively poor, needing all the common necessaries of life to be supplied to them during her sickness, by her neighbors. In examining an old family chest for articles to lay out the dead in a decent manner, Mrs. Lake discovered a large stocking leg, filled with silver dollars, several hundred in number. On questioning the man why he feigned such extreme poverty, with all this money in his possession? he replied, quite unconcerned, *"0, that is to buy land with."*

Her husband was appointed a Deputy-Commissary to the hospital, and ranged the adjacent country, providing vegetables, and other necessaries suitable for the sick. It is well known that Gen. Washington often visited the hospitals to examine the condition of the sick and wounded soldiers, encourage those who were in despair by his voice and kind looks, and inquire into their wants, which were always supplied, so far as he had the power to direct. In these benevolent visits, Mrs. Lake more than once received his personal thanks in their behalf, for her tender, vigilant, and unremitting care of the sick; an evidence that she richly merited praise; for Washington flattered no one with undeserved commendation. After the peace, when the hospital was broken up, and army disbanded, the family returned to New York, and her husband resumed his former occupation.

She became pious when quite young, and united with Dr. Rogers' Church, one of the oldest in the city, of the Presbyterian order, and at the close of the war it contained but two churches of this denomination. Her early piety and religious feelings were no doubt the secret impulses which supported and urged her on in this work of charity and mercy; for her pay while thus employed was no better than that of all the others engaged in their country's cause—depreciated, worthless, continental paper. But love for her divine Master and charity for the sick and distressed, constrained her, and she felt it a duty to do all in her power for their relief.

After the war, ship-building was a poor business, and hearing accidentally from Gen. Putnam, of the new colony forming at Marietta, in the rich country of the Ohio, they became attracted by the glowing descriptions published, of its advantages and future prospects. Having little to expect where they were, hope pointed them to plenteous and happy days in the west. In 1789, he moved his family, consisting of eight children, to Marietta. Three of the sons, James, Thomas, and Andrew, were young men and able to assist in their support. The spring after their arrival, the smallpox broke out amongst the inhabitants, who were chiefly living in Campus Martius, in such close quarters that it was very difficult to prevent its spreading by contagion. The larger number of the settlers had never gone through with the disease and was to be inoculated. This was done by the Physician and Mrs. Lake's skill as a nurse was now in full requisition, and was unsparingly applied. Her experience was of great use, even to the surgeons, who were all young men, and had seen but little of this disease except in books, in directing the regimen and treatment during its course. Her services on this trying occasion, when several who took it by contagion died, were often spoken of by the inhabitants in after years, as well as at the time, with gratitude. The kind, benevolent heart and Christian feeling of Mrs. Lake, led her constantly to endeavor to do good to the souls, as well as the bodies, of her fellow creatures.

Probably one of the first Sunday Schools in America was taught by her in 1791, and continued for several years during the Indian War, at Campus Martius, in Marietta. Having brought up a family herself, and knowing the advantages of early religious instruction, she took compassion on the younger children of the garrison, who were spending their Sabbath afternoons in frivolous amusements, and established a school in the single and only room occupied by the family. After the regular religious exercises of the day by Mr. Story were closed, which consisted of only one service, or half the day, she regularly assembled as many of the children as she could persuade to attend, and taught them the Westminster catechism and lessons from the Bible, for an hour or more. The school usually contained about twenty. She was very kind and affectionate toward them, so that they were fond of assembling and listening to her instructions. Her explanations of scripture were so simple and child-like that the smallest of the little ones could understand them, and rendered very pleasant by her mild manner of speaking. The accommodations for the children were very rude and simple, consisting only of a few low stools and benches, such an article as a chair being a rarity in the garrison. One of the scholars, then a little boy of four years old, says that one day, being scant of seat, he was placed, by the kind old lady, on the top of a bag of meal that stood leaning against the side of the room. The seed thus charitably sown in faith and hope was not scattered in vain, as several of her scholars are now prominent members of the church. This school was kept in the lower room of the northeast blockhouse.

Soon after the peace of 1795, she moved with the family on to a farm, eight miles up the Muskingum.

She died in 1802, aged sixty years.

Her children were all pious, and two of her sons, now very aged men, are reckoned amongst the elders of Israel, adorning that religion instilled into their youthful minds by their pious mother.

Chapter XIV
REV. DANIEL STORY

Soon after the organization of the Ohio Company at Boston, in the year 1787, it seems that the enlightened men, who directed its concerns, began to think of making arrangements for the support of the gospel, and the instruction of youth in their new colony, about to be established in the western wilderness. Having been and brought up in a land where more attention was paid to the religious, moral, and literary instruction of the people, than at any other spot on the globe, being the country of the Puritans, and themselves the descendants of the Plymouth colonists, they naturally turned their attention to its vast importance to the settlement just budding into existence under their care. Accordingly a resolution was passed, at a meeting of the directors and agents, on the 7th of March, 1788, at Providence, R. I., for the support of the gospel, and an instructor of youth; in consequence of which, the Rev. Manasseh Cutler, one of the directors, in the course of that year engaged the Rev. Daniel Story, then preaching at Worcester, Mass., to go to the west as a Chaplain to the settlement at Marietta.

Mr. Story was born in Boston, in 1755, and graduated at the Dartmouth College, in Hanover, N. H. He was an uncle of the late Judge Story, of Cambridge, Mass.

After a tedious and laborious journey over the Allegheny Mountains, he arrived at Marietta, in the spring of 1789, and commenced his ministerial labors. The settlements were just beginning, and situated at various points, a considerable distance from each other. Nevertheless, he visited them in rotation, in conformity with the arrangement of the directors, by which he was to preach about one-third of the time at the settlements of Waterford and Belpre. His first visit to Waterford was in the summer of that year, and as there was no house large enough to contain all the people, he preached under the shadow of a wide-spreading tree, near the mills of Wolf Creek, a temple not reared by the hands of man.

During the Indian War, from 1791 to 1795, he preached the larger portion of the time in the northwest blockhouse of Campus Martius, in Marietta. The upper story in that building was fitted up with benches and a rude, simple desk, So as to accommodate an audience of a hundred and fifty or two hundred persons. It was also used for a school, which was first taught by Maj. Anselm Tupper.

During this period, a committee appointed by the directors, to report on the religious and literary instruction of the youth, resolved that one hundred and eighty dollars be paid from the funds of the company, to aid the new settlements in paying a teacher, with the condition that Marietta support him for one year, Belpre seven months, and Waterford three months. If they complied with this arrangement, that sum was to be divided amongst them in proportion to the time. Near the same period, twenty dollars were appropriated to pay Col. Battelle for his services on the Sabbath, already performed at Belpre. These testimonials sufficiently prove the interest the directors of the company felt for the spiritual welfare, as well as the temporal comfort of the colonists.

Mr. Story also preached occasionally at a large room in the upper story of a frame house in the garrison at the Point, being at the junction of the Muskingum with the Ohio on the left bank; Fort Harmar being on the right bank. At periods when the Indians were quiet, he visited and preached at the settlements of Belpre and Waterford, fifteen and twenty miles from Marietta. These pastoral visits were made by water, in a log canoe, propelled by the stout arms and willing hearts of the pioneers. There were no roads at that day, by which he could travel by land, and beside there was less danger in this mode, than by the obscure paths of the hunters.

In the year 1796 he united and established a Congregational Church, composed of members residing in Marietta, Belpre, Waterford, and Vienna in Virginia. In 1797 he visited his native state, and remained there until he received *a call* to the pastoral charge of the church he had collected in the *wilderness*. He was ordained on the 15th of August,

1797, in Danvers, Mass., there being no clergyman to perform that office on the west side of the mountains, to the care of the church in Marietta and vicinity. It was composed of thirty-two members, nine of whom were officers of the Revolution. The ordination sermon was preached by Rev. Manasseh Cutler, and printed at the time, a few copies of which are yet extant. This relation continued between Mr. Story and the church until the 15th of March, 1804, when he was dismissed at his own request, his health being too much impaired for the performances of a pastor any longer. He died the 30th of December following.

After the Marietta Academy was built in 1797, public worship was held in that edifice, it being constructed and so finished as to answer for that purpose.

Mr. Story was in the ministry for some time before he came to Marietta, and when selected by Dr. Cutler, the choice was much approved by those who knew him. In coming to Marietta, then a wilderness, he sacrificed his interest and his comfort; but knowing the necessities of the people, he was willing to part with many things for their good and the cause of his divine Master. What little wealth he possessed was invested in new lands before coming out, with an expectation of a reasonable support from the Ohio Company, until the rents of the lands set apart for the support of the gospel should be available; but this was prevented by the Indian war, and no money was raised from that source until the year 1800. The inhabitants were generally much impoverished from the same cause, and most probably his receipts for preaching from 1789 to 1797, could not have paid for his board and clothing. He was obliged to draw upon his former earnings, by the sale of some of his lands. However, the hospitality of one or two kind Christian friends, who gave him a welcome seat at their tables during a part of this period, relieved him from some of his difficulties. At his death, the proceeds from the sale of his remaining lands were insufficient to discharge the debts incurred while laboring in the new settlements; so that, like a faithful servant, he spent not only his life, but all his substance in the service of the cause to which he was devoted.

In person he was rather tall and slender; quick and active in his movements; manners easy, with a pleasant address; cheerful and animated in conversation; and always a welcome guest in the families he visited. After the war he frequently went out to the new settlers, and sometimes spent a week at their houses, in the most familiar and pleasant intercourse. His sermons were practical; logically and methodically written after the manner of that day; and were said, in matter and manner, to be fully equal to those of the best preachers in New England. In prayer he was greatly gifted, both in diversity of subject, propriety and fervency, as well as in beauty of language. He was never married, but lived a single life after the manner and advice of St. Paul. Placed as he was, in the midst of a people trembling for their lives, and filled with anxiety for the support of their families, in the midst of the careless habits and dissolute manners of the soldiery, it is not to be expected that much could be done, by a humble minister of the gospel, in advancing the spiritual condition of the people; nevertheless, he did what he could for the support of the cause in which he was engaged, and his name is still held in grateful remembrance, by the few living remnants of the first settlers of Marietta.

Chapter XV
DR. JABEZ TRUE

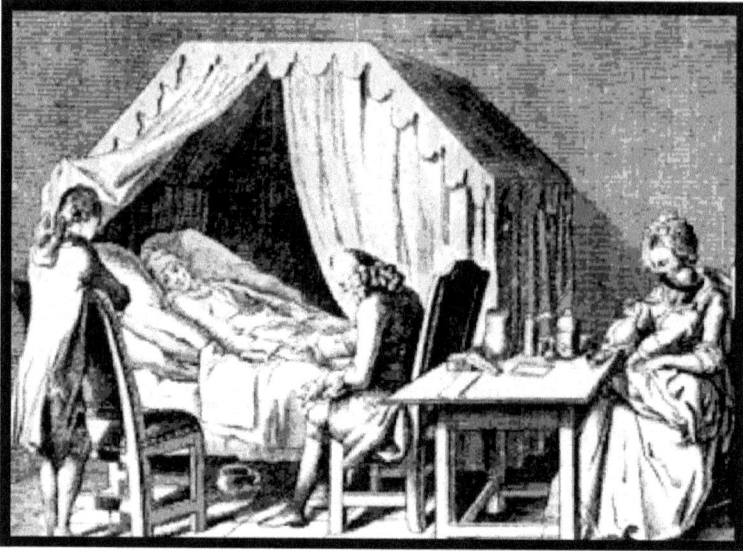

Dr. Jabez True was born in Hampstead, N. H., in the year 1760. His father was the Rev. Henry True, a native of Salisbury, Mass., and was for many years the pastor of a church in the former place. When a boy he was a student at the old Dammer Academy, and completed his education at Cambridge University. In 1752, he was settled in the ministry after the Puritan order. In the French War he served as the Chaplain of a brigade of the Colonial Troops at Ticonderoga and Fort Edward. He was a fine scholar, of sound judgment and exemplary piety, *"making Revelation his guide, and Reason its companion,"* as is inscribed on his tombstone.

It was the custom of that day, before many high schools or academies were founded, for the clergymen of New England to fit young men for college. Mr. True had a class of this kind before the War of the Revolution, in which was his son Jabez. He read a competent share of the classics to prepare him for the study of medicine, which, in due time, he pursued under the instruction of Dr. Flagg, of Hampstead, an eccentric man, but eminent in his profession, and highly esteemed by his friends. He completed his studies sometime after the commencement of hostilities between the colonies and the mother country, when feeling the spirit of resistance strong upon him, he engaged in the war as a Surgeon on board a privateer ship from Newburyport, a small seaport in the northeast corner of Massachusetts, distant about twelve miles from his home, and sailed for Europe. After a short cruise and limited number of captures, the privateer was wrecked on the coast of Holland, thus abruptly terminating his hopes of a fortune.

After about two years spent amongst the Hollanders, who were friends of the young republic, at the close of the war he returned to America in a merchant-ship. He now gave his attention to the practice of medicine, and commenced business in Gilmanton, N. H., where he remained two years.

The Ohio Company was formed in 1787, and feeling a strong desire to visit the enchanting region along the shores of the Ohio, so admirably described by the writers and travelers of that day, he purchased a share of their lands, and concluded to leave the home of his forefathers, and come out to Marietta in company with a family from Newburyport. The emigrants arrived at the mouth of the Muskingum early in the summer of 1788. The settlement at that time had but few persons in it; the country was covered with a thick forest, and there was more employment for able bodied men in clearing lands and building log cabins, than for physicians.

In the following year several young men from Boston, who had become enamored with the country from the glowing descriptions of its fertility and beauty, came out to the city of Marietta. They built a long, low log cabin, in which they kept Bachelors' Hall, on the corner where the Bank of Marietta now stands, and commenced clearing some land. It was a new business to those who had been brought up in a city, and when the novelty of the change had subsided, they began to think of the comfortable homes they had left, and to sigh for a return. The breaking out of the Indian War, put a stop to any further progress of the settlement for the present, and leaving all their improvements, returned to Boston. Not so with Dr. True; he had come out with the intention of spending his life in the west, and nothing but imperious necessity could turn him from his purpose. His steady habits and good character gained for him the favor of the influential men, and in the beginning of the war he was appointed a Surgeon's Mate to the Ohio Company's troops, at a salary of twenty-two dollars a month, which, was a welcome and timely aid in this season of privation.

During this distressing, and often perplexing period, he was many times exposed to the attack of the Indians, as he passed up and down the Ohio in his visits to Belpre, and still lower on the river, to minister to the sick and wounded in the garrisons. During the continuance of the small-pox, and then again in the sickness of the scarlet fever, numerous trips were made in a canoe, accompanied, generally, by two men. The most hazardous of these, was one made to Flinn's Station, or Bellville, as it was afterward called, thirty miles below Marietta, the second year of the war, to visit Mrs. Sherwood, who was attacked by the Indians and severely wounded, at the same time her husband was taken prisoner.

Late in the spring of the year 1792, Stephen Sherwood, an inmate of the garrison, went out very early one morning to feed his hogs in a pen a few rods above the station on the bank of the river. His wife, a fearless, bold woman, who had always lived on the frontiers, about fifty years old, went out at the same time to milk a cow, standing in the path near the corner of the upper blockhouse, about twenty yards from the gate. After throwing the corn into the pen, he stepped into the thicket by the side of the road to cut a stick for an ox-goad, intending to plow that day amongst the young corn. While engaged in this employment, eight or ten Indians, who were lying in the bushes, sprang upon him and overpowered him, making him a prisoner. Two of them remained with him, while the others hurried down to the garrison, and seeing the old lady milking the cow, two of them seized upon her, intending to make a prisoner of her also; but she resisted their efforts so stoutly, and screamed so loud to the men in the garrison for help, that they abandoned that plan. One of them knocked her down with a blow of his tomahawk, while the other proceeded to take off her scalp. In the meantime, Peter Anderson and Joel Dewey had just risen from their beds, and were putting their rifles in order for a hunt. Anderson's gun was lying across his knees, with the lock in his hand, having just finished oiling it, when, hearing the screams of Mrs. Sherwood, and readily guessing the cause, he clapped on the lock without fastening the screws, and sprang up the stairway to a port-hole in the block-house. As he was about to fire at the Indians, the lock dropped on to the floor, greatly to his vexation. At this instant, Joel Dewey, whose rifle was in better order, sprang to his side, and taking aim at the Indian who was in the act of scalping his victim, shot him through the elbow of the very arm that wielded the scalping knife, before he could complete the operation. Fearing the effects of other shots, the two Indians retreated. Before they had time to rally and repeat the attempt, Anderson and Dewey ran out, and seizing the old lady by the shoulders and feet, brought her into the block-house, amidst a volley of rifle shots from the other Indians. It was a foggy morning, and they both escaped injury, although the bullets were left sticking in the logs on each side of the doorway. Mrs. Sherwood remained for a long time without sense, or signs of life, from the stunning effects of the blow, which gashed her head in the most shocking manner, while the settling of the effused blood about her eyes gave her a deadly aspect. After a considerable period, signs of returning sensibility appeared, and Joshua Dewey, the brother of Joel, offered his services to go to Marietta for surgical aid. It may seem to us to have been a dangerous offer, but the old borderers knew there was far less danger immediately after an attack of the Indians than at any other time, as they always left immediately, the vicinity of their depredations, for fear of a pursuit or an attack on themselves. This journey was performed in a light canoe, with no companion but his trusty rifle, which he pushed to Marietta, a distance of thirty miles, the same day before nightfall, and returned by midnight with Dr. True, whose benevolent feelings and kind heart were ever ready to the calls of the distressed. By his judicious treatment, she was finally restored to health, and lived many years with her husband, who effected his escape from captivity in a short time.

In after life he was celebrated for his sympathy for the sick, having himself suffered much from disease. So tender was he to the prejudices of his patients, that he seldom prescribed without first consulting their opinion as to the medicine to be taken, and if they had any particular objection to the article which he thought proper, it was changed to suit their taste, unless it was really necessary in managing the disease, that the objectionable remedy *should* be taken. His attitude by the bedside of the sick was peculiar and striking. Leaning a little forward in the chair, with his long slender legs crossed over each other, his compassionate but single eye intently fixed on the patient, having lost the use of the other from a long and painful disease of the optic nerve, with one hand on the pulse and the other diligently employed in switching about a long cue, for he kept up the good old fashion of wearing the hair carefully dressed with a black ribbon. It was a habit he had insensibly fallen into when his mind was engaged on any subject of deep thought, and no doubt aided in fixing his attention. The result of his calm, deliberate judgment, was generally very correct, and his treatment of disease remarkably successful, which was, doubtless, in part, owing to its simplicity. It is a lamentable fact that many die from the effects of too many and often improper remedies, as well as from disease itself.

After the close of the war, he built a small dwelling-house and office at the Point, and turned his attention, when not occupied with his profession, to the clearing and cultivation of a small farm, about a mile above the town. He still remained a bachelor, boarding for several years in the family of Mr. Moulton, with whom he emigrated to Ohio. He subsequently boarded with Mrs. Mills, the widow of Capt. William Mills, a very amiable and excellent woman, whom he finally married in the autumn of 1806.

In the year 1799, he became united to the Congregational Church in Marietta, the earliest religious society in Ohio. Of this church he was for many years a deacon, fulfilling the duties of that sacred office with great fidelity and propriety.

His charity for the poor, and especially the sick poor, was unbounded, and only limited by his scanty means, often bestowing on them, in addition to his own services, the larger portion of the avails of his attendance on richer patients. It was many years after the close of the war before bridges were built and roads opened between the settlements, and during this period he was the principal physician in Marietta and for the country round. His rides often extended to twenty or thirty miles by bridle paths or old Indian trails, marked out by blazes on the trees. The people were many of them poor and just beginning life in a new country—had but little to spare for the services of the physician. With him, however, it made no difference whether the patient was poor or rich; he was always ready, when his health permitted, to attend to the calls, and to divide his last dollar with those who were in want. A practical proof of his equanimity of temper, generosity and forgiving disposition, even to those who had done him an injury, was related by the transgressor himself.

The doctor was a lover of fine fruit, and had cultivated, with much care, some of the choicest varieties of apples and pears, in a small garden near his house. Amongst them was a tree of the richest kind of summer sweeting apples, to which the neighboring boys paid daily visits whenever the doctor was out of the way. James Glover, a partially blind, near-sighted man, well known to the inhabitants of Marietta, many years since, for his natural, ready, and keen wit, but then a stout boy of fourteen or fifteen years of age, hearing the other lads speak of the fine apples in the doctor's garden, concluded he would also try them; so, one night, a little after bedtime, he mounted the tree, and began filling his bosom and pockets with the fruit; making a rustling among the branches, the doctor happened to hear him, and coming out into the garden, peering up into the trees, he espied James, and hailed him. James was obliged to answer, and give his name. "*Ah James is that you; why you are on the wrong tree; that one is the summer sweeting. Come down, come down, my lad.*" This was indeed the fact, but in his hurry he had not yet made the discovery of his mistake. James came down very slowly, expecting rough treatment, and the kind language of the doctor only a ruse to get him within his reach. But he was very pleasantly disappointed. Instead of using harsh words, or beating the aggressor, as most men would have done, he took a long pole and beat off as many apples as he could carry, and dismissed him with the request, that when he wanted any more, to call on him, and he would assist him in getting them. James, however, never visited the tree again, and did all in his power to persuade the other boys to do so.

As the country became more thickly settled, the roads better, and the people more wealthy, other physicians came in, and divided with him the medical business, which he bore without murmuring or complaining, willing to see all prosperous and happy, even at his expense. For several of the last years of his life, he held the office of county treasurer, which afforded him a small remuneration without much toil, and enabled him to further extend his charities to benevolent societies, and other objects for the support of religion and morals, which came into use about thirty years ago, and of which he was a zealous promoter. Samuel J. Mills, the projector of foreign missions, and other benevolent societies, spent two weeks at his house in 1812, when was formed the Washington County Bible Society, being the first in the valley of the Ohio. His house was the home of all traveling preachers of the Congregational or Presbyterian order, who visited the town, or were engaged in promoting the spread of the gospel. He was the Gaius of Marietta; although, for its population, it numbered many men who were zealous and liberal in all good works.

In his domestic relations the doctor was very happy. His wife was a cheerful, humble, and sincere Christian, with a lively, benevolent temperament, ever ready to promote the happiness and comfort of her companion, and to aid him in all deeds of charity. By this union he had no issue; but the children of his wife were treated with all the love and kindness he could have bestowed on his own. In person Dr. True was tall, with simple, but not ungraceful manners; his eyes grey and small, with full, projecting brows, nose large and aquiline; forehead rather low; face mild, and expressive of the benevolence of the mind and heart within. He was a man of whom no enemy could say hard things, and whom everyone loved and respected.

He died, after a short illness, of the prevailing epidemic fever of 1823.

The memory of this good man is still cherished by the descendants of the pioneers, for his universal charity, simplicity of manners, and sincere, unaffected piety.

Chapter XVI
CAPTAIN WILLIAM DANA

The progenitor of the Danas was a French Huguenot, who fled from the Catholic persecutions to England, at the period of the edict of Nantz. Near the middle of the seventeenth century, Richard Dana, the son of William Dana, who was the Sheriff of Middlesex, under Queen Elizabeth, came to Boston, and settled in that vicinity. He was the great grandfather of Capt. William Dana, the subject of this brief biography. From this man sprang all of that name in New England. He was born at Little Cambridge, now Brighton, Mass., in the year 1745. He had three older brothers, Jonathan, Samuel, and Benjamin, and two younger, Josiah and Ezra, with three sisters. The latter settled in Amherst, N. H., where he held the first rank in society. His son Samuel was a lawyer, and a member of Congress from that state, in the year 1813, and held many public stations in the Democratic ranks.

Capt. Dana married Miss Mary Bancroft, the daughter of Esq. Bancroft of Peperil, Mass. She had but one brother, who was a staunch patriot, and entered the service of his country at the Battle of Bunker Hill, where he discharged his musket sixteen times; and when the ammunition was all expended, came off with the retreating troops. That summer he died with the small-pox.

Mary Bancroft Dana
1752 - 1831

After Capt. Dana's marriage, he resided in Charleston; but just before the Battle of Lexington, sold his house and lot, and moved his family to the vicinity of Worcester, where he was living, on the Mount Farm, at the commencement of hostilities. This is quite a noted place, and now owned by the Roman Catholic College. Here he was chosen Captain of a company of artillery, and was stationed with his men a mile or two out of Charleston, at the time of the Battle of Bunker hill. An express from Gen. Putnam, near its close, arrived, with orders to hasten on to the hill and reinforce the flagging provincials. He started at full speed, but met his countrymen on Charleston neck, on their retreat. He continued in the service for two or three years, attached to the command of Gen. Knox, who was at the head of the artillery corps. Having a tempting offer, about the year 1778, he sold his possession for continental money, in which he had the fullest confidence. Before he could again invest it, the paper perished on his hands, leaving him, like many others of that day, in poverty. Having no means of supporting his young and growing family but his pay in the service, which would not even support himself, he reluctantly resigned his commission, and moved his family to Amherst, N. H. Here he rented a small farm, which required all his efforts, with the aid of his extra work as a carpenter, to supply his family with food;

provisions being both scarce and dear. A portion of the time of his living here, from 1779 to 1788, he was employed as a Deputy-Sheriff.

In the spring of the latter year he decided on removing his rapidly increasing family to the banks of the Ohio, where the soil was more fertile, and the climate less severe than that of New Hampshire. Hither several of his military associates had already gone. Leaving his wife and family at Amherst until he could visit Ohio, he, after a wearisome journey, arrived with his two oldest sons at Marietta the last of June, and built a log-cabin on the corner of market-square, where the post-office building now stands. As it was too late in the season to plant a crop of corn, he cleared off a small piece of ground on the land occupied by the female seminary, for a brickyard, and made and burnt a small kiln that summer, which were the first bricks made in the territory. These were in demand for chimneys, and aided him in supplying his present wants.

In 1789, he moved out his family and joined the Belpre associates, and drew a lot of land in that wide, beautiful bottom on the Ohio River, just above the head of Blennerhassett's Island. The first labor was chiefly devoted to clearing the land of the immense growth of forest trees which covered it, shutting out the rays of the sun, and inclosing it with fence. This left but little time for the erection of a comfortable cabin, and the winter was passed in a hut built like a large corn-crib, and so small that all the family could not be accommodated at night, and two of the oldest boys slept in a large covered road-wagon. The next year, or in 1790, he built a more comfortable house. That was the year of the famine, in which Capt. Dana's family suffered largely with the other settlers. During the Indian War, they lived in Farmers' Castle. In a few years after its close, his land was cleared, a convenient frame house built, orchards of fruit trees in bearing, and smiling plenty crowned his table, around which he could assemble eight sons and three daughters.

In person Capt. Dana was tall, and in his manhood sustained the post and bearing of a soldier. In disposition cheerful and social, and never happier than when surrounded by his old associates at the festive board.

He died in the year 1809, and has left a numerous train of descendants, who rank in vigor of mind, intelligence, civil and moral usefulness, with the first families in the community.

Chapter XVII
COLONEL NATHANIEL CUSHING

Col. Nathaniel Cushing was a branch of the illustrious Cushing family of Boston, which is classed with the first citizens of the cradle of liberty.

He was born in Pembroke, Mass., on the 8th of April, 1753. But little has been preserved of his early life, by his relatives, except that he received a good common school education. At a suitable age he served an apprenticeship to the trade of a house-carpenter, a common occurrence among the New England yeomanry, who often added to the calling of a farmer that of some useful trade or handicraft, giving them vigorous health and strength of limbs, fitting them to wield effectively the implements of war, as well as the tools used in their daily occupations.

He married Miss Elizabeth Heath, in November, 1775, the year the struggle for independence commenced. The fruits of this union were twelve children, six sons and six daughters, several of whom are now living in Ohio, amongst the most respectable and wealthy of her citizens. Mrs. Cushing was an accomplished, well educated lady, of refined manners, and accustomed to the best society of that day.

At the commencement of the war he was living in or near Boston, and offered his services in defense of the country. In July, 1775, while the Americans were investing the town under Gen. Washington, he was commissioned by Congress as a Lieutenant in Capt. Trescott's Company and Col. Brewer's Regiment. In January, 1776, he was commissioned as First Lieutenant in the same company, but in the Sixth Regiment of

Massachusetts Infantry, under Col. Whitcomb. In 1777 he was promoted to a Captain, and in this capacity served the remainder of the war, being at its close made a Major by brevet. He was engaged in many battles and skirmishes, and noted as one of the most brave and successful of the partisan officers. By his kindness to those under his command, and watchful care for the best interests of his men, he became a great favorite with the soldiers. As a disciplinarian he was very strict, and the men often remarked that they could always depend on his word; and whether it was to reward them for their good conduct, or to punish them for their faults, it was sure to be accomplished.

In 1780 Capt. Cushing was attached to Col. Rufus Putnam's Regiment of Light Infantry, while the main army was stationed on the North River, and the enemy held possession of New York. At this time there was a large district of country between the contending armies, called the Neutral Ground that was nearly deserted by the inhabitants and ravaged by both parties, especially by the Tories, who, from this and the adjacent country, supplied the British in New York with forage and fresh provisions. The Americans, to watch the incursions of the enemy, and keep the Tories from robbing the peaceable inhabitants near the lines, kept strong outposts, or detachments of soldiers, on the borders between Kingsbridge and the White Plains. It was a dangerous position for the troops; and none but the most active and vigilant of the partisan officers were ordered on this service. They were not only liable to sudden and night attacks, from the bands of Tories who were born and brought up here, and familiar with every road and by-path, but also exposed to a corps of light-horse, under the noted partisan officer, Col. Simcoe, who had cut off and destroyed several advanced parties of American troops. To avoid the latter casualty, the order of the Commanding General was that they should not advance beyond a certain line into the neutral ground, but keep within their own defenses, lest they should be surprised by the light-horse, and cut to pieces.

Amongst others ordered on this hazardous service, was Capt. Cushing, with a detachment of men in addition to his own company. Soon after arriving and taking up his position, information was brought by some of the Whig inhabitants, that there was a considerable body of Tories posted at no great distance from him, on the road to New York. The opportunity thus offered, of distinguishing himself and the detachment under his orders, was too great to be resisted; beside, if successful, would be doing a service to the cause, and wipe away some of the disgrace attached to the defeat of other officers who had preceded him in this service. With the main body of his men, he early that night commenced a rapid march across the country by an unfrequented road, and about midnight surprised and captured the whole party. Col. Simcoe, with his mounted Rangers, was posted in that vicinity, and received early notice of the event, by some friend of the British, and acting with his usual promptness, immediately commenced a pursuit, with the expectation of cutting to pieces the detachment and releasing the prisoners. Capt. Cushing, with all haste, posted off the captive Tories in advance, under a small guard; charging the officer to rush on toward the lines as rapidly as possible, while he followed more leisurely in the rear, with the main body of his troops. Expecting a pursuit from Simcoe, he marched in three ranks, and arranged the order of defense if they were attacked by the cavalry; a kind of troops much more dreaded by the infantry than those of their own class. When about half way back, the clattering hoofs of the Rangers' horses were heard in hot pursuit. As they approached, he halted his detachment in the middle of the road, ready to receive the charge. It fortunately happened that he found, in the house with the captured Tories, a number of long spears or lances, sufficient to arm the rear rank. When called to a halt, and face the enemy, it brought the spearmen in front. Standing in close array, shoulder to shoulder, with one end resting on the ground, they received their enraged enemies on their points, while the other two ranks poured upon them a deadly fire, leaving many of the horses without riders. This unexpected result threw them into disorder, and their leader directed a retreat. Cushing now renewed his march in the same order. Simcoe, enraged and chagrined at the failure of his charge, again ordered a fresh and more furious onset, but was received by his brave antagonist in the same cool and resolute manner, and met with a still more decided repulse, losing a number of his best men and horses. Not yet satisfied to let his enemies escape, he made a third unsuccessful attempt, and gave up the pursuit, leaving Capt. Cushing to retire at his leisure. He reached his post unmolested, with all the prisoners, and the loss of only a few men wounded, but none killed. The following day he was relieved by a fresh detachment, and marched into camp with the trophies of this brave adventure.

The morning after his return, in the orders of the day, by the Commander-in-Chief, notice was taken of this affair, and any similar attempt by the troops on the lines forbidden, thereby apparently censuring the conduct of Capt. Cushing. This was rather a damper to the feelings of a brave officer, who was peculiarly sensitive, and sustained a nice sense of military honor. Soon after the promulgation of the order, and he had retired to his tent, brooding over the event of the morning, and half inclined to be both angry and mortified at the nice distinctions of the commander, an aid of Gen. Washington entered with a polite invitation to dine with him. He readily complied with the request, and at the table was placed in the post of honor, at Washington's right hand. A large number of officers were present, in whose hearing he highly complimented Capt. Cushing for the gallant manner in which he conducted the assault on the Tories, and the bravery and skill with which he defeated the charges of Simcoe; and that there were few, indeed, who could have conducted the retreat with the coolness and success he had done; but, at the same time, added that for the strict and orderly discipline of the army, it was necessary to discountenance every act that contravened the orders of the commander-in-chief. This satisfied all his mortified feelings, and increased his love and respect for his revered general.

After the close of the war he lived in Boston, from whence, on the formation of the Ohio Company, he removed with his family to Marietta, in the summer of 1788. Soon after his arrival, in August, he was commissioned by Gov. St. Clair as a Captain in the First Regiment of Territorial Militia, and in 1797, by the same, as Colonel of the regiment. When the Belpre colony was formed, in 1789, he joined the association, and was one of the most active, brave, and intelligent men, in arranging and conducting the military and civil affairs of that settlement. After the capture of Capt. Goodale by the Indians, he was chosen to command the garrison of Farmers' Castle. At the close of the war he settled on his farm, and pursued agriculture for the support of his family, and was a very successful cultivator. He paid great attention to the education of his children, who now rank with the most worthy and useful citizens of Ohio.

Thomas H. Cushing was a younger brother, and faithfully served his country, not only in the war of 1776, but also in that of 1812. In 1815 he was Collector of the United States revenue in the port of New London, Conn., which office he held until his death, in 1822. He is spoken of as a very excellent man.

In person, Col. Cushing was rather short, but very muscular and stout-limbed; eyes black, and of the keenest luster, piercing and intelligent; face well formed, with an expression of firmness and dignity seldom seen; manners gentlemanly and refined; very courteous and affable in his intercourse with mankind, whether poor or rich. He was highly esteemed by Mr. Blennerhassett, and both he and Mrs. Cushing treated with marked attention.

They died in August, in the year 1814; but their names will be long cherished by the descendants of the early settlers, as amongst the most worthy of that heroic band.

Chapter XVIII
MAJOR JONATHAN HASKELL

Maj. Jonathan Haskell

Major Jonathan Haskell was born in Rochester, Mass., the 19th of March, 1754. Like the larger portion of the New Englanders of that day, he was brought up on a farm, and received only a common school education, which fitted him for conducting the usual concerns of life to which he might be called.

At the commencement of the War of Independence, when he was twenty years old, he was engaged in agriculture. How early he entered the army is not known. In 1779 he was Aid-de-Camp to Gen. Patterson, of the Massachusetts line, and was commissioned as a Lieutenant. He continued to serve until the close of the war, either as an aid, or in the line of the army.

When the Ohio Company was formed, he became an associate, and moved out there in company with Capt. Devol's family, in the autumn of 1788. In 1789 he united with the Belpre settlement, and commenced clearing his farm. On the breaking out of the Indian War, in January, 1791, he received the appointment of Captain in the regular service, and went to Rochester, Mass., where he recruited a company, and returned to Marietta in December; where he was stationed for the defense of that, and the adjacent settlements; as the troops had been withdrawn from Fort Harmar in the fall of 1790. After the defeat of Gen. St. Clair, he remained at Marietta until March, 1793, when he was commissioned as a Captain in the Second Sub-Legion under Gen. Wayne, and joined the army on the frontiers that summer. He was stationed at Fort St. Clair, where he remained until June, 1794, when he was appointed to the Command of the Fourth Sub-Legion, ranking as a Major, although his commission was not filled until August, 1795. In a letter to Griffin Greene, Esq., whose relative he married, he gives a sketch of the campaign which defeated the combined forces of the Indians and closed the war.

"Head Quarters, Miami of the Lake, August 29th, 1794.

Sir:

The 28th of July the army moved forward, consisting of about eighteen hundred regulars and fifteen hundred militia, from the state of Kentucky, passing by the way of St. Clair's battle-ground, now Fort Recovery. We then turned more to the eastward, and struck the St. Mary's in twenty miles, where we erected a small fort, and left a sub-altern's command. We then crossed the St. Mary's, and in four or five days' marching found the Auglaize River, and continued on down that stream to its junction with the Miami of the Lake; distant one hundred miles from Greenville, by the route we pursued. At this place we built a garrison, and left a Major to command it. The army then marched down the river forty-seven miles from the new garrison, and on the 20th inst., at nine o'clock in the morning, came up with the Indians, who had posted themselves in a position chosen as most favorable for defense. The troops charged upon them with the bayonet, and drove them two miles, through a thicket of woods, fallen timber, and underbrush, when the cavalry fell upon and entirely routed them. Our line extended two and a half miles, and yet it was with difficulty we outflanked them. One of the prisoners, a white man, says the number of the Indians engaged was about twelve hundred, aided by two hundred and fifty white men from Detroit. Our loss in the action was two Officers killed, and four wounded, with about thirty Privates killed, and eighty wounded. The Indians suffered much; about forty or fifty of their dead fell into our hands. The prisoner was asked why they did not fight better? He said that we would give them no time to load their pieces, but kept them constantly on the run. Two miles in advance of the battleground, is a British garrison, established last spring, which we marched round within pistol shot, and demanded surrender; but they refused to give it up. Our artillery being too light, and the fort too strong to carry by storm, it was not attacked; but we burnt their outhouses, destroyed all their gardens, cornfields, and grass, within musket shot of the place, and all below for eight or nine miles without any opposition. On the 27th we arrived at this place, where we have a fort, and shall halt a few days to rest. We have marched through the Indian settlements and villages for about sixty miles, destroyed several thousand acres of corn, beans, and all kinds of vegetables, burned their houses, with furniture, tools, &c A detachment has gone into Fort Recovery for a supply of provisions for the troops, and when it returns, we shall march up the Miami sixty miles, to where the St. Mary's unites with the St. Joseph's, and destroy all the corn in that country."

This letter describes, in plain terms, the ruin and devastation that marked the course of the American army. It might have been considered a *wise policy* to devote to destruction the dwellings, cornfields, gardens, and in fact every species of property that belonged to the hostile savages, but it was also a *most cruel policy*. The British troops, in their inroads amongst the rebel settlements of the Revolutionary War, never conducted more barbarously. The Indian villages on the Miami and the Auglaize were snugly and comfortably built—were furnished with many convenient articles of house-keeping and clothing. They had large fields of corn and beans, with gardens of melons, squashes, and various other vegetables. Mr. Joseph Kelly, of Marietta, then a boy of twelve years old, and for several years a prisoner with the Indians, who treated him kindly, and was adopted into a family as one of their own children, was living at this time with them at the junction of the St. Mary's and Auglaize, the spot where Maj. Haskell says the army would next go, to complete their work of destruction. Mr. Kelly was there when an Indian runner announced that the American troops had arrived in the vicinity of the village. His friends had not expected them so soon, and with the utmost haste and consternation, the old men, with the women and children, the warriors being absent, hurried aboard their canoes, taking nothing with them but a few kettles and blankets, not having time to collect any provisions from their fields and gardens. The sun was only an hour or two high when they departed, in as deep sorrow at the loss of their country and homes, as the Trojans of old when they evacuated their favorite city. Before the next day at noon, their nice village was burnt to the ground; their cornfields of several hundred acres, just beginning to ripen, were cut down and trampled underfoot by the horses and oxen of the invaders, while their melons and squashes were pulled up by the roots. The following winter, the poor Indians deprived of their stock of corn and beans, which were grown every year and laid up for their winter food as regularly as among the white people, suffered the extreme of want. Game was scarce in the country they retreated to on the west of the Miami, and what few deer and fish they could collect, barely served to keep them alive. It was a cruel policy; but probably subdued their Spartan courage more than two or three defeats, as for many years thereafter, until the days of Tecumseh, they remained at peace.

After the close of the war, Maj. Haskell returned to his farm at Belpre, where he died in December, 1816. He was considered a brave man and a good officer. Several of his descendants are living in Washington County.

Chapter XIX
COLONEL EBENEZER BATTELLE

Col. Ebenezer Battelle was a descendant of the Puritan race, and the only son of Ebenezer Battelle Esq., of Dedham, Mass. His father was one of the industrious, honest yeomanry of the good old bay state, who duly appreciated the value of learning, more farmers' sons being liberally educated in that state than in any other of the Union. At a suitable age he pursued a full college course at Cambridge, and graduated in the year 1775. He was intended for the ministry, as were a large share of the educated men before the Revolution; but the war breaking out in the last year of his course, his attention was diverted from the study of divinity to that of a martial nature. He held the commission of a Colonel under the Governor of Massachusetts, in the militia, during or at the close of the war.

In 1781, he commenced business in Boston, as the active partner in a bookstore, in company with Isaiah Thomas, of Worcester, a man who delighted in being useful, and assisted many young men in their commencement of life. He remained in this occupation six years; and during the time, married Miss Anna Durant, the daughter of Cornelius Durant, Esq., a rich merchant of that place. She was a woman of superior intellect, beautiful person, and great excellence of character, the impress of which descended to her children.

Anna Durant Battelle
Wife of Ebenezer Battelle

This bookstore was the second one ever opened in Boston, the first being kept by Mr. Guile, to which was added a circulating library to aid in keeping up the establishment. While here he was elected to the command of the Ancient and Honorable Artillery Company, a noted band of military men, composed of officers of good standing and character.

Webſter's Grammatical Inſtitutes,
Recommended by ſome of the principal Literary Characters in Pennſylvania, New-Jerſey,
New-York, Connecticut and Maſſachuſetts,
as the beſt Spelling-Book now in uſe, ſold by

Ebenezer Battelle,

STATE-STREET, BOSTON,
At which place may be had,

B O O K S,

In the various Branches of Literature, and

STATIONARY,

As uſual.

Advertisement from the
American Hearald, Boston
April 26, 1784

On the formation of the Ohio Company, he became an associate, and was appointed one of their agents. On the sixth of April, 1788, the day before the pioneers landed at Marietta, he left Boston in company with Col. John May and others, by water, for the mouth of the Muskingum, by way of Baltimore. After a six weeks' tour in crossing the mountains, by almost impassable roads, with their heavy loaded wagon, they reached the place of destination the last of May. During the following summer he was employed in erecting a dwelling-house, in the front curtain of Campus Martius, for the reception of his family. The first Court of Quarter Sessions, held the 9th of September, was opened in his house, as appears by the old records of that court. In October, 1788, he re-crossed the mountains to meet his family at Baltimore, and guide them over the Alleghenies. He found them under the care of Mr. Daniel Mayo, a young gentleman who had recently graduated at Cambridge, and became a resident of Newport, Ky., after the close of the Indian War. Their journey, at this late season of the year, was very trying to Mrs. Battelle, who had all her life been nurtured in the comforts of a city. At Simrel's Ferry, a noted place of embarkation for emigrants, they met with several other New England families, amongst them, Isaac Pierce, Charles Green, and Capt. Zebulon King, who, the next spring, was killed by the Indians. The last of November, eight families embarked in one boat, and that not a large one, and arrived at Marietta in December. Here they met with a hearty welcome from the five or six females and heads of families who had come on in August preceding. The winter was passed very pleasantly in Campus Martius, in the company of such men as Generals Varnum, Parsons, Putnam and with Gov. St. Clair and the officers of Fort Harmar. The Indians were yet all friendly, and an abundance of wild game, with a good stock of provisions from Pittsburg, rendered this as delightful a season as any that occurred for many years thereafter.

That winter an association was formed for the settlement at Belpre, composed almost entirely of the old officers of the Continental Line. Col. Battelle united himself with these enterprising and intelligent men, and in the spring of 1789 proceeded to clear his land and erect a stout blockhouse for the reception of his family. On the 1st day of May, one of the associates, Capt. King, from Rhode Island, was killed by the Indians, while peaceably at work on his new land. The following day Col. Battelle, with two of his sons and Griffin Greene, Esq., embarked at Marietta in a large canoe, with farming tools, provisions, &c. On their way down they were hailed by someone from the shore, and informed of this sad event. They landed and held a consultation on what was best to be done. Some were for returning; but they finally decided on proceeding. The blockhouses of the two emigrants were near each other, and nearly opposite to the middle of Backus' Island, on the spot afterward occupied by Farmers' Castle. After landing, the other settlers came and joined them for mutual defense, and through the night kept up a military guard, in the old Revolutionary style, the sentinel calling out every fifteen minutes, *"All's well,"* not thinking this would give the skulking Indians notice where to find them. No enemy, however, molested them during the night, and their fears of attack gradually subsided. They were not again disturbed until the winter of 1791.

Early in April, before any families had moved on to the ground, a party of officers from Fort Harmar, with their wives, and a few ladies from Marietta, made a visit to the new settlement, in the officer's barge, a fine, large boat, rowed with twelve oars. These were the first white females who ever set foot on the soil of Belpre. On their return Col. Battelle, with several others, accompanied them by water in a canoe, and another party by land. While on the voyage, a large bear was discovered swimming across the river. The landsmen fired at him with their muskets and rifles, but without effect. The canoe then ranged alongside, when Col. Battelle seized him by the tail, and when the bear attempted to bite his hand, he raised his hind parts, throwing his head under water, and thus escaped his teeth. One of his companions soon killed him with an axe. He weighed over three hundred pounds, and afforded several fine dinners to his captors. In 1790, owing to early frosts and late planting the year previous, the inhabitants were left without bread-stuff, corn being their chief dependence. Their sufferings were very great, until the crop of 1790 was gathered, which proved to be plentiful, and after that time they did not suffer again for food. During the Indian War his family was sheltered in Farmers' Castle, and all escaped injury, though often in danger. Several of the inmates were killed.

In the plan of Farmers' Castle, his blockhouse occupied the northeast corner. In their lower room of this building, regularly on the Sabbath, divine worship was kept up by the inhabitants. His son Ebenezer, a lad of fourteen years, was drummer to the garrison, and at the hour of service marched with his drum the whole length of the castle, summoning the people to worship. Col. Battelle officiated as chaplain, sometimes delivering his own discourses, and, at others, reading the sermons of a standard divine; so that the Sabbath was honored and generally respected by the inhabitants.

He died at the residence of his son, in Newport, Washington County, Ohio, in the year 1815.

He left three sons and one daughter, Cornelius, Ebenezer and Thomas.

Cornelius and Thomas, at the close of the war, went to the West Indies, where a rich uncle put them into lucrative business. Thomas married the daughter of Gov. Livingston, of New York, and Cornelius the daughter of a rich planter. Louisa remained single, and lived in Boston with her mother's relatives. Ebenezer settled on a farm in Newport, and has a numerous family of children, noted for their intelligence and respectability.

Chapter XX
COLONEL ISRAEL PUTNAM

Col. Israel Putnam was the eldest son of Gen. Israel Putnam, of Pomfret, Conn., but was born in the town of Salem, Mass., in 1739. He had three brothers, Daniel, David and Schuyler, whose native place was Pomfret. His early days were passed on the farm, and he was bred to the noble art of agriculture, an art without which all other arts are useless. This gave him a vigorous, healthy frame, and fitted him for the turmoil of the camp or the labors of the field.

His education was similar to that of the sons of the surrounding yeomanry, equal to all the common concerns of life. As a proof that Gen. Putnam highly valued learning and the cultivation of the mind, he collected a large library of the most useful books; embracing history, belles-lettres, travels, &c, for the benefit of himself and children, called the Putnam family library. After his death they were divided amongst the heirs, and quite a number of them found their way to Ohio, being brought out by his son and grandchildren.

About the year 1764, he married Miss Sarah Waldo, of an ancient and honorable family in Pomfret, and a woman of excellent qualities, with whom he passed a long and happy life.

On the 20th of April, 1775, when the news of the Battle of Lexington arrived, flying on the wings of the wind, his father, Col. Putnam, was plowing in the field with four oxen. He left them standing in their yokes, and hastening to the stable, mounted one of his fleetest horses, without even changing his dress, and started for the scene of action. The distance was one hundred miles, which he accomplished by a relay of horses, in twenty-four hours. Shortly after his departure, his son Israel raised a company of volunteers, of which he was the Captain, and marched to Cambridge, where he remained under his father's orders until the arrival of Gen. Washington. Soon after this time, Col. Putnam was commissioned by Congress as a Major-General, and on the 22d of July, Capt. Putnam and Lieut. Samuel Webb were appointed his aids. He accompanied his father to New York, where he took command of that division of the army, and to the posts on the Hudson River. Having but little taste for military life, to which calling neither his address nor personal appearance fitted him, being diffident and awkward in his manners, but naturally fearless and brave like all his name, after spending about three years in the army, he concluded to quit the service and devote his attention to the farm, for which he was eminently fitted, both by inclination and practice. While absent from his home, his wife took charge of the family of six children. She was a woman of great spirit, and as firm a patriot as the General himself, hating, with all her soul and strength, the British oppressors of her country, who were technically called Redcoats, and loving with equal ardor the American soldiers, supplying them with food and clothing to the extent of her abilities. In the winter of 1779, when the patriot troops suffered so much from the want of warm garments, she had spun and wove in her own house, a number of blankets made of the finest wool in the flock, and sent on for their relief. Numerous pairs of stockings were also manufactured by her own hands, and contributed in the same way. No one at this day knows or can appreciate the value of the labors of American females in achieving our freedom. They wrought and suffered in silence, bearing many privations in common with their husbands and sons in the days which tried the patriotism of the colonists. She was a woman of elevated mind and great personal courage, worthy of the family to which she was allied. In the absence of her husband, when the vultures and hawks attacked the poultry, she could load and fire his light fowling-piece at them, without dodging at the flash.

While at Harlem Heights, Col. Putnam purchased two fine bulls, to improve his stock of cattle; one was black, and a full-blooded English animal; the other, an American, of a mottled color. From these, crossed with his best native cows, was raised a very superior stock, celebrated for size, and their excellent qualities for the dairy. Oxen of this breed were brought out to Ohio in the year 1788 and cows in 1795, which were as famous for milk as the noted Durhams of this day. During the period of the Revolution, amidst all their other cares, intelligent American farmers found time to attend to the improvement of their farming operations, as well as to the calls of military duties.

When the Ohio Company was formed, he became an associate; and with two of his sons crossed the mountains, bringing a wagon load of farming utensils; but left his wife and other children in Pomfret, until a farm was provided for their comfort in the wilderness. His team was composed of two yokes of oxen, sprung from this famous stock. The adventure in crossing the North River, related in the biography of his son Waldo, took place on this journey; and his life was saved by one of these fine oxen. At the formation of the settlement in Belpre, in the spring of 1789, he joined that community, locating his farm in the broad, beautiful bottom on the Ohio River, opposite to the mouth of the Little Kanawha. Here he remained, clearing and fencing the land, until the fall of 1790, when he returned to Connecticut for his family. The Indian War broke out in January following, and he did not return until after the peace of 1795. His wealth, although not great, yet gave him facilities for improving his lands and erecting buildings, rather superior to most of the other associates, who were generally in very moderate circumstances. He was a practical and intelligent agriculturist, who, by his example and precepts, was the means of giving a correct tone to the progress of farming in Belpre, thus conferring a direct benefit on the country. In all public improvements on the roads and bridges, so useful in new settlements, he was a leading and influential man; also, in the support of schools and the gospel; reading on the Sabbath, in their social meetings, when they had no preacher, the prayers of the Episcopal Church, and a sermon from the work of some pious divine; thus doing all in his power for the good of his fellow men.

He was the father of a numerous family; five sons and three daughters, viz.: Israel, Aaron Waldo, David, William Pitt, and George Washington. These all settled in Ohio, and three of them as farmers. William Pitt Putnam was a physician, and came to Marietta in 1792, in the midst of the war, and practiced medicine. David Putnam also settled in Marietta, in 1798, as a lawyer, and is now the only survivor. The daughters married as follows: Sarah to Samuel Thornily, Mary to Daniel Mayo, and Elizabeth to Joel Craig; the two latter settled in Newport, Ky., opposite to Cincinnati, where their descendants now live.

Col. Putnam was a man of sound, vigorous mind, and remarkable for his plain, common sense; abrupt and homely in his manners and address, but perfectly honest and upright in his intercourse with mankind. He was a strict utilitarian; esteeming the useful much more highly than the ornamental. In his life he practiced all the Christian virtues, and died in the full hope of a blessed immortality.

Chapter XXI
MAJOR NATHAN GOODALE

Maj. Nathan Goodale was born in Brookfield, Mass., about the year 1743. His father died when he was quite young, and his mother married a Mr. Ware, of Rutland, where he was removed to his new home, and passed his early years, to the time of manhood, on a farm, and in learning the trade of a bricklayer; thus laying the foundation for that vigorous, muscular frame, which enabled him to undergo the fatigues and exposures of a military life, at a time when the army afforded few facilities for the comfort of the soldier. No other set of men could have borne up under the trials of want, famine, and a lack of all the common necessaries of life, for several years in succession, as did the American soldiers, but such as had been inured like the Spartans, in childhood, to bear suffering with patience. His education was rather above that of the common schools of that day, for we find him, at an early period of the war, employed by Gen. Putnam as an assistant engineer.

At a suitable age he married Elizabeth Phelps, of Rutland, on the 11th of September, 1765. About the year 1770 he moved his family to Brookfield, where he purchased a farm two miles from the center of the town. His three oldest children were born in Rutland, as we learn from the town records.

From this time to the rupture with the mother country, in 1775, he continued to labor on his farm, and to work at his trade of bricklaying; but as nearly all the houses of that day were made of wood, his mechanical work was chiefly confined to chimneys. For some time previous to the first hostilities, he had, with thousands of his countrymen, been preparing for the day of strife, which every thinking man foresaw must soon arrive, by practicing military exercises, and collecting arms and ammunition. Many of these volunteer companies were aptly called, by the New Englanders, who are never at a loss for a phrase to express exactly their meaning, "Minutemen." They were, indeed, minute men, and when the first notice of alarm echoed from hill to hill, all over the country, at the bloodshed at Lexington, they were ready, at a moment's warning, to pour their thousands on thousands into the vicinity of Boston, the stronghold of the British, which nothing but the lack of battering cannon and ammunition hindered them immediately from storming. Mr. Goodale here first saw the actual movements of military life, and immediately entered into the service of his country, as a Lieutenant. It being uncertain how long he might remain in the army, the homestead of his early manhood was sold, and his family resided, during the war, in rented premises. With what spirit and enterprise he entered into the service, and how well his activity and talents were adapted to the trying exigencies of a partisan officer, the most difficult of all military duties, will be best shown by a letter from Gen. Rufus Putnam to Gen. Washington, near the close of the war:

"Massachusetts Huts, June 9th, 1783.

Sir:

I do myself the honor to enclose a letter I received a few days since from Capt. Goodale, of the Fifth Massachusetts Regiment. I confess I feel a conviction of neglect of duty in respect to this gentleman; that I have not, till this moment, taken any measures to bring his services to public view, has been owing to the confidence I had, that Gen. Gates would have done it, as the most extraordinary of them were performed under his own orders, and as he gave repeated assurances that they should not be forgotten. I am sorry that Gen. Gates is now out of camp, for were he not, I should appeal to him on the subject, but as I am sure so worthy a character, and such important services, ought not to be buried in oblivion, or pass unrewarded, I beg your Excellency's patience a few moments, while I give a short detail of them. Capt. Goodale was among the first who embarked in the common cause in 1775. He served that year as a Lieutenant in the same regiment with me. I had long before known him to be a man of spirit, and his probity and attention to service soon gained him the character of a worthy officer. In 1776, he entered again as a Lieutenant, but served with me the most of the year as an Assistant Engineer, and the public are much indebted to him for the dispatch and propriety with which several of the works about New York were executed. In the dark month of November, 1776, Mr. Goodale entered the service as a Captain in the regiment under my command, and was in the field early the next spring; but, although he always discovered a thirst for enterprise, yet fortune never gave his genius fair play till August, 1777. It is well known into what a panic the country and even the Northern Army, were thrown on the taking of Ticonderoga. When Gen. Gates took command in that quarter our army lay at Van Shaick's Island; and Mr. Burgoyne, with his black wings and painted legions, lay at Saratoga. The woods were so infested with savages that for some time none of the scouts who were sent out for the purpose of obtaining prisoners or intelligence of the enemy's situation, succeeded in either. Gen. Gates being vexed at continual disappointments desired an officer to procure him a man that would undertake, at all hazards, to perform this service. Capt. Goodale, being spoken to, voluntarily undertook the business under the following orders from Gen. Gates.

"Sir:

You are to choose out a sergeant and six privates, and proceed with them to the enemy's camp, unless you lose your life or are captured, and not return until you obtain a full knowledge of their situation.

Capt. Goodale, in his report of this scout, says it was not performed without great fatigue, as the party was much harassed by the Indians, which occasioned their being in the woods three days without provisions. However, he succeeded beyond expectation; first throwing himself between their out-guards and their camp, where he concealed his party until he examined their situation very fully, and then brought off six *prisoners, which he took within their guards, and returned to Gen. Gates without any loss. This success induced Gen. Gates to continue him on that kind of service. A full detail of all the art and address which he discovered during the remainder of that campaign, would make my letter quite too long. It may be enough to observe that before the capture of the British army, one hundred and twenty-one prisoners fell into his hands. But as Capt. Goodale is no less brave and determined in the open field, where opposed to regular troops, than he is artful as a partisan of the woods, I beg your patience while I recite one instance of this land. A day or two after Mr. Burgoyne retreated to Saratoga, in a foggy morning, Nixon's brigade was ordered to cross the creek which separated the two armies. Capt. Goodale, with forty volunteers, went over before the advance guard. He soon fell in with a British guard of about the same number. The ground was an open plain, but the fog prevented their discovering each other till they were within a few yards, when both parties made ready nearly at the same time. Capt. Goodale, in this position reserving his fire, advanced immediately upon the enemy, who waited with a design to draw it from him; but he had the address to intimidate them in such a manner, by threatening immediate death to any one that should fire, that not more than two or three obeyed the order of their own officer, when he gave the word. The event was that the officer and thirty-four of the guard were made prisoners. These, sir, are the services which Capt. Goodale and his friends conceive have merited more attention than has been paid to them; and, at least, merit a Majority as much as Maj. Summers' unsuccessful command of a boat a few months on Lake Champlain. But if the tables are reversed, and the ill luck of a brave man should be the only recommendation to promotion, Capt. Goodale, I believe, has as great pretensions as most men, for he is the unfortunate officer who commanded about forty white men, and being joined by about the same number of Indians, fought more than one thousand of the enemy below Valentine's Hill in 1778, until near two-thirds were killed, himself and most of the rest made prisoners. But I mention this not so much to show his bravery, for he takes no merit from that action, but always lamented the necessity he was under from the orders he received, to do what he did. In writing to me on the subject, he says: "At this time a number of brave men were sacrificed to bad orders; but, as they were not my orders, I hope the candid will not censure me."*

Having stated these facts, I beg leave to request your Excellency will lay them before Congress, &c.

He goes on to say, Gen. Washington forwarded my letter to the secretary of war; but as about this time Congress came to a resolution to raise the rank of all officers one grade who had not been promoted since their entrance into service, the 1st of January, 1777, Maj. Goodale received promotion with the rest, and thus never had that justice done him which he so highly merited.

Thus far Gen. Putnam testifies to the valuable services of this brave and noble-minded man. Had Gen. Gates, as in duty bound, given notice to Congress of the heroic exploits of Capt. Goodale, in collecting information of the movements of Burgoyne, so essential to the welfare of the American Army, he would no doubt have received the promotion so justly his due. But Gates was a selfish, proud man, who cared little for the interest of others, provided his own personal wishes were accomplished.

From another hand a more detailed account is given of the action at Valentine's Hill. It seems that the commander of the troops to which he was attached, had ordered him to keep possession of a certain pass, important to the Americans, at all hazards, without any discretionary power as to contingencies. His command consisted, as above-stated, of about forty light-infantry and a number of Indians, who stood the attack of a large body of the enemy and a company of cavalry, until there were only seventeen men left alive out of the forty. Near the close of the combat, the officer who led the charge rushed upon him with his sword. Capt. Goodale, with a loaded musket which he had probably picked up from one of his fallen men, shot the Briton dead from his horse as he approached. In a moment, another of the enemy, seeing the fall of his leader, sprung at him in desperation, with full purpose to revenge his death. The musket being discharged, the only resource was to parry the descending blow, aimed at his head, in the best manner he could, with the empty piece. It fell obliquely, being turned a little from its course by the musket, and instead of splitting the skull of its intended victim, glanced on the bone, peeling up a portion of the scalp several inches in length. The stunning effects of the blow felled him to the earth, but directly recovering, he rose to his feet. In the meantime, the cavalry man, who had leaned forward in the saddle further than prudent to give a certain death-stroke, lost his balance, when the heavy sword glanced from the skull and fell to the earth. The bayonet of Capt. Goodale instantly pinned him to the ground, and left him dead by the side of his leader. Thus two of the enemy fell by his hand in a space of time less than a minute. Seeing all prospect of further resistance useless, he retreated with the balance of his men to an open woodland, near the scene of action, and secreted himself under a pile of brush. An Indian had hidden under another heap, where they might have remained in safety until dark and then escaped; but the savage having an opportunity to shoot one of the enemy who had approached their hiding-place, he could not resist the chance of adding another scalp to his trophies, and shot him. The report of the shot revealed their hiding place and being discovered, they were made prisoners. How long he remained in durance does not appear from the imperfect memorials left of his military life. It is probable he was shut up in the old Jersey prison-ship at New York, as his children have a tradition that he was poisoned, from the fact of a long sickness he suffered after his return home. But it is more probable that the poison was that of human malaria, received in that pest-house of British cruelty, which killed more Americans than all those who fell in battle during the whole war, being estimated at twelve or fourteen thousand. It is one of the foulest stains on the English nation that ever disgraced their character.

During the war he received one other wound in the leg, from a musket or grape shot. Could all his adventures be collected they would make one of the most interesting of biographies; but time, and a fire which destroyed his papers at Belpre some years after his death, have put this matter to rest, and these scanty gleanings are all that are left of his military life.

At the close of the war he entered into mercantile business, in company with Col. Cushing, a brother officer. Not succeeding in this to his expectations, he sold out, and bought a farm on Coit's Hill, in the north part of the town of Brookfield. In the pursuits of agriculture he was as much at home as in military matters, having a natural taste for cultivation, and engaged in this primitive employment with his characteristic ardor and perseverance, at a time when improvements of all kinds were at a low ebb; the country during the war having retrograded, amidst the trials of that eventful period. Mr. Goodale was remarkable for his industry, and thorough, neat manner in which he conducted all the operations of the farm. The forecast and wisdom of the man may be seen before setting out on his journey to Ohio, in the course he pursued in preparing for it. Knowing that a superior breed of neat cattle is all-important to the farmer, and more especially to one beginning in a new country, instead of taking a team of oxen, or horses, as all other men did, to haul their wagons, he, after deciding on joining the new colony, selected three of the best cows and one of the finest bulls to be found in that vicinity, and trained them to work together in a team. With this novel working power, he drew on the wagon, with a part of his family and household goods, to Marietta, performing the journey with as much ease, and in as short a time, as the best of oxen. He had also the profit of their milk for the use of the family along the road. The stock from this breed of cattle has been spread through the county, and is held in high estimation at this day, for their perfect forms, gentle dispositions, and great abundance of rich milk; constituting them, on all accounts, the best dairy stock ever introduced to the country. They are known as the "Goodale Breed," still retaining many of their original characteristics.

Maj. Goodale arrived at the mouth of the Muskingum on the 2d of July, 1788, in company with several other families from Massachusetts, descending the Ohio, from Wheeling, in a flatboat. In August he was appointed, by Gov. St. Clair, who soon organized the militia, Captain of a Company of Light-Infantry, selected from amongst the most active men of the colony. This company held regular musters, until the commencement of the war, when each man was confined to the defense of his own garrison, in the settlement where he lived. His experience in military affairs rendered him a very able and efficient officer, familiar with all the details of actual service.

In April, 1789, he moved his family to Belpre, being a leading associate of the colony. During the short period he was permitted to live in that place, he was considered to be one of the most industrious, persevering, and thoroughly educated farmers in the county; clearing his land in the most rapid manner, fencing and cultivating it in the best style. In the famine of 1790 his family suffered, with the rest of their neighbors, for wholesome bread-stuff. When the war broke out in 1791, he was one of the most active and resolute men in planning and erecting the fortified village called Farmers' Castle, in which they all resided during the first two years of the war. In making the arrangements for the defense and military government of the garrison, he was the leading man; and the command was, by unanimous consent, given to him, as the most experienced in warlike matters. In the winter of 1793 the place had become too strait for the numerous families congregated within its walls, and it was decided to erect two additional stockades; one a mile and a half below, on Maj. Goodale's farm, and one on Capt. Stone's land, just below the mouth of the Little Kanawha, called the "Upper Settlement."

He had been but a week in his new garrison, when the colony met with the most serious loss it had yet sustained from their Indian enemies, in the captivity and death of Maj. Goodale. On the first day of March, 1793, he was at work in a clearing on his farm, distant about forty or fifty rods from the garrison, hauling rail timber with a yoke of oxen. It lay back of the first bottom, on the edge of the plain, in open view of the station. An Irishman, named John Magee, was at work, grubbing or digging out the roots of the bushes and email trees, on the slope of the plain, as it descends on to the bottom, but out of sight of Maj. Goodale. The Indians made so little noise in their assault, that John did not hear them. The first notice of this disaster was the view of the oxen seen from the garrison, standing quietly in the field, with no one near them. After an hour or more they were observed to be still in the same place, when suspicion arose that some disaster had happened to Mr. Goodale. John was still busy at his work, unconscious of any alarm, when one of the men sent up from the garrison, passed him to inquire what was the matter. In the edge of the woods there was a thin layer of snow, on which the messenger discovered several moccasin tracks. It was now apparent that Indians had been there, and taken him prisoner, as no blood was seen on the ground. A small party followed the trail some distance, but soon lost it. The following day a larger body of men, with some of the Rangers, were sent in pursuit, but returned without making any discovery. The Ohio River at this time, with many of the smaller streams, was at nearly full banks, and less danger was apprehended on that account; it was also rather early in the season for Indians to approach the settlements. The uncertainty of his condition left room for the imagination to fancy everything horrible in his fate; more terrible to bear, than the actual knowledge of his death.

Great was the distress of Mrs. Goodale and the children, overwhelmed with this unexpected calamity. His loss threw a deep gloom over the whole community, as no man was so highly valued amongst them, neither was there any one whose council and influence were equally prized by the settlement. He was, in fact, the life and soul of this isolated community, and left a vacancy that none of his companions could fill. One of the early colonists thus speaks of him: *"His memory was for many years fresh and green in the hearts of his cotemporary pioneers, now all passed away, and is still cherished with respect and affection by their descendants."*

(Judge Barker's notes.)

So greatly depressed were the inhabitants at his loss, that they awoke with new feelings in regard to their dangerous position on the outer verge of civilization. While he was living amongst them a certain degree of safety was felt, that vanished at his loss.

On the 14th of March they forwarded a petition to Gen. Washington, whom they regarded with parental veneration, a copy of which has been preserved, setting forth their exposed situation and losses by the Indians. It is stated that six of their number have been killed, besides the recent loss of Maj. Goodale; that one-third of their cattle, and produce of their lands, had been destroyed by the Indians, and they were fearful of a total breaking up of the settlement, unless the government afforded them a larger number of men for protection, their usual United States guard being only a Corporal and four Privates, detailed from the post at Marietta. The numbers of the settlers at the three stations were fifty-two men, and one hundred and forty-nine women and children.

At the treaty of Greenville, in 1795, when the captives were given up by the Indians, some intelligence was obtained of nearly all the persons taken prisoners from this part of the territory, but none of the fate of Maj. Goodale. A deep mystery seemed to hang over his destiny, never to be revealed. At length, about the year 1799, Col. Forrest Meeker, since a citizen of Delaware County, Ohio, and well acquainted with the family of Maj. Goodale, and the circumstances of this event, when at Detroit, fell in company with three Indians, who related to him the particulars of their taking a man prisoner at Belpre, in the spring of 1793. Their description of his person left no doubt on the mind of Col. Meeker, of its being Maj. Goodale. They stated that a party of eight Indians was watching the settlement for mischief; and as they lay concealed on the side of the hill back of the plain, they heard a man driving, or talking to his oxen, as they expressed it. After carefully examining his movements, they saw him leave his work and go down to the garrison, in the middle of the day. Knowing that he would return soon, they secreted themselves in the edge of the woods, and while he was occupied with his work, sprang out and seized upon him, before he was aware of their presence, or could make any defense, threatening him with death if he made a noise or resisted. After securing him with thongs, they commenced a hasty retreat, intending to take him to Detroit and get a large ransom for him. Somewhere on the Miami, or at Sandusky, he fell sick and could not travel, and that he finally died of this sickness. A Mrs. Whitaker, the wife of an Indian trader at Lower Sandusky, has since related the same fact. She says the Indians left him at her house, where he died of a disease like the pleurisy, without having received any very ill usage from his captors, other than the means necessary to prevent his escape. This is probably a correct account of his fate; and although his death was a melancholy one, amongst strangers, in captivity, and far away from the sympathy and care of his friends, yet it is a relief to know that he did not perish at the stake, nor by the tomahawk of the savages.

Chapter XXII
MAJOR ROBERT BRADFORD

The Battle of Bunker Hill

Maj. Robert Bradford was born in old Plymouth, Mass., in the year 1750. He was a lineal descendant of Gov. Bradford, of about the fifth remove. His wife was Kezia Little, the daughter of Capt. Nathaniel Little, of Kingston, Plymouth County.

He entered early, and with all his heart, into the service of his country during the Revolutionary War, and for the larger portion of that period commanded a company of light-infantry. His military life commenced at the Battle of Bunker Hill, and ended with the capture of Cornwallis at Yorktown, being actually engaged in nearly all the pitched battles fought in the eastern and middle states. With many others of the American Officers, he received the gift of an elegant sword, from the Marquis Lafayette, as a mark of his esteem, which yet remains in the hands of his only surviving son, O. L. Bradford, of Wood County, Va.

He also has in his possession, as family relics, some of the old furniture that came over in the Mayflower. Amongst them was a pair of hand-irons, one only now being preserved; the other was destroyed accidentally a few years since. Being of an ardent temperament, and ambitious to excel in military exercises, and to do his whole duty, Lafayette one clay witnessed the exactness of the evolutions of his company, and spoke in the warmest terms of their merits. When he was in Marietta, in the year 1826, he inquired particularly after Maj. Bradford; and when told that he was dead, he expressed his regret with much feeling. The lapse of more than forty years had consigned the larger portion of his old comrades to their graves, and his inquiries after his Revolutionary associates, were often answered with that short and melancholy phrase, *"He is dead!"*

At the close of the war he received an honorable discharge, and the brevet rank of Major. With others of his brother officers, he suffered great loss by the depreciation of the United States securities, and the worthlessness of the paper currency, in which his long and arduous services were paid. But the main object of his taking up arms was secured, the liberty of his country, which he lived to enjoy for many years.

When the Ohio Company was formed, he became an associate, and moved his family to Marietta, in the year 1788. In 1789 he joined the band of old officers who settled Belpre, where he suffered the privations of famine, and the dangers of the rifle and scalping-knife of the Indians, having several narrow escapes from these wily sons of the forest. During the prevalence of the putrid sore throat in 1792, he suffered a greater loss of children than any other family. Out of four or five, all died but one, with that disease.

In 1794, during the Indian War, he went out into the Indian country, about eighty miles from the settlements, in company with Griffin Greene, and others, to discover the site of the Scioto Salt Springs, of which vague rumors had been heard from the reports of white prisoners. After several days' search, they were found by following the Indian and buffalo paths which led to them and by long use had been worn to a depth of more than a foot, for several miles in extent. Another indication was the remains of the fires, where the squaws had recently boiled the brine collected from a cavity in the rock, cut with their tomahawks, in the bed of the creek, and now full of saline water. On their return, they narrowly escaped pursuit from a large party of Indians who came in sight on the hank of the river, a few minutes after their boat had left the shore.

Mr. Bradford and the inmates of Farmers' Castle never expected to see them again amongst the living.

He died in the year 1823, during the period of the great epidemic fever, which removed a number of the old soldiers, aged seventy-two years.

Maj. Bradford was a man of a warm heart, cheerful, lively temperament, and sound judgment. He ranked with the most worthy cultivators of the soil in the settlement. In person he was rather tall, erect, and active; strongly marked and bold features, indicative of courage and resolution; with the bearing of a soldier. He was a man whose virtues and name are worthy of preservation, amongst the defenders of an infant colony, and the pioneers of the valley of the Ohio.

Chapter XXIII
AARON WALDO PUTNAM

Aaron Waldo Putnam, the second son of Col Israel Putnam, was born in Pomfret, Connecticut on the 18th of April 1767.

During his boyhood and youth he assisted his father in cultivating the farm; the larger portion of that name being tillers of the earth. In the summer of 1788 when he was twenty-one years old, he accompanied his father on his long and tedious journey to Marietta, where the Ohio Company had just commenced a settlement. Colonel Putnam did not, at this time, move his family, taking only a few household goods, with agricultural implements and mechanical tools, the heavy load being transported by a team of two yoke of oxen, this patient but steady animal being well suited to the difficult passes of the mountains, and when at the journey's end less likely to be stolen by the Indians than horses.

In crossing the North River, at Fishkill, a serious accident happened, which served to display the coolness and presence of mind of the Putnam race, in cases of unexpected danger. The oxen were crossed in a flatboat, separate from the wagon, under the care of young Waldo. The river is here a mile wide, or more. A sudden gale of wind raised such a sea, that the boat filled and began to sink. In this extremity, seeing that the oxen must leave the boat, he unyoked them that they might swim more freely, putting the iron pins of the bows carefully into his pocket. Being unable to swim himself, he selected one of the most active of the oxen, and seizing him by the tail with one hand, and brandishing the whip with the other, he directed him, with his voice and an occasional touch of the lash, to the western shore, distant full half a mile. The wind and the tide carried them down about a hundred rods below the landing, where they reached the solid earth in safety, after a voyage of more than a mile. The other oxen having no encumbrance, made the land higher up. Finally all were collected without any loss of yokes, pins, or team.

The rest of the journey to the Ohio was accomplished without further accident, but with immense labor and fatigue in crossing the mountain ranges, by roads which, in these days, would be called impassable; but the persevering, bold men of that day, overcame all difficulties but absolute impossibilities. The following winter was passed in Campus Martius, and in making preparations to begin the settlement in Belpre, where they moved the following spring. Waldo Putnam's land fell to him in the Middle settlement, where he immediately commenced clearing and putting up a small log cabin. In the fall of 1790, his father, Col. Putnam, returned to Pomfret for his family. That winter the war began, and he did not return until after the peace.

In 1791, the settlers had to leave their houses and go into garrison, which they all united in building for their common defense. In this Mr. Putnam passed the time during the five years that followed, boarding in the family of Judge Loring, and performing the duties of a soldier in the defense of the castle, every able-bodied man and boy of sixteen years being enrolled. During this period he became acquainted with Miss Bathsheba Loring and was united to her in marriage amidst the dangers and perils of the savages who constantly watched the garrison for prey. In the spring of the year 1791, for the better security of their cattle from the Indians, the settlers ferried a part of them across the Ohio into Virginia, above the head of the island, where they roamed in safety.

On one of these occasions Mr. Putnam was in a flatboat with his Negro boy Kitt, who had been brought up in the family, and two other men. The cattle became alarmed, and running to one end of the flat, sunk it. They directly swam to the shore without his having an opportunity to seize one by the tail, as on North River, leaving him and the others, as the boat party rose to the surface, standing up to their breasts in the water. A small canoe was sent out to their rescue that carried but two persons. The black boy became much alarmed, as the water was up to his chin, and was eager to go first to the shore, but to this the two whites objected. Between the effects of the cold water and fear, Kitt's teeth chattered at a great rate, and he must have perished but for the stern rebukes and encouragement of Mr. Putnam, who bid him rise on to his toes, if the water came too near his mouth, and that he must not disgrace the family name by any symptoms of fear, although in the greatest extremity. At the third trip, Kitt, almost exhausted, was helped into the canoe with great difficulty by Mr. Putnam, who, now that the others had left him, felt quite safe, as the boat became more buoyant. He was finally relieved, after floating two or three miles, without any harm but the chilling effects of the cold water; and thus, by his calm, collected manner, were all saved, while in similar circumstances, many timid men have been drowned.

Mr. Putnam's improvement lay about half a mile below the garrison. Here the stacks of grain and fodder for the cattle were deposited, and every day during the winter months he had to visit the yard to feed them, and to milk the cows. In these trips, one or more men usually went with him for the same object, and for greater safety.

On one of these occasions, he had just sat down to milk when Nathaniel Little, who was with him and on the lookout, caught sight of an Indian in the edge of the clearing, in the attitude of firing at him. He instantly cried out *"Indians!"* At the alarming sound, Mr. Putnam sprang to one side as the gun cracked, and the ball struck the ground a few feet from him, passing across the spot where he sat. They instantly fled to the garrison and escaped, though hotly pursued by two or three other Indians.

At the second narrow escape, the year after, he was on the top of the stack, throwing down hay for the cattle. A small dog that they had with them began to growl and show signs of alarm. At this juncture, in the still calmness of a frosty morning, he heard the well-known click of a gun lock. Turning his head in the direction of the sound, he saw, at the distance of forty or fifty yards, an Indian behind the fence, in the act of re-cocking his gun, it having missed fire. He instantly sprang to the ground and ran. The Indian now fired, but missed his mark. With a tremendous yell, he gave chase, in which two others joined from the edge of the woods, trying to cut them off at a ravine they had to pass on a log. The fleetness of the whites disappointed their hopes, and the log was crossed before their pursuers reached it. A sally was made from the garrison on the report of the Indian's rifle, and a gun fired at them by a spirited little fellow named Bull; on which they retreated back to the fodder-yard, and out of sheer spite at their defeat, shot down a fine large yoke of oxen belonging to Capt. Benjamin Miles, from Brookfield, Mass. These cattle were the pride of the settlement, being eight feet in girt, and of proportionate height, vying with the best breeds of modern days.

Thus were the settlers in constant danger, and their lives in jeopardy, from a skulking, invisible foe, every time they left the walls of the garrison to follow the labors of the farm. In cultivating their crops, for the first years of the war, they worked in common, on each man's land, in parties of thirty or forty men, well armed; and in the autumn divided the crop amongst the laborers, in proportion to the days' work done, of which a regular account was kept by a stated clerk. Generally, before the laborers left the garrison, the Rangers made a circuit in the woods adjacent to the field or scene of their labor that day. With this precaution, it was seldom that Indians came very near the settlement, without leaving some signs of their approach, discoverable by the Rangers.

In the spring of the year 1793, after the green feed had become good in the forests, the oxen and cows of Mr. Putnam one night failed to come home as they usually did. The following morning he took his gun and sallied out into the woods in search of the absent animals. Expecting to find them in the adjacent hills, he did not ask the aid of any one to accompany him. After a little examination he discovered their trail, and followed it that day to Fort Harmar, distant fifteen miles from Farmers' Castle. Here he ascertained that they had been seen the evening before, and passed the night. In the morning he again discovered their trail up the Muskingum, and followed it all that day, alone in the woods, not choosing to ask anyone to risk his life with him in this dangerous enterprise. That evening he reached Tyler's Blockhouse, at Waterford, twenty miles from Marietta, where, to his joy, he found the strayed animals. Here he passed the second night, very uneasy at the alarm and distresses his young wife and friends would feel at his long absence. In the morning he took the precaution of removing the clapper from the bell of the leading ox, whose noisy tinkle might give notice of his approach to some watchful Indian, and commenced his return to the castle, across the country between the waters of Wolf Creek and Little Hocking, by an obscure trail frequented by the Rangers, and reached home, eighteen or twenty miles, just before dark. His long absence, three days and two nights, had caused him to be given up as a prisoner, or killed by the savages, his well known, daring character rendering the latter the most probable, and all the agonies of reality were suffered by his young and lovely wife, now the mother of one child, who, in the last sleepless night, had time to give full scope to her imagination, and picture all the cruelties practiced by the savages on their foes. His return was so unlooked for and unexpected, that he was like one risen again from the dead, and all sorrow was turned into joy at his providential preservation.

After numerous difficulties and dangers, borne for five years by the stern pioneers of Farmers' castle, with the greatest fortitude and equanimity, peace was at length established; and in 1796 Mr. Putnam was permitted to resume the clearing and cultivating his farm, unmolested; a privilege which none in these days can understand, or fairly appreciate. In a few years he had a large plantation under fence, and divided into fields, several acres of orchard, composed of the best varieties of the fruits of the New England and Middle states, sent out in 1795, by his brother Israel, who selected them with great care, and packed them with bees-wax, so that few, if any of the scions failed to grow. A young man named Waldo, and a relative, brought them over the mountains on horseback, in a large pair of saddlebags. Fruit trees in the virgin soil of the Ohio bottoms, grew with astonishing rapidity, and in six or eight years were loaded with apples. The peach often produced the second year from the pit, bearing fruit of a size and quality not now seen in Ohio. The depredations of the peach insect were unknown for more than twenty years, and the tree flourished and grew, undisturbed by the yellows or any other enemy. Before temperance societies were known, large orchards of fifteen or twenty acres were devoted to the manufacture of peach brandy, which bore a liberal price on the borders of the Mississippi, and was an article of export. As early as 1802, or 1803, the log cabins of several of the farmers at Belpre, were abandoned, and large, commodious houses of wood or brick, built in their place. Mr.

Putnam was one of the first to make improvements of this kind; and his capacious, white house, surrounded by orchards, on the margin of the plain, or second bottom, became a conspicuous and beautiful object to travelers on the *"Belle Riviere,"* who saw little else but the wilderness and the log huts of the new settlers, from Pittsburg to Cincinnati. Belpre, at this period, was like an oasis in the desert, the only spot where the eye could rest with delight. A thriving dairy was added to his other operations, composed of the cows raised from his father's famous Harlem breed, and celebrated for their rich milk. A numerous family of boys and girls grew up around him, and everything prospered under his wise and thrifty administration. After Mr. Blennerhassett settled on the island, he became one of his most intimate and useful friends, giving him much valuable information in the management of his new and untried farming operations. The genteel, easy manners, and beautiful person of Mrs. Putnam early attracted the attention of Madam Blennerhassett, and she became one of her most intimate associates, visiting each other with the familiarity of sisters. When this unfortunate woman, after the flight of her husband, in December, 1806, left the island in the midst of winter, he was the last to visit her in the boat, and furnished her with many necessaries, to make her voyage comfortable, denied her by the military posse from Wood County, who had taken forcible possession of her house.

Mr. Putnam and his wife both died in the fatal epidemic of 1822, aged forty-five years, in the midst of his usefulness.

In person he was of a medium size, with dark, expressive eyes, and a countenance beaming with intelligence and kind feelings. For public stations he had little inclination, the highest post being a Major in the militia. His delight was centered in his domestic relations, and in his farm. The elder son, William Pitt, born in Farmers' castle, possesses the homestead. His children, six of whom are now living, are settled at various points in the valley of the Mississippi, and rank with the most reputable of its citizens.

Chapter XXIV
CAPTAIN JONATHAN STONE

Capt. Jonathan Stone was born in New Braintree, Mass., in the year 1751. He was the son of a soldier, Francis Stone, who lost his life in the service of the King during the period of the colonial vassalage, while serving as a private soldier in the army of Gen. Wolfe, at the conquest of Quebec. Large numbers of the provincials sacrificed their lives for the good of their country during the period of the old French War, and especially at the siege of Havana in 1762. His father was killed when he was eight years old. After the death of his parent, his mother married a Mr. Pearson, by whom she had several children. Francis, the elder brother, inherited the patrimonial estate, and pursued the occupations of farming and tanning leather, which had been followed by his father before him.

The education of Jonathan extended only to reading, writing, and arithmetic, for which latter study he had probably a decided relish, as in after life he became an accomplished land surveyor. At a suitable age he was bound as an apprentice to his brother Francis. Connections of this kind between near relatives, are seldom fortunate or happy, and are much more likely to be agreeable with a stranger. Dr. Franklin has given us a sample of this kind, with its unpleasant results, in his apprenticeship to an elder brother. There seems to be a disposition on one side to act the tyrant, and on the other to render obedience with reluctance, as if the tender tie of relationship was severed when forced by the indenture of apprenticeship to perform certain duties, whether willing or not. In this they conflicted so roughly with each other, that before the expiration of the term of service, Jonathan left his brother, and entered on board a whale-ship at Newport, R. I., and was absent two years. What adventures he experienced in this voyage, are unknown; but, doubtless he learnt one salutary thing, that he must obey his new master, both in foul and fair weather; and that he could not leave the ship so easily as he did the house of his brother Francis.

Soon after his return, hostilities commenced between the colonies and Great Britain, and he entered the service of his country as a volunteer, being an Orderly-Sergeant in Col. Learned's Regiment. By his letters of the 29th of May, 1775, he was then at Roxbury with the army, besieging the town of Boston, then the headquarters of the King's troops in America. He seems to have possessed the true spirit of patriotism, for he says that himself and each one of the company to which he belonged, *"Are animated with the glorious cause in which they are engaged, hoping to deliver the country from vassalage and slavery, tyranny and oppression, that those blood-thirsty hirelings may not again be allowed to imbrue their filthy hands in the innocent blood of our neighbors,"* referring, no doubt, to the Lexington murders of the 19th of April, which had filled the whole country with the spirit of resistance and revenge. In August of this year he was sick with a fever, and he observes that the "camp distemper," as the dysentery was called, prevailed amongst the troops, and extended into the country towns, as was thought by contagion from the sick soldiers.

As a testimony of his bravery and good conduct during the year 1775, he was appointed a Lieutenant, for on the 11th of March, 1776, in writing to a female correspondent, he directs her to put *Lieut.,* after his name, in Col. Learned's Regiment. He also says, *"We have had a great deal of cannonading lately. Last Saturday night I was on Dorchester Heights and of our party, one surgeon and three soldiers were killed by one shot. They are now firing from Boston, and not less than thirty or forty cannon have been discharged since I have been writing this letter;"* and it was but a brief one. It was at this time that the celebrated fascine battery was erected by Col. Putnam, on the heights, that soon after forced the British to evacuate the town, as the American guns commanded the inner harbor, and endangered the shipping. In all these stirring scenes, Lieut. Stone took an active part, but the particular incidents are not noticed in his letters, and none of his old comrades are living to narrate them.

In the course of the year 1776 he was married to Susannah Mathews, of New Braintree, a young lady to whom he had for several years been attached. She was a daughter of Daniel Mathews, and her mother a sister of Gen. Rufus Putnam. She possessed an agreeable person, good, sound sense, plain, country manners, and industrious habits, being the child of a farmer. She displayed great energy of character, and after her husband's death, in 1801, conducted the affairs of a large dairy farm with judgment and profit.

On the 1st of January, 1777, Lieut. Stone was commissioned as Paymaster in Col. Putnam's Regiment. In August of that year he was with the army at Saratoga, and in September at Stillwater, quartering with Capt. Goodale, some of whose partisan exploits are noticed in his letters to his wife. He remained with the troops, partaking in all the dangers of the numerous engagements with the enemy, until the surrender of Burgoyne. In 1778 he was stationed at West Point, attached to Col. Putnam's Regiment. In 1779 he received a Lieutenant's commission in the Fifteenth Regiment, and in 1781 that of Captain, in which post he served to the close of the war. Several of these commissions are signed by John Hancock, in that strong, bold hand so conspicuous among the signatures of the Declaration of Independence. The seals attached are remarkable for having a huge rattlesnake figured over the cap of liberty, as if threatening his enemies with death, and to defend it against all opposers; the other emblems are implements of war. Under the new Constitution, of 1788, the United States selected the eagle to represent their dignity and sovereignty to the nations of the earth; and if less terrific, is a much more beautiful and noble emblem of the grandeur and magnanimity of the republic.

After the close of the war he returned to the peaceful occupations of agriculture, and purchased a farm, with the remains of his seven years' hard service in the cause of liberty, in the town of Brookfield, Mass., then the home of Gen. Putnam, with whom he had been intimate during this long period. Having become familiar with the science of field surveying, he was employed by Gen. Putnam, in 1786 and 1787, to assist him in surveying the lands of the state of Massachusetts, on the eastern shore of the District of Maine, then a part of her territory.

It was during the winter after the first year of this survey, or that of 1786, that he found, on his return, the adjacent counties deeply involved in an insurrection against their own government, commonly known as "Shays' Insurrection." It was one of the strangest anomalies in nature that a people who had just escaped from the thralldom of a tyrannical monarch, and had established a government of their own choosing, should so turn against it, and like the shark, or the alligator, devour their own progeny. So wide-spread and universal was this spirit of disaffection, that nearly one-third of the inhabitants of the Counties of Hampshire, Berkshire, and Worcester, were engaged in it, beside many in all other portions of the state. The saying of our Savior in regard to the reception of the gospel amongst mankind, in the division of families, households, and neighborhoods, was here exemplified, in relation to their political sentiments, the father being opposed to the son, and the brother against his brother. In the family of Capt. Stone, his brother Francis was a Shays man, and his wife's father was on the same side; while he enlisted, with all his powers of body and soul, in aid of the government, in opposition to the principles of the insurgents. In support of the laws and good order, were found nearly all the Officers of the Revolutionary army, and most of the well-informed and substantial citizens.

The cause of this unnatural outbreak seems to have arisen from the general oppression felt from the immense load of public and private debt, contracted during the war. The debt of the state amounted to more than five million dollars, and their portion of the national debt, to nearly as much more. During the war stay laws had been enacted to prevent the regular collection of debts, by which the amount had greatly accumulated. Paper-money, their hope and stay during the war, had run down to a mere nominal value, and state bonds had depreciated to a few shillings on the pound. What specie the French troops had left in the country, was gathered up by the merchants, and sent to Europe, to purchase merchandise, of which the states were woefully destitute at the close of the war. The country was so much exhausted by their long struggle, that they had no produce to send abroad to buy either goods or specie. Their fisheries and whaleries, which, before the war, had brought millions into the provinces, were ruined by that event, and had not yet revived.

In this wide-spread distress, a general clamor arose against the merchants, and against the courts; but more especially against the lawyers who executed the decrees of the courts, in collecting the debts due to the wealthier portion of the people. Private contracts, as early as 1782, had been made to give place to the payment of public taxes, from an idea that the scarcity of specie did not admit of the payment of both. The former, therefore, were made payable in other property than money, by an act called "The Tender Act." By this, executions issued for individual demands, might be satisfied by neat cattle and other personal property, on an appraisement by impartial men. This only suspended the payment of debts; as many would not collect under it, but waited for its expiration, in a year from its origin. It was the first signal for hostilities between creditors and debtors, the rich and the poor, the few and the many.

With such high-wrought notions of freedom, in a people just escaped from the fetters of the mother country, it was a difficult matter for their rulers to make laws that satisfied them. They, therefore, commenced holding conventions of the disaffected, in which they censured the conduct of their public officers. They voted the senate and the judicial courts to be grievances, and called for a revision of the constitution, which they had so lately formed, and was considered one of the best in the Union. Advantage was taken of these commotions to clamor against lawyers, and in their public addresses to say, that this class ought to be abolished, and none of them returned as representatives in the General Court for 1786. So far was this principle carried, that in the House of that year a bill was passed, *"to admit all persons of a moral character into the practice of the law, before the judicial courts;"* also to fix their fees, and oblige them to take an oath, previous to their pleading, not to receive more than the lawful fees, of their clients. When the bill came to the Senate, they laid it over, for examination, to the next Assembly. As this body had continued to act with wisdom and dignity, opposed to the wild, Jacobin principles of the disaffected people, they, at a convention of delegates from fifty towns in the county of Hampshire, held at Hatfield, on the 22d of August, published a statement of their grievances in twenty articles; the first of which was *"the existence of the Senate,"* as if this body was one cause of their troubles; fifth, *"the existence of the Courts of Common Pleas and General Sessions of the Peace;"* so that every man might do what was right in his own eyes. In the eighteenth they voted that their representatives be instructed to use their influence in the next General Court, to emit paper-money, subject to a depreciation, making it a tender in all payments, equal to silver and gold, to be issued in order to call in the state securities; thinking, no doubt, that an abundance of paper-money would relieve all their embarrassments. The state of Rhode Island was then trying this experiment, and its results only added to their troubles instead of relieving them.

The last of August, a body of more than a thousand of these misguided people, led on by designing demagogues, assembled at Northampton, took possession of the courthouse, and prevented the sitting of the court. The same thing was attempted at Worcester, and the courts adjourned without doing any business. Amidst these scenes of commotion and misrule, the inhabitants of Boston and several of the adjacent counties remained firm and true to their government, constitution, and laws; supporting their excellent Governor, Mr. Bowdoin, in all necessary measures for the public weal, and advancing money from their private resources, when the time came for calling out an armed force in aid of the laws.

A similar effort was made to put down the court at Springfield, by a body of men under Daniel Shays, but it was prevented by an assembly of six hundred well armed citizens, from the most respectable and influential inhabitants of the County of Hampshire, who took possession of the courthouse, and protected the Judges in their official duties, so that, although this was the stronghold of the insurrection, there was yet patriotism enough amongst them to save from utter ruin the forms of civil society.

The General Court met at Boston in October, and finding that the opposition to the courts of law, and the necessary restraints of government were increasing, rather than diminishing, they authorized the Governor to call out the militia for their protection. Accordingly, four thousand four hundred men were assembled and put under the command of Gen. Benjamin Lincoln, who marched to Worcester and protected the sitting of the court. Gen. Shepherd also collected nine hundred of the militia at Springfield, where was the arsenal of the state, and principal deposit of arms. On the 25th of January, Shays, with eleven hundred men, well armed, attempted to drive Gen. Shepherd from the town, but was defeated without any serious attack, by discharging one round of artillery amongst the insurgents, by which three men were killed and one badly wounded. Well knowing the badness of their cause, the main body broke and fled. They were pursued by the state troops a short distance, without overtaking them, and took up their quarters in the town of Hadley, from the inclemency of the weather, being in the midst of a severe winter. A company of men from Brookfield, amongst which was Capt. Stone, volunteered in putting down this rebellion, in which was engaged his brother Francis Stone, and some of the connections of his wife.

"The morning after the arrival of the army at Hadley, information was received that a small number of Gen. Shepherd's men had been captured at Southampton, and that the enemy's party still continued there. The Brookfield volunteers, consisting of fifty men, commanded by Col. Baldwin, were sent in sleighs with one hundred horses, under Col. Crafts, to pursue them. They were soon found to consist of eighty men with ten sleighs, and at twelve o'clock the same night, were overtaken at Middlefield.

They had quartered themselves in separate places, and about one-half of them, with one Ludington, their Captain, being lodged in a house together, were first surrounded. It was a singular circumstance that among the government's volunteers happened to be Gen. Tupper, who had lately commanded a Continental Regiment, in which Ludington had served as Corporal. The general, ignorant of the character of his enemy, summoned the party to surrender. How astonished was the Corporal at receiving the summons in a voice to which he had never dared to refuse obedience! A momentary explanation took place, which but lightened the General's commands. Resistance was no longer made, the doors were opened, and surrender was agreed upon. By this time the rest of the party had paraded under arms, at the distance of two hundred yards, where they were met by a number of men prepared for their reception. Both sides were on the point of firing, but upon an artful representation of the strength of the Government's troops, the insurgents laid down their arms, and fifty-nine prisoners, with nine sleigh loads of provisions, fell into the hands of the conquerors, who returned to the army on the day following."*

* Minot's History of the Rebellion.

The insurgents under Shays having taken a strong position on the hills of Pelham were summoned by Gen. Lincoln to lay down their arms, and subscribe the oath of allegiance to the state, or he should be obliged to attack them and apprehend their leaders, thus occasioning much bloodshed. To this they replied that they were willing to disband, but could not until they heard from the General Court on the matter, to which body they had sent a messenger with a petition.

"On the next day three of the insurgent leaders came to head-quarters with the following letter:

'The Honorable Gen. Lincoln:

Sir:

As the officers of the people, now convened in defense of their rights and privileges, have sent a petition to the General Court, for the sole purpose of accommodating our present unhappy affairs, we justly expect that hostilities may cease on both sides until we have a return from our Legislature. Your honor will, therefore, be pleased to give us an answer.

Per order of the Committee for Reconciliation,

> *Francis Stone, Chairman,*
> *Daniel Shays, Captain,*
> *Adam Wheeler.*

Pelham, January 31st, 1787.'"*

* *Minot's History of the Rebellion.*

To this communication, Lincoln returned a decided negative. The Legislature met on the 3d of February, and declared the commonwealth in a state of rebellion, approved the Governor's doings, and proceeded in earnest to put down the insurrection. The insurgents did not wait for the return of their messenger from Boston, but on the 3d of February, left the hills and marched to Pelham, where provisions were more plenty. They were pursued by Lincoln, through a tremendous snow-storm and excessive cold, to Petersham, a distance of thirty miles without halting, a march unequaled in the American annals. About one hundred and fifty were taken prisoners, and the rest dispersed over the country, some to their own homes, but the leaders and the most violent of their followers, fled from the state into New York and Vermont.

In both these states they found many abettors, and during the following spring, occasionally made inroads into the commonwealth for plunder and the capture of persons particularly obnoxious to them. It was late in the year before order was entirely restored in the disaffected portions of the state. The leniency of the government finally pardoned nearly or quite all who were concerned in the rebellion, and thus ended one of the most dangerous and singular insurrections that ever happened amongst a free people.

On the formation of the Ohio Company, Capt. Stone sold his farm in Brookfield, and invested the proceeds in two shares of the Ohio

Company lands, being about two thousand acres. To this he was doubtless the more readily induced from the ill conduct of several of his near connections in the late insurrection, and that he might still be favored with the society of such men as Gen. Putnam, Tupper and Goodale, with whom he had been so long and so intimately associated. In the fall of 1788, he visited Marietta and made preparations for the reception of his family. On the 4th of July, 1789, he left Brookfield with a wagon drawn by four oxen, containing his household goods and three children. Two cows were driven on ahead, while his wife traveled the whole distance on horseback to Simrel's Ferry, the western rendezvous for emigrants to Marietta. At Buffalo, or Charleston, he bartered one yoke of the oxen for provisions to support his family until he could raise a crop himself. He reached Belpre the 10th of December and put up a log-cabin on his lot, drawn the winter before, making the floors and doors from the planks of the boat in which he descended the river. His farm lay in the wide bottom, opposite and a little below the mouth of the Little Kanawha, and is now in the possession of his son, Col. John Stone. In the Indian War he moved his family into Farmers' Castle, and was one of the most active and efficient defenders of that garrison. In the spring of 1793, he, with several others, erected a palisade and several blockhouses on his own farm, and remained there until the peace of 1795. In 1792, he was appointed Treasurer of the County of Washington, by Winthrop Sargent, then acting as Governor of the Northwest Territory. After the peace he was employed by the Ohio Company, with Jeffery Mathewson, to complete the surveys of their lands, which was done in a masterly manner.

He died after a short illness, on the 25th of March, 1801, aged fifty years.

Capt. Stone was a man with a well-formed, agreeable person, gentlemanly manners and social habits. By his contemporaries he was highly esteemed, and his early death greatly lamented. A number of his children and grandchildren are living in Ohio, holding respectable stations in society.

Chapter XXV
COLONEL ROBERT OLIVER

Shay's Rebellion

Col. Robert Oliver was born in the vicinity of Boston, in the year 1738. His parents were emigrants from the north of Ireland. When he was quite young they moved to the town of Barre, Worcester County, Mass., and purchased a farm. His early years were devoted to agriculture, which gave him a hardy, vigorous frame, fitted to meet and sustain the fatigues of the camp. His education was good for that period, embracing reading, writing, and arithmetic, which, added to his naturally strong mind, prepared him for transacting any ordinary public business, as well as his own private affairs, in a creditable manner.

About the year 1775, he married Miss Molly Walker, by whom he had a large family of children.

At the commencement of the Revolution, he entered the service as a Lieutenant, marching with a company of Minutemen to Cambridge, where he was advanced to a Captaincy by the Provincial Government, in the Third Massachusetts Regiment. In 1777, he was commissioned as a Major, and in 1779, promoted to a Lieutenant-Colonel of the Tenth Regiment, and at the close of the war a Colonel by brevet. In the campaign which humbled Gen. Burgoyne, he was engaged in all the principal battles, and especially in storming the German lines on the 7th of October, under Col. Rufus Putnam, to whose regiment he was attached. He was celebrated as a disciplinarian, and for a time acted as Adjutant General of the Northern Division of the Army. Baron Steuben highly applauded his superior tact in the discipline and evolutions of the troops.

At the close of the war, having served through the whole period, he returned to his family and purchased a farm in the town of Conway, Mass. Nearly eight years of the most valuable period of his life were spent in the service of his country, for which he received payment in final settlement securities, which, in the market, were worth about ten cents on the dollar.

In the fall and winter of 1786-7, true to the cause of liberty and the country he had assisted in gaining its independence, he volunteered in suppressing the insurrection in Massachusetts, under Shays and others, which came nigh overturning the government, then barely established, in tumult and ruin.

The Ohio Company was soon after formed, and he invested the remains of his property in two shares of their land, and moved his family to Marietta in the summer of 1788, where he was united with many of his old friends and companions in arms. In 1789, in company with Maj. Haffield White and Capt. John Dodge, both Massachusetts men, he erected a saw and grist-mill on Wolf Creek, in Waterford, about a mile from its mouth. These were the first mills ever built in the present State of Ohio. The situation is very picturesque and beautiful, with solid limestone banks, overhanging cedar trees, and other evergreens. There is a considerable rapid, or falls, at this spot, making a suitable site for a mill. The drawing which accompanies this memoir is a good representation of the mills and scenery, with the log-cabins of the three proprietors as built in 1789.

In 1790, after the death of Gen. Parsons, he was elected a Director of the Ohio Company, and was a very active and efficient member of that important board. In forming the settlements at Wolf Creek and Waterford, he was one of the principal leaders, giving energy and zeal to these frontier establishments, and by his military knowledge, directing the best models for their works of defense against the attacks of the hostile tribes. So formidable and strong was the post at Waterford that the Indians did not venture a serious attack upon it, but only killed their cattle and such of the inhabitants as they found outside of its walls. After the destruction of the Big Bottom settlement, in January, 1791, and the war was fairly commenced, he removed his family to Marietta, where his services were constantly needed as a Director of the Company; who, for the first year or two of the war, provided the means, and were at all the expense of defending the country, so that their continual watchfulness was as much required as that of the civil government of a province in the time of actual war or invasion. Some estimate may be formed of their duties, when it is stated that they expended upwards of eleven thousand dollars of the company funds in providing for and protecting the colonists.

In the formation of the first territorial Legislature in 1798, he was elected a Representative from Washington County. Out of the assembled representatives, the Governor selected five men who were to act as a Legislative Council, performing the duties of a Senate. Col. Oliver was one of this number, and in company with Jacob Burnet, James Findlay, H. Vanderburg, and David Vance, was commissioned by John Adams, then President of the United States, on the 4th day of March, 1799. In 1800 he was elected President of the Council, and continued in that post until the formation of the state government in 1803. When the standing and character of the men who constituted the council is considered, it was no ordinary honor to be elected as their presiding officer.

Col. Oliver possessed a clear, discriminating mind, and was truly dignified in his manners; had a perfect command of his passions, and was very amiable in his intercourse with his associates. He had a good fund of anecdote, which he related in a very interesting manner.

After the close of the Indian War, he returned to his farm at the mills, where he resided until his death. He was appointed by Gov. St. Clair Lieutenant-Colonel of the First Regiment of Territorial Militia, and Colonel of the Second Regiment, in 1795. He also appointed him one of the Judges of the Court of Common Pleas in the same year, and made a very efficient magistrate. He was a man of great activity and usefulness, both as a civil and military officer. Soon after the territory became a state, the men whose eyes had grown dim, and their heads gray in their country's service, were *"laid upon the shelf,"* if they differed in political opinion from the ruling powers. Col. Oliver was a disciple of

Washington, and followed his political precepts; therefore he received no more favors from the government. The inhabitants of his township, however, thought him still a worthy man, and elected him a Justice of the Peace, and kept him in office as long as he lived.

In person, he was about five feet ten inches high, stoutly built, and commanding appearance; face full, mild, and bland, with a pleasant expression when in conversation with his friends, but severe and terrible to the vicious and undeserving. His head was finely formed, but early became bald. Once, at Chillicothe, in a convivial party, one of the company, an influential and noted man of that day, being rather full of wine, laid his hand familiarly and somewhat roughly on the bald head of the Colonel. With one of his stern looks he thus addressed him: *"General, you must not lay your hand on my bald pate, which has many times stood where you would not dare to show your face."*

In early life he became a professor of religion, and although his calling exposed him to the dissolute habits of an army, and was not calculated to promote his growth in grace, yet he was always a consistent follower of the Lord Jesus Christ, and at the formation of the first Congregational Church in Marietta, in 1796, he was a member, and remained an ornament to the profession of a Christian.

He died in May, 1810, aged seventy-two years.

The impress of his character still remains on the early settlement he formed, and it is hoped will long remain for their best good.

Chapter XXVI
MAJOR HAFFIELD WHITE

The Battle of Trenton

Maj. Haffield White was a native of Danvers, Massachusetts.

At the commencement of the war, on the 19th of April, 1775, by the attack of the British troops on the militia, at Lexington, and the destruction of the stores at Concord, he was an officer in a company of Minutemen. The news of that attack was spread through the country with great rapidity; and men who in the morning were thirty miles from the scene of action, were on the ground before night, in time to harass the jaded and retreating Britons, from their first inroad into the possessions of the Massachusetts yeomanry. The result of that day taught them to be cautious in venturing far beyond the cover of the guns of their navy, into the land of these modern Spartans. The alarm reached Danvers in time for Lieut. White, with the company of Minutemen, to reach the flanks of the flying enemy, and, from behind the stone walls, throw several destructive fires into the ranks of the British. His own men suffered considerably; losing eight killed out of the company. Soon after this affair he was commissioned as a Captain, and raised a company of men, which was among the most efficient and active in the service, especially at the Crossing of the Delaware, and Battle of Trenton, in December, 1761; many of them being sailors, and very useful in manning the boats to cross the army. He was with Gen. St. Clair in the retreat from Ticonderoga; and under Col. Francis fought manfully at the Battle of Hubbardston; thereby checking the pursuit of the British troops, and enabling the Americans to reach Stillwater, and form the nucleus of that army which soon after conquered Burgoyne, and turned the tide of conquest against our foes. He was engaged in many of the battles that preceded this overthrow, and thus shared in the glories and triumphs of Saratoga, on the 13th of October, 1777. At the time of the retreat from Ticonderoga, he was Paymaster of the Regiment, and in that disastrous affair lost a large sum of money, which was not allowed by the United States. When Col. Pickering took charge of the Commissary Department of the Army, being acquainted with the integrity and activity of Capt. White, living in the same town, he was selected for one of his assistants, and remained in that branch of the service until the close of the war, when he was made a Major.

At the formation of the Ohio Company, he became one of the proprietors, and was appointed, by the directors, commissary and conductor of their first detachment of pioneers, which left Danvers in December, 1787. On their arrival at Marietta, he was continued as their steward for the first year; after which that office was no longer needed. His son Peletiah was one of the forty-eight who landed from the "Mayflower" at Marietta, on the 7th of April. In 1789 he engaged with Col. Oliver and Capt. Dodge, in erecting mills on Wolf Creek. When the war with the Indians commenced, he left the mills, as they were much exposed to hostile attacks, and came to Marietta, where he remained until after the peace of 1795. He then resumed his possessions, a farm, near the mills, and lived with his son until his death.

In person Maj. White was below the medium size, but thickset and robust; very active, and brisk in his motions; prompt to execute any business on hand in the most expeditious manner; complexion florid, and sanguine temperament. He was a brave soldier, and a very useful and industrious citizen.

Chapter XXVII
DEAN TYLER

Dean Tyler, Esq., was a native of Haverhill, Mass., and liberally educated at one of the New England colleges. He possessed a brilliant mind, an agreeable person, and refined manners.

In early life he formed an attachment to a young lady, who returned it with equal affection. But the wayward course of lovers sometimes crosses all their purposes; a misunderstanding occurred, which induced Tyler to embark for Europe, to flee from that which had really become necessary to his happiness. He took passage in a letter of Marque for Bordeaux. On the voyage out and back, he met with some fighting, some storms, and had several narrow escapes. These incidents probably helped to cure him of his jealousy, or whatever it was that caused him to go on this adventure. He returned with a full determination to confess his fault, and unite himself with her whom he had so abruptly parted from. But it was too late; he had broken the heart of his loved one, and the first news he heard on landing, was, that she was dead—had died of a broken heart. The shock entirely overcame him; he was attacked with a violent illness, followed with delirium, and narrowly escaped that death he would willingly have suffered, could it atone for his error. His recovery was slow and tedious; and it was a long time before he could attend to any business.

As soon as he was able to travel, he joined the Ohio Company adventurers, then in the opening of their enterprise to occupy the great west, and redeem' it from the wilderness. He attached himself, in 1789, to the settlement of Waterford, and, with them, drew a donation lot of one hundred acres. He was a brave and active pioneer; exposing himself to danger on every occasion, and doing all he could for the benefit of the inhabitants. During the winter months, he taught school; and on the Sabbath officiated as Chaplain, reading the sermons of some able divine, and conducting the public devotions, which were regularly kept up during the period of the war, as well as subsequently.

As a man, he was much respected by the pioneers, and the garrison built for their protection, was called Fort Tyler. He never married, but continued a bachelor to the end of his days. His habits were rather studious and sedentary; except when danger threatened the inhabitants from an Indian attack, when he was alert and active. In his latter years he became rather intemperate, probably hoping to drown his melancholy reflections in the inebriating bowl. His name is still fondly cherished by the descendants of his pioneer companions.

Chapter XXVIII
CAPTAIN WILLIAM GRAY

The Attack at Stony Point

Capt. William Gray was born in Lynn, Mass., on the 26th of March, 1761.

Being of a warm, active temperament, and the struggle for independence occupying the thoughts and conversation of all around him, he became early inspired with the determination of doing all in his power to aid the cause of his country, and entered the service of the United States, as a private soldier, at the age of seventeen years, or in the year 1778, and served to the close of the war. At the attack on Stony Point, he had been promoted, for his good conduct, to a Lieutenant, and was among the first who scaled the walls of that fortress.

At the close of the war he returned to his home, and married Miss Mary Diamond, of Salem. His uncle, the rich merchant, William Gray, for whom he was named, lived at that time in Salem and from a humble situation in life, being bred a shoemaker, rose to be one of the richest merchants in Boston. He treated his nephew with great kindness; and for many years, even after he moved to Ohio, annually sent him a sum of money, sufficient to aid very materially in the support of his family. Soon after his marriage he resided in Danvers, where his two oldest children were born.

In the autumn of 1787 he joined the Ohio Company, and had the charge of one of the wagons that transported the first band of pioneers on to the waters of the Ohio. On this wagon was written, in large letters, *"For Ohio."* His family was left in Danvers, and did not come out until 1790, in company with Maj. Ezra Putnam, from the same place. He joined the settlement at Waterford, and when the war of 1791 broke out, was chosen Commander of the Garrison erected for its defense, called Fort Tyler. By his good conduct and prudence, this fortress was preserved unharmed, although several times in great jeopardy. The situation was a very exposed one, on the extreme frontier. On the head waters of the Muskingum, which washed its foundations, were seated numerous tribes and villages of the hostile Indians, who, at almost any season of the year, could embark their whole force in canoes, and in forty-eight hours land at the garrison. Their approach might have thus been made in the most secret manner, without even the knowledge of the Rangers, who constantly scoured the country, watching for signs of the Indians. But an overruling Providence diverted their attention to other quarters, and they passed the four years of war with but little loss of life, but much of property. Soon after the peace and men could till the earth in safety, he bought a farm near the present town of Beverly, and lived there, highly respected, until the time of his death, in July, 1812.

He was the father of ten children, nearly all of whom married, and their descendants are living in this county.

Chapter XXIX
COLONEL WILLIAM STACEY

Col. Stacey was a native of Massachusetts, and a proprietor in the Ohio Company. He came early to the Northwest Territory, and settled in Washington County.

In the forepart of his life he lived on the sea-coast, probably Salem, and was engaged in sea-faring business. Finding himself surrounded by a rapidly increasing family, he removed to New Salem, in the county of Hampshire, Mass., and entered on the life of a farmer. He was much respected by his fellow townsmen, and was promoted in the military service. In Barber's Historical Sketches of Massachusetts, is the following notice of Col. Stacey, copied from the Barre Gazette:

"The news of the Battle of Lexington flew through New England like wild-fire. The swift horseman with his red flag proclaimed it in every village, and made the stirring call upon the patriots to move forward in defense of the rights so ruthlessly invaded, and now sealed with the martyrs' blood. Putnam, it will be recollected, left his plow in the furrow, and led his gallant band to Cambridge. Such instances of promptness and devotion were not rare. We love the following instance of the display of fervid patriotism, from an eye witness, one of those valued relics of the band of '76, whom now a grateful nation delights to honor.

When the intelligence reached New Salem, in this state, the people were hastily assembled on the village green by the notes of alarm. Every man came with his gun and other preparations for a short march. The militia of the town was then divided into two companies, one of which was commanded by a Capt. G. This company was paraded before much consultation had been held on the proper steps to be taken in the emergency, and while determination was expressed on almost every countenance, the men stood silently leaning on their muskets, awaiting the movement of the spirit in the officers. The Captain was supposed to be tinctured with Toryism, and his present indecision and backwardness were ample proofs, if not of his attachment to royalty, at least of his unfitness to lead a patriot band. Some murmurs began to be heard, when the First Lieutenant, William Stacey, stepped out of the line, took off his

*hat, and addressed them. He was of stout heart, but of few words.
Pulling his commission from his pocket, he said, "Fellow soldiers, I
don't know exactly how it is with the rest of you, but for one, I will no
longer serve a king that murders my own countrymen;' and tearing the
paper in a hundred pieces, he trod them under his feet. Sober as were the
people by habit and natural disposition, they could not refrain from a
loud huzza, as he stepped back into the ranks. Capt. G still faltered, and
made a feeble endeavor to restore order, but they heeded him as little as
the wind. The company was summarily disbanded, and reorganization
took place on the spot. The gallant Stacey was unanimously chosen
Captain, and with a prouder commission than was ever borne on
parchment, he led a small but resolute band to Cambridge. He continued
in service during the war, reaching, before its close, the rank of
Lieutenant-Colonel, under the command of Putnam."*

In 1778, Capt. Stacey had risen by his merits to the rank of a
Lieutenant-Colonel, not in Col. Putnam's Regiment, but in Col. Ichabod
Alden's, of the Massachusetts Line.

The first of July, that year, the Indians and Tories sacked and
destroyed the settlement of Wyoming, on the Susquehanna River. They
now threatened, and had partly depopulated, the settlement of Cherry
Valley, which lies on the head waters of the eastern branch of that
stream, fifty-two miles northwest of Albany, in the present County of
Otsego, but then Tryon County, N. Y. It was a beautiful valley, noted for
its fertility and picturesque scenery, being first settled as early as 1739,
but greatly harassed by the Tories, who formed nearly half of the
inhabitants of that county, and were friends to the crown, to which they
were partly induced from the popularity and high standing of Sir Guy
Johnson, who lived in the northern part of the county, and probably from
respect to the Governor of the state while under the king, for whom it
was named. Late in the summer of 1778, Col. Alden's regiment was
ordered up to Cherry Valley, for the protection of the inhabitants. A
stockaded garrison had been previously built around their little church,
and the regiment of about two hundred men took possession of it. Being
rather straitened for quarters, several of the officers lodged at the houses
of the adjacent inhabitants. Alden and Stacey, with a small guard of
soldiers, quartered in the house of a Mr. Wells, not more than a quarter

of a mile from the garrison. On the 6th of November, Col. Alden received a letter from Fort Schuyler, now in Oneida County, distant about forty miles northwest, near the head of the Mohawk, saying that an Oneida Indian, whose tribe was friendly to the United States, had told them that the Indians and Tories, under a son of Col. Butler, were assembling on the Tioga River, a northerly branch of the Susquehanna, which passes through the country of the Seneca Indians, for the purpose of attacking the fort and settlement of Cherry Valley. Butler had been a prisoner with the Americans, and confined in Albany jail, a short time before, but had escaped, and was now seeking revenge. Being notified of this intended attack, he sent out scouting parties to watch their approach, although he did not actually apprehend any danger, even after this timely warning. The inhabitants, better aware of their peril, made application to the Commander to be admitted within the fort, but as it was only large enough for his own men, he declined, saying it would be time enough when they were certain of the approach of the enemy. Being unacquainted with Indian warfare, he did not take shelter within the fort himself. The scout, which was sent down that branch of the river which waters the valley, having kindled a fire, were surprised in their camp and taken prisoners, so that they could not give the alarm of the advance of the Indians as he had expected. From these prisoners, Butler and Brant learned the condition of the settlement and the houses where the officers slept, being themselves familiar and acquainted in the valley before the war.

Early on the morning of the 11th of November, an army of five hundred Indians and two hundred Tories entered the settlement undiscovered, and began the attack on the scattered dwellings near the fort. Before they reached Wells', the house where he quartered, a man on horseback gave notice of their approach. He was still persuaded there was only a small body of Indians, but on their coming in sight he directly ran for the fort, closely pursued by an Indian who, after calling on him to surrender, which he refused, snapping his pistol at him, he threw his tomahawk, striking him on the head and felling him to the ground. The Indian then scalped him, *"and thus he was the first to suffer from his criminal neglect."** Before Col. Stacey could leave the house, it was surrounded by the Indians, and he was taken prisoner with a few of the guard, while all the women and children were killed. It was a damp, rainy morning, and the powder of the out-door guards was wet, so that their arms were useless, which was one reason of there being so little resistance. After a feeble attack on the fort, they departed with their scalps and prisoners, killing about forty of the inhabitants. Joseph Brant, who commanded the Indians, saved the lives of a number of families, making them prisoners, while Butler and the Tories under his command, spared very few that fell into their hands.

*Annals of Tryon County

The Indians, in their return to their own country on the Genesee River, passed down the Cherry Valley branch of the Susquehanna to its junction with the Tioga Fork, and up that stream over to the Seneca Lake, and onward to an Indian town that stood near the present beautiful village of Geneva, distant more than two hundred miles, by the route they traveled, from Cherry Valley. Here the revengeful savages who had taken Col. Stacey prisoner, after holding a council, decided on burning him at the stake. It has for ages been the practice of the Indians in their attacks, to take some prisoners for this purpose, that the young Indians and squaws may share in their revenge on their enemies. Being devoted to this dreadful death, he was tied to the stake, the fire kindled, and he thought his last hour was come. Seeing the noble-minded Brant in the throng, and having probably heard that he was a Freemason, he made the well known sign of the fraternity, which was instantly recognized by the quick eye of the Indian. His influence was almost unlimited amongst the northern tribes of New York, and he persuaded them to release their victim, thus adding one more to the number of lives saved by his humanity.

Soon after this he was adopted into an Indian family. At the time of the invasion of the country of the Senecas in 1779, by Gen. Sullivan, when their villages, orchards, and crops of corn, were totally destroyed, many of them retreated to Fort Niagara, then in the hands of the British. Amongst others, Col. Stacey was taken there by the family to which he was attached. While here, Mr. Campbell, the author of the history of Tryon County, from whom some of these events are copied, says, "Lieut. Col. Stacey, who had been taken prisoner at Cherry Valley, was also at the fort. Molly Brant, the sister of Joseph, and former mistress of Sir William Johnson, had, from some cause, a deadly hostility to him. She resorted to the Indian method of dreaming. She told Col. Butler that she dreamed she had the Yankee's head, and that she and the Indians were kicking it about the fort. Col. Butler ordered a small keg of rum to be painted and given to her. This, for a short time, appeased her, but she dreamed a second time that she had the Yankee's head, with his hat on, and she and the Indians kicked it about the fort for a football. Col. Butler ordered another keg of rum to be given to her, and then told her, decidedly, that Col. Stacey should not be given up to the Indians. Apart from this circumstance, I know nothing disreputable to Molly Brant. On the contrary, she appears to have had just views of her duties. She was careful of the education of her children, and some of them were respectably married.

Col. Stacey remained a prisoner over four years, and was then exchanged. He returned to his home in New Salem, and in 1789 moved with his family, consisting of his wife, five sons, and a son-in-law, with their families, to the Ohio, and settled in Marietta. Two of his sons, John and Philemon, joined the settlement in Big Bottom, formed in the fall of 1790. The 2d of January, following, the blockhouse was taken by surprise, and fourteen of the inmates were killed; amongst the slain was his son John, while Philemon, a lad of sixteen years, was taken prisoner, and died in captivity. Col. Stacey feeling anxious for the safety of the new settlement, and the welfare of his sons, visited the post the day before the attack; and although the Indians pretended to be friendly, well knowing their wiles from former experience, gave the young men strict orders to keep a regular guard, and strongly bar the door of the house at sunset, and not open it again until sunrise, even although it was the depth of winter. They neglected his advice, and perished. During the war he lived in a small block-house, at the Point in Marietta, on the bank of the Ohio, and is figured in the drawing of that place, in the preceding volume. He had the charge of overseeing the construction of these works in January, 1791. His remaining sons and son-in-law settled in this county, and left a numerous posterity, who still resides here. His youngest son, Gideon, settled in New Orleans, and established a ferry across Lake Pontchartrain, and was there lost.

After the death of his first wife, Col. Stacey married Mrs. Sheffield, a widow lady from Rhode Island, and owned four shares of land in the Ohio Company. She was the mother of the wife of Maj. Zeigler, Mr.

Charles Green, and Isaac Pierce, Esq., a woman of highly cultivated mind, lady-like manners, and agreeable person.

He died in Marietta, in the year 1804, and was a man greatly esteemed for his many excellent qualities.

Chapter XXX

THE FIRST SETTLEMENT OF ATHENS COUNTY

WITH

BIOGRAPHICAL NOTICES OF SOME OF THE EARLY SETTLERS

BY EPHRAIM CUTLER, ESQ.

The Indian war, which was brought to a close by the Treaty of Greenville, in August, 1795, had caused an almost entire stop to the wave of population, which, by the settlement of Marietta and Cincinnati, had begun to swell and move. It was not until 1797 and 1798 that the symptoms of what has astonished the whole civilized world, began again to appear in the west. In those years, that kind of boats to which the pioneers gave the cognomen of broadhorns were seen continually floating down the Ohio. Many of these contained the families of persons of strong, adventurous minds, and hardy frames, but generally of little or no property. They of course sought for opportunities to locate themselves on lands that they could obtain on easy terms.

In the early part of 1797, Marietta was crowded with this kind of population, seeking for some place to make a home. It is well known that in the purchase of the Ohio Company's lands, they made it a condition that two townships of land should be conveyed which were to be forever for the use and benefit of a university. These lands were in the trust of the directors of the Ohio Company, and were thus to remain until they should resign that trust to the future Legislature. Gen. Putnam, who was the Superintendent of the surveys of the land of the Ohio Company, had these two townships surveyed into sections in 1796. The trustees were convinced that it would be good policy to early make these lands productive, and thus provide a fund to commence an institution, which they foresaw would soon be much needed, and if established, promised most important results. They believed that the public interest would be served by encouraging substantial men to occupy these lands, make improvements, and wait until a more permanent title could be made to them by an act of Legislature, which, it was expected, would soon (as was the case,) be acquired as the second step provided for by the ordinance of 1789, providing for the government of the territory northwest of the river Ohio.

These lands, with a large surrounding region, were one of the most favorite portions of the hunting ground which the Indians had surrendered in their several treaties; and the treaty of 1795 seemed to close the last fond hope of ever after enjoying them. Yet the hunters living about Sandusky, and on the different branches of the Muskingum, continued not only to visit there, but until the winter before the last war with Great Britain commenced, they were in large parties during the hunting season, coursing through that extensive range of country, comprising the lands watered by the Raccoon, Monday, Sunday Creeks, and the head of Federal Creek. It was here they formerly found the buffalo, the elk, and the bear. The buffalo and elk were not exterminated until the year 1800. The bear continued in considerable abundance until their last great hunt in the winter of 1810-11. That winter was a favorable season for them to effect the object they seemed to have in view, which was to destroy the game, the weather being cold, with several falls of snow. The carcasses of many deer were found in the woods bordering the settlements in Washington and Athens Counties, which appeared to be wantonly destroyed by the savages. A young buffalo, believed to be the last seen in this part of the country, was taken a few miles west of Athens, on a branch of Raccoon, in the spring of 1799, brought to the settlement, and reared by a domestic cow. The summer after it was two years old, it was taken by its owner over the mountains, and for a considerable time exhibited from place to place. At first it was easily managed, but at length became ungovernable, and gored its owner, who died of the wounds, and the animal was then killed.

Gen. Putnam probably would not, at this time, have encouraged the commencement of this settlement, had he not foreseen that these lands would soon be occupied, and that it was important, in order to establish a peaceable and respectable settlement, to select, from the emigrants already at Marietta, men possessing firmness of character, courage, and sound discretion. He accordingly gave every facility in his power, relating to the surveys, &c, to Capt. Silas Bingham, Judge Alvin Bingham, John Wilkins, Esq., Capt. John Chandler, John Harris, Robert Lindsey, Jonathan Watkins, Moses Hewitt, Isaac Barker, William Harper, Barak, Edmond and William Dorr, and Dr. Eliphaz Perkins. Some of these individuals, with their families, and some others, made their way up the Hockhocking, in pirogues, early in the spring of 1797;

and were the first in felling the interminable forest, and to erect dwellings. Immediately after the settlement commenced, as was anticipated, large numbers came to take possession of these lands, many of whom seemed disposed to practice the principle that, might makes right; this soon occasioned a state of things which required much courage and prudence to counteract. Alvin Bingham was commissioned a Magistrate, and Silas was appointed a Deputy-Sheriff. The cases of taking forcible possession of the land and improvements had commenced, and it required no common share of prudence and firmness to keep the peace, and give an effectual check to these outrages. Add to these, a Canadian Frenchman, by the name of Menour, who had resided with the Indians, was in the habit of stealing horses from the savages, and bringing them into the settlement, on the college lands, where he had men ready to take them and convey them away to some settled region, and dispose of them. The Indians found no difficulty in tracing their horses to this point, but could follow them no further. They, of course with great justice, made their complaints. Menour had collected around him quite a number who were well armed, and showed a determination to defend him. Judge Bingham issued a warrant for his apprehension, and entrusted it with Silas, who made an attempt to perform his duty, but found quite a party of desperate characters in arms to protect him. He very adroitly retired; giving out the idea that he should not venture to arrest him, unless he could obtain assistance from Marietta. Menour's house was a strong building for those times; the only access to the chamber was a small opening in the gable-end. Menour and his wife, who used it for a lodging room, ascended a ladder, then drew it up after them, and closed the aperture. The lower part of the house was, at this time, occupied by a large party of desperate men, horse thieves, and outlaws, who slept on their rifles, and were ready at any moment to do their leader's bidding. In the meantime, Bingham, with the utmost secrecy and dispatch, collected the well-disposed citizens of Athens and Ames, and proceeded that night to make the arrest. The night was very dark, and they approached and surrounded the house, without being discovered by its inmates. E. Cutler burst open the door and the citizens rushed in upon the desperadoes, and secured them before they were fairly awake. Robert Lindsey and Edmond Dorr broke into the opening that formed the entrance to the chamber, and captured Menour; who was taken to Marietta, where he was convicted of the offense, on the testimony of the Indians, and punished; he, however, afterward went to Sandusky, and it was said, was there killed by an Indian.

Judge Bingham was not lax in punishing breaches of the peace. Some cases of forcible entry and detainer took place, which required a jury and two magistrates to decide them; and at this time there were but two in this portion of the country, Judges Bingham and Cutler. These cases sometimes showed a threatening aspect; a certain number of disorderly persons were always ready to attend such courts. At one of these trials the leaders of this class came forward, and threatened violence; the Magistrates ordered them to leave the room; they retired; but expressed an intention to put a stop to such courts. The Magistrates issued warrants, and ordered the Sheriff to apprehend them immediately, and take them to Marietta. He was not slow in arresting them. It is not easy to conceive of men more frightened; the idea of being taken to Marietta, to be tried by a court that had established its character for firmness and strict justice, filled them with terror. Silas Bingham, (who, to great shrewdness and dispatch in business, united an unconquerable love of fun,) did nothing to allay their fears, but told them the better way would be to come into court, and, on their knees, ask forgiveness, and promise amendment. The prominent man of the offending party replied, that *"it was too bad to be compelled to kneel down, and ask forgiveness of two Buckeye justices;"* but he would submit rather than be taken to Marietta. This anecdote was often repeated by the facetious Col. Sproat and Bingham, and might have aided in fixing the cognomen on the state.

The Binghams were natives of Litchfield County, Conn., and although quite young, they were volunteers at the capture of Ticonderoga, by Ethan Allen, in 1775. Silas was with the army which invaded Canada, and both served most of the time during the Revolutionary War. Judge Bingham was a substantial, clear-headed man, sober and dignified in his manners, stern and uncompromising in his sense of right. Silas was full of anecdote and humor, social and kind in his feelings, a man of excellent sense, and a terror to evil doers. The promptness with which these men acted in enforcing the laws and in protecting the rights of the weak, had the effect to rid the settlement of a large portion of this disorderly population; and Athens, many years ago, established its character as an orderly and respectable community, embracing as much intelligence and refinement as any other town of equal size. For this happy result, it was in no small degree indebted to Dr. Eliphaz Perkins. Few men were better calculated to introduce a mild and refined state of manners and feelings. He was a native of Norwich, Conn., born in 1753, graduated at an eastern college, and removed to Athens in 1800, the time when a disposition to trample on the laws prevailed. The services of a physician were greatly needed in the settlement, and his arrival was hailed with joy. By his attention to the sick, skill in his profession, and by his urbanity and kindness, he at once became popular. The influence thus acquired, he exerted in the most salutary and unostentatious manner, while he frowned upon every breach of law and decorum. His own deportment was a bright and living example of purity and benevolence. He was truly a patron of learning. He did much to establish and sustain common schools in that region. He contributed liberally to the Ohio University, was early appointed a trustee, and for many years was Treasurer of the institution. He died, much lamented, on the 29th of April, 1828, in the lively exercise of that Christian faith of which he had been many years a professor. His descendants are numerous and highly respectable; seven of them have graduated at the Ohio University.

Soon after the settlement of Athens and Ames, the venerable Elder Quinn, then a young man, found his way through the wilderness, with little more than blazed trees to guide his steps, enduring like a true soldier of the cross, extreme toil and privation. He may be regarded as the founder of the Methodist Church in that county.

Chapter XXXI
MAJOR JERVIS CUTLER

Jervis Cutler
1768 - 1844

Maj. Jervis Cutler was the son of the Rev. Manasseh Cutler, who for fifty-two years was pastor of the Congregational Church in Hamilton, Mass. He was also the negotiator with Congress in the year 1787, for the purchase of a million and a half of acres for the Ohio Company, by means of which the settlement of the now great State of Ohio was effected. From the year 1800 to 1804, Dr. Cutler was a representative in Congress from the Lynn district in Massachusetts.

Maj. Cutler was born at Edgerton, on Martha's Vineyard, in the year 1768. Being educated for the mercantile business, he was placed, at the age of sixteen years, under the care of Capt. David Pearce, of Gloucester, who sent him on a voyage to Havre de Grace, in France. If the father deserves the credit of paving the way for the settlement of this then savage wilderness, the son is entitled to be considered a pioneer of the settlement itself. In the year 1788, when only nineteen years old, he joined the little band of forty-eight, who emigrated from New England, under Gen. Rufus Putnam, and pitched their tents at Marietta, in the center of the Indian country. He has been often heard to say that he was the first to leap on shore at the mouth of the Muskingum, on the seventh of April, and actually cut the first tree to make a clearing for a habitation in the new settlement. Of that little band of hardy pioneers, not more than one or two are now living.* *American Almanac, 1845.

The following summer he taught a school about four miles from Simrel's Ferry, on the Youghiogheny River, and was there when his father made his visit to Marietta in August, 1788. In 1789 he returned to Marietta, and aided in forming the settlement of Waterford, being one of the first associates, but did not long remain there.

In the autumn of that year he joined a party of the Ohio Company land surveyors, not as a regular hand, but out of curiosity to see the country, who were running the east and west township lines of the fourteenth and fifteenth ranges, between the Big Hockhocking and Raccoon Creek. It consisted of twelve men, of whom Daniel Mayo, of Boston, was one, and Benoni Hurlburt, afterward killed by the Indians, was the hunter. The following interesting sketch of his being lost in the woods, was taken from his own lips, about three years before his death, and is a specimen of the exposures to which the early settlers were all liable.

Having quite a relish for hunting, and expert with the rifle, he one day went out with Hurlburt in quest of provisions for the party, whose supply was nearly exhausted. He ascended one side of a large creek, and his companion the other, which would give them a chance for mutual assistance in killing the game, as it crossed from bank to bank. Mr. Cutler, not being accustomed to the woods, presently left the main stream and followed up a large branch. He soon discovered his mistake, and retraced his steps, but could find no signs of his trail. Just at night he met a fine bear, which he shot at and wounded. A small dog, now his only companion, gave it chase, but as the bear declined taking a tree, as they usually do, he soon gave up the pursuit. Finding that he was actually lost, he fired his gun several times, in hopes the party would hear it and answer his signal of distress. Night now rapidly approaching, he prepared to encamp, and selected a dead, dry beech tree, the top of which was broken off about twenty feet from the ground, against which he kindled the fire. He lay down on some leaves before it, and being excessively tired, dropped into a sound sleep. The flame soon ran to the top of the dry beech, and a large flake of the burning wood, aided by the current of air, dropped on to the breast of his hunting shirt, burning his skin severely. With some effort he succeeded in extinguishing his burning garment, and slept at intervals during the night. He rose at daylight, directing his course eastwardly, with the hope of striking the Hockhocking, which he knew lay in that direction. All that day he traveled diligently, with the little dog by his side, without discovering the object of his search. That night he encamped near a small stream of water, but without fire, as he dreaded a repetition of the last night's accident; besides, he had nothing to cook for supper, and the weather was not cold. The night was passed quietly, with the little dog coiled up at his feet. The third morning he started early, and saw many signs of buffaloes, but no animals; and traveled all day without seeing any game. Toward evening the little dog, which seemed aware of his master's necessities as well as his own, ranged either to the right or left of the course, in search of game; and toward night, barked vehemently at something he had discovered. Mr. Cutler hastened up to the spot in expectation of at least seeing a fat bear, but only found a little, poor, starved opossum. Thinking this better than no meat, he killed and dressed it, roasting it by his camp fire. A part of it was offered to the dog, but he declined partaking such poor fare, and his master consumed the whole of it. It was now three days since he left his companions, and this was his only meal. On the fourth morning, after a sound night's sleep by his fire, he felt quite refreshed, and pushed manfully onward, as he thought on an easterly course, but doubtless making many deviations from a right line. Soon after getting under way, his faithful companion started up a flock of turkeys, the sight of which greatly animated his spirits. His gun was soon leveled and discharged at one of the largest, not more than thirty feet distant. In the agitation and eagerness of the moment, he missed his mark, and the bird flew unharmed away, much to the chagrin of the little dog, which looked quite astonished and mortified at his master. His first impression was that his gun had been bent or injured, and would not shoot with any accuracy. Despair now succeeded to his recent joy, as he thought he must inevitably starve before he could escape from the woods. After shedding a few tears over his hopeless condition, and resting awhile on a log, he carefully wiped out his rifle and loaded it with great nicety. In the meantime the turkeys had all disappeared but a solitary one, perched on the top of a high tree. He now rested his gun against the side of a tree, and taking deliberate aim, he fired once more, and to his great joy the turkey came tumbling to the ground. A fire was soon kindled, the feathers pulled, and the bird roasted on the coals. A hearty meal was then made, of which the little dog now readily partook. This food was the sweetest he had ever tasted, and put fresh courage into the wanderers. The remains of the turkey were stowed away in the bosom of his hunting shirt, and he pursued his solitary way more cheerfully. Soon after, in passing up a ridge, a fine deer came round the point of the hill, which he shot. From the skin of the animal he formed a kind of sack, which he slung to his shoulders, with strips of leatherwood bark, filled with the choicest pieces of the meat. He now traveled on quite cheerily, in which the little dog also participated, knowing he had food for several days, or until he could reach the settlements. That night he camped by the side of a little run, made a cheerful fire, roasted his venison, and ate his supper with a fine relish. After sleeping soundly, he awoke with renovated strength and spirits. This was now the fifth day of his wandering, and luckily, a little before noon, he came on to the Hockhocking, at a place which he at once recognized as being about a mile and a half below the point from which the surveying party had started out on their work. He felt so much animated at the successful termination of this adventure, that instead of going down stream to the cabin of John Levins, seven miles below, he determined to go up to the line of the surveyors, and follow that until he found them. It was easily distinguished by the blazes, or marks on the trees, and before night reached the camp they had left two weeks before, and found a little fire still smoking in a dry sugar tree, which retains fire longer than any other wood. Feeling weary and low spirited, he proceeded no further that night, but slept on the old camping ground. In the morning, knowing where he was, and freed from the harassing feelings known only to those who have been lost in the woods, he started with fresh vigor on the trace. His little companion seemed to understand their more hopeful condition, and capered along ahead, barking heartily for joy. He now killed as much game as he needed, without leaving the trail, and on the eighth day of his solitary ramble, came up with the surveyors. There was great joy in the party at meeting their lost companion, but as they supposed he had gone back to the settlement, not being a regular hand, they were not so much alarmed at his long absence.

Soon after this adventure he returned to New England, and resided for some time with his brother Ephraim, at Killingly, Conn., where he married Miss Philadelphia Cargill, the daughter of Benjamin Cargill, who owned, at that time, valuable mills on the Quinebog River, the site of the present Wilkinson factories and village in Pomfret. His roving propensities led him to spend some months in Carolina and Virginia; but his brother having removed to Ohio, he came again to Marietta, in the year 1802, with the intention of establishing a tin manufactory; but meeting with little encouragement at that early day, he went to Chillicothe, and finally established himself at Bainbridge, on Paint Creek, and engaged in the fur trade.

In the years 1806 and 1807 there was great excitement respecting Louisiana, and Aaron Burr's expedition; the militia was organized, and he was elected a Major in Col. McArthur's Regiment. His fine personal appearance, and some experience in military affairs in Connecticut, enabled him to fill the post with great credit. When additional troops were raised for the purpose of taking possession of New Orleans, he received the appointment of Captain, and soon enlisted a full company of men. He was stationed at Newport, Ky., and for some time had the command of the post at that place. In the spring of 1809 he was ordered, with his company, to New Orleans. A French gentleman, engaged in the fur trade on the Missouri, and toward the Rocky Mountains, was taken on board his boat, as they descended the Mississippi, as a passenger. Being able to speak the French language fluently, he obtained from him much valuable information, which he carefully noted down, respecting these regions. In 1812 he published a work, being a topographical description of that country, including much of Ohio, with an account of the Indian tribes residing therein. His two subaltern officers, Jessup and Cutler, have since attained the rank of General Officers in the Army of the United States. At New Orleans he had a severe attack of yellow fever, which reduced his strength and health so much, that he left the army, and returned to New England, where he remained until 1818, when he removed his family to Warren, near Marietta. Here he lost his wife, in 1822.

Two years after he married Mrs. Eliza Chandler, of Evansville, Indiana, and soon after moved to Nashville, Tenn., where he was engaged in engraving copper plates for bank notes, for the banks of that state, and for Alabama. He possessed great taste for the fine arts; sketched remarkably well, and made some very creditable attempts at sculpture. With much versatility of talent, he lacked that singleness of purpose, and perseverance in one pursuit, necessary to success. He possessed a well cultivated mind, and was an acute observer of men and things.

He died at Evansville, the 25th of June, 1844, aged seventy-six years.

Chapter XXXII

A HISTORY OF THE FIRST SETTLEMENT OF AMESTOWN
IN ATHENS COUNTY, OHIO
WITH SKETCHES OF THE EARLY INHABITANTS.

BY EPHRAIM CUTLER.

In the summer of 1797, Ephraim Cutler, the proprietor of several shares in the Ohio Company's purchase, ascertaining that a considerable amount of his lands were situated on the waters of Federal Creek, in the sixth township of the thirteenth range, accompanied by Lieut. George Ewing, explored a way through the wilderness, and cut out a packhorse path, twenty miles in length, from Waterford to Federal Creek. They returned, and accompanied by Capt. Benjamin Brown, made a second and more thorough exploration. They found the lands exceedingly fertile, with rich limestone hills and valleys, and chestnut ridges; which afforded a plentiful supply of food for animals of every description, and promised an abundant reward to the labors of the farmer. The Indians had not yet quite exterminated the buffalo and elk; the bear, deer, wolf, and panther abounded, while the wild turkeys were innumerable. Mr. Cutler proposed to furnish them with land, if they would unite with him in forming a settlement. They accordingly made their selection; and about the 1st of March, 1798, Lieut. Ewing removed his family, and in April, 1799, Cutler and Brown went over to build their cabins, and make preparation for the accommodation of their families. On their way back to Waterford, they found Wolf Creek impassable, from recent heavy rains. They cut a large bitter-nut hickory tree, that stood on the bank, peeled thirty feet of bark from the trunk, sewed up the ends with leatherwood, and launched it upon the stream; when themselves, with two young men, who accompanied them, embarked in this frail vessel. They had proceeded but a short distance downstream, when they discovered a large bear on the bank of the creek, which was shot, and taken on board. This Indian canoe, with its passengers and freight, performed the voyage of fifteen miles, to Waterford, in safety. The goods and furniture of the two families were put on board pirogues, and sent down the Muskingum and Ohio Rivers, to the mouth of the Big Hockhocking and up that stream to Federal Creek, a distance of eighty miles; while the women and children were taken on horseback, through the wilderness, and over the rough hills, to their woodland abodes. The creeks were much swollen, and difficult to pass. One large stream was crossed on a raft of driftwood, at great peril. They reached the place of destination on the 6th of May. About the year 1800, Deacon Joshua Wyatt and family, with Sylvanus Ames and his accomplished and intelligent wife, joined them, making a very pleasant addition to the little colony. Other settlers also came, but the increase was small until 1804.

After the arrival of Deacon Wyatt, public worship on the Sabbath was established, by reading a sermon, and prayer. The settlers very early entered into an agreement, not to use ardent spirits on any public occasion, such as raisings, 4th of July, &c, which was strictly adhered to for several years. Schools of an elevated character were soon established. Two gentlemen, graduates of Harvard University, Moses Everett, son of the Rev. Moses Everett, of Dorchester, Mass., and Charles Cutler, taught successively for several years. During a number of years, the youth enjoyed no other means of acquiring knowledge. But one newspaper was taken, the United States Gazette, and that, except by accident, did not arrive much oftener than once in three months.

In the autumn of 1804, the settlers of Dover, Sunday Creek, and Ames were convened in public meeting, to devise means to improve the roads. At this meeting the intellectual wants of the settlement became a subject of remark. In their isolated position, the means of acquiring information were extremely limited. It was suggested that a library would supply the deficiency. But the difficulty of obtaining money, to make the purchase of the books, presented an insuperable obstacle. Josiah True, Esq., of Dover, proposed that they should collect furs, and send on to Boston, to effect the object. This project was acceded to by acclamation. The young men of the colony had become expert hunters. Surrounded by a vast wilderness, with a boundless ocean of woods and prairies, inhabited by savages, who still regarded it as their favorite hunting grounds, their fatherland, amidst dangers and privations, unknown in more cultivated regions, a hardy and adventurous character was early developed. John Jacob Astor employed agents in this country, to purchase furs, especially bear skins. At the commencement of winter, the bear seeks a hollow tree, or a cavern amongst the rocks, for his winter's sleep. The entrance of those cavities in which this animal takes refuge, is generally small. These were often entered by the hunters, and the bear dispatched, by shooting, or stabbing with the knife. In one instance the bear being wounded, determined to surrender his fortress, and retreat. The young man, who had entered the narrow aperture, had no other resource than to lie flat upon his face, and let the animal squeeze his passage over him. At the outlet of the den, another hunter stood with his rifle, and shot him through the head; young Brown soon crawled out, covered with blood from the wounded bear, saying, *"That Bruin had given him a harder squeeze than he ever had before."*

In order to obtain the proposed library, the settlers, during the ensuing winter, procured a sufficient quantity of raccoon and other skins to make the desired purchase. Samuel Brown, Esq., who was returning to New England that spring in a wagon, took charge of the skins. He was furnished with letters to the Rev. Thaddeus M. Harris, and the Rev. Dr. Cutler, who accompanied Mr. Brown to Boston, and selected a valuable collection of books. It is worthy of note, that this was the first public library in Ohio, and perhaps the first west of the mountains, and certainly was the first incorporated in the state. It has since been divided, after accumulating several hundred volumes, and part taken to Dover. Both branches are still in a flourishing condition. About sixty youth have been reared under these influences, and gone forth to the world with fully developed physical powers, uncorrupted morals, and well cultivated minds; but as most of them are now in active life, it would appear invidious to mention them. It may perhaps be proper to say that ten of them have graduated at the Ohio University. Many others have received more or less instruction at that institution. Two have been professors in colleges, three ministers of the gospel, and five lawyers, of established reputation. All of them occupy respectable, and many of them responsible stations in society.

The Hon. Ambrose Rice, son of Mr. Jason Rice, of Ames, attended the institution at Athens in its earlier stages. He manifested great aptness in mathematical science, solving the most difficult problems, almost by intuition. He settled in the northwest part of this state, where he occupied stations of trust and profit. His reputation as a man of probity and talent was high. He died leaving a large fortune.

The first physician in Ames was Dr. Ezra Walker, a native of Killingly, Conn. He still lives, at an advanced age.

Mrs. Cutler was a woman of uncommon fortitude and great excellence of character. Though in feeble health, and reared amidst the quiet and peaceful scenes of a New England village, she never shrunk from the dangers and hardships of frontier life. In the early days of the settlement the Indians were in the habit of encamping within a mile of her house. Her husband was obliged to be absent four times in a year, to attend the courts at Marietta. On one of these occasions several Indians came to her house. Two hired men, or striplings, being alarmed, caught up their guns and ran over to Capt. Brown's, leaving her and the children unprotected. One of the Indians approached Mrs. Cutler with threatening gestures, brandishing his tomahawk, and pointed to a decanter of brandy upon the cupboard. She knew if they tasted the liquor her life was in danger. With the spirit of a veteran, she seized the fire shovel and ordered him to set down the bottle and leave the house. The Indian told her, *"She was brave squaw; he would give her some meat."* They left the house and returned to their camp. She was much relieved by the speedy arrival of Capt. Brown, who came immediately on hearing of the unwelcome visit of the Indians. This incident is mentioned to show the trials and dangers to which the females of this settlement were exposed. She was a member of the Congregational Church in Marietta, and an exemplary Christian. She died of consumption, in 1809.

Mrs. Wyatt was an intelligent, pious woman. Her maiden name was Shaw. She died some years after Mrs. Cutler.

Mrs. Ames was the daughter of a New England clergyman. She still lives, honored and cherished by her numerous and respectable family.

It may be proper to give some sketch of the lives of Lieut. Ewing and Capt. Brown, men whose history belongs to that of their country. It was the efforts of such men, under the blessing of God on their labors and daring that brought our country into existence as a distinct nation of the earth. They have already been mentioned as the individuals who first commenced the settlement at Ames, a movement which, considering the attendant difficulties and perils, required no little courage and perseverance. It seemed like plucking an inheritance from the mouth of the lion, situated as it was, in the heart of the Indian hunting grounds, much valued and often visited by them in large parties until 1812; literally a frontier settlement, isolated and unsupported.

Lieut. George Ewing was a native of Salem County, N. J., and though but a youth at the commencement of the Revolutionary War, when his native state was invaded, and the sound of battle heard, he took his stand to defend it to the last. He was soon noticed for his bravery and good conduct, and received the commission of a First Lieutenant in the Jersey Line of the Army, a proud mark of distinction thus to be placed in that noted corps, the Jersey Blues. He continued in the army until the return of peace, when it was disbanded. He soon, with his wife and young family, left New Jersey for the west, and resided a few years near Wheeling, Va. In 1793, with other families of that vicinity, he removed to Waterford, the frontier settlement on the Muskingum, in the midst of the Indian War. They were entitled to lands on the tract donated by Congress to those who, at that period, ventured their lives to defend the frontiers from the savage foe, and made a selection about four miles above Fort Frye, at the mouth of Olive Green Creek, on the bank of the Muskingum River. They prepared a stockade garrison, to which they removed, and commenced improving their lands. The Indians watched them closely, and one of their number was killed by them, but with prudence and vigilance they maintained their post without further loss.

As a member of the new settlement of Ames,* Mr. Ewing was ever ready to promote schools, the library, and every measure calculated for the general good. He was fond of reading; was intelligent; possessed a fund of sterling sense, combined with lively wit and good humor. He sometimes indulged in a natural propensity for poetic and sarcastic descriptions: often served on juries at the freehold courts, held to settle the conflicting claims on the college lands at Athens. There were one or two individuals sometimes employed as advocates, demagogues, who frequently made sad havoc with the King's English. He could not help versifying some of these bombastic speeches, which he did in a masterly manner, but always in a vein of good humor. He finally removed to Indiana, and died about the year 1830. He was the father of the Hon. Thomas Ewing, well known for his talents and the public stations he has held.

*The name of the township was suggested by Gen. R. Putnam, in honor of Fisher Ames, of Massachusetts. It is now one of the richest farming townships in the Ohio Company's purchase.

Chapter XXXIII

CAPTAIN BENJAMIN BROWN

The sketch of Capt. Brown was furnished by his grandsons,
G. Brown and Ephraim Cutler, Esqs.

Battle of White Plains

Capt. Benjamin Brown was born in Leicester, Worcester County, Mass., on the 17th of October, 1745. He was the son of Capt. John Brown, who served with distinction among the Colonial troops in the French war, and before and subsequently to the Revolution, for twenty years, represented the town of Leicester in the General Court of the state. His grandfather, William Brown, while a youth, came from England to America, and was the first settler in the town of Hatfield, on the Connecticut, at the mouth of Deerfield River, and was often engaged in the Indian wars of that early period. The maiden name of his mother was Elizabeth Jones, a near relative of John Coffin Jones, a man somewhat distinguished during and after the Revolution. His father's family was large, numbering nineteen children: five by a former wife.

At the age of twenty-seven, he married Jane Thomas, who survived him, and died at Athens, in 1840, aged eighty-six years. Soon after his marriage he settled on a farm in the town of Rowe, then in the northwest corner of Hampshire County, but now in Franklin, Mass.

In February, 1775, he connected himself with a regiment of Minutemen, as they were then called, commanded by Col. Barnard, filling the post of Quartermaster. This regiment, under the command of Lieut. Col. Williams, of Northfield, at the first sound of war at Lexington, marched to Cambridge, on the 21st of April. Here he received a Lieutenant's commission in Capt. Maxwell's Company, of Col. Prescott's Regiment and Massachusetts Line, in which he continued until December, 1776. In June, 1775, he was engaged with a party of Americans in a very hazardous service, removing the stock from Noodle's Island, in Boston Bay, to prevent their falling into the possession of the British, and also in burning the enemy's packet, "Diana", ashore on Maiden Beach.

He took an active part in the Battle of Bunker Hill, on the 17th of June, where his commander, Col. Prescott, highly distinguished himself by his judicious conduct and bravery. In this battle his oldest brother, John Brown, who died in Adams, Washington County, Ohio, in 1821, aged eighty-seven years, was dangerously wounded in two places, by musket shots, one of which ranged the whole length of his foot, shattering the bones in a dreadful manner. He was borne from the field on the shoulders of his brother Pearly to a place of safety, showing the rare spectacle of three brothers engaged in this first of American battles.

After the evacuation of Boston, in March, 1776, he marched with his regiment to New York, and was present in several engagements during the retreat from Long Island. At the Battle of White Plains, where he took an active part, his brother Pearly was killed; and his brother William died in the hospital at New York. On the 1st of January, 1777, he received a Captain's commission in the Eighth Regiment of the Massachusetts Line, of which Michael Jackson was Colonel, and John Brooks, afterward Governor of Massachusetts, Lieutenant-Colonel, and William Hall, subsequently Governor of Michigan, Major. He remained in this regiment until the close of the year 1779. In December, 1776, he assisted at the capture of Hackensack, by Gen. Parsons. In the summer of 1777, his regiment was ordered to Albany to check the progress of the enemy under Gen. Burgoyne.

About the middle of August, Col. Jackson, with his regiment, was detached with a body of troops under Gen. Arnold, to raise the siege of Fort Schuyler, and to check the advance of St. Leger's men down the Mohawk toward Albany, of which there was great apprehension, after the defeat of Gen. Herkimer at Oriskany, on the 7th of August. On his arrival at the German Flats, he received information that at the stone house of Maj. Tenbreck, near where he was encamped, Maj. Walter Butler, a notorious Tory leader, had hoisted the British flag, and that the house and buildings contained a large amount of military stores and provisions. Tenbreck held unlimited sway over the Tory inhabitants of that region, and all the disaffected were flocking to him for arms and provisions. It was known to be a place of great strength, and In addition to the other difficulties, it was said that Maj. Butler had with him a detachment of British troops, besides his Tory allies. But as it was of great importance to get possession of these two men, it was decided to make an immediate attack, before they were aware of the approach of their enemies. The Colonel selected Capt. Brown, with a chosen corps, to proceed in advance a little before the break of day. He marched with the utmost caution, until they came near the house, when, halting his men, he silently approached the sentinel, who, on his duty, advanced a few rods from the door, and then turning, marched back toward the house. Brown was a man of great strength and activity, and as he turned round he sprang upon him, securing his arms, and ordered his men to surround the house. He then with several of his trusty lads, tore some heavy rails from the fence, and using them as battering rams, stove in the stout door and entered the building. He there met the two Majors, who surrendered the post without resistance, and when the regiment came up they had nothing to do but take possession, and thus, by this happy device, much bloodshed was prevented, and the troops proceeded without delay to the relief of Fort Schuyler, then in the most imminent danger from the army of Indians and Tories that surrounded the brave Gansevoort and his gallant companions. On the approach of Arnold, the siege was raised, and the garrison saved.

Soon after this event, his regiment returned to the vicinity of Saratoga, and was engaged in nearly all the battles which preceded the surrender of the army under Gen. Burgoyne. At the storming of the German redoubts, on the 7th of October, Capt. Brown was eminently distinguished. The events of this day sealed the fate of the British troops. The Eighth Regiment, under Col. Jackson, led the attacking column. Brown, being the senior Captain, commanded the front division; on approaching the redoubt, he found an abatis in front of the works, formed of fallen treetops. Being a man of uncommon muscular strength, as was also his Armor-Bearer, or Covering-Sergeant, they together almost instantly cleared a sufficient opening for his men, and were the first to enter the redoubt. In doing this they received the full fire of the Germans, which killed his brave Sergeant, his Lieutenant, and several Privates; but he, with the remainder, and a free use of the bayonet, soon drove the enemy from the works, and closed this important day in triumph. Col. Breyman, the Commander of the Germans, was killed in this redoubt, and from concurrent circumstances, and his own confession, it is quite certain that he lost his life in a personal contest with Capt. Brown, as he entered the works.

After the surrender of Burgoyne, he was not present in any important battles, but was with the army until his resignation. The station of Aid-de-Camp to Baron Steuben, was offered to him a short time before the Battle of Camden; but he declined the honor, from a sense of his deficient education to fill the post with credit, being that of all the New England farmers of that period.

During his absence in the army, his family, in common with many others, suffered severe privations, incident to the condition of the country.

At the time of his resignation, in 1779, the continental currency had so greatly depreciated, that his month's pay would not purchase a bushel of wheat for his family, and he was thus forced to leave the service, and return home, to provide for their wants, by his personal efforts. About the year 1789, he removed from Rome, to Hartford, Washington County, N. Y., then a new settlement, where he remained until September, 1796; when, with several families, he left there, to seek a new home in the territory northwest of the Ohio River; the fertility and beauty of the country having spread, by the voice of fame, through the middle and eastern states. He reached Marietta in the spring of 1797, and in 1799 moved, with Judge Cutler, to Ames Township, and assisted in the first settlement of that place. In 1817, his health being much impaired, he went to live with his son, Gen. John Brown, in Athens. In 1818 he applied for, and received a pension.

He was a professor of religion, and died, much lamented, in October, 1821, aged seventy-six years.

The descendants of John and Benjamin Brown have multiplied in the west to hundreds. Some of them have occupied highly respectable public offices, with ability. Among the number is our late worthy member of Congress, P. B. Johnson, M. D., whose mother was the daughter of John Brown. Those two old pioneers may well be compared to the oaks of our forest, which nothing but the terrible tornado that levels all before it, can overthrow.

The following is a copy of the certificate of Gov. Brooks, given to Capt. Brown on applying for a pension:

"Medford, Mass., August 24th, 1818.

This is to certify that Benjamin Brown was a Captain in the late Eighth Massachusetts Regiment, commanded by Col. Michael Jackson—that he (Brown) ranked as such from January 1st, 1777—that he was with me in the capture of Majors Tenbreck and Butler, near German Flats—in raising the siege of Fort Stanwix, and in the several battles which immediately preceded the capture of Gen. Burgoyne and his army, all in the year 1777, and that he always acted as a spirited and brave officer. The time of Capt. Brown's resigning is not within my knowledge, but he continued in service until after the 11th of September, 1778, at which time I left the Eighth, being promoted to the command of the Seventh Regiment. I have no doubt of his having continued in service until the time he has mentioned in his declaration.

J. Brooks, late Lieutenant-Colonel
Eighth Massachusetts Regiment."

Chapter XXXIV
COLONEL JOSEPH BARKER

Col. Joseph Barker was a native of New Market, Rockingham county, N. H., and was born on the 9th day of September, A. D. 1765. His father was Ephraim Barker. The maiden name of his mother was Mary Manning, of Ipswich, Essex County, Mass. At the age of six years, he lost his mother, who left six children. A few years after her death, Joseph was sent to Exeter Academy, one of the earliest classical seminaries in New England, and ranking with the best in reputation, for sound scholarship and correct discipline. He remained in the academy for a considerable time, and laid the foundation of a good English education, which, in after-life, by reading, a clear, discriminating mind, and close observation of mankind, enabled him to appear in the several posts he occupied, of a public nature, with honor to himself, and the credit of his patrons.

His father having married again, in the year 1774, moved his family to Amherst, N. H., where he followed the occupation of a house carpenter, to which he was bred; few of the New England men of that day being without some industrial pursuit. His oldest son, Jeremiah, was educated as a physician, and settled in Portland, Me., where he became one of the most eminent practitioners of his time; furnishing numerous articles on the diseases of that region, for the Medical Repository, from its first establishment by Drs. Mitchell and Miller, of New York city. This work was continued for many years, and was not only the first medical periodical published in America, but is said to have been the first in the world; opening the way to the vast amount of medical literature which is now sent forth to the public

Joseph was continued at Exeter until sometime during the war, probably until he was about fourteen or fifteen years old, when he returned to his father, and commenced the acquirement of the art of a house-joiner and carpenter, under the guidance of his parent. He was a youth of great spirit, courage, and activity; and many stories are related, of his pugilistic feats and wrestling, not only with the boys of his own age, but with those much his superiors in years and size. His father lived near the courthouse and jail, and Joseph became a great favorite of the

Sheriff of the county, who was fond of such sports as were common during the period of the Revolution, and encouraged him in the practice. These athletic exercises invigorated and strengthened his muscular frame, and gave him that manly bearing and contempt of danger, which characterized his after-life. When a boy, he possessed a rare fund of wit and humor, with a taste for the ludicrous, which was very amusing to his companions. One of his boyish feats was related, a few years since, by an old man of Amherst, to Mr. G. Dana, his brother-in-law, while there on a visit.

"In the spring of the year, it was common for the nice housekeepers in New England, to have their rooms and dooryards fresh whitewashed annually. Joseph had been set at this work, and when he had about completed the job, an old red mare, that belonged to a crabbed, ill-natured neighbor, came up to the gate, as she had been in the habit of doing for some time, giving him considerable trouble in driving her away. The conceit immediately came into his head, that it would be a good joke to metamorphose the old mare, by giving her a coat of the whitewash. She was accordingly tied up to the fence, and the operation commenced, of giving her a white masquerading dress over her red one. When finished, she was turned loose, and went directly home. The owner, seeing a strange horse at the stable door, threw stones at her, and drove her away, not once suspecting that this white horse could be his. The next morning, finding the strange animal still about his premises, he set his dog on her, in great anger, following her with many curses and brickbats, determined to break up her unwelcome visits. Several curious disquisitions were held, by the old man and his wife, on the pertinacity of the animal, while the mare was in the greatest wonder at the strange conduct of her master. One or two of the neighbors, who were in the secret, as the man was no favorite among them, enjoyed the joke exceedingly, especially when he began to make inquiries after his own horse, which had somehow strangely disappeared. It was not until after two or three days, when the coat of white was rubbed off in patches, showing the natural red, that he could be convinced of her identity, and that he had been harassing and starving his own beast during all that time. This piece of fun was long remembered in the village, and gave

Joseph no little éclat in the estimation of the real lovers of a little harmless mischief."

After working a year or two with his father, he went to live with a relative of his mother in New Ipswich, where he perfected his knowledge of the carpenter's business, becoming a skillful architect. He followed his occupation for several years. In 1788 he worked as a journeyman carpenter in the erection of a meeting-house in New Boston, where he remained until 1789.

In the latter year he married Miss Elizabeth Dana, the eldest daughter of Capt. William Dana, of Amherst, with whom he had long been acquainted. His father-in-law having visited the Ohio country in 1788, and determined on moving his family there, Mr. Barker concluded to join his fortune to theirs, and embark with them in the enterprise of seeking a home in the far west. They left Amherst in September, 1789. The mode of travel was in wagons drawn by oxen. One favorite cow was brought with them, which furnished milk for the children on the way; and on their arrival at Belpre, their future home was named Old Amherst, in remembrance of their former place of residence. The fatigues of a journey of seven hundred miles, and across the mountains, at that day, cannot be estimated by those born amongst the facilities of steamboats and railroads. Such were the difficulties in passing these lofty ranges, that sometimes the wagons were actually taken in pieces, and the separate parts carried by hand over the impassable barrier of rocks and ledges. On the route one of their oxen became lame, and had to be exchanged for a sound one, and as is usually the case in such events, they were sadly cheated, the new ox being nearly valueless for the draught. But the resolution of Capt. Dana and Mr. Barker was equal to any emergency, and surmounted every obstacle. The rugged mountains were finally passed, and in November the party arrived at Simrel's Ferry, the grand embarking port of the New England emigrants in their descent of the Ohio River. As was usual at this early period, they were detained several days for a boat to be made ready for their use. No facilities of passenger boats of any kind were then known on the western waters, but every traveler furnished his own conveyance, or united with others, his companions, in procuring one. While waiting at this place, Isaac Barker, with his family, from Rhode Island, arrived, and they all lived under the hospitable roof of Thomas Stanley, a citizen of Connecticut then living at that place, and who subsequently became a respectable and valuable citizen of Marietta, and after the Indian war in 1797, erected mills on Duck Creek, in the present township of Fearing. As soon as the boat was prepared, the three families embarked in their unwieldy craft, built after the fashion of a large oblong box, covered half its length with a roof to shelter the people and their goods from the weather, while the open space contained their teams and wagons. The water on the Youghiogheny and Monongahela, as it usually is at this season of the year, was low, and every mile or two the boat grounded on the sand-bars and rocks, requiring the voyagers to leap over the side into the cold water, and pry her off into the current, rendering the passage both slow and painful. When they reached Pittsburg, a favorable rise in the river accelerated their progress and rendered the rest of the voyage more comfortable. On their arrival at Marietta, where they proposed to pass the winter, they found the few houses then built so crowded with inhabitants, that they concluded to pass on to Belpre, a settlement just commenced, where Capt. Dana's land was located.

The appearance of Marietta at that time is thus described by one of the party now living. *"On ascending the bank of the river to look at the town we had been nearly three months toiling to see, a very cheerless prospect was presented to our view. A few log huts were scattered here and there, raised only a few feet above the tall stumps of the sturdy trees that had been cut away to make room for them. Narrow footpaths meandered through the mud and water from cabin to cabin; while an occasional log across the water-courses afforded the pedestrian a passage without wetting his feet".*

The people were very kind and hospitable to the new comers, to the extent of their ability; but after waiting a day or two, Capt. Dana proceeded on with his boat to his future home, where he arrived late in November. Much to his disappointment, he found that the log house he had built the spring preceding, by accident was burned up, and the family had to remain in the boat until another was erected.

Mr. Barker, who depended on the proceeds of his mechanical labor for the support of his family, concluded to stay for the present in Marietta, where carpenters were in demand, and immediately began putting up a cabin on the corner of the square where the post office building now stands. Early in January, 1790, the small-pox was introduced amongst the inhabitants by a moving family, and it was thought prudent for Mrs. Barker to go to Belpre and live in her father's family, until the danger was passed. Mr. Barker not having had the disease was inoculated about the middle of January, as were a large portion of the inhabitants of Marietta. For pest-houses, several small log buildings were put up on the border of the plain. On the 30th of that month he wrote to his wife. *"I am living in a little, clean log-cabin that is six feet wide, seven feet long, and four and a half high. We make out to sit up, but cannot stand straight. We lodge very well."*

This shows the narrow accommodations to which some of the inhabitants had to submit. Those in Campus Martius had larger rooms, but were also very much crowded. He passed through the disease favorably, but was not allowed to visit his wife at Belpre, on account of the danger to the inhabitants, until the forepart of March.

On the 28th of February, Mrs. Barker gave birth to a son, the present honorable Joseph Barker, of Newport. He was the first child born in that township, and has several times represented Washington County in the state Legislature. Sometime in the spring of the year 1790, he moved his wife and little son to Marietta, where he remained until the autumn of 1793.

The Indian War began in January, 1791, yet, notwithstanding the danger, he lived in his own house during a part of the time, retiring to the stockade at the Point when the Rangers reported signs of Indians in the vicinity, and returning to his own domicile when the danger was at a distance. Soon after the war broke out, he was appointed an Orderly-Sergeant, in the pay of the United States by Col. Sproat, who was the Military Agent, with the rank of a Lieutenant-Colonel.

The condition of the Ohio Company's settlements at the time of his arrival, and for a year or two after, cannot be better described than in his own words.

"In November, 1789, at the time of my arrival, ninety families had landed, and associations embracing two hundred and fifty settlers had been formed, and improvements had commenced in several of them. By May, 1790, there were very few lots in Belpre and Newbury without a settler. On a return of all the men enrolled for militia duty in the county, made to the Secretary of War in March, 1791, their number amounted to one hundred and ninety-five. But after that I think the number increased and the one hundred thousand acres granted by Congress for donation purposes, induced many to remain, and many more to come in, to avail themselves of the terms of the donation.

In January, 1790, a new arrangement was made in the militia, a company of artillery was formed, commanded by Capt. William Mills, of Marietta, Lieut. George Ingersoll, of Belpre, and the late Gen. Joseph Buck, Orderly-Sergeant. The infantry company was commanded by Maj. Nathan Goodale, of Belpre, and Anselm Tupper, of Marietta, Lieutenant. Early in the spring, some alterations were made, by which I was transferred from the artillery, and made Orderly-Sergeant of the company of infantry, and it became my duty to keep a roll of every person amenable to military service; to attend at the place of public worship, with my roll; call every man's name, examine his arms and ammunition, and see that he was equipped according to law. I had also to note down and report all delinquencies."

The territorial militia law made it the duty of the troops, to assemble on Sunday morning, at ten o'clock, for inspection; those who attended public worship, and there were few who did not, after the inspection, marched from the parade ground to the room where service was held, preceded by the clergyman and Col. Sproat, the Commandant at the Point garrison, with his Revolutionary sword drawn, and the drum and fife, and by Gen. Putnam and Gen. Tupper, at Campus Martius. The citizens generally fell into the ranks and the procession moved, in military array, to wait on divine service; the fife and drum supplying the place of the church going bell, in the eastern states. In case of an alarm on the Sabbath, that portion of the congregation who were armed, rushed out of the meeting, to face the danger, or pursue the Indians, which several times happened. After the war commenced, the troops under pay, were the special guard for the garrisons, in the daytime, but were not connected with the citizens in their military duties. The latter were held in preparation, to be called on for scouts and pursuing parties; while the guard was not allowed to leave the garrison, or the sentinel his post, but they were both inspected at the same hour by their respective officers, to see if they were prepared for action at all times. Before the arrival of the Rev. Daniel Story, who was the stated pastor, Thomas Lord, Esq., of Connecticut, who had been educated at Yale College and studied theology preparatory to the ministry, officiated as clergyman for the settlement. Previous to the commencement of hostilities by this weekly inspection on the Sabbath, when the most of the people were at home, but absent on other days, the Commandant was informed what proportion of them were armed and equipped to defend the settlement; emigrants frequently arrived without arms, so that the number of guns fell short of the number of men, and the deficiency could not be made up in the settlement, and those persons only who were known to have arms, were proceeded against as delinquents. A short time previous to hostilities, Col. Sproat had been authorized by the secretary of war to enlist a company of men into the service of the United States, out of the settlers, to be employed in guarding and defending the settlements and also to superintend and distribute them at the posts which most needed their aid. He was directed to appoint a commissary to furnish provisions to these troops, and employed Paul Fearing, Esq.; Col. Sproat being Commander-in-Chief, his aid was solicited in procuring arms for the citizens, who were deficient. He immediately wrote to the commanding officer at Fort Pitt, who sent down about thirty old muskets which had been laid aside as unfit for use; they were put into the hands of the blacksmiths, who repaired them as well as they could, and distributed where most needed. Powder and lead were furnished, and cartridges made to suit each caliber and deposited in the blockhouses ready to be distributed in case of an attack. In June, 1792, Col. Sproat received two boxes containing twenty-five stands each of United States muskets with bayonets fresh from the factory. These were distributed to the soldiers and citizens on their signing a receipt to return them when called for, to Col. Sproat. The arms were never called for and are still in the county. The inhabitants were now thought to be well armed; many rifles were procured and brought into the country. The northern men, previous to their coming here, were unacquainted with the rifle and the woods, but by practicing on the example of those who had been educated among the Indians and the forests, they soon became good hunters and expert woodsmen. Those who were well armed and good marksmen, were commonly selected as sentries for the working parties in the fields, and were always ready to start on any discovery of the enemy, or pursue an Indian trail. Thus, by being familiar with danger, and inured to the hazard of an encounter with their enemies, they gained that confidence in themselves which promised, in case of meeting an Indian, the odds in their own favor. Several followed hunting continually: others were out with the Rangers, or small parties, so that it was difficult for an Indian to make a track within five miles of a garrison without being detected. Thus a large portion of the inhabitants became fearless of danger from the Indians, and preferred some employment or enterprise abroad, to being confined in the garrisons, which is evident from the fact that nearly all the one hundred thousand acres of donation land had been taken up, surveyed and deeded away, with improvements made on many of the lots, previous to Wayne's treaty. Where the lots bordered on large streams, many had made considerable improvements during the war, and others were ready to do so on the news of peace. All the lots settled along the Ohio River below the Muskingum, belonged to the Ohio Company's purchase, It is an axiom with military men that Rangers are the eyes of an army. It proved true with respect to our settlements. The measure of employing Rangers was adopted previous to the commencement of hostilities, and they were stationed at Marietta and Waterford three months before the massacre at Big Bottom; and as the safety of the lives and property of the inhabitants depended much on the vigilance and honesty of these men, none were selected but such as possessed these qualities. Their pay, under the Ohio Company, was one dollar a day; but under the United States, it was eighty four cents, or twenty-five dollars a month.

After naming and describing the persons of a number of the Rangers, he says, *"Two men, Benjamin Patterson and John Shepherd, from the state of New York, were employed as Rangers three of the first years of the war, and then moved down the river."* At the time of the controversy between Pennsylvania and Connecticut relative to their conflicting land claims on the Susquehanna River, the State of Pennsylvania appointed Timothy Pickering, of Salem, Mass., the honest old Federalist, to go upon the ground and meet others to adjust the difference. While there, this same Benjamin Patterson was one of two or three men who took Pickering from his bed at night, and conveyed him three miles into the woods, and bound him fast to a white-oak sapling and left him there to starve to death; but after two or three days Patterson returned, and went and unbound him, setting him at liberty, for which outrage he fled from Wyoming to the state of New York, and from thence to Marietta. It was not uncommon for such characters to call at our settlement, but finding neither plunder nor speculation, and their characters soon pursuing them, they floated down the river.

To the plan early adopted of employing Rangers, may be attributed the general safety and success of the settlement of Washington county. It was first proposed by Gen. Putnam, and afterward adopted by Congress. The Indians finding themselves so closely watched by men, who were their compeers in their own arts of warfare, as well as more vigilant and untiring soldiers, became indifferent to enterprises where they were likely to meet with more loss than profit. The hope of reward is the great spring of human action. Men, who are not paid, nor fed nor clothed, may make good partisans for a short emergency, but never make good soldiers. Their patriotism soon cools. The hope of plunder is the main stimulus with the Indians. Therefore they crossed the Ohio River below and above—passing by us, went a hundred miles beyond, on to the waters of the Monongahela, where there was more plunder and less watchfulness. Revenge is sweet, but must not be bought too dear. Parties of fifty or a hundred, who came on to attack us, seldom remained about the settlements more than a week; and larger bodies of a thousand or more, such as attacked Gen. St. Clair and Fort Recovery, could not keep together more than four or five days, as they had no means to provide food for the soldier or his family, when fighting the battles of his tribe. It is estimated, that in the seven years previous to the war of 1791, the Indians, along the frontiers south of the Ohio River, killed and took prisoners, fifteen hundred persons, stole two thousand horses, and other property to the amount of fifty thousand dollars. This was the declared object of the party who killed Mr. Carpenter and the family of Armstrong.

The first physician who came to settle in Marietta was Dr. Jabez Farley, a son of Gen. Farley, of Old Ipswich, Mass. He had been educated for a physician, and studied medicine with old Dr. Holyoke, walking with him, as his friends said, three years in the streets of Salem. He was a modest, amiable, young man; always ready to obey the calls of humanity, and had the good-will and confidence of all who knew him. But as there were but few people and those young and healthy, (except the disease of an empty purse,) his practice was very limited. As he was not fitted for any other business, in the autumn of 1790, his medicine being exhausted, he returned to Ipswich, and did not come out again.

In the first settlement of the country, intermittent fever, or fever and ague, was the prevailing disease, among all classes, along the water-courses. It commenced about the 1st of August, and continued at intervals, until sugar-making in February or March. Maple sugar was a valuable article of diet, in families who had little or no salt meat, as this food was scarce and dear. Sugar was a substitute for many things, and where they could get it, as most people could, who took the pains of making it, was used freely, and sometimes exhausted their store, before the sickly season, in August, arrived; when they were almost certain to be sick; while those who had more substantial and solid food, escaped. Remitting or bilious fevers were not so common, until long after the war. Industry and temperance were preventives of most disorders, and a remedy for many more.

Gen. Putnam used to relate an anecdote of his own experience in the fever and ague. After concluding a treaty of peace with the Wabash and Illinois Indians, in September, 1792, he was attacked with the fever and ague, and suffered severely with this disorder, on his voyage up, performed in a superb, twelve-oared barge, rowed by United States soldiers. He had a surgeon on board, who prescribed for him, but debarred him from the use of stimulating food and drink. His disease continued unabated, under this course, until he reached this side of Gallipolis, when the boat landed at nightfall, at a camp of hunters on the bank of the Ohio. They had a profusion of bear meat, venison, and turkey. They feasted themselves, and made every person welcome; but the General was interdicted the savory contents of the camp kettle, by his surgeon, the very fumes of which were quite a feast to a hungry stomach. He lay down on his blanket, before the camp-fire, and tried to sleep, but the thoughts of the rich contents of the camp-kettle, only a few feet from him, prevented. As soon as all around him were lost in slumber, he crept up to the side of the kettle, and feasted his craving appetite on the well-seasoned bear meat and venison, as long as he dared to indulge it. He had not a single return of the ague after this night; showing that all he needed, was more stimulating food than he had been allowed to use for several weeks preceding.

As the Indians came into the treaty at Fort Harmar in the fall of 1788, they employed themselves in hunting and destroying the game, for which they had no use, (as they were supplied with rations from the garrison,) except for the skins of the deer. So great was their industry and perseverance, that in the fall and winter they brought in deer and turkeys, piling them up on the bank of the Muskingum, at the Point, like a stack of hay, until the inhabitants were obliged to assemble and throw them into the river, to abate the nuisance. They left the carcasses about the woods, which brought in the wolves and panthers, but destroyed all the deer. A man by the name of Bagley, who was a fiddler, and lived at Wolf Creek Mills, on his way to Marietta one cold, snow-stormy day in March, was attacked by a gang of wolves, who drove him up a tree, where he had to sit and play the fiddle for them all night, until they left him in the morning. When the Indians were asked why they destroyed and wasted the game in such a manner, they answered they meant to destroy and starve out every white man north of the Ohio. They frequently alluded to the prospect of repossessing their lands, and recovering their good hunting grounds. One old Indian, when he drew his blanket at the treaty, threw it over his shoulders, saying he had got his cornfield on his back, but he would have it to walk on next year. It was said there were four hundred Indians, men, women, and children; and so thoroughly did they destroy the game within ten miles of Marietta, that scarcely a deer could be seen; where, before, a good hunter could kill from fifteen to twenty in a day. I have heard Hamilton Kerr say, that the hills between Duck Creek and Little Muskingum were the best hunting ground he had ever seen; that he could easily kill fifteen deer in a day, and frequently in a morning. The Indians, by burning the woods every year, kept down the undergrowth, and made good pasture for the game and good hunting for themselves. The famine of 1790 was much aggravated by this destruction of the wild animals.

Early in March, 1791, Capt. Joseph Rogers, one of the Rangers, was killed by the Indians. He was a native of Pennsylvania, and about fifty years old; a gentlemanly, brave, humane soldier, and had been an officer in Col. Morgan's Rifle Corps at the capture of Burgoyne. Having served honorably through the Revolution, he, with many an old soldier, marched toward the setting sun, on the formation of the Ohio Company, in the hope of finding a new home in the west. He was in company with Edward Henderson, another of the Rangers, on their return from a tour of duty, and was shot by a party of four Indians, on the side of a hill a mile north of Campus Martius. Henderson had several balls shot through his clothes, but made his escape after being chased several miles, and reached the garrison at the Point about twelve o'clock at night, where he was recognized by the sentinel on duty, and admitted at the gate on Ohio street. The Commander was roused, the cannon fired, and answered at Campus Martius and Fort Harmar. The alarm ran through the garrison that Rogers was killed, and Henderson chased into the post by a large body of Indians, who were now at the gate making an attack. All was consternation in the darkness of night, but everyone hastened to his alarm post. Some incidents occurred which marked the propensities of different individuals. The first person for admittance into the central blockhouse was Col. Sproat, with a box of papers. Then came some young men with their arms; Then a woman with her bed and children; Next old Mr. William Moulton, from Newburyport, aged seventy, with his leather apron full of old goldsmith tools and tobacco; Close at his heels came his daughter Anna, with the China teapot, cups and saucers: Lydia brought the great Bible; but when all were in, their mother was missing. Where was mother? She must be killed! No, says Lydia, mother said she would not leave the house *looking so;* she would put things a little more to rights, and then she would come. Directly mother came, bringing the looking-glass, knives and forks, &c.

Messengers were soon exchanged with Campus Martius, and no appearance of hostilities was discovered. All returned to their homes in the morning, and peace was restored to the little anxious community. A strong party of men went out that forenoon, brought in the dead body of Rogers, and buried him in Second Street, near the brink of the plain."

Mr. Barker, as Orderly-Sergeant, had charge of the blockhouse at the Point, where the inhabitants assembled at the alarm of Indians and was an eye-witness of the scene described.

During the continuance of the war, he was exposed to many dangers and trials, which he met with the fortitude of a brave man, and was ready at all times to lead or to follow wherever duty called him. Soon after the massacre at Big Bottom, he was on the ground with a party of volunteers from Marietta, and assisted in burying the burnt and mutilated bodies of his countrymen. Also in the autumn of 1791, when Capt. Carpenter and four others were killed by the Indians seven miles above Marietta, in Virginia, he was early at the spot, and assisted in committing to the earth their mangled bodies, which was a dangerous service, as the savages might still be lurking in the vicinity of the place, watching for their approach.

In August, 1793, the small-pox again visited Marietta, and to avoid the infection in his family, he moved to Stone's Garrison, in the upper settlement of Belpre, built in the spring of that year. But this enemy of the human race, more subtle than the savage, could not be eluded, and Mrs. Barker took the disease in the natural way. It proved to be of the malignant, confluent kind, and she barely escaped with her life, bearing about her person the marks of its violence the rest of her days. All the inhabitants of Belpre, who had not previously had the small-pox, were now inoculated, turning their garrisons into so many hospitals. Between the Indians without their walls, and disease and want within, they suffered extremely.

In the spring of 1794, a family by the name of Armstrong, on the Virginia shore of the Ohio, in sight of Stone's Garrison, was attacked by the Indians, four killed and three taken prisoners. On this occasion he was one of the volunteers who, on the first alarm, turned out from the garrison to pursue the Indians, bury the dead, and give succor to such of the family as escaped by not being in the house at the time. These melancholy scenes were common during the war, and tried the courage and the hearts of the bravest of the settlers.

In the winter of 1793-4, he taught a school in the garrison. This post was about one hundred yards in length by fifty yards in breadth, and contained five blockhouses, and six log dwelling houses, with a schoolhouse. The whole were enclosed with stout palisades. The inmates consisted of twelve families, and being generally prolific in children, averaging from three or four to eight or ten in a family, they could furnish a school of forty between the ages of four years and twenty years. The heads of families in this garrison were Capt. Jonathan Stone, Capt. William Dana, Capt. Elias Gates, Col. Silas Bent, Stephen Guthrie, Israel Stone, Simeon Wright, Isaac Barker, Joseph Barker, Wanton Cosey, Benjamin Patterson, and Stephen Smith. The school was an interesting one, and he spent the winter very pleasantly in teaching the young idea how to shoot.

In February, 1795, the inhabitants of this little garrison were doomed to lose one of their own number by the Indians. Jonas Davis, an intelligent young man from New England, and at the time living in Mr. Barker's family, incautiously left the station one morning alone, and went about three miles up the bank of the Ohio, for the purpose of getting the boards and nails from a small boat he had discovered wrecked in the ice on the shore, as he came down from Marietta the day before. Not returning that night, fears were felt for his safety. The following morning all the inhabitants of the garrison fit to bear arms, excepting Capt. Dana and Col. Bent, who were rather infirm, were mustered to go out in search of Davis. After cautiously reconnoitering their way, he was found killed and scalped near the mouth of Crooked Creek, stripped of all his clothing but a shirt. Preparations were soon made, for bringing the dead body to the garrison, by lashing it with hickory withes to a pole.

In the meantime, one of the party, unused to such scenes, became much alarmed at the sight of the dead and mangled body, together with the surmises of Patterson, the Ranger, that the Indians were still lurking in the vicinity, watching their motions, suffered his fears to get the better of his reason, and started, full speed, for home. So much alarmed was the man, that he fancied an Indian in every bush, and thought he could see their dusky forms stalking from tree to tree, ready to intercept him. In the meantime, the inmates of the garrison were waiting, in anxious suspense, the return of the party, and to hear the result of their search. At length the person in the watch-tower gave notice of the approach of a messenger, at his utmost speed. A general rush of the women and children was made to the gate, to learn the tidings. The man, out of breath, and pale with affright, had hardly strength enough to relate that he had been chased by the Indians, who filled the woods, and barely escaped with his life, and he had no doubt the whole party were either killed or taken prisoners. The gates were immediately closed and barred, while every preparation in their power, was made for defense, by the two old veterans, Dana and Bent, who had both seen service in the American Revolution. Grief, anguish, and confusion, for a short time pervaded this wretched group of mothers, wives, and children, at the false intelligence of the fate of their dearest friends. On more closely questioning the alarmed fugitive, as to the particulars of the fight with the Indians, from his incoherent account, they were led to hope the matter was not so disastrous as represented, and quiet began to be restored, while they waited, in great anxiety, the return of the party.

It was a slow and laborious task, to bring the dead body on their shoulders, and not regarding the flight of the runaway as of any importance, or that he might cause needless alarm to their friends at home, they returned cautiously along, keeping a good lookout for their wily foes, if any were near. They, at length, to the great relief of the inmates of the garrison, made their appearance with the dead body; and as it was naked, they halted a few rods from the gate, and called for a blanket to cover it. The article required, was carried out to them by Mr. Barker's little son, Joseph, then only four years old, who, to this day, remembers that distressing scene, with the anguish and alarm of the occasion, with all the vividness of a recent event. This was the last trial they had with the savages, as in August following, the peace of Greenville was completed with the western tribes.

From the time of his first coming to Marietta, Mr. Barker's intention was, to become the owner of a farm, but had thus far been prevented by the hostilities of the Indians. The donation lands of one hundred acres, had previously been distributed to actual settlers, and his lot fell in Wiseman's Bottom, seven miles above Marietta; to this he subsequently added three other lots, making a fertile and valuable farm, of four hundred acres, the seat of his future home.

In April, 1795, he left the garrison, in a canoe, with two of his wife's brothers, William and Edmond Bancroft Dana, to assist him in making the first opening on his wilderness farm, taking with him—, in addition to his cooking utensils, farming tools, and provisions — fifty young apple, and twelve cherry trees; it being one of the first acts of the thrifty New Englanders, to provide their families with fruit, as well as bread. The name of Wiseman's Bottom originated from a backwoodsman, who, while Virginia claimed the right to all the lands northwest of the Ohio River, had made an entry at this spot, of four hundred acres, called a settlement right. It was upon this little improvement, that Mr. Barker began his first clearing. There was yet considerable danger from the Indians, as peace was not yet concluded, and a man was killed by them about ten miles distant, on Wolf Creek, in a short time after. Nevertheless, the adventurers proceeded up the Muskingum and commenced their labor. About the time of their arrival a blockhouse had been built at Rainbow Creek, on the opposite side of the river, by Gen. Putnam, where he proposed to erect a mill, distant about a mile. In this building, during the time of their stay, the party took shelter every night, returning to their work in the morning with a gun on each one's shoulder, and an axe in the hand. While at their work chopping down the trees, one of the party was constantly kept on the lookout for danger. In addition to their own watchfulness, they had the aid of a faithful old dog, called Pedro, who accompanied them from New Hampshire, and had been with them during the war in Belpre. He would instinctively post himself on some elevation, such as a big log, or the stump of a tree, on the watch for the approach of an enemy, ready to give the alarm on the least sign of its appearance, whether from wild beast or savage.

They were thus occupied for three weeks, and made the first permanent improvement in the Wiseman's bottom settlement, a tract embracing two or three thousand acres, and which subsequently became one of the most beautiful, well cultivated tracts, and intellectual community on the Muskingum River. During this time they had cleared about two acres of ground in the rich bottom, which was thickly covered with immense trees of black walnut and sugar maple, the labor of removing and burning which no one can tell, but him who has actually tried it. Holes were dug in the fresh virgin soil, and apple trees planted out amidst the gigantic sons of the forest, whose lofty heads were made to bow at the presence of civilized man. The cherry trees were not yet set, as they intended to remain a day or two longer; but old Pedro notified them one afternoon that danger was near. With the hair erect on his back, he would rush into the thick woods on the side of the clearing, threatening instant attack on some unseen enemy, but which his acute olfactories enabled him to detect; then returning to his master, seemed to say, "*It is time to be off.*" This was repeated at intervals for several hours, until near night, when the party thought it would be more prudent to go. In the meantime, as the apple trees were not all set, when the dog began his warning, two of the party stood on the watch with their guns ready, while the third one finished the work by setting the remaining trees near the bank of the river, further from the edge of the woods, and from the concealed danger, whatever it might be. They now stepped on board the canoe with their faithful watchdog, just at evening, and by the aid of a rapid current and the vigorous application of their paddles, they reached Stone's Garrison, a distance of nineteen miles, before ten o'clock that night.

In May, Mr. Barker returned to his farm and cleared an additional piece of woodland, making in all about three acres, which was planted in corn. He visited the little field two or three times during the summer, to dress the corn and witness its progress. Once he came alone, and staid three nights, lodging as before in the blockhouse. These early fields were planted without plowing. The seed corn being committed to the rich, loose, vegetable soil grew with astonishing vigor; and where it received plenty of sunshine, yielded fine crops. His little field produced about one hundred and twenty-five bushels, which very fortunately escaped the ravages of the squirrels and raccoons, there being an abundant supply of food for them that year in the forest.

The final articles of peace were signed in August, 1795. As soon as the intelligence reached the garrisons on the Ohio and Muskingum, their inmates prepared to leave their rude fortresses, where they had suffered much from the three greatest scourges of the human race, war, famine, and pestilence.

In December following, Mr. Barker, with his wife and three children, left the garrison and landed at his new home on the 18th of the month.

The first thing that attracted the notice of little Joseph on their going ashore at the new farm, now the old homestead, was the fresh cut stumps of the small willow trees that lined the water's edge, the work of the half-reasoning beaver. These sagacious animals had a lodge behind an island about a mile below, and another a short distance above, at the mouth of Rainbow Creek. They were the last families of the race seen in this part of the country, and were in a year or two after caught by that venerable old trapper, Isaac Williams. The new dwelling house of the Barkers was a log cabin sixteen feet square. One side of this was occupied by a corncrib four or five feet in width, made of poles, containing the crop of the little clearing. On entering the future home of the family, in a cold December night, it may be safely said that no future visitors of the dwelling of Mr. Barker, ever met so cold a reception as they themselves did, on that long remembered evening. The nearest neighbor was at Marietta, seven miles below; the next at Waterford, fifteen miles above. The fortitude and perseverance requisite to meet the hardships and privations of a settlement in the wilderness were found centered in this family. Mrs. Barker possessed patience, resolution, industry, and good sense; all needed, in no small degree, in trials of this kind. During that winter the clearing was considerably enlarged, and two hundred peach trees were added to the orchard in the spring. Mills for grinding were scarce and remote; and the hand mill at the block-house across the river was their only dependence for meal; but with a good crib of corn, and this resource, famine was kept at a respectful distance.

In the following year, or 1796, the families of Capt. J. Devol, John Russel, and Israel Putnam, moved into Wiseman's Bottom, and lessened by their vicinity the sense of loneliness, as they were all social and well informed persons. During the year, he put up a convenient hewed log house, with a brick chimney, a degree of refinement to which but few new settlers arrive short of several years.

In January, a serious accident befell him, which was sensibly felt for a long time. The little cabin which they had recently left, accidently took fire, and was destroyed. It was occupied as a workshop, storehouse, &c, and contained a large stock of carpenter's tools, while in the loft was stored away the crop of well rotted flax, ready for dressing, and on which, before the introduction of cotton, the inhabitants depended for their domestic cloth, and was a very important article in every family. On one side of the building was the pen containing the fat hogs, and were saved from the flames with difficulty. In their fright they fled across the river on the ice, into the woods and were not found until they were much lessened in value. All his bread-stuff for the ensuing year was destroyed, as well as his tools brought from New England. The intrinsic value of the articles was not great, but to him was a serious affair, as it took away his whole stay of bread and meat, with his main dependence for clothing, and was a more afflicting loss than the burning of a whole block of buildings, filled with goods, would be to a rich Wall Street merchant.

To repair this disaster, Mr. Barker set to work at his trade, like a sensible, resolute man, and followed the business of a house carpenter for several years in Marietta, erecting dwelling houses for the Hon. Paul Fearing, William Skinner, Rev. Daniel Story, and many others, with the Muskingum academy. In 1799 and 1800, he built the splendid mansion of Mr. Blennerhassett, on the island since called by his name.

About this time, ship-building commenced at Marietta and on the Muskingum River, where many a tall oak which had nourished for ages on its banks, two thousand miles from the ocean, was destined to toss upon its waves, and to visit far distant lands. In this new business, Mr. Barker took an active part, and in 1802, built two vessels at his farm. One was the Brig Dominic, for Messrs. Blennerhassett and Woodbridge, and named for Mr. B's oldest son. The other was a schooner for E. W. Tupper, called the "Indiana". In 1803, he built a brig called the "Louisa", for the same man.

During the autumn of 1800, he was employed by Mr. Blennerhassett to build fifteen large batteaux, to be used in the famous Burr expedition. After having been so extensively employed, by the former gentleman, as an architect, and to his entire satisfaction, it was very natural for him to select Mr. Barker for this purpose, of constructing boats so necessary to the enterprise. They were calculated for the ascent of water-courses, and were doubtless intended to transport troops and munitions of war up Red River, to Natchitoches, from which point a short land journey would reach New Mexico, then a province of old Spain. To revolutionize the Mexicans, was, beyond controversy, the object of that ardent, bold, and restless man, Aaron Burr. The result is well known to history.

As early as 1799, Mr. Barker was commissioned, by Gov. St. Clair, as a Justice of the Peace, for Washington County, at that time embracing a large portion of the southern territory of Ohio. He also received a Captain's commission from the same source, and was advanced, from time to time, through the various grades of promotion, to that of Colonel of the regiment. These were offices of distinction and honor in those days, when every citizen deemed it his duty to appear on parade, armed and equipped according to law. It was during this period in our history, that the present Senator, in Congress, from Michigan, Hon. Lewis Cass was Orderly-Sergeant in Capt. Burlingame's company of militia at Marietta.

In the year 1800 the House of Representatives in the territorial Legislature, issued an address to the citizens, requesting them to assemble in county conventions, and instruct their representatives on the question of forming a state government. It was a subject on which there was great division of sentiment. At a meeting of the citizens of Adams Township, Col. Barker was Chairman of a committee to report on this measure, at a subsequent assembly. He wrote a very full and able report in opposition to the question, which received the approbation of the committee. On the 17th of June, 1801, the delegates met at Marietta, as follows: for Marietta, Paul Fearing, and Elijah Backus; Belpre, Isaac Pearce, and Silas Bent; Waterford, Robert Oliver, and Gilbert Devol; Adams, Joseph Barker; Newport, Philip Witten, and Samuel Williamson; Middletown, (or Athens,) Alvin Bingham; Gallipolis, Robert Safford. Gilbert Devol was chairman, and Joseph Barker, clerk. Col. Barker presented his views in a well written argument, in opposition to the policy of entering into a state government; especially setting forth the injurious effects, of the measure, to the settlers in the Ohio Company's purchase. They had been struggling with the hardships of first opening the wilderness, since the year 1788; and for a large part of the time, pressed by the merciless savage to the extremes of want, danger, and even death. The population was sparse, and generally poor. The expenses of government would be heavy in proportion to the inhabitants, while the advantages of a state government, over the territorial, would be few, perhaps none, in their present situation. The taxes to support it, would fall on the actual settlers and landholders, as the Ohio Company lands would all be brought on the tax list, while Congress lands, daily becoming more valuable by the improvements of the settlers, were to be free from taxation. These, with various other reasons, were used in support of the position taken, and were so satisfactory to the convention, that the report was unanimously adopted, and the following resolution passed:

"Resolved, That in our opinion, it would be highly impolitic, and very injurious to the inhabitants of this territory, to enter into a state government, at this time. Therefore, we, in behalf of our constituents, do request that you would use your best endeavors to prevent, and steadily oppose the adoption of any measures that may be taken for the purpose."

This, with the usual preamble, was signed by the Chairman, and sent to their representatives.

In the Legislature as well as among the people, there was a great division on this important question. Those who were fond of office and expected promotion, with a share of the loaves and fishes of the new dynasty, were the leaders in favor of the measure, and clamorous for its adoption, while the sober, judicious, and thinking men, were opposed to it. The advocates of the proposition, however, succeeded in rallying sufficient force in the Legislature, to carry the measure, and the eastern portion of the territory became the State of Ohio. So anxious were the ambitious men of the territory for the change, that they relinquished the right of taxing the lands owned by Congress until five years after they had been sold and in the possession of the purchaser; when, in equity, they should have been liable to taxation as soon as they were in his occupancy. The apprehensions of the evil results to the Ohio Company settlers, were soon realized, as the taxes for the support of the new government fell very heavily on them, and were very oppressive on the inhabitants of this district, as well as Symmes' purchase and the Connecticut reserve. This inequality remained until the year 1825, when the ad valorem system took place, and removed this long continued injustice.

Although an un-aspiring man, yet Col. Barker was called by his fellow citizens to hold many stations of trust and honor during his life. In 1818, he was elected a Representative for Washington County, in the State Legislature. He served for a number of years as a County Commissioner, and planned the model for the new courthouse, built in 1822, which is considered both a convenient and beautiful edifice.

He was often called on to deliver Fourth of July orations and agricultural addresses, in all which he acquitted himself with much credit. He possessed a good share of poetic genius, as well as imagination, and wrote a number of pieces quite well adapted to the occasion. One of these, for the Fourth of July, 1815, abounds in humor, and is well worth preserving as coming from the backwoods. It appears much better when sung than in simply reading.

THE BIRTHDAY OF UNCLE SAM
TUNE OF GOOD QUEEN BESS
Will you hear me, my friends, if I jingle in rhyme?
On the day Uncle Sam was first out of his prime, sir,
If I sing of the times, and the deeds he has done,
How he dress'd, how he fought, how the battle was won, sir?
Hail to the memory of old Uncle Sam,
Merry be the *birthday* of old Uncle Sam!
The family was young, and the farm rather new;
They had their odd notions like us, not a few, sir,
Had full faith in witches, gave conjurors devotion,
And to the oldest boy they gave a double portion, sir.
Proud be the birthday of old Uncle Sam,
Long live the memory of old Uncle Sam.
Our grandsires wore buckles on their shoes for to please;
Their jackets and their breeches both came to their knees, sir,
With a wig on the head and a cue tail so trim,
Nine inches on a hat was a fashionable brim, sir.
These were the boyish days of old Uncle Sam,
Long live the memory of old Uncle Sam.
Our grandmothers, too, were the patterns of good taste,
Three-quarters of a yard was the length of a waist, sir;
A cushion on the head, and a cork on the heel,
With a hoop in the gown quite as broad as a wheel, sir.
Such were the minor days of old Uncle Sam,
Long live the memory of old Uncle Sam.
They were tenants at will of the famous Johnny Bull,
Who demanded high rents and collected them in full, sir;
He tax'd them direct for each article they wore,
While his army and his stamp act vex'd them very sore, sir.
These were the sorry days of old Uncle Sam,

Merry be the birthday of old Uncle Sam.
"He'd a right to tax the colonies," so Johnny Bull declared,
"In any case whatever." Uncle Sammy thought it hard, sir,
But when he tried to make them pay a tax on their tea,
'Twas steep'd in Boston harbor, for the fishes in the sea, sir.
These were the spunky days of old Uncle Sam,
Long live the memory of old Uncle Sam.
Then Johnny Bull was wrath, and to give his passion vent,
He fell on Uncle Sam, and at fisticuffs they went, sir.
The squabble lasted long, and it proved very sore,
For Johnny Bull was pelted both behind and before, sir.
These were the fighting days of old Uncle Sam,
Long live the memory of old Uncle Sam.
Every farmer owned a short gun, and if he had good luck,
Could bring down a redcoat as easy as a buck, sir.
And when they fell in with Burgoyne and his men,
They took them as easy as turkeys in a pen, sir.
Proud be the birthday of old Uncle Sam,
Long live the memory of old Uncle Sam.
Every boat was a ship, every ship was a fleet;
Every boy was a sailor, every fisherman a mate, sir;
And then if the British but peep'd from their holes,
They hook'd them as easy as cod from the shoals, sir.
Proud be the memory of old Uncle Sam,
Long live the memory of old Uncle Sam.
Uncle Sam now obtained some *allies* and a fleet,
Some bayonets and men, with some rations to eat, sir;
Then in taking Cornwallis, so light was the job,
That they shelled him as farmers do corn from the cob, sir.
These were the proud days of old Uncle Sam,
Long live the memory of old Uncle Sam.
At length, Johnny Bull thought 'twas best to make a peace;
For in fighting for the feathers, he had lost all the geese, sir.
Then each made a promise they would do no more harm,
So he left Uncle Sam and his boys with the farm, sir,
Proud be the birthday of old Uncle Sam,
Long live the memory of old Uncle Sam.

In the year 1830, Col. Barker was elected an Associate Judge of the Court of Common Pleas, and at the expiration of the term in 1837, was again re-elected, which post he held until his declining health led him to resign in 1842. The duties of this office were discharged with great dignity and propriety, while his intimate knowledge of the principles of law enabled him to give correct and satisfactory decisions when his opinion was required.

His acquaintance through the State of Ohio was extensive, and his friends numerous. In hospitality, he was unsurpassed; fond of social intercourse, gifted with a ready flow of language, and a mind well stored with historical facts, his conversation was both instructive and interesting. This rendered his society very pleasing to both young and old. From the time of his settlement on the Muskingum, in 1795, to the period of his death, in 1843, nearly half a century, his house was open to receive the weary and destitute emigrant, the transient traveler, or the familiar friend; ever delighting in the opportunity of rendering a kindness to his fellow-man.

He was the father of ten children, four sons and six daughters, who, all but one, were living at his death, and most of them have large families of children, making numerous descendants to bear onward the family name.

Mrs. Barker died in 1835.

Nearly all those with whom he had "stood shoulder to shoulder" during the Indian War, and the trials incident to a new country, had been called away before him, and he felt that he was somewhat alone in the world, but he still retained the vigor of mind incident to younger days.

He died in September, 1843, aged seventy-eight years.

In person, Col. Barker was tall and commanding, with a stout, muscular frame; finely formed features, of rather a Roman cast, indicating manly firmness and intellectual vigor. His manners were easy, naturally graceful and gentlemanly, with the appearance and bearing of a man of superior mind and talents; born to lead in the councils, and to command the respect of the community in which he dwelt.

Chapter XXXV
HAMILTON KERR

This bold, active, and enterprising borderer was one of the spies, or Rangers, employed for the defense of the Ohio Company settlements during the Indian War. He was a finished backwoodsman, an adept in all the wiles and craft of the hunter, as well as in the arts of partisan warfare. He possessed the coolness and caution of old Isaac Williams, with the bravery and activity of Lewis Wetzel, having been trained under the instruction and example of both these noted pioneers.

Matthew Kerr, the father of Hamilton, was of Scotch descent, from one of the northern counties of Ireland. He immigrated to America, before the Revolutionary War, and lived in Philadelphia, where his son Hamilton was born. Soon after the close of the war, he moved his family west of the mountains, and settled on Chartier Creek, below Pittsburg. After staying here a short time, he removed to Wheeling, and lived in the vicinity of the Wetzels for several years. In 1787 he transferred his residence to the island, just above the mouth of the Muskingum, and Hamilton, then in the prime of manhood, engaged as a hunter for the garrison of Fort Harmar, supplying them with wild meat.

While living on Wheeling Creek, he was often the companion of Lewis Wetzel, the most famous hunter, and killer of Indians, in all that region; having killed, it is said, thirty-seven in the course of his life. His athletic frame, and bold bearing when a boy, won for him the goodwill of Lewis, and he promised to give him the first opportunity that occurred, of firing at an Indian, provided he felt certain that he could *"draw a sight"* at one, without trembling. The well-grown lad, then in his eighteenth year, answered, fearlessly, that he would. It was not long before Lewis, in one of his hunting trips, fell on the trail of a party, and traced up their camp. He directly hastened back for his young friend, whom he found ready and willing for the attack. They crept silently up to within a sure distance of their camp fire, and at the dawn of day, each selecting his man from a party of five or six, who were sitting in a circle round the fire, having just risen from sleep, fired at the same time. Hamilton's victim was sitting on a log, eating a roasted goose egg, and fell dead, into the ashes; while Wetzel's man was mortally wounded, but fled, and secreted himself in a tree top. They immediately rushed out from their covert, and with loud yells, calling out, *"Come on, boys, come on; why don't you head 'em;"* as if there were quite a number of white men in the attack. The remaining Indians took to flight, without waiting to count their foes, and secreted themselves in the thickets. After taking the scalp of the dead Indian, they left the ground; and coming out the next day with a larger party, traced the wounded Indian by his blood, and found him dead in the spot where he had hidden. This was Kerr's first adventure with the Indians, and might be construed as an omen of future success; although his next encounter was less propitious.

The time of a large portion of the young men who lived on the frontiers, was occupied in hunting and trapping; little attention being paid to cultivation of the earth, beyond the wants of the family for bread, which was chiefly made from corn meal. There was no market for produce; while there was a steady demand for skins and peltry, by the traders, who collected them at various points along the water-courses, and transmitted them, on pack-horses, across the mountains, to Baltimore or Philadelphia. This manner of dealing, made hunting a regular employment, like farming in these days.

In the spring of the year 1784, before Fort Harmar was built, or any settlements made by the whites, between Baker's Station and the mouth of Big Kanawha, a party of young men left the post in a large canoe on a trapping and hunting expedition. It was composed of Lewis and George Wetzel, John Greene, Hamilton Kerr, and one other man. They dropped down the river as low as Muskingum Island, where they encamped. The next day at evening they went over to the mouth of the Muskingum, and set their traps for beaver, returning to the island as a safe place for their camp, against the attack of the Indians. The following morning they went down again, and thirty or forty rods above the mouth, landed two of their party to reconnoiter, and examine the woods for signs of an enemy, while the other three remained in the canoe, and went into the Muskingum to examine their traps. They directly discovered that several of them were missing, and immediately concluded that a party of Indians had discovered their marks, and stolen them. George Wetzel soon returned to the canoe, and reported that he had seen no Indians, but plenty of signs of bears, which had been wallowing and tearing down the weeds in several places. This confirmed their suspicions that they were in the vicinity of a large party of Indians. Taking George on board, they pushed up the Ohio, and had proceeded twenty or thirty rods on their return, when four Indians stepped on to the bank, and from behind trees fired upon the men in the canoe. George Wetzel was shot through the head, and fell dead into the boat. Kerr was shot in the left arm above the elbow, splintering the bone, and received a bullet at the same time through the fleshy portion of his side. His dog, a noble, large animal standing by his master, was also killed. The other two men escaped injury; and pushing out into the stream before they could reload, were soon out of danger.

John Greene, who rambled farther into the woods than George, had returned to within a few rods of the bank, when the Indians fired, and hearing the report of their rifles, rushed up to see what his comrades had shot at. As he approached within twenty yards of the bank, he saw an Indian behind a tree, in the act of pushing down a bullet in his rifle. Comprehending at once the condition of the parties, he instantly raised his piece, fired, and the Indian fell dead, tumbling headlong down the bank, near the brink of which he was standing, and rolled close to the water's edge. The other Indians, hearing the report of the shot and seeing their dead companion, came rushing upon their new enemy before he could reload. His only safety was now in flight; and running toward the swamp a short distance back from the river, in the windings and turnings of the pursuit, counted not less than ten or twelve Indians, whom the shots and the war cry of the savages had called into the chase. After wading in the water for some time, and seeing no chance for escape by flight, he secreted himself under the tops of a fallen tree, whose leaves and branches sheltered him from observation. As a further precaution, he buried himself beneath the water, leaving only so much of his face uncovered as allowed of respiration. This was a common mode of eluding pursuit, practiced by the natives, as well as cunning white men. The Indians, a few rods behind, traced him by the turbid appearance of the water, and walked directly on to the trunk, beneath whose top he lay concealed. Looking up through his leafy covert, he plainly saw his enemies, peering into every crevice and behind every twig for their victim, vociferating in angry tones their vengeful thoughts, and pointing with their gun-sticks to the recent signs of his flight. Greene lay perfectly quiet, hardly daring to breathe, fearing lest even the beating of his heart should agitate the water; watching with intense anxiety their movements, until finally, to his great relief, they gave up the search as hopeless. As soon as the darkness of night concealed his movements, he left his watery bed, wet, weary, and hungry. Having a long journey before him, he instantly commenced his march for home, thankful that he had been able to escape the scalping knife of his foes. He traveled across the ridges, the nearest route, well known to the hunters of that day. In the course of his journey he passed no less than three deserted Indian hunting camps, so recently left that the fire was still burning, without being discovered. So rapid was his march, that he reached Baker's before his companions in the canoe, who pushed up stream as rapidly as they could, and buried the dead man on an island twenty-five miles above Marietta, now known as Williamson's. This mournful work detained them some time, as they had no spades but their wooden paddles with which to dig the grave. The favorite dog of Kerr, whose dead body had made a pillow for the head of his wounded master, was buried at the same place.

A few miles above this island at the head of the Long Reach, a spot well known to old as well as modern boatmen, they discovered just at evening, during a heavy shower of rain, on the Virginia shore, a white horse tied to a stake near the water. On the top of the bank they saw a hickory tree just stripped of the bark. The quick apprehension of the borderers instantly understood these signs as denoting a party of Indians who had stolen the horse, and were preparing a bark canoe for crossing the river. The shower coming on when they had finished it, the canoe was turned bottom up, and the Indians had crept under as a shelter from the storm. This prevented the whites from being seen. They directly crossed to the other shore, and pushed rapidly on until a turn in the river hid them from sight.

Kerr's arm was several months in healing, the bone being splintered, and no remedies but slippery elm bark and such other simples as the woods afforded. The injuries received in this excursion, kept Hamilton from any other adventures for some time. When able, he hunted deer in the neighboring hills and visited the stations at Grave Creek, where Isaac Williams lived, and with whom he had become quite a favorite, making various short tours of trapping and hunting in his company, so that his house was as free to him and nearly as much his home as that of his own father.

In 1785, the Indian depredations were frequent and destructive. Notice having been received of a large war party fitting out for the attack of Grave Creek, the settlement was abandoned, and Mr. Williams moved his family, with the rest of his neighbors, to Wheeling. Kerr also made this place his home with his father. It was during this period that he had a second narrow escape from death by the Indians.

In the summer of 1785, in company with Thomas Mills and Henry Smith, he went up the Ohio a few miles, near the head of the first island above Wheeling, spearing fish by torchlight. While busily occupied with their sport, thinking of no danger, in a quiet, shallow eddy near the shore, ten or twelve Indians who had been attracted by the light, rose up on the top of the bank, and fired a volley at them. Mills, who was in the bow of the canoe near the torch, received several balls in his body and limbs and fell, apparently dead, into the bottom of the boat. The others were unharmed, but also fell down on the bottom of the boat, to screen themselves from a repetition of the shots. The Indians seeing the effect of their fire, dropped their guns, rushed down the bank, and into the river, with the intention of dragging the canoe ashore, and securing the scalps of their dead enemies. The splashing of the water gave notice of their approach; when Kerr, who was in the waist of the boat, sprang into the bow, and brandishing his fish-spear, made motions to stab the first man who came within his reach. The long, barbed points of the instrument, made it a formidable weapon to the half-naked bodies of the savages, while the resolute bearing of the man who wielded it, made them cautious of approaching too near. Although he could have plunged it into several of them, he did not think it prudent to do so, lest they should seize it, and drag him ashore, or pull him out of the canoe. After one or two minutes spent in this mimic warfare, the boat gradually receded, by the whirl of the eddy, into deeper water, and the man in the stern, having so far recovered his senses from the first shock, as to begin to apply his paddle, they were soon out of their reach. The Indians, now with loud yells, and aggravated rage at their disappointment and folly, in leaving all their guns on the top of the bank, rushed up to regain them, and running along the sandy beach ahead of the boat, waded into the water, breast-high, to bring them nearer the canoe, which was now in the middle of the stream. While exulting at the prospect of escape, a new enemy sprang up on the opposite side of the river. A party of Indians on their own shore, heaving the firing and shouts of their countrymen, began to fire at them. The balls passed all around, and through the sides of the canoe, but missed the mark, as they generally dropped into the bottom, at the sight of the flash, and were hid by the sides of the boat. After a pursuit of one or two miles, Kerr concluded that this slow progress would be their destruction, and pushing manfully ahead, regardless of their shots, was soon out of their reach. When the enraged Indians saw that their victims would escape, they fell to taunting them with insulting language and obscene attitudes. Kerr then keenly felt the want of his trusty rifle, with which he could have shot several of them; but no one had taken his arms with him, not expecting to meet an enemy, or to have use for anything, but the fish-spear. When they reached the garrison at Wheeling, Mills was still alive, and taken into the town, where, under the care of Mrs. Rebecca Williams, and one other skillful matron, he finally recovered from his hopeless condition, having not less than twelve or fourteen different wounds, with an arm and a leg broken by the shots of the savages. On this occasion, the intrepidity and presence of mind in Kerr, no doubt saved their lives from the tomahawk, and knives of the Indians; while his mode of defense, in their condition, was the only one that could have been effectual.

The winter after this adventure was passed in Wheeling.

Early in the spring of 1786, Kerr, in company with Isaac Williams and a Dutchman named Jacob, made a visit to the deserted plantations at Grave Creek, to look after the cattle and hogs that had been left there. They passed the night in an empty cabin at Little Grave Creek, about a mile above the larger stream. Soon after daylight in the morning, they heard a rifle shot in the direction of Mr. Williams' farm. Not thinking of Indians, he attributed the shot to moving boatmen, who sometimes, when short of provision, landed at the deserted clearings and killed a hog. It so happened that a party of four Indians, who had been scouting on Wheeling Creek, had that morning reached the Ohio with their plunder, one white prisoner and some horses; seeing Mr. Williams' hogs, they killed one with the rifle and put it into their canoe, which had been secreted in the mouth of the creek. Three of the Indians took possession of the canoe with their prisoner, while the fourth was busied in swimming the horses across the river. At this critical juncture, Kerr and his companions started at a rapid gait to arrest the marauders. Being in the prime of life and more active than his companions, he reached the mouth of the creek first, and looking down the bank, saw the three Indians standing in the canoe. At the feet of the one in the middle of the boat lay four rifles and a dead hog, while a fourth Indian was swimming a horse over the Ohio, a few rods from the shore. An Indian in the stern had his paddle in the water, in the act of shoving the canoe from the mouth of the creek into the river. Before they were aware of his presence, Kerr shot the Indian in the stern, who fell into the river. The crack of his rifle had scarcely ceased when Williams came on to the bank, and shot an Indian in the bow of the canoe, who also fell overboard. At this time Jacob came up, and handing his rifle to Kerr as the better marksman, he shot the other Indian in the waist of the boat, who also fell into the water, but still held on to the side of the canoe with one hand. So amazed was the latter Indian at the fall of his companions, that he never offered to raise one of the rifles at his feet in self defense, but acted like one deprived of his senses. By this time, the canoe impelled by the impetus given to it by the first Indian, had reached the current of the Ohio, and was some rods below the mouth of the creek. Kerr now reloaded his own gun, and seeing a man in the bottom of the boat, raised it in act of firing, when he, discovering the movement, called out, *"Don't shoot, I am a white man!"* He was directed to knock loose the Indian's hand from the side of the canoe, and paddle to shore. In reply, he said his arm was broken. The current, however, set it near some rocks not far from land, on to which he jumped and waded out. Kerr now aimed his rifle at the Indian on the horse, who was near the middle of the river. The shot struck close by him, splashing the water on to his naked skin. Seeing the fate of his companions, the Indian, with the bravery of an ancient Spartan, immediately slipped from the horse, and swam for the abandoned canoe, in which were the rifles and ammunition of the whole party. This was in fact an act of necessity, as well as of noble daring, for he well knew he could not reach his country without the means of killing game by the way. There was also in this act but little hazard, as his enemies could not cross the creek without a canoe, while the current had now set the object of his solicitude beyond the reach of rifle shot. He soon gained possession of the canoe, crossed with it to the other shore, and taking out the arms and ammunition, mounted the captive horse, and with a shout of defiance, escaped into the woods. The canoe was turned adrift and taken up near Maysville, with the dead hog still in it, which had caused their discovery by their shooting, and been the source of all their misfortunes.

The following year he moved with his father to Devol's Island, near Fort Harmar, where the latter kept several cows and supplied the officers with milk, while Hamilton was employed as a hunter to furnish the garrison with buffalo meat and venison. Isaac Williams and several other families also moved at the same time, being the spring of 1787, and opened a plantation in the forest, opposite the mouth of the Muskingum, on the Virginia shore. In the spring of 1791, after the death of Capt. Rogers, one of the Ohio Company's Rangers, he was hired to supply his place, and was esteemed the most active and brave man in that hazardous employment. He continued to serve during the whole war, and several Indians fell by his hand, as related in the preceding history of the Ohio Company settlements. During this period, his father's family left the island, and lived within the walls of the garrison at the Point. The Indians killed his father early in the war, at the mouth of Duck Creek, which still further sharpened his revenge and hate of the red men.

At the close of the war he married Susannah, the daughter of Col. John Nighswonger, one of the heroes of the Battle of Point Pleasant. She was well educated, and could read German and English, while Hamilton could do neither, having never been a day to school in his life. He owned a share of land in the Ohio Company, the purchase money for which was earned in the course of a single fall and winter hunt; so profitable was that business in early times to skillful hunters. With the most intelligent men amongst the Ohio Company's settlers, Kerr was a great favorite, for his manly, upright conduct, vigilance, and bravery in guarding the settlements from the attack of the Indians.

In person, he was of a full medium size, being five feet ten inches in height, as ascertained from one of Col. Sproat's old payrolls, with limbs fashioned in nature's finest mould; form erect, and movements agile as any red man of the forest; of a pleasant, cheerful temperament; light complexion, blue eyes, and reddish hair, denoting his Scotch descent; fine, full forehead, with all the marks of a superior mind and intellect. This had received no training but what his own remarks on men and things had produced; but for reflection and strong reasoning powers, was far superior to men of his class, causing him always to be looked up to as a leader in any dangerous emergency by his companions.

He was born in the year 1764, making him twenty years old at the time the Indians wounded him at the mouth of the Muskingum.

After the war, he settled on his land at the outlet of Leading Creek; learned to read and write, became a substantial farmer, a Major in the militia, and highly esteemed by all his neighbors! He has been dead several years, leaving a large family of descendants, who live in Meigs and Gallia counties.

Chapter XXXVI

ISAAC WILLIAMS AND MRS. REBECCA WILLIAMS

To those who are now enjoying the benefits of the toils and dangers of the early explorers and pioneers of the valley of the Ohio, there ought to be no more pleasant employment than that of recounting their exploits and preserving the remembrance of their names. It is a duty we owe to their memory. Amongst that hardy list of adventurers, on the left bank of the Ohio, none are more worthy of preservation than those at the head of this article.

Isaac Williams was born in Chester County, Penn., the 16th of July, 1737. While he was yet a boy, his parents moved to Winchester, Va., then a frontier town. Soon after this event his father died, and his mother married Mr. Buckley. When he was about eighteen years old, the colonial government employed him as a Ranger, or spy, to watch the movements of the Indians, for which his early acquaintance with a hunter's life eminently fitted him. In this capacity he served in the army of Gen. Braddock, during his short, but disastrous campaign. He was also attached to the party which guarded the first convoy of provisions to Fort du Quesne, after its surrender to Gen. Forbes, in 1758. The stores were carried on pack horses over the rough declivities of the mountains, continually exposed to the attack of the Indians, for which the deep ravines and narrow ridges of the mountains afforded every facility.

After the peace made with the Indians in 1765 by Col. Bouquet, the country on the waters of the Monongahela began to be settled by the people east of the mountains. The fertility of the soil, and the immense growth of the forest trees, so different from that on the eastern side of the mountain ranges, gave a romantic charm to the new regions on the waters of the Ohio, and made it a desirable abode to the backwoodsmen, especially as it abounded with wild game. Amongst the early emigrants to this region were the parents of Mr. Williams, whom he conducted across the mountains, in 1768, but did not finally locate himself in the west until the following year, when he settled on the waters of Buffalo Creek, near the present town of West Liberty, Brooke County, Va. He accompanied Ebenezer and Jonathan Zane when they explored and located the country at and about Wheeling, in the year 1769. Previous to this period, however, he had made several hunting and trapping excursions to the waters of the Ohio, and was familiar with its topography. In returning from one of these adventurous expeditions in company with two other men, in the winter of 1769, the following incident befell him.

Early in December, as they were crossing the *glades,* or table-lands of the Alleghany Mountains, they were overtaken by a violent snowstorm. This is always a stormy, cold region, but on the present occasion the snow fell to the depth of five or six feet, and put a stop to their further progress. It was succeeded by intensely cold weather. While thus confined to their camp, with a scanty supply of food and no chance of procuring more, one of his companions was taken sick and died, partly from disease, and having no nourishment but the tough, indigestible skins of their peltry, from which the hair was first burned off and then boiled in their kettle. Soon after the death of this man his remaining companion, from the difficulty of procuring fuel to keep up their fire, was so much frozen in the feet that he could render no further assistance. He managed, however, to bury the dead man in the snow. The feet of the poor fellow were so badly frosted that he lost all his toes and a part of each foot, rendering him unable to walk for nearly a month. During this time their food consisted of their skins, of which they had a good supply, boiled into soup with the water of melted snow. The kind heart of Mr. Williams would not allow him to leave his friend in this suffering condition, while he went to the settlements for assistance, lest he should be attacked by the wolves, or perish for want of food. With a patience and fortitude that would have awarded him a civic crown in the best days of the chivalrous Romans, he remained with his helpless companion until he was so far recovered as to be able to accompany him in his return home. So much reduced was his own strength from the effects of starvation, that it was several months before he was restored to his usual health.

In 1769 he became a resident of the western wilds, and made his home on the waters of Buffalo Creek, as before noted. Here he found himself in a wide field for the exercise of his darling passion, hunting. From his boyhood, he had discovered a great relish for the hunter's life, and in this employment he for several years explored the recesses of the forest, and followed the water-courses of the great valley, to the mouth of the Ohio, and from thence, along the shores of the Mississippi, to the banks of the turbid Missouri. As early as the year 1770, he trapped the beaver on the tributaries of this river, and returned in safety, with a rich load of furs. During the prime of his life, he was occupied in hunting, and in making entries of lands. This was done by girdling a few trees, and planting a small patch of corn, which operation entitled the person to four hundred acres of land. Entries of this kind were aptly called tomahawk improvements. An enterprising man could make a number of these in a season, and sell them to persons, who, coming later to the country, had not so good an opportunity to select the best lands, as the first adventurers. Mr. Williams sold many of the rights for a few dollars, or the value of a rifle-gun, which was then thought a fair equivalent; of so little account was land then considered; and besides, like other hunters of the day, thought wild lands of little value, except for hunting grounds. There was, however, another advantage attached to these simple claims; it gave the possessor the right of entering one thousand acres adjoining the improvement, on condition of his paying a small sum of money per acre into the treasury of the State of Virginia. These entries were denominated *"Pre-emption Rights*;" and many of the richest lands on the left bank of the Ohio River are now held under these titles. After the conquest of Kaskaskia and Post Vincent, by Gen. Clark, in 1778, Virginia claimed the lands on the northwest side of the Ohio; and many similar entries were made in the present State of Ohio, especially on the Muskingum River, as high up as Duncan's Falls. One tract, a few miles above Marietta, is still known as Wiseman's Bottom, after the man who made an entry there.

While occupied in these pursuits he became acquainted with Rebecca Martin, the daughter of Mr. Joseph Tomlinson, of Maryland, then a young widow, and married her in October, 1775. Her former husband, John Martin, had been a trader among the Indians, and was killed on the Big Hockhocking, in the year 1770. A man by the name of Hartness, her uncle on the mother's side, was killed with him at the same time. As a striking proof of the veneration of the Indians for William Penn, and the people of his colony, two men from Pennsylvania, who were with them, were spared. The two killed, were from Virginia. The fact is referred to by Lord Dunmore, in his speech at the Indian treaty, near Chillicothe, in the year 1774. Mr. Williams accompanied Dunmore, in this campaign, and acted as a Ranger until its close.

By this marriage he was united to a woman whose spirit was congenial to his own. She was born on the 14th of February, 1754, at Will's Creek, on the Potomac, in the province of Maryland, and had removed, with her two brothers, Samuel and Joseph, into the western country, in 1771, and was living with them as their housekeeper, near the mouth of Grave Creek; and for weeks together, while they were absent on tours of hunting, she was left entirely alone. She was now in her twenty-first year, full of life and activity, and as fearless of danger as the man who had chosen her for his companion. One proof of her courageous spirit is related by her niece, Mrs. Bakey, now living near Marietta, in Wood Co., Va.

In the spring of the year 1774, she made a visit to a sister, Mrs. Baker, then living on the Ohio River opposite to the mouth of Yellow Creek. It was soon after the massacre of Logan's relatives at Baker's station. Having finished her visit, she prepared to return home in a canoe, by herself, the traveling being entirely done by water. The distance from her sister's to Grave Creek was about fifty miles. She left there in the afternoon, and paddled her light canoe rapidly along until dark. Knowing that the moon would rise at a certain hour, she landed, and fastening the slender craft to the willows she leaped on shore, and lying down in a thick clump of bushes, waited the rising of the moon. As soon as it had cleared the tops of the trees, and began to shed its cheerful rays over the dark bosom of the Ohio, she prepared to embark. The water being shallow near the shore, she had to wade a few paces before getting into the canoe; when just in the act of stepping on board, her naked foot rested on the dead, cold body of an Indian, who had been killed a short time before, and which, in the gloom of the night, she had not seen in landing. Without screaming or flinching, she stepped lightly into the canoe, with the reflection that she was thankful he was not alive. Resuming the paddle, she arrived at the mouth of Grave Creek without any further adventure, early the following morning.

Walter Scott's Rebecca, the Jewess, was not more celebrated for her cures, and skill in treating wounds, than was Rebecca Williams amongst the honest borderers of the Ohio River. About the year 1784, while living a short time at Wheeling, on account of Indian depredations, she, with the assistance of Mrs. Zane, dressed the wounds of Mr. Mills, fourteen in number, from rifle shots. He, with Hamilton Kerr and one other man were spearing fish by torch-light about a mile above the garrison, when they were fired on by a party of Indians secreted on the shore. Mills stood in the bow of the canoe holding the torch, and as he was a fair mark, received the most of the shots. One leg and one arm were broken, in addition to the flesh wounds. Had he been in the regular service, with plenty of surgeons, he probably would have lost one or both limbs by amputation. These women, with their fomentations and simple applications of slippery elm bark, not only cured his wounds, at the time deemed impossible, but also saved both his limbs. In a conversation many years after, she said her principal dressings were made of slippery elm, the leaves of stramonium, and daily ablutions with warm water. Many similar cures of gunshot wounds are related, as performed by her in the first settlement of the country.

Their marriage was as unostentatious and simple as the manners and habits of the parties. A traveling preacher happening to come into the settlement, as they sometimes did, though rarely, they were married at her brother's house, without any previous preparation of nice dresses, bride-cakes, or bride-maids; he standing up in his hunting dress, and she in a short gown and petticoat of homespun, the common wear of the people.

In the summer of 1774, the year before her marriage, she was one morning busily occupied in kindling a fire preparatory to breakfast, with her back to the door, on her knees, puffing away at the coals. Hearing some one step cautiously on the floor, she looked round and beheld a tall Indian close to her side. He made a motion of silence to her, at the same time shaking his tomahawk in a threatening manner, if she made any alarm. He, however, did not offer to harm her, but looking carefully around the cabin, espied her brother's rifle hanging over the fireplace. This he seized upon, and fearing the arrival of some of the men, hastened his departure without any further damage. While he was with her in the house she preserved her presence of mind and betrayed no marks of fear; but no sooner had he gone than she left the cabin and hid herself in the cornfield until her brother Samuel came in. He was lame at the time, and happened to be out of the way; so that it is probable his life was saved from this circumstance. It was but seldom that the Indians killed unresisting women or children, except in the excitement of an attack, and when they had met with resistance from the men.

In 1777, the depredations and massacres of the savages were so frequent that the settlement at Grave Creek, now consisting of several families, was broken up. It was the frontier station, and lower on the Ohio than any other above the mouth of Big Kanawha. This year the Indians made their great attack on the garrison and settlement of Wheeling. Mr. Williams, with his wife and the Tomlinsons, moved over on to the Monongahela River, above Red Stone' old fort. Here he remained until the spring of the year 1783, when he returned with his wife's relations to their plantations on Grave Creek. In the year 1784 he had to remove again from his farm into the garrison at Wheeling. Sometime in the spring of the succeeding year he had the following adventure with the Indians.

John Wetzel, a younger brother of Lewis, the noted Indian hunter and *Indian hater,* (having killed above thirty of them,) then about sixteen years old, with a neighboring boy of the same age, was in search of horses that had strayed away in the woods on Wheeling Creek, where the father of John resided. One of the stray animals was a mare with a young foal, belonging to John's sister; and she had offered the colt to John as a reward for finding the mare. While on this service they were captured by four Indians, who, having come across the horses in the woods had taken and placed them in a thicket, expecting that their bells would attract the notice of their owners, and they could then capture them or take their scalps. The horse was ever a favorite object of plunder with the savages, as not only facilitating their own escape from pursuit, but also assisted them in carrying off the spoils. The boys, hearing the well known tinkle of the bells, approached the spot where the Indians lay concealed, and were taken prisoners. John, in attempting to escape, was shot through the arm. On their march to the Ohio, his companion made so much lamentation on account of his captivity, that the Indians killed him with the tomahawk; while John, who had once before been a prisoner, made light of it, and went along cheerfully with his wounded arm.

The party struck the Ohio River early the following morning at a point near the mouth of Grave Creek, just below the clearing of Mr. Tomlinson. Here they found some hogs belonging to Mr. Williams, and killing one of them with a rifle shot, put it into a canoe they had secreted when on their way out. Three of the Indians took possession of the canoe with their prisoner, while the other Indian was occupied in swimming the horses across the river. It so happened, that Mr. Williams, with Hamilton Kerr, and Jacob, a Dutchman, had come down from Wheeling, the evening before, to look after the stock left on the plantation, and passed the night at the deserted cabin of Tomlinson. While at the outlet of Little Grave Creek, about a mile above, they heard the report of a rifle shot, in the direction of his plantation. *"Dod rot 'em,"* exclaimed Williams, *"a Kentuck boat has landed at the creek, and they are shooting my hogs."* Immediately quickening their pace to a rapid trot, they, in a few minutes, were within a short distance of the creek, when they heard the loud snort of a horse. Kerr being in the prime of life, and younger than Williams, reached the mouth of the creek first. As he looked down into the stream, he saw three Indians standing in a canoe; one was in the stern, one in the bow, and one in the middle of the boat. At the feet of the latter lay four rifles and the dead hog; while the fourth Indian was swimming a horse across the Ohio, only a few rods from shore. The one in the stern was in the act of shoving the canoe from the mouth of the creek into the river. Before they were aware of his presence, Kerr shot the Indian in the stern, who fell into the water. The crack of the rifle had barely ceased, when Mr. Williams came on to the bank, and shot the Indian in the bow of the canoe, who also fell overboard; Jacob was now on the ground, and Kerr seizing his rifle, shot the remaining Indian in the waist of the boat. He fell over into the water, but still held on to the side of the canoe, with one hand. The whole process did not occupy more than a minute of time. The canoe, impelled by the impetus given to it by the Indian first shot, had reached the current of the Ohio, and was a rod or two below the mouth of the creek. Kerr had now reloaded his gun, and seeing another Indian, as he thought, laying in the bottom of the canoe, raised it in the act of firing, when he called out, *"Don't shoot, I am a white man!"* Kerr told him to knock loose the Indian's hand from the side of the boat, and paddle it to the shore. He said his arm was broken, and he could not. The current, however, set it near some rocks not far from land, on to which he jumped, and waded out. Kerr now aimed his rifle at the Indian on horseback, who, by this time, had reached the middle of the Ohio. The shot struck near him, splashing the water on to his naked skin. He, seeing the fate of his companions, with the bravery of an ancient Spartan, slipped from the back of the horse, and swam for the abandoned canoe, in which were the rifles of the four Indians. This was, in fact, an act of necessity, as well as of noble daring, as he well knew he could not reach his country, without the means of killing game by the way. He also was aware, that there was little danger in the act, as his enemies could not cross the creek to molest him. He soon gained possession of the boat, crossed, with the arms, to his own side of the Ohio, mounted the captive horse, which, with the others, had swam to the Indian shore, and with a yell of defiance, escaped into the woods. The canoe was turned adrift, and taken up near Maysville, with the dead hog still in it, which had led to their discovery by the shot, and was the cause of all their misfortunes.

It has been stated that Mrs. Williams, before her marriage, acted as housekeeper for her brothers several years; in consideration of which service, Joseph and Samuel made an entry of four hundred acres of land on the Virginia shore of the Ohio River, in that broad, rich bottom, directly opposite to the mouth of the Muskingum River, for their sister; girdling the trees on four acres of land, fencing, and planting it with corn, and building a cabin, in the spring of the year 1773. They spent the summer on the spot, occupying their time with hunting during the growth of the crop.

In this time they had exhausted their small stock of salt and bread-stuff, and lived for two or three months on the boiled meat of turkeys, which then filled the woods, and was used without salt. So accustomed had Samuel become to eating his food without this condiment, that it was some time before he could again relish the taste of it; a fact that has often been verified in others under similar circumstances; showing that the use of salt is acquired by habit. The following winter the two brothers hunted on the Great Kanawha, where bears and beavers greatly abounded. Sometime in March, 1774, they arrived at the mouth of the river on their return, and were detained some days by a remarkably high freshet in the Ohio River, which, from certain fixed marks on Wheeling Creek, is supposed to have been fully equal to that of February, 1832. This year was long known among the borderers as that of Dunmore's War; serving as a date for domestic events, and noted for Indian depredations.

The land entered thus early for Mrs. Williams still remains in the possession of her descendants, but was for many years contested, in law, by other more recent claimants, like all the Virginia western lands; causing great expense and anxiety to the rightful owners.

The renewed and oft repeated inroads of the Indians, led Mr. Williams to turn his attention toward a more safe and quiet home than that at Grave Creek. Fort Harmar, at the mouth of the Muskingum, having been erected in 1786, and garrisoned by United States troops, he decided on occupying the land belonging to his wife, which embraced a large share of rich alluvions, and was in sight of the fort. The piece opened by the Tomlinsons, in 1773, had grown over with young saplings, but could be easily reclaimed. He visited the spot, and put up a log cabin in the winter, and moved his family thither the 26th of March, 1787, being the year before the arrival of the Ohio Company.

Soon after the removal to his forest domain, his wife gave birth to a daughter; and was the only issue by this marriage. He was now fifty-two years, old, so that she might be called the child of his old age. She was named Drusilla; and married Mr. John Henderson; but died when about twenty years old, leaving no children.

Soon after the associates of the Ohio Company had settled at Marietta, a very friendly intercourse was kept up between them and Mr. Williams; and as he had now turned his attention more to farming than hunting, he was pleased to see the new openings made in the forest, and the wilderness changing into the home of civilized man. From the destructive effect of an untimely frost in September, 1789, the crops of corn were greatly damaged; and where late planted, entirely ruined.

In the spring and summer of 1790, the inhabitants in the new settlements of the Ohio Company, began to suffer from the want of food, especially wholesome bread-stuffs. Many families, especially at Belpre, had no other meal than that made from moldy corn; and were sometimes destitute even of this, several days in succession. This moldy corn commanded the price of a dollar and a half, and even two dollars a bushel. When ground in their hand-mills, and made into bread, few stomachs were able to digest, or retain it, more than a few minutes. The writer of this article, has often heard Charles Devol, Esq., then a small boy, relate, with much feeling, his gastronomic trials with this moldy meal made into sap-porridge; which, when made of sweet corn meal, and the fresh saccharine juice of the maple, was both a nourishing and a savory dish. The family, then living at Belpre, had been without food for two days, when his father returned from Marietta, just at evening, with a scanty supply of moldy corn. The hand-mill was immediately put in operation, and the meal cooked into sap-porridge, as it was then the season of sugar-making. The famished children swallowed eagerly the unsavory mess, which was almost as instantly rejected; reminding us of the deadly pottage of the children of the prophet; but lacking the healing power of an Elijah to render it salutary and nutritious. Disappointed of expected relief, the poor children went supperless to bed, to dream of savory food and plenteous meals, not realized in their waking hours.

It was during this period of want, that Isaac Williams displayed his benevolent feelings for the suffering colonists. From the circumstance of his being in the country earlier, he had more ground cleared, and had raised a large crop of several hundred bushels of good, sound corn. This he now distributed amongst the inhabitants at the low rate of fifty cents a bushel, when at the same time he had been offered, and urged to take, a dollar and twenty-five cents for his whole crop, by speculators; for man has ever been disposed to take advantage of the distresses of his fellows. *"Dod rot 'em!,"* said the honest hunter, *"I would not let them have a bushel!"* He not only parted with his corn at this cheap rate, the common price in plentiful years, but he also prudently apportioned the number of bushels to the number of individuals in a family. An empty purse was no bar to the needy applicant, but his wants were equally supplied with those who had money, and a credit given until more favorable seasons should enable him to discharge the debt.

Capt. Devol, hearing of Mr. William's corn, and the low rate at which he sold it, made a trip to Marietta, directly after the adventure, with the sap-porridge, to procure some of it. The journey was made by land, and in the night, traveling on the ridges adjacent to the river, as the stream was so swollen by the spring flood, as to prevent the ascent by water in a canoe. He chose to come in the night, on account of danger from the Indians; and the intrepidity of the man, may be estimated, from his traveling this distance, twelve or fourteen miles, alone. He reached Fort Harmar at daylight; and Maj. Doughty, after giving him a warm breakfast, directed two soldiers to set him across the Ohio, in the garrison boat. Mr. Williams treated him with much kindness; and after supplying him with corn, also furnished him with his only canoe, in which to transport it to his home. Capt. Devol was unwilling to take it;

but he urged it upon him, saying he could soon make another. In after years, when Capt. Devol owned a fine farm and mill on the Muskingum River, Mr. Williams used often to visit him, and pass a night or two at his house, which was the temple of hospitality, in the most social and pleasant manner, talking of the trials and sufferings of bygone days.

He retained a relish for hunting to his latest years; and whenever a little unwell, forsaking his comfortable home, would take his rifle, and favorite old dog "Cap," accompanied by one of his black servants, retire to the woods, and encamping by some clear stream, remain there drinking the pure water, and eating such food as his rifle procured, until his health was restored. Medicine he never took, except such simples as the forest afforded. The untrodden wilderness was to him full of charms; and before the close of the Revolutionary War, he had hunted over a large portion of the valley of the Ohio, sometimes with a companion, but oftener alone, leaving his favorite Rebecca to oversee and take charge of the little plantation, which was never very extensive, until he moved to his new home, opposite the mouth of the Muskingum.

From his sedate manners and quiet habits, the trapping of the beaver was a favorite pursuit; and after he was seventy years old, if he heard of the signs of one being seen within fifty miles of his home, would mount his horse with his traps, and not return until he had caught it. This was a great art amongst the hunters of the west, and he who was the most successful in this mystery, was accounted a fortunate man. The proceeds of a few months hunt often realizing three or four hundred dollars to the trapper. He stood high in this branch of the hunter's vocation, and no man could catch more beavers than himself; being eminently qualified for this pursuit, both by disposition and by practice. He was a close observer of nature; taciturn in his manners, and cautious in his movements; never in a hurry, or disturbed by an unexpected occurrence. In many respects he was an exact portrait of Cooper's beau ideal of a master hunter, so finely portrayed in the Pioneer, and other backwoods legends.

During the Indian War, from 1791 to 1795, he remained unmolested in his cabin, a view of which is seen in the sketch of Fort Harmar, on the opposite shore of the Ohio, protected, in some measure, by the vicinity of that fort, as well as by the stockade around his dwellings, which sheltered several families besides his own.

He seldom spoke of his own exploits, and when related, they generally came from the lips of his companions. There was only one situation in which he could be induced to relax his natural reserve, and freely narrate the romantic and hazardous adventures that had befallen him in his hunting and war excursions; and that was when encamped by the evening fire, in some remote spot, after the toils of the day were closed, and the supper of venison and bear meat ended. Here, while reclining on a bed of fresh autumnal leaves, beneath the lofty branches of the forest, with no listeners but the stars and his companion, the spirit of narration would come upon him, and for hours he would rehearse the details of his youthful and hazardous adventures by forest, flood, and field. In such situations, surrounded by the works of God, his body and his mind felt a freedom that the hut and the clearing could not give. In this manner the late Alexander Henderson, a man of refined taste, and cultivated manners, has said that he passed some of the most interesting hours of his life, when hunting with Mr. Williams on the head waters of the Little Kanawha.

In person, he was of the middle size, with an upright frame, and muscular limbs; features firm, and strongly marked; a mild expression of countenance, and taciturn, quiet manners. In his youth he does not appear to have been addicted to the rude sports and rough plays so congenial to most of the early borderers, but preferred social converse, and an interchange of good offices with his fellows. Although he lived at a time and in a situation where he was deprived of all opportunity for religious instruction, yet he appears to have had an intuitive dread of all vicious words or actions. The writer distinctly recollects hearing him reprove a keel-boatman, a class of men whose language was intermingled with oaths, in the most severe manner, for his profanity, as he passed the boat where the man was at work. Like Isaac and Rebecca of old, this modern Isaac and Rebecca were given to good deeds; and many a poor, sick, abandoned boatman, has been nursed and restored to health beneath their humble roof. So intimately connected are their names with the early settlers of the Ohio Company that they deserve to go down to posterity together. Many years before his death, he liberated all his slaves, six or eight in number, and by his will left valuable tokens of his love and good feeling for the oppressed and despised African.

Full of days and good deeds, and strong in the faith of a blessed immortality, Mr. Williams resigned his spirit to Him who gave it, the 25th of September, 1820, aged eighty-four years, and was buried in a beautiful grove, on his own plantation, surrounded by the trees he so dearly loved when living.

Chapter XXXVII
HARMAN AND MARGARET BLENNERHASSETT.*

• These celebrated individuals, although not attached to the Ohio Company settlers, yet came into the territory so early as to be ranked among its pioneers. They fill so large and interesting a space in the history of this region, and did so much for the pecuniary benefit of the country of their adoption, that they deserve a place amongst the settlers of Washington County.

Harman Blennerhassett
1764 - 1831

Harman Blennerhassett, Esq., was a descendant of a noble family of Ireland, in the county of Cork. He was born in Hampshire, England, in the year 1767, while his parents were there on a visit. The family residence was Castle Conway, in the County of Kerry, to which they shortly after returned. He was educated with great care, and when a boy attended the Westminster School, celebrated for its classical excellence, completing his studies at Trinity College, Dublin, whose honors he shared in company with his relative, the celebrated T. A. Emmitt. They read law together at the King's Inn Courts, Dublin; were admitted to the bar on the same day in the year 1790, and between them existed ever after the warmest friendship. Having spent some time in traveling in France and the Netherlands, he returned and practiced at the bar in Ireland. Expecting, however, to fall heir to a large estate in a few years, he made but little effort to excel in the law, rather cultivating his taste for the sciences, music, and general literature.

At the death of his father, in 1796, he became possessed of a handsome fortune; but on account of the troubles in Ireland, in which he became politically involved, he sold the estate to his cousin, Lord Ventry, and went to England, where, he soon after married Miss Agnew, daughter of the Lieutenant-Governor of the Isle of Man, and granddaughter of Gen. Agnew, who fell at the Battle of Germantown. Lord Kingsale, and Admiral De Courcey, of the navy, both married sisters of Mr. Blennerhassett; who, expressing rather freely his republican principles, in opposition to his relations, finally concluded to visit the United States, and make that country his future home, where he could utter his sentiments, and enjoy the benefits of freedom, undisturbed by spies or informers.

Before sailing for America, he visited London and purchased a large library of classical and scientific books, with a philosophical apparatus, embracing various branches, and arrived in New York in 1797. By the aid of his letters, wealth, and his own personal and literary merit, he became acquainted with some of the first families in the city. Amongst others of his newly acquired friends, was Mr. Joseph S. Lewis, a rich merchant of Philadelphia, who became his business agent, and for many years his firm friend. Mr. Blennerhassett named his youngest son Joseph Lewis, in token of his regard for him. He was finally a considerable loser by this connection, and after Mr. Blennerhassett's failure, and the destruction of his house and property, became the owner of the island.

His stay in New York was of only a few months' continuance; when, hearing of the rich valleys and beautiful country on the Ohio River, he crossed the mountains, and after spending a few weeks in Pittsburg, took passage for Marietta, in the fall of the year 1797. Here he passed the winter, examining the vicinity of that place for a spot on which to make his permanent residence. He finally decided on purchasing a plantation on an island in the Ohio River, twelve miles below the mouth of the Muskingum, within the jurisdiction of the State of Virginia. The situation was wild, romantic, and beautiful; and as it was chiefly in a state of nature, a few acres only being cleared, he could reclaim it from the forest, adorn and cultivate it to his own taste. Its location also gave him the privilege of holding colored servants as his own property, which he could not do in the Northwest Territory. The island was, moreover, near the settlement of Belpre, composed chiefly of very intelligent and well-educated men, disbanded officers of the American army, whose society would at any time relieve him of ennui. The island itself was a picture of beauty, as well as all of its kind, at that early day, before the hand of man had marred its shores. The drooping branches of the willow laved their graceful foliage in the water, while the more lofty sycamore and elm, with their giant arms, protected them from the rude blasts of the storm, and gave a grandeur and dignity to these primitive landscapes, now only to be seen in the more remote regions of the west.

The island at present known as "Blennerhassett's," was then called "Backus's," who had owned it since 1792. It is said to have been located by Gen. Washington, as he owned a large tract of land immediately below, called "Washington's Bottom," entered by him in the year 1770.

It was first surveyed in May, 1784, on a land warrant, issued in 1780, and a patent made out by Patrick Henry, Governor of Virginia, in 1786, to Alexander Nelson, of Richmond, Va.; who was a member of a mercantile firm in Philadelphia. By a bill in chancery, of the High Court of Virginia, procured by Mr. Blennerhassett, to perfect his title, it appears that Elijah Backus, of Norwich, Conn., bought of James Herron, of Norfolk, Va., in the year 1792, two islands in the Ohio River; the principal one being the first below the mouth of the Little Kanawha, then in the county of Monongalia, containing two hundred and ninety-seven acres, for the sum of two hundred and fifty pounds, Virginia currency, or about eight hundred and eighty-three dollars and thirty-three cents. This island is of a very peculiar form, narrow in the middle, and broad at both extremities.

In March, 1798, Mr. Blennerhassett purchased the upper portion, containing about one hundred and seventy acres, for the sum of four thousand, five hundred dollars, and soon after moved, with his wife and one child, on to his new purchase, living in a large old blockhouse, standing about half a mile below the upper end of the island, built in the time of the Indian War, by Capt. James. Here he resided while conducting the improvements near the upper end of the island, and building his island mansion, which was completed in 1800. A good deal of labor and heavy expense was necessary in preparing the ground for his buildings and the gardens. It was covered, at this spot, with forest trees, which had to be removed, and stumps eradicated, so as to leave a smooth, level surface, with extensive landings up and down the banks on both sides of the river, for convenient access to and from the island. Boats of various sizes were also to be procured, and a company of eight or ten black servants purchased, as waiters, grooms, watermen, &c. His outlays, when the improvements were completed, amounted to more than forty thousand dollars. This sum, expended chiefly amongst the mechanics, laborers, and farmers of this new region, where money was scarce, and hard to be obtained, was of very great advantage to their interests; and Mr. Blennerhassett may be considered as the greatest benefactor, in this respect, that had ever settled west of the mountains.

The island mansion was built with great taste and beauty; no expense being spared in its construction, that could add to its usefulness or splendor. It consisted of a main building, fifty-two feet in length, thirty in width, and two stories high. Porticoes, forty feet in length, in the form of wings, projected in front, connected with offices, presenting each a face of twenty-six feet, and twenty feet in depth, uniting them with the main building; forming the half of an ellipsis, and making, in the whole, a front of one hundred and four feet. The left-hand office was occupied for the servant's hall; and the right for the library, philosophical apparatus study, &c. The drawing which accompanies this memoir is a correct likeness of the mansion, taken from the description of Col. Barker, one of the principal architects.

Blennerhassett Mansion
On the island 12 Miles downriver from Marietta

A handsome lawn of several acres occupied the front ground; while an extended opening was made through the forest trees, on the head of the island, affording a view of the river for several miles above, and bringing the mansion under the notice of descending boats. Nicely graveled walks, with a carriage-way, led from the house to the river, passing through an ornamental gateway, with large stone pillars. A fine hedge, of native hawthorn, bordered the right side of the avenue to the house, while back of it lay the flower garden, of about two acres, enclosed with neat palings, to which were traced gooseberry bushes, peaches, and other varieties of fruit-bearing trees, in the manner of wall fruits. The garden was planted with flowering shrubs, both exotic and native; but especially abounding in the latter, which the good taste of the occupants had selected from the adjacent forests, and planted in thick masses, through which wandered serpentine walks, bordered with flowers, imitating a labyrinth. Arbors and grottoes, covered with honeysuckles and eglantines, were placed at convenient intervals, giving the whole a very romantic and beautiful appearance. On the opposite side of the house was a large kitchen garden, and back of these, orchards of peach and apple trees of the choicest varieties, procured from abroad, as well as from the Belpre nurseries. Lower down on the island was the farm, with about one hundred acres under the nicest cultivation; the luxuriant soil producing the finest crops of grain and grass. For the last three or four years of his residence, a large dairy was added to his other agricultural pursuits, under the management of Thomas Neal, who also superintended the labor of the farm. The garden was conducted by Peter Taylor, a native of Lancashire, England, who was bred to the pursuit, but under the direction of Mr. Blennerhassett, whose fine taste in all that was beautiful, ordered the arranging and laying out the grounds.

The mansion and offices were frame buildings, painted with the purest white, contrasting tastefully with the green foliage of the ornamental shade trees, which surrounded it. An abundance of fine stone for building could have been quarried from the adjacent Virginia shore, but he preferred a structure of wood, as less liable to be damaged by earthquakes. The finishing and furniture of the apartments were adapted to the use for which they were intended. The hall was a spacious room; its walls painted a somber color, with a beautiful cornice of plaster, bordered with a gilded molding, running round the lofty ceiling; while its furniture was rich, heavy, and grand. The furniture of the drawing room was in strong contrast with the hall; light, airy, and elegant; with splendid mirrors, gay-colored carpets, rich curtains, with ornaments to correspond, arranged by his lady with the nicest taste and harmonious effect. A large quantity of massive silver plate ornamented the sideboards, and decorated the tables. Yet they had not entirely completed their arrangements, when the destroyer appeared, and frustrated all their designs for comfort and future happiness. The whole establishment was noble, chastened by the purest taste, without that glare of tinsel finery, too common among the wealthy.

Their style of living was in unison with the house and furniture, elegant, easy, and comfortable.

Mr. Blennerhassett was a highly intellectual man, greatly devoted to scientific pursuits, which his ample library and leisure time afforded every facility for pursuing. He was studious, and fond of experimenting in chemistry, electricity, and galvanism. His apparatus, though not extensive, was ample for such experiments as an amateur would wish to make. Astronomy was also a favorite study; for which he had a fine telescope to examine the constellations in their courses, and a solar microscope, to inspect the minute bodies of the earth. In music, he possessed the nicest taste, and an uncommon genius, composing harmonious and beautiful airs, several pieces of which are now remembered and played by a gentleman, who, when a youth, was intimate in his family. His favorite instruments were the base-viol and violoncello, on which he played with admirable skill. The spacious hall of the mansion being constructed so as to give effect to musical sounds, the tones of his viol vibrated through it with thrilling effect, calling forth the admiration of his guests. Electricity and galvanism received a share of his attention, and many experiments were tried in both these wonderful branches of modern science.

Amongst his trials in chemical operations, was that of converting beef into adipocere, large pieces of which were submerged in the beautiful little cove between the landing and the sand-bar at the head of the island. He fancied it might be used in place of spermaceti, for light; but the catfish and perch interfered so much with his trials, that he could never bring the adipocere to perfection. He was a good classical scholar, and so highly was he enraptured with Homer's Iliad, that it was said he could repeat the whole poem in the original Greek.

His manners were gentlemanly, and disposition social, hospitable, and kind, especially to those with whom he wished to associate, but rather haughty to others. In mind, he could not be said to be masculine and strong, but was rather wavering and fickle; easily duped and deceived by the designing and dishonest. He had quite a taste for medicine, and read many authors on that subject, which, with his natural propensities, often led him to think himself attacked with imaginary diseases, and it was sometimes difficult to convince him they were merely ideal. To his sick neighbors and servants, he was kind and attentive, often visiting and prescribing for their complaints; freely tendering his medicines, of which he always kept an ample supply. His own heart being perfectly honest and *free* from deceit, he was unsuspicious of others, and very credulous in regard to their statements, which often led him into pecuniary losses in his business transactions.

In bargaining with a notorious cheat for a quantity of the shells of the river clam, which, in the early settlement of the country, before quarries of limestone were opened, were calcined in log-heaps, and used for plastering rooms, the fellow said it was a difficult matter to collect them, as he had to dive under the water where it was six or eight feet deep, and must charge fifty cents a bushel, when, in fact, he could collect any quantity, where it was only a few inches.

Thinking the man told the truth, he paid him the price, which was at least five times as much as they were worth.

He was very kind and charitable to the poor and unfortunate backwoodsmen. A Virginian, who had lost his house and furniture by fire, was soon after invited, with his wife, to dine with him. This man owed him a considerable sum of lent money. After dinner he told him he would either cancel the debt, or give him an order on his store at Marietta for an equal sum, and let the debt stand. The sufferer was a man of honorable mind and just feelings. He, therefore, chose not to add to his present obligations, but accepted the canceling of the debt, which was immediately done. This man still lives, and related the incident in 1846. Many such facts were known to have occurred while he lived on the island.

His wife was still more charitable to the sick and poor in the vicinity, many of whom felt the benefit of her gifts.

With all these kind acts fresh in their memories, several of these men were found among the banditti, who ransacked his house and insulted his wife, after he had been forced to leave the island from the hue and cry of treason, which maddened and infuriated the public mind in the valley of the Ohio.

In person, Mr. Blennerhassett was tall, about six feet, but slender, with a slight stoop in the shoulders. His motions were not very graceful, either as an equestrian, or on foot; forehead full, and well formed; with rather a prominent nose, and good proportioned face; eyes weak, and sight imperfect; seeing objects distinctly only when near; so that in reading, the surface of the page nearly touched his nose. They had a nervous, restless agitation, which probably arose from weakness of the optic nerves, requiring the constant aid of glasses. Yet with this permanent and continual annoyance, he was a great student and operator in experiments.

He was also much attached to hunting, shooting quails, and other small game on the island. To enjoy this sport, he had to call in the aid of some other person, whose vision was more acute than his own, who pointed the gun for him at the game, and gave the word when to fire. This person was often his wife, who, with the greatest kindness, attended him in his short excursions, and with the tact of an experienced sportsman, pointed out the object, leveled the gun, and stood by with the most perfect coolness, while he discharged the piece.

His general habits were sedentary and studious; preferring the quiet of his library to the most brilliant assemblies. In conversation, he was interesting and instructive; confining his remarks to the practical and useful, more than to the amusing.

As a lawyer, his wife, who had probably heard his forensic eloquence, has been heard to say that he was equal to Mr. Emmitt; and frequently urged him to enter as an advocate at the higher courts of Virginia and Ohio, instead of wasting his time in obscurity, at his philosophical pursuits on the island. His library contained an ample supply of law books. A list of thirty volumes, loaned to James Wilson, a lawyer of Virginia, a few days before he left the island, is now among his papers in the hands of his agent at Marietta.

Mr. Blennerhassett dressed in the old English style, with scarlet or buff-colored small clothes, and silk stockings, shoes with silver buckles, and coat generally of blue broadcloth. When at home, his dress was rather careless; often, in warm weather, in his shirt-sleeves, without coat or waist-coat; and in winter, wore a thick woolen roundabout, or short jacket.

In this quiet retreat, insulated and separated from the noise and tumult of the surrounding world, amidst his books, with the company of his accomplished wife and children, he possessed all that seemed necessary for the happiness of man; and yet he lacked *one thing,* without which no man can be happy: a firm belief in the overruling providence of God. Voltaire and Rousseau, whose works he studied and admired, had poisoned his mind to the simple truths of the gospel, and the Bible was a book which he seldom or never consulted. At least this was the fact while he lived on the island; whatever it might have been, after misfortune and want had humbled and sorely tried him.

Mrs. Blennerhassett was more aspiring and ambitious; with a temperament in strong contrast to that of her husband. Her maiden name was Margaret Agnew; the daughter of Capt. Agnew, a brave officer in the British service, and at one time the Lieutenant-Governor of the Isle of Man. Gen. Agnew, who fell at the Battle of Germantown, in the American Revolution, was her grandfather, and a monument was erected to his memory by his granddaughter, after her arrival in America. She was educated and brought up by two maiden aunts, who took great care to instruct her in all the useful arts of housewifery, laundry, pastry, sewing, &c, which was of great use to her in after-life, when at the head of a family. They were led to this, in part from their own limited means, teaching them to be frugal, and the need there is, for every woman who expects to marry, to be acquainted with all the useful branches of housekeeping.

In person, Mrs. Blennerhassett was tall and commanding, of the most perfect proportions, with dignified and graceful manners, finely molded features, and very fair, transparent complexion; eyes dark blue, sparkling with life and intelligence; hair, a rich, deep brown, profuse and glossy, dressed in the most elegant manner. When at her island-home, she often wore a head-dress of colored silk stuff, folded very full, something in the manner of an eastern turban, giving a noble and attractive appearance to the whole person.

These were of various colors, but always composed of a single one, either of pink, yellow, or white, adjusted in the most becoming manner and nicest taste; in which particular, few women could equal her. White was a favorite color for dress in the summer and rich colored stuffs in the winter. Her motions were all graceful, and greatly heightened by the expression of her countenance. No one could be in her company, even a few minutes, without being strongly attracted by her fascinating manners. A very intelligent lady, who was familiarly acquainted with her in her best days on the island, and has since visited and seen the most elegant and beautiful females in the courts of France and England, as well as Washington City, says that she has beheld no one who was equal to her in beauty of person, dignity of manners, elegance of dress, and in short, all that is lovely and finished in the female person, such as she was, when *"Queen of the fairy isle."*

When she rode on horseback, her dress was a fine, scarlet broadcloth, ornamented with gold buttons; a white beaver hat, on which floated the graceful plumes of the ostrich, of the same color. This was sometimes changed for blue or yellow, with feathers to harmonize. She was a perfect equestrian; always riding a very spirited horse, with rich trappings, who seemed proud of his burthen; and accomplished the ride to Marietta, of fourteen miles, in about two hours; dashing through and under the dark foliage of the forest trees, which then covered the greater part of the distance, reminding one of the gay plumage and rapid flight of some tropical bird, winging its way through the woods. In these journeys she was generally accompanied by Ransom, a favorite black servant, who followed on horseback, in a neat, showy dress, and had to apply both whip and spur to keep in sight of his mistress. She sometimes came to Marietta by water, in a light canoe, (the roads not being yet opened for wheel-carriages,) navigated by Moses, another of the colored servants, who was the principal waterman, and had charge of the boats for the transport of passengers from the island to the main. Her shopping visits were made in this way, as she directed the purchase of groceries, &c, for the family use, as well as for the clothing. She possessed great personal activity; sometimes in fine weather, choosing to walk that distance, instead of riding. In addition to her feats in riding and walking, she could vault, with the ease of a young fawn, over a five-rail fence, with the mere aid of one hand placed on the top rail, and was often seen to do so, when walking over the farm, and a fence came in the way of her progress. It was performed with such graceful movement, and so little effort, as to call forth the wonder and admiration of the beholder.

She was passionately fond of dancing, and greatly excelled in this healthful and charming exercise, moving through the mazes and intricacies of the various figures, with the grace and lightness of the "Queen of the fairies." Her tastes in this respect were often gratified in the numerous balls and assemblies, given at that day in Marietta and Belpre, as well as at her own house; where the lofty hall frequently resounded to the cheerful music and lively steps of the dancers.

With all this relish for social amusements, Mrs. Blennerhassett was very domestic in her habits; being not only accomplished in all the arts of housewifely, but was also an excellent seamstress; cutting out and making up with her own hands much of the clothing of her husband, as well as preparing that for the servants, which was then made by a colored female. At that period, when tailors and Mantua makers were rare in the western wilderness, this was an accomplishment of real value. She being willing to practice these servile acts, when surrounded by all the wealth she could desire, is one of the finest and most remarkable traits in her character; indicating a noble mind, elevated above the influence of that false pride so often seen to attend the high-born and wealthy.

She was a very early riser; and when not prevented by indisposition, visited the kitchen by early dawn, and often manipulated the pastry and cakes to be served up on the table for the day; when this service was completed, she laid aside her working dress, and attired herself in the habiliments of the lady of the mansion. At table she presided with grace and dignity, and by her cheerful conversation and pleasant address, set everyone at ease about her, however rustic their manners, or unaccustomed they might be to genteel society.

Her mind was as highly cultivated as her person. She was an accomplished Italian and French scholar; and one of the finest readers imaginable; especially excelling in the plays of Shakespeare, which she rehearsed with all the taste and spirit of a first-rate actor. In history and the English classics, she was equally well read; and was often called upon to decide a disputed point in literature, under discussion by her husband and some learned guest. Her decisions were generally satisfactory to both parties, because founded on correct reasoning, and delivered in so gracious a manner. Few women have ever lived, who combined so many accomplishments and personal attractions. They strongly impressed not only intellectual and cultivated minds, who could appreciate her merits, but also the uneducated and lower classes. One of the young men, a farmer's son, of Belpre, rented and cultivated a field of corn on the island, near the avenue leading from the house to the river, for the sole purpose of stealing a look at her beautiful person, as she passed by, on her way to ride or walk, as she was wont to do every pleasant day. Wirt's celebrated panegyric on this lady was in no way undeserved; although in appearance so much like romance.

Eight years had passed rapidly and happily away since they took possession of their island home. Two children, Harman and Dominic, had been added to their domestic blessings, whose lively prattle and cheerful smiles served to make life still more desirable.

Parties of the young people from Marietta, Belpre, and Wood County, with occasional visits from more distant regions, whom the far-famed beauty of this western Eden had called to see and admire, often assembled at their hospitable mansion. Social parties of the older and more sedate portions of the community, were invited to visit them, and spend several days and nights on the island; especially females of the families where they visited themselves; so that they were as abundantly provided with social intercourse, as if living on the main land. A large portion of their visitors came by water, in rowboats, or canoes; as the country was so new, and destitute of bridges across the numerous creeks, that carriages were but little used. If travelers came by land, it was on horseback. A gentleman of taste, who visited the island in 1806, describes it as *"a scene of enchantment, a western Paradise, where beauty, wealth, and happiness, had found a home."* The wild condition of the surrounding wilderness, and the rude log cabins in which the inhabitants generally lived, by their striking contrast, added greatly to the marvelous beauty of the improvements on this remote island. Steamboats were then unknown, and traveling on the western rivers was slow and painful. Each man or family provided their own vessel; usually fitted for the temporary voyage in the rudest manner. A journey of one hundred miles was a long one; more formidable than five hundred or a thousand at this day. The settlement of Belpre was the only one from Marietta to Cincinnati, that showed marks of civilization, in its well built houses, nicely cultivated farms, and blooming orchards; indicating an intelligent and refined population, who could appreciate the worth of their accomplished neighbors. A gentleman who once lived in Marietta, and was a great favorite in the family, from his many personal and mental attractions, says, *"I was but a boy when they left the island, but I had been a favorite in the family for years, and had passed many of my happiest days in their society. My intimacy in the family of Blennerhassett, is like an oasis in the desert of life. It is one of those green spots in the memory's waste, which death alone can obliterate; but the verdure of the recollection is destroyed by the knowledge of their ruin and misfortunes."*

In an evil hour this peaceful and happy residence was entered by Aaron Burr, who, like Satan in the Eden of old, visited this earthly Paradise, only to deceive and destroy. *"Like some lost, malignant spirit, going to and fro upon the earth, to harass and sneer at poor humanity; was always so courteous, so polite and decorous; so interesting, nay, fascinating, when he strove to engage the attention, that it was impossible to resist his influence. It was the atmosphere of his presence that poisoned all who came within its reach."*

In the spring of the year 1805, this intriguing and artful man first visited the valley of the Ohio, his mind restless and uneasy, a disappointed, vexed man, whose hands were still red with the blood of the great and noble-minded Hamilton. No ordinary occupation could satisfy the mind of such a being; but some vast, difficult and grand scheme of ambition must be sought out, on which he could employ his exuberant faculties. Filled with his future project of founding a vast empire in the provinces of Mexico, with a portion of the valley of the Mississippi, then, as he had ascertained, ripe for revolution, (but the plan chiefly confined, at that time, under a cloud of mystery, purporting to be a settlement of the lands he had bargained for on the Washita River.) He descended the Ohio in a boat, landing as a passing traveler, merely to see and admire the far-famed improvements of the island. Mr. Blennerhassett, hearing that a stranger was on his lawn, sent a servant to invite him to the house. The wily serpent sent his card, with an apology; but Mr. Blennerhassett, with his usual hospitality, walked out and insisted on his remaining a day or two. He, however, made a visit of only a few hours; long enough to introduce the subject of a splendid land speculation on the Red River, and to allude to the prospect of a war of the United States with Spain, and the ease with which the Mexicans might, with a little aid, throw off the foreign yoke which had so long oppressed them. He then proceeded on his way.

Aaron Burr
1756 - 1836

A large portion of the following winter was spent by Mr. Blennerhassett and his lady, in Philadelphia and New York, on a visit to his old friend Emmitt, where, it is probable, he saw Burr again, and matured the plan for a participation in the purchase of Baron Bastrop's lands on the Washita, as he had addressed a letter to him on that subject before leaving home, in December, wishing to become a partner in any purchase he might make of western lands: also offering to aid in the Mexican enterprise, as was afterward ascertained in the trial at Richmond.

The next August we find Aaron Burr at Pittsburg, in company with his accomplished daughter, Mrs. Theodosia Alston, on his way down the Ohio River. He again visited the island, with his daughter, where he spent several days; he, in the meantime, taking up his abode at Marietta, where several of the inhabitants received him with marked attention;

while others looked upon him with contempt and abhorrence, as the murderer of Col. Hamilton; especially the old officers, friends and associates of that excellent man. It was in September, at the period of the annual militia muster; the regiment was assembled on the commons, and Col. Burr was invited by the commander to exercise the men, which he did, putting them through several evolutions. In the evening there was a splendid ball, at which he attended, and was long after known as the Burr Ball.

Early in this month the contract was made for boats to be built on the Muskingum River, six miles above the mouth, for the purpose, as was said, of conveying the provisions and adventurers to the settlement in the new purchase. There were fifteen large bateaux; ten of them forty feet long, ten feet wide, and two and a half feet deep; five others were fifty feet long, pointed at each end, to push, or row up stream as well as down. One of these was considerably larger, and fitted up with convenient rooms, a fireplace, and glass windows; intended for the use of Mr. Blennerhassett and family, as he proposed taking them with him to the new settlement, and is evidence he did not then think of any hostile act against the United States. To these was added a keel-boat, sixty feet long, for the transport of provisions. A contract for bacon, pork, flour, whisky, &c, was made, to the amount of two thousand dollars, and a bill drawn on Mr. Ogden, of New York, for the payment. The boats cost about the same sum, for which Mr. Blennerhassett was responsible. One main article of the stores was kiln-dried, or parched corn, ground into meal; which is another evidence that the men engaged in the expedition, were to march a long distance by land, and carry this parched meal on their backs; of which, a pint mixed with a little water, is a day's ration, as practiced by the western Indians. Several hundred barrels of this article were prepared; some of which was raised on the island and parched in a kiln built for that purpose. The boats were to be ready by the 9th of December; rather a late period, on account of ice, which usually forms in this month; but they were tardy in making the contract.

Col. Burr remained in the vicinity three or four weeks, making a journey to Chillicothe. His son-in-law, Alston, came out and joined his wife at the island, and with her and Mr. Blennerhassett, who accompanied them, proceeded on to Lexington, Ky., early in October. Many young men in the vicinity of Marietta, Belpre, and various other points on the river, were engaged to join in the expedition; of which Col. Burr was the leader. They were told that no injury was intended to the United States; that the President was aware of the expedition and approved it; which was to make a settlement on the tract of land purchased by the leaders in the Baron Bastrop grant, and in the event of a war breaking out between this country and Spain, which had for some time been expected, they were to join with the troops under Gen. Wilkinson, and march into the Mexican provinces, whose inhabitants had long been ready for revolt, and prepared to unite with them. This was no doubt the truth, as believed by Mr. Blennerhassett, and those engaged under him, whatever may have been the ulterior views of Burr. Not one of all that number enlisted on the Ohio, would have hearkened for a moment, to a separation of the western from the eastern states; and when the act of the Ohio Legislature was passed, to suppress all armed assemblages, and take possession of boats with arms and provisions, followed by the proclamation of the President, they, almost to a man, refused to embark further in the enterprise.

The bateaux were calculated to carry about five hundred men; and probably a large portion of that number had been engaged, expecting to receive one hundred acres of land for each private, and more for officers. As to their being required to furnish themselves with a good rifle and blanket, it was of itself no evidence of hostility; as it is customary, in making all new settlements, for men to be armed; as was the case with the forty-eight pioneers of the Ohio Company settlers, in 1788.

In the meantime, a rumor had gone abroad, that Col. Burr and his associates were plotting treason on the western waters, and assembling an army to take possession of New Orleans, rob the banks, seize the artillery, and set up a separate government west of the Alleghany Mountains, of which he was to be the Chief. From the evidence on the trial at Richmond, and other sources, it appears that Mr. Jefferson was acquainted with the plan of invading Mexico, in the event of a war with Spain, and approved it; so that Burr had some ground for saying that the government favored the project. But when no war took place, and the parties had become deeply involved in building boats, collecting provisions, and levying men, to which the baseness and treachery of Wilkinson directly contributed, it was thought a fitting time to punish the arch enemy of the President, who, by his chicanery, had well nigh ousted him from the chair of state, and had since taken all opportunities to vilify and abuse him. Another evidence that the government was supposed to favor the enterprise, is the fact, that nearly all its abettors and supporters in the west, until the proclamation appeared, were of the party called Republicans, or friends of Mr. Jefferson, and was opposed by the Federalists, who hated and despised Burr and all in which he was engaged, as, from the character of the man, they thought it boded nothing good.

By the last of October, rumor, with her thousand tongues, aided by hundreds of newspapers, had filled the minds of the people with strange alarms of coming danger, to which the mystery which overshadowed the actual object of these preparations greatly added, and many threats were thrown out, of personal violence to Mr. Blennerhassett and Col. Burr. Alarmed at these rumors of coming danger, Mrs. Blennerhassett dispatched Peter Taylor to Kentucky, with a letter requesting her husband immediately to return; where he had gone on a visit with Mr. Alston. The history of this journey, as related by Peter in his evidence on the trial, is an amusing sketch of simplicity and truth. He was the gardener on the island for several years, and was a single hearted, honest Englishman, who, after his employer's ruin, purchased a farm at Waterford, in Washington County Ohio, where he lived many years, much respected for his industry and integrity.

During the month of September, and forepart of October, there appeared a series of articles, four or five in number, published in the Marietta Gazette, over the signature of Querist, in which the writer advocated a separation of the western from the eastern states, setting forth the reasons for, and advantages of, such a division. These were answered in a series of numbers, condemning the project, over the signature of Regulus. They were well-written, spirited articles. The former were probably written by Burr; and the author of the last has remained concealed. The result, however, was unfavorable to the project, and roused the public mind in opposition both to the man and the cause he had espoused. Some of the articles by Regulus were much applauded by the editor of the Aurora, a leading government paper of that day, who considered the writer a very able and patriotic man.

The last of November, Mr. Jefferson sent out John Graham, a clerk in one of the public offices, as a spy, or agent, to watch the motions of the conspirators in the vicinity of the island, and to ask the aid of the Governor of Ohio in suppressing the insurrection, by seizing on the boats and preparations making on the Muskingum. While at Marietta, Mr. Blennerhassett called on the agent once or twice, talking freely with him on the objects of the expedition, and showed him a letter he had recently received from Col. Burr, in relation to the settlement on the Washita, in which he says that the project of invading Mexico was abandoned, as the difficulties between the United States and Spain were adjusted. He also mentioned his arrest and trial before the Federal Court, on charge of *"treasonable practices,"* and *"a design to attack the Spanish dominions, and thereby endanger the peace of the United States;"* of which he was acquitted. But all this would not satisfy Mr. Graham. He visited the Governor at Chillicothe, laid before him the surmises of Mr. Jefferson; and the Legislature, then in session, on the second day of December, with closed doors, passed an act authorizing the Governor to call out the militia, on his warrant to any Sheriff or Militia Officer, with power to arrest boats on the Ohio River, or men, supposed to be engaged in this expedition; and might be held to bail, in the sum of fifty thousand dollars, or imprisoned, and the boats confiscated. One thousand dollars were placed at the disposal of the Governor, to carry out the law.

Under this act a company of militia was called out, with orders to capture and detain the boats and provisions on the Muskingum, with all others descending the Ohio, under suspicious circumstances. They were placed under the command of Capt. Timothy Buell. A six-pounder was planted in battery on the bank of the Ohio, in Marietta, and every descending boat examined. Regular sentries and guards were posted for several weeks, until the river was closed with ice, and all navigation ceased. Many amusing jokes were played off on the military during this campaign, such as setting an empty tar barrel on fire, and placing it on an old boat, or a raft of logs, to float by on some dark, rainy night. The sentries, after hailing, and receiving no answer, fired several shots to enforce their order; but finding the supposed boat escaping, sent out a file of men to board and take possession, who, approaching in great wrath, were still more vexed to find it all a hoax.

On the 6th of December, just before the order of the Governor arrived, Comfort Tyler, a gentleman from the state of New York, landed at the island with four boats and about thirty men, fitted out at the towns above, on the Ohio. On the 9th, a party of young men from Belpre went up the Muskingum to assist in navigating the bateaux and provisions of parched meal from that place to the island. But the militia guard received notice of their movements, and waylaying the river a little above the town, took possession of them all but one, which the superior management of the young men from Belpre enabled them to bring by all the guards, in the darkness of the night, and reach the island in safety. Had they all escaped, they would have been of little use, as the young men engaged had generally given up the enterprise, on the news of the President's proclamation, and the act of the Ohio Legislature.

Mr. Blennerhassett was at Marietta on the 6th of December, expecting to receive the boats; but they were not quite ready for delivery. On that day he heard of the act of the assembly, and returned to the island, half resolved to abandon the cause; but the arrival, that night, of Tyler, and the remonstrance of his wife, who had entered with great spirit into the enterprise, prevented him. Had he listened to the dictates of his own mind, and the suggestions of prudence, it would have saved him years of misfortune and final ruin.

In the course of the day of the 9th of December, he had notice that the Wood county militia had volunteered their services, and would that night make an attack on the island, arrest him, with the boats and men there assembled, and perhaps burn his house. This accelerated their departure, which took place on the following night. They had learned that the river was watched at several points below, and serious apprehensions felt for their future safety; although the resolute young men on board, well armed with their rifles, would not have been captured by any moderate force. The Ohio River, from the Little to the Big Kanawha, is very crooked and tortuous; making the distance by water nearly double that by land.

Col. Phelps, the commander of the Wood county volunteers, took possession of the island the following morning, and finding the objects of his search gone, determined not to be foiled, and started immediately on horseback across the country, for Point Pleasant, a village at the mouth of the Big Kanawha, and arrived there several hours before the boats. He directly mustered a party of men, to watch the river all night and arrest the fugitives. It being quite cold, with some ice in the stream, large fires were kindled, for the double purpose of warming the guard and more easily discovering the boats. Just before daylight, the men being well filled with whisky, to keep out the cold, became drowsy with their long watch, and all lay down by the fire. During their short sleep, the four boats seeing the fires, and aware of their object, floated quietly by, without any noise, and were out of sight before the guard awakened. They thus escaped this well laid plan for their capture, arriving at the mouth of the Cumberland, the place of rendezvous, unmolested.

On the 13th, Mr. Morgan Nevill and Mr. Robinson, with a party of fourteen young men, arrived and landed at the island. They were immediately arrested by the militia, before the return of Col. Phelps. A very amusing account of this adventure is given in the "Token," an annual of 1836, written by Mr. Nevill, in which he describes their trial before Justices Wolf and Kincheloe, as aiders and abettors in the treason of Burr and Blennerhassett. So far was the spirit of lawless arrest carried, that one or two persons in Belpre, were taken at night from their beds, and hurried over on to the island for trial, without any authority of law. This was a few days before the celebrated move in the Senate of the United States, for the suspension of the act of *habeas corpus*, so alarmed had they become; but was prevented by the more considerate negative of the House of Representatives After a detention of three days, the young men were discharged, for the want of proof.

Mrs. Blennerhassett, who had been left at the island, to look after the household goods, and follow her husband at a more convenient period, was absent at Marietta, when they landed, for the purpose of procuring one of the large boats that was fitted up for her use, and had been arrested at Marietta; but was unsuccessful, and returned the evening after the trial.

The conduct of the militia, in the absence of their commander, was brutal and outrageous; taking possession of the house and the family stores in the cellar, without any authority, as their orders only extended to the arrest of Mr. Blennerhassett and the boats. They tore up and burnt the fences for their watch-fires, and forced the black servants to cook for them, or be imprisoned. One of them discharged his rifle through the ceiling of the large hall, the bullet passing up through the chamber, near where Mrs. Blennerhassett and the children were sitting. The man said it was accidental; but being half-drunk, and made brutal by the whisky they drank, they little knew or cared for their actions.

On the 17th of December, with the aid of the young men, and the kind assistance of Mr. A. W. Putnam, of Belpre, one of their neighbors and a highly esteemed friend, she, with her children, was enabled to depart, taking with her a part of the furniture, and some of her husband's choice books. Mr. Putnam also furnished her with provisions for the voyage, her own being destroyed by the militia, in whose rude hands she was forced to leave her beautiful island home, which she was destined never again to visit. They kept possession for several days after her departure living at free quarters, destroying the fences, and letting in the cattle, which tramped down and ruined the beautiful shrubbery of the garden, barking and destroying the nice orchards of fruit trees, just coming into bearing; and this too, was done by men, on many of whom Mr. Blennerhassett had bestowed numerous benevolent acts. It is due lo the commander, Col. Phelps, to say that these excesses were mostly perpetrated in his absence, and that on his return he did all he could to suppress them, and treated Mrs. Blennerhassett with respect and kindness. This spot, which a short time before was the abode of peace and happiness, adorned with all that could embellish or beautify its appearance, was now a scene of ruin, resembling the ravages of a hostile and savage foe, rather than the visitation of the civil law.

Before leaving the island, Mr. Blennerhassett, not expecting to return, had rented it to Col. Cushing, one of his worthy Belpre friends, with all the stock of cattle, crops, &c. He did all in his power to preserve what was left, and prevent further waste. Col. Cushing kept possession of the island one or two years, when it was taken out of his hands by the creditors, and rented to a man who raised a large crop of hemp. The porticoes and offices were stowed full of this combustible article; when the black servants, during one of their Christmas gambols, in 1811, accidentally set it on fire, and the whole mansion was consumed. The furniture and library, a portion of which only was removed with the family, were attached, and sold at auction at a great sacrifice, to discharge some of the bills endorsed by him for Aaron Burr, a few months after his departure.

With her two little sons, Harman and Dominic, the one six, and the other about eight years old, she pursued her way down the Ohio to join her husband. The young men, her companions, afforded every aid in their power to make her situation comfortable; but the severity of the weather, the floating ice in the river, and the unfinished state of her cabin, hastily prepared for her reception, made the voyage a very painful one. Late in December she passed the mouth of the Cumberland, where she had hoped to find her husband; but the flotilla had proceeded out of the Ohio into the rapid waters of the Mississippi, and landed at the mouth of the Bayou Pierre, in the Mississippi Territory. The Ohio was frozen over soon after the boat in which she was embarked left it, and was not again navigable until the last of February, the winter being one of great severity. Early in January she joined the boats of Col. Burr, a few miles above Natchez, and was again restored, with her two little boys, to her husband, who received them with joy and gratitude from the hands of their gallant conductors.

The whole country being roused from Pittsburg to New Orleans, and the hue and cry raised on all sides to arrest the traitors, Col. Burr abandoned the expedition as hopeless; and assembling his followers, now about one hundred and thirty in number, made them a spirited speech, thanked them for their faithful adherence, amidst so much opposition, and closed by saying that unforeseen circumstances had occurred, which frustrated his plans, and the expedition was at an end. All were now left, the distance of one thousand or fifteen hundred miles from their homes, to shift for themselves. Several of the young men from Belpre, six or eight in number, returned in the course of the spring. Two brothers, Charles and John Dana, remained and settled near the Walnut Hills; purchased lands, and entered into the cultivation of cotton.

Sometime in January, Col. Burr and Mr. Blennerhassett were arrested, and brought before the United States Court, at Natchez, on a charge of treason, and recognized to appear in February. Blennerhassett did appear, and was discharged *in chief;* no proof appearing to convict him of any treasonable design. Burr did not choose to appear; but soon after the recognizance, he requested John Dana, with two others, to take him in a skiff or rowboat, to a point about twenty miles above Bayou Pierre, and land him in the night; intending to escape across the country by land. The better to conceal his person from detection, before starting he exchanged his nice suit of broadcloth clothes and beaver hat with Mr. Dana, for his coarse boatman's dress, and old slouched white wool hat, which would effectually disguise him from recognition by his intimate acquaintance. He proceeded safely for some days; but was finally arrested on the Tombigbee River, and with many taunts and insults taken on to Richmond, where he arrived the 26th of March, 1807. No bill was found by the grand jury, until the 25th of June, when he was indicted on two bills; one for treason and the other for a misdemeanor. After a long and tedious trial, he was acquitted, on a verdict of "*not guilty.*"

Mr. Blennerhassett supposing himself discharged from further annoyance, sometime in June started on a journey to visit the island, and examine into the condition of his property; which, from various letters, he was told was going fast to waste and destruction. Passing through Lexington, Ky., where he had many friends and acquaintances, he was again arrested, on a charge of treason, and for some days confined in the jail; as an indictment had been found against him, as well as Burr, at Richmond. He employed Henry Clay as his counsel; who expressed deep indignation at the illegality of his client's arrest. *"He had been discharged already in chief, and why should he be again arrested on the same supposed offense?"* But the government was unrelenting, and nothing but the conviction of the offender could appease their wrath. He was taken, with much ceremony and parade of the law, to Richmond, where he again met Burr, the originator of all his troubles and misfortunes. The magnanimity of the man is well shown, in that he never recriminated or accused his destroyer with deceiving him, inasmuch as he had entered voluntarily into his plans, and therefore did not choose to lay his troubles on the shoulders of another; although it is apparent, that if he had never seen Aaron Burr, he would have escaped this sudden ruin to his prosperity and happiness. The following letter is from the pen of Mrs. Blennerhassett, addressed to her husband at Lexington, and displays her noble and elevated mind, as well as her deep conjugal affection. It is copied from the sketch of Mr. Blennerhassett, by William Wallace, published in vol. ii, of the American Review, 1845.

"Natchez, August 3d, 1807

My Dearest Love:

After having experienced the greatest disappointment in not hearing from you for two mails, I at length heard of your arrest; which afflicts and mortifies me, because it was an arrest. I think that had you of your own accord gone to Richmond and solicited a trial, it would have accorded better with your pride, and you would have escaped the unhappiness of missing my letters, which I wrote every week to Marietta. God knows what you may feel and suffer on our accounts, before this reaches, to inform you of our health, and welfare in every particular; and knowing this, I trust and feel your mind will rise superior to every inconvenience that your present situation may subject you to; despising, as I do, the paltry malice of the upstart agents of government. Let no solicitude whatever for us, damp your spirits. We have many friends here, who do the utmost in their power to counteract any disagreeable sensation occasioned me by your absence. I shall live in the hope of hearing from you by the next mail; and entreat you, by all that is dear to us, not to let any disagreeable feelings on account of our separation, enervate your mind at this time. Remember that all here will read with great interest, anything concerning you; but still do not trust too much to yourself; consider your want of practice at the bar, and don't spare the fee of a lawyer. Apprise Col. Burr of my warmest acknowledgments for his own and Mrs. Alston's kind remembrance, and tell him to assure her she has inspired me with warmth of attachment which can never diminish. I wish him to urge her to write to me.

    God bless you, prays your wife,

M. Blennerhassett."

On Burr's acquittal, Mr. Blennerhassett was never brought to trial, but discharged from the indictment for treason, and bound over in the sum of three thousand dollars, to appear at Chillicothe, Ohio, on a misdemeanor; *"for that whereas he prepared an armed force, whose destination was the Spanish territory."* He did not appear, nor was he ever called upon again; and thus ended this treasonable farce, which had kept the whole of the United States in a ferment for more than a year, and, like *"the mountain in labor, at last brought forth a mouse."*

After the trial at Richmond, in 1807, he returned to Natchez, where he stayed about a year, and then bought, with the remains of his fortune, a plantation, of one thousand acres, in Claiborne County, Miss., seven miles from Gibson Port, at a place called St. Catharine's, and cultivated it with a small stock of slaves. While here he continued his literary pursuits, leaving Mrs. Blennerhassett to superintend both indoors and out. The embargo destroyed all commerce, and the war which soon followed put a stop to the sale of cotton, and blasted his hopes of reinstating his fortune from that source. In a letter to his attorney, at Marietta, in 1808, wherein he proposes the sale of his island for slaves, he says, that with thirty hands on his plantation, he could in five years clear sixty thousand dollars. Cotton was then in demand, and brought a high price.

His lady, with her characteristic energy, rose at early dawn, mounted her horse and rode over the grounds, examining each field, and giving directions to the overseer as to the work to be done that day, or any alteration to be made in the plans, which circumstances required. They here had the society of a few choice friends in Natchez, and among the neighboring planters. On this plantation they passed ten years; in which time one son and daughter were added to the number of their children. The daughter died when young. Retaining still a fond recollection of his Marietta and Belpre friends, he, in the year 1818, sent one of his sons to the college in Athens, Ohio, under the care of W. P. Putnam, the son of his old friend, A. W. Putnam.

Here he remained a year, at the end of which time, finding his fortune still decreasing, and means much cramped by his endorsements for Col. Burr, amounting to thirty thousand dollars, ten thousand of which were repaid by Mr. Alston, he in 1819 sold his plantation, and moved his family to Montreal; the Governor of the province, an old friend, having given him hopes to expect a post on the bench, for which he was well qualified. Misfortune having marked him for her own, soon after his arrival his friend was removed from office, and his expectations frustrated.

He remained here until the year 1822, when he removed his family to England, under an assurance of a post from the government, which was never realized, and resided in the town of Bath, with a maiden sister.

It was at Montreal, with the prospects of poverty and blighted hopes thickening around her, that she wrote those beautiful and touching lines describing "The Island," and her once happy home, that may well be called her "Lament," and are given below, as well worthy of preservation.

THE DESERTED ISLE

Like mournful echo from the silent tomb,
That pines away upon the midnight air,
Whilst the pale moon breaks out with fitful gloom,
Fond memory turns with sad, but welcome care,
To scenes of desolation and despair;
Once bright with all that beauty could bestow,
That peace could shed, or youthful fancy know.

To thee, fair isle, reverts the pleasing dream;
Again thou risest in thy green attire;
Fresh, as at first, thy blooming graces seem;
Thy groves, thy fields, their wonted sweets respire;
Again thou'rt all my heart could e'er desire.
0 why, dear isle, art thou not still my own?
Thy charms could then for all my griefs atone.

The stranger that descends Ohio's stream,
Charm'd with the beauteous prospects that arise,
Marks the soft isles, that 'neath the glistening beam,
Dance in the wave, and mingle with the skies;
Sees also *one,* that now in ruin lies,
Which erst, like fairy queen, towered o'er the rest,
In every native charm by culture dress'd.

There rose the seat where once, in pride of life,
My eye could mark the queen of rivers flow;
In summer's calmness, or in winter's strife,
Swoln with the rains, or baffling with the snow;
Never again my heart such joy shall know.
Havoc, and ruin, and rampant war, have past
Over that isle with their destroying blast.

The black'ning fire has swept throughout her halls,
The winds fly whistling through them, and the wave
No more in spring-floods o'er the sand-beach crawls;
But furious drowns in one o'erwhelming grave,

Thy hallowed haunts it watered as a slave.
Drive on, destructive flood! and ne'er again
On that devoted isle let man remain.

For many blissful moments there I've known;
Too many hopes have there met their decay,
Too many feelings now forever gone.
To wish that thou wouldst e'er again display
The joyful coloring of thy prime array.
Buried with thee, let them remain a blot;
With thee, their sweets, their bitterness forgot.

And 0, that I could wholly wipe away
The memory of the ills that work'd thy fall:
The memory of that all eventful day,
When I return'd and found my own fair hall
Held by the infuriate populace in thrall,
My own fireside blockaded by a band,
That once found food and shelter at my hand.

My children, (0, a mother's pangs forbear,
Nor strike again that arrow through my soul,)
Clasping the ruffians in suppliant prayer,
To free their mother from unjust control;
While with false crimes, and imprecations foul,
The wretches, vilest refuse of the earth,
Mock jurisdiction held, around my hearth.

Sweet isle! methinks I see thy bosom torn,
Again behold the ruthless rabble throng,
That wrought destruction, taste must ever mourn;
Alas, I see thee now, shall see thee long,
Vet ne'er shall bitter feelings urge the wrong;
That to a mob would give the censure due,
To those that arm'd the plunder-greedy crew.

Thy shores are warm'd by bounteous suns in vain,
Columbia, if spite and envy spring
To blast the beauty of mild nature's reign,
The European stranger, who would fling
O'er tangled woods refinement's polishing,
May find (expended every plan of taste,)
His work by ruffians rendered doubly waste.

In addition to the expectation of office in England, he also had hopes of recovering an interest he held in an estate in Ireland. Both of these, however, failed. He ultimately resided in the island of Guernsey, where he died in 1831, aged sixty-three years.

Eleven years after his death, in 1842, when his widow and children were reduced to extreme want, she returned to New York with one of her sons, both of them in very poor health, with the purpose of petitioning Congress for remuneration in the destruction of the property on the island, by the Wood County militia, in December, 1806. The petition is couched in very feeling and appropriate language, in which she sets forth the outrages offered to herself and family, with the damages done to the house and property on the island.

"Your memorialist does not desire to exaggerate the conduct of the said armed men, or the injuries done by them; but she can truly say, that before their visit the residence of her family had been noted for its elegance and high state of improvement, and that they left it in a state of comparative ruin and waste; and as instances of the mischievous and destructive spirit which appeared to govern them, she would mention that while they occupied as a guard-room one of the best apartments in the house, (the building of which had cost nearly forty thousand dollars,) a musket or rifle ball was deliberately fired into the ceiling, by which it was much defaced and injured; and that they wantonly destroyed many pieces of valuable furniture."

She would also state, that, *"being apparently under no subordination, they indulged in continual drunkenness and riot, offering many indignities to your memorialist, and treating her domestics with violence.*

Your memorialist further represents, that these outrages were committed upon an unoffending and defenseless family in the absence of their natural protector; your memorialist's husband being then away from his home; and that in answer to such remonstrance as she ventured to make against the consumption, waste, and destruction of his property, she was told by those who assumed to have the command, that they held the property for the United States, by order of the President, and were privileged to use it, and should use it, as they pleased. It is with pain that your memorialist reverts to events, which, in their consequences, have reduced a once happy family from affluence and comfort, to comparative want and wretchedness; which blighted the prospects of her children, and made herself, in the decline of life, a wanderer on the face of the earth."

This memorial was directed to the care of Henry Clay, then in the Senate of the United States, enveloped in a letter from R. Emmitt, a son of the celebrated man of that name. He says, *"She is now in this city, residing in very humble circumstances, bestowing her cares upon a son, who, by long poverty and sickness, is reduced to utter imbecility, both of mind and body, unable to assist her, or provide for his own wants. In her present destitute situation, the smallest amount of relief would be thankfully received by her. Her condition is one of absolute want, and she has but a short time left to enjoy any better fortune in this world."*

Mr. Clay presented the memorial to the Senate, with some very feeling and appropriate remarks; having been formerly well acquainted with the family, and employed as his attorney, when arrested at Lexington, Ky. It was taken up, and referred to the Committee of Claims; of which the Hon. William Woodbridge was Chairman. His report on the memorial is a very able and feeling document, in which he advocates the claim as just, and one which ought to be allowed, notwithstanding it had now been thirty-six years since the events transpired. He says, *"Not to do so, would be unworthy of any wise or just nation that is disposed to respect, most of all, its own honor."*

This report sets forth all the circumstances attending the "Burr treason," as described in the foregoing biography. The documents which accompany the report are very interesting, especially the statement of Morgan Neville and William Robinson, jr., two of the young men who were arrested and tried on the island, as partisans of Burr, in December, 1806, and written for the future use of Mr. Blennerhassett, a few days after these events transpired. It is given as a correct history of the outrages on the island.

Statement of Messrs. Neville and Robinson, and Affidavit of Margaret Blennerhassett:

"On the 13th day of December, 1806, the boat in which we were, was driven ashore, by ice and wind, on Backus's Island, about one mile below Mr. Blennerhassett's house; we landed in the forenoon, and the wind continuing unfavorable, did not afford us an opportunity of putting off until after three o'clock in the evening, at which time we were attacked by about twenty-five men, well armed, who rushed upon us suddenly, and we, not being in a situation to resist the fury of a mob, surrendered; a strong guard was placed in the boat, to prevent, we presume, those persons of our party who remained in the boat, from going off with her, while we were taken to the house of Mr. Blennerhassett. On our arrival at the house we found it filled with militia; another party of them were engaged in making fires, (around the house,) of rails dragged from the fences of Mr. Blennerhassett. At this time Mrs. Blennerhassett was from home. When she returned, (about an hour after,) she remonstrated against this outrage on the property, but without effect; the officers declared that while they were on island, the property absolutely belonged to them. We were informed, by themselves, that their force consisted of forty men the first night; and on the third day it was increased to eighty. The officers were constantly issuing the whisky and meat, which had been laid up for the use of the family; and whenever any complaint was made by the friends of Mrs. Blennerhassett, they invariably asserted that everything on the farm was their own property. There appeared to us to be no kind of subordination among the men; the large room they occupied on the first floor presented a continued scene of riot and drunkenness; the furniture appeared ruined by the bayonets, and one of the men fired his gun against the ceiling; the ball made a large hole, which completely spoiled the beauty of the room. They insisted that the servants should wait upon them, before attending to their mistress; when this was refused, they seized upon the kitchen, and drove the Negroes into the wash-house. We were detained from

Saturday evening until Tuesday morning; during all which time there were never less than thirty, and frequently from seventy to eighty men living in this riotous manner entirely on the provisions of Mrs. Blennerhassett. When we left the island, a cornfield near the house, in which the corn was still remaining, was filled with cattle, the fences having been pulled down to make fires. This we pledge ourselves to be a true statement of these transactions, as impression was made on us at the time.

> *Morgan Neville,*
> *Wm. Robinson, Jr."*

Charles Fenton Mercer, Esq., also, in September, 1807, soon after the trial at Richmond, made a full statement of his knowledge of the events on which the accusation against Mr. Blennerhassett was founded; as they transpired between the 20th of September and 6th of December, 1806, having been himself at the island in November; with his opinion of the objects of the expedition, in which he fully clears Mr. Blennerhassett of any designs against the peace and quiet of the United States. Mr. D. Woodbridge, of Marietta, in a letter to the chairman, of the 2d of April, 1842, makes a statement of the loss of property, from the attachment of the government, and the riotous conduct of the Wood County volunteers on the island.

In August, 1842, while this subject was under consideration, news arrived of the death of Mrs. Blennerhassett at New York; and nothing more was done in the matter. She, who had lived in wealth and splendor, and imparted charity to hundreds of the poor, was indebted to others for a grave. She died in the most destitute condition; and her last days passed under the soothing care of a charitable society of Irish females in New York, by whom she was buried. The reverses in this accomplished woman's fortune, and in that of her amiable husband, illustrate the uncertainties of human life, and unfold the mysterious doings of Providence with the children of men. More than forty years have passed away since these events were transacted, and not a vestige now remains of the splendid and happy home of Harman and Margaret Blennerhassett. All has passed away like the vision of a pleasant dream; while the thousands of passengers, who annually travel up and down the Ohio on steamboats, still eagerly inquire after, and gaze upon *"The island of Blennerhassett,"* with wonder and delight.

APPENDIX

[Note A.]

The acquaintances formed during his college residence at Cambridge, in many cases ripened into close intimacy and friendship. Among his early friends and correspondents, is the name of *John Adams*. The following extract of a letter, written by this distinguished statesman, at Braintree, Mass., December 5, 1760, exhibits at that early period, their mental character and their insatiable thirst for intellectual improvement, upon which were based their subsequent elevation. The perusal may stimulate others to imitate so laudable an example.

Braintree, December 5th, 1760.

Sir:

I presume upon the merit of a brother, both in the academical and legal family, to give you this trouble, and to ask the favor of your correspondence. The science which we have bound ourselves to study for life, you know to be immensely voluminous, perhaps intricate and involved; so that an arduous application to books at home, a critical observation of the course of practice, the conduct of the older practitioners in courts, and a large correspondence with fellow students abroad, as well as conversation in private companies, upon legal subjects, are needful to gain a thorough mastery, if not to make a decent figure in the profession of law. The design of this letter, then, is to desire that you would write me a report of any cause of importance and curiosity, either in Courts of Admiralty or Common Law that you hear resolved in your colony. And on my part, I am ready and engage to do the same of any such causes that I shall hear argued in the province. It is an employment that gives me pleasure, and I find that revolving a case in my mind, stating it on paper, recollecting the arguments on each side, and examining the points through my books, that occur in the course of a trial, makes the impression deeper on my memory, and lets me easier into the spirit of law and practice.

In view I send you the report of a cause argued in Boston last term, and should be glad to know if the points, whether the statutes of mortmain were ever stirred in your colony and by what criterion you determine what statutes are, and what are not extended to you." (Here follows the case reported, which is too long for insertion.)

[Note B.]

"In the House of Representatives of the Colony of Connecticut,

Friday, 21st of May, 13th, George iii, 1773.

Mr. Speaker:

Having laid before the House a letter from the Speaker of the House of Burgesses of the Colony of Virginia, containing certain resolutions entered into by said house on the 12th of March last; this House taking into consideration the contents of said letter, the above-mentioned resolutions, and the reasons on which they are grounded, are of opinion that they are weighty and important in their nature and design, calculated and tending to produce happy and salutary effects, in securing and supporting the ancient legal and constitutional rights of this and the colonies in general, do approve and adopt the measure, and thereupon

Resolved, That a *Standing Committee of Correspondence and Inquiry,* to consist of nine persons, viz.: The Hon. Ebenezer Silliman, Esq., William Williams, Benjamin Payne, Samuel Holden Parsons, Nathaniel Wales, Silas Dean, Samuel Bishop, Joseph Trumbull, and Erastus Wolcot, Esq., whose business it shall be to obtain all such intelligence, and take up and maintain correspondence with our sister colonies, respecting the important considerations mentioned and expressed in the aforesaid resolutions of the patriotic House of Burgesses of Virginia, and the result of such their proceedings from time to time to lay before this house.

Resolved, That the Speaker of this House do transmit to the Speakers of the different Assemblies of the British colonies on this continent, copies of these resolutions, and request that they would come into similar measures, and communicate, from time to time, with the said committee, on all matters wherein the common welfare and safety of the colonies arc concerned.

[Note C]

In the House of Representatives of the Colony of Connecticut, June 3, 1774. Whereas a Congress of Commissioners from the several British Colonies in America, is proposed by some of our neighboring colonies, and thought necessary: and whereas, it may be found expedient that such Congress should be convened before the next session of the Assembly,

Resolved, by this House, that the Committee of Correspondence be, and they are hereby, empowered, on application to them made, or from time to time as may be found necessary, to appoint a suitable number to attend such Congress or Convention of Commissioners, or Committees of the several colonies in British America; and the persons thus to be chosen, shall be, and they hereby are, directed, in behalf of the colony, to attend such Congress, to consult and advise on proper measures for advancing the best good of the colonies; and such conferences from time to time to report to this House,

[Note D.]

"New London, July 28th, 1774.

Dear Sir:

On the refusal of three of our commissioners to attend the Congress, I have received a notification to attend a meeting of the Committee of Correspondence, at Hartford, next Wednesday, to make a further appointment, and also a desire to notify you of the time and place of our meeting. If you will come to New London on Monday, we will go together. I hope no business of a private nature will divert you from attending this important public business. As the eyes of all the continent are upon the Congress for relief, so I think we should be unpardonable, to suffer small things to divert us from attending to make the appointment.

I am, sir, your friend,

Samuel H. Parsons.

Col. Joseph Trumbull, Norwich."

The following letter, written June 7, 1774, to Samuel Adams, by a member of the Committee of Correspondence, soon after the passage of the resolution of June 3d, by the Connecticut Assembly, illustrates the ardent patriotism which inspired the gentlemen composing that committee, and their earnest desire and efficient influence in promoting the important object of a Convention of the Colonies, or General Congress. It alludes to a letter which may be found in Force's Archives.

"Sir: Yon will have received a letter from our General Committee of Correspondence before this comes to hand. By that you will find that a General Congress of Commissioners from all the colonies is expected, and that in the opinion of people *here,* that will be a necessary step to unite the several colonies in the most effectual measures to oppose the designs of Administration; who doubtless expect that the other governments will sit still, tame spectators, while they wreak their vengeance on Boston, if they are left untouched.

This town had a full meeting yesterday, in which it was easily seen that the spirit of our people is as high as ever, and full as determined to oppose, with vigor and resolution, the wicked and unjust attempts of our enemies. The Committee of Correspondence have this day written to the Committee of Correspondence for the town of Boston, on the subject."

[Note F.]

"To The Honorable General Assembly now sitting, the memorial of *Samuel E. Parsons,* humbly showeth:

That in April, 1775, the memorialist, Mr. Silas Dean and Col. Samuel Wyllys, with others, were induced, from the particular situation of public affairs, to undertake surprising and seizing the enemy's post at Ticonderoga, without the knowledge and approbation of the Assembly; and to prosecute the business, were necessitated to take out a quantity of money from the treasury, for which they gave their promissory receipt; that the whole moneys were delivered to the gentlemen sent on that service, and were actually expended therein. That said receipts are still held against the promissors, notwithstanding the public have taken the post into their own hands, and repaid the expense. Your memorialist therefore prays your honors to order said receipts to be given up; that the sums thereof he allowed the treasurer in settlement; and he, as in duty bound, &c.

Dated in Hartford, the 30th of May, 1777.

Samuel H. Parsons.

The action of the Legislature, and the original receipts, are recorded in the office of the Secretary of State at Hartford.

[Note G.]

Gen. Parsons to Gen. Washington:

"New Haven, May 25th, 1777.

Dear General:

Having received information that the enemy were collecting forage, horses, &c, on the east end of Long Island, I ordered a detachment from the several regiments then at this place, consisting of one Major, four Captains, viz.: Troop, Pond, Mansfield, and Savage, and nine subalterns, and two hundred and twenty men, commissioned officers and privates, under the command of Col. Meigs, to attack their different posts on that part of the island, and destroy the forage, *Etc.,* which they have collected. Col. Meigs embarked his men here, in thirteen whaleboats, the 21st inst., and proceeded to Guilford, but the wind proving high, and the sea rough, could not pass the sound until Friday, the 23d. He left Guilford, at 10 o'clock on the afternoon of the 23d, with one hundred and seventy of his detachment, and under convoy of two armed sloops, and in company with another unarmed, (to bring off prisoners,) crossed the sound, to the north branch of the island, near Southold, where he arrived about 6 o'clock in the evening; the enemy's troops on this branch of the island had marched for New York two days before; but about sixty of the enemy remaining at a place called Sagg Harbor, about fifteen miles distant, on the south branch of the island, he ordered eleven whale-boats, with as many men as could be safely transported across the bay, over the land to the bay, where they re-embarked, to the number of one hundred and thirty, and at about 12 o'clock, arrived safe across the bay, within about four miles of the harbor; where, having secured the boats in the woods, under the care of a guard, Col. Meigs formed his remaining little detachment in proper order for attacking the different posts and quarters of the enemy, and securing the vessels and forage at the same time. They marched in the greatest order and silence, and at 2 o'clock arrived at the harbor. The several divisions, with fixed bayonets, attacked the guards and posts assigned them, whilst Capt. Troop, with the detachment under his command, secured the vessels and forage lying at the wharf. The alarm soon became general, when an armed schooner of twelve guns and seventy men, within one hundred and *fifty* yards of the wharf, began a fire upon our troops, which continued, without cessation, for three quarters of an hour, with grape and round shot; but the troops, with the greatest intrepidity, returned the fire upon the schooner, and set fire to the vessels and forage, and killed and captured all the soldiers and sailors, except about six, who made their escape under cover of the night. Twelve brigs and sloops, one an armed vessel with twelve guns, about one hundred and twenty tons of pressed hay, oats, corn, and other forage, ten hogsheads of rum, and a large quantity of other merchandize, were entirely consumed. It gives me the greatest satisfaction to hear the officers and soldiers, without exception, behaved with the greatest bravery, order, and intrepidity. Col. Meigs, having finished the business on which he was sent, returned safe, with all his men, to Guilford, by 2 o'clock, P. M., yesterday, with ninety prisoners; having, in twenty-five hours, by land and water, transported his men full ninety miles and succeeded in his attempts, beyond my most sanguine expectations, without losing a single man, either killed or wounded.

It gives me singular pleasure to hear no disposition appeared in any one soldier, to plunder the inhabitants, or violate private property, in the smallest degree, and that even the clothing and other articles belonging to the prisoners, the soldiers, with a generosity not learned from British troops, have, with great cheerfulness, restored to them, where they have fallen into their hands.

Maj. Humphreys, who waits on your Excellency, with the account, was in the action, with Col. Meigs, and will be able to give any further necessary information, etc., etc."

[Note H.]

"Peekskill, July 30th, 1777.

Dear General:

The designs of the enemy, and the importance of the posts in the various; parts of the country, are, doubtless, better understood by your Excellency, than I can pretend to know them. This ought not to prevent my proposing my sentiments to your Excellency's consideration: in this I do no more than my duty, and if I am mistaken, it can be no ill consequence to anyone but myself. The posts on the North River have always appeared to me of greater importance to the enemy, than any in America, and the most difficult to obtain, if any considerable body of men were left to defend them. In this light they have been generally viewed, as the communication between the eastern and southern states will be almost wholly cut off, if the enemy holds the passes in or near the river. When I was last at headquarters, it was thought of so much importance, that Gen. Nixon's brigade was ordered not to march for Albany, until I should arrive within a day's march of Peekskill, when three brigades and the militia would have then been loft at the post. If the post is of so much importance to be held, and the intention of the enemy not fully known, it appears to me very necessary that a body of troops, sufficient for the defense of it, should be left here. The militia are to leave us tomorrow; two brigades are ordered over the river for Philadelphia. About two thousand men are then left to defend the forts, man the ships, and other commands, and to defend the passes through the mountains; one thousand of which will be necessarily detached over the river, and in the ships, and to other posts; the remaining number much too small to answer the expected purposes. That the enemy do not design to attack any other place at present, I think most probable for these reasons: That no object can be of so much importance toward subjugating the country; and if a junction of Mr. Howe's army, with that at the northward, is an event they wish to take place, it can no other way

~ 454 ~

be so easily effected, as by this river. The force left in and about York Island, is certainly much larger than is necessary for the defense of New York. I think there can be doubt but they have six thousand men left there, and unless this army is much greater than I conceive it to be, he cannot have with the fleet, men sufficient to effect anything considerable against the force he would expect to meet at any other place southward of this post. On these grounds, I am still of opinion the enemy are designed here, and the present maneuver is to draw off our troops from this place. The difficulty of carrying the post, if a good body of troops were left here, I think will fully justify the maneuver of the enemy. They have never attempted to obstruct our passage over the river, which was always in their power. This I think strengthens the opinion they design to attack here. Under these circumstances I feel myself exceedingly concerned that so many of the troops are drawn to so great a distance; 'tis not my own reputation only which gives me so much concern, though I am very sensible the little I have will be forever lost, if the post is not maintained, and I think the most sanguine person can have very little hope of it, with no greater force than will remain here; with the four brigades, and what assistance we can have from the militia, there might be a prospect of maintaining it against the main body of the enemy until your Excellency's arrival here; otherwise I see very little prospect of holding out one day. However, I hope I may be mistaken in my conjecture; if I should be, I shall be heartily rejoiced. The two brigades should join yon, and I wish I may be added to the number. I am your Excellency's obedient servant,

Samuel H. Parsons.

To Gen. Washington.

[Note L.]

Gen. Parsons to Gov. Trumbull:

THE ATTACK ON FORT MONTGOMERY.

Extract. Danbury,   October 7th, 1777.

Sir:

I came this morning to forward, with all possible expedition, such troops as I should find coming to our aid from Connecticut. I am much pleased to find my countrymen seem again roused from the stupor which had seized them. I think by appearances that we shall soon receive a re-enforcement of *two thousand men from this State.* Happy would I have been had the fourth of this body arrived yesterday.

I am sorry to inform your Excellency that the enemy made a successful attack on fort Montgomery yesterday. The 5th, they landed about fifteen hundred men at King's Ferry, on the east side of the river, under cover of their ships and armed vessels, and the night after, re-embarked most of them. Which, with a large additional number, (about twenty-five hundred in the whole,) were landed on the west side (the 6th) in the morning, keeping a large reserve on board and at King's Ferry.

About 10 o'clock the enemy began the attack on the fort, which lasted without cessation, until near half-after six in the evening, when the fort was carried by storm, after eight or ten unsuccessful attempts, in which they were repulsed, with great loss. The courage and bravery displayed by the troops (principally militia from New York) who defended the post, would do honor to the best disciplined regiment. No terms would be accepted, but with fortitude seldom found, they undauntedly stood the shock, determined to defend the fort or sell their lives as dear ns possible. The fort was finally taken, merely for want of men to man the lines, and not for want of spirit in the men. But about five hundred was afforded to man the post and outworks belonging to them: a number of men not more than sufficient to defend the largest fort. The post on the east side was left in a weak, defenseless state, and could afford but little aid.

Thus was a post of importance, and the lives and liberties of some of the bravest men, made a sacrifice to the careless inattention of our countrymen to objects of great and extensive public importance. The enemy must have suffered much, as more than three hours of this attack the musketry was incessant within forty yards, and less a greater part of the time. Gov. Clinton, who commanded, and Col. Lamb and some other officers, escaped after the enemy had entered. Gen. James Clinton was wounded, and is a prisoner. Maj. Humphrey, Col. Dubois, Lieut. Col. Livingston, and sundry other officers, arc missing.

This event is unfortunate, but I hope will not be attended by any very ill consequences. I think a little more patience and public virtue, (which is now very scarce,) will set all things right again.

I am, with esteem, your Excellency's obedient servant,

Samuel H. Parsons.

Letter from Gen. Parsons to Gov. Trumbull:

THE CAPTURE OF FORT MONTGOMERY AND THE ADVANCE OF GEN. CLINTON UP THE NORTH RIVER.

Fishkill, October 9th, 1777

Sir:

I wrote yesterday, from Danbury, an account of the misfortune which had befallen this post, merely for the want of a timely re-enforcement of men sufficient to man the lines. On that head I can only add, that should this misfortune have the happy effect to rouse my countrymen to more vigorous exertions, and to the exercise of a degree of patience, submission and perseverance, necessary to accomplish anything great, or save the country from inevitable ruin, we may consider the event as fortunate, rather than as an event from which any ill effects will follow.

Gov. Clinton, his brother, Gen. James Clinton, Col. Lamb, Col. Maj. Humphrey, and most of the officers, and a great part of the men, who were supposed to be lost, have got in, many of them badly wounded. Tho garrison was defended with the utmost bravery: no men could do more. Our loss cannot yet be ascertained: I hope not so considerable as we feared. The army of the enemy arc now advancing. We have no doubt Albany is their object. Should they attack this post, from which they are seven miles distant, and the same spirit of inattention seize our countrymen. I fear you will hear no better news from here. We shall fight the enemy if possible. We shall do our utmost to defend ourselves, if attacked. The troops are in good spirits. The issue is in the disposal of the great Arbiter of all events. I think it of absolute necessity that all who can bear arms, and can be spared, should be immediately sent forward to Poughkeepsie, except those on their march for this post, who will join us here.

Gen. Clinton, who commands the British forces in person, must be defeated at Albany, or before he arrives there, or Gen. Gates will be undone. Every exertion is necessary to animate end encourage the people, in this important crisis. That we are embarked in the cause of justice and truth—in the cause of God and mankind—is beyond a doubt. That we shall finally succeed, I think equally certain. When public spirit prevails over private interest—and injustice (so scandalously prevalent at this time) is restrained, and religion, and virtue, and a sense of our dependence on Heaven for all our mercies, and especially deliverance from imminent danger, takes place of the vain confidence in our own arm and on our own strength: then, and not till then, will our salvation be brought out; but I cannot say that a profound belief of these things, and a careless neglect of using the means put into our hands for our own deliverance, is any evidence of the sincerity of our profession. As Gen. Putnam ii exceedingly busy, I have wrote by his desire. I have the honor to be,

Your Excellency's obedient servant,

Samuel H. Parsons.

Letter from Gen. Parsons to Gov. Trumbull.

THE RETREAT OF GEN. CLINTON DOWN THE NORTH RIVER.

Peekskill, Oct. 22d, 1777.

Sir:

The enemy prevented our designed attack upon them by *a very sudden embarkation of their troops* on board their ships, which still lie off Verplank's Point. Every favorable opportunity has offered for their going to New York, but no movements have taken place. Their Northern Army is more within your Excellency's knowledge than mine. If we should soon be ordered toward New York, I think some aid from Connecticut will be much wanted. As I understand fourteen hundred men are ordered from the east side of Connecticut River to join Gen. Gates, under his present situation would it not be best to order them to join this part of the army as soon as possible. The militia from this post are all returned home.

I am your Excellency's obedient servant,

S. H. Parsons.

[Note K.]

Gen. Parsons to Gen. Washington.

THE STATE OF THE GARRISON AT WEST POINT, AND THE CONTINUANCE OF HIS COMMAND AT THAT POST.

West Point, June 5th, 1779.

Dear General:

In answer to your questions, by Capt. Christie, of the Pennsylvania regiment, I have given him general information of the state of this garrison, which will be explained by the proper key. The garrison are in high spirits, and are very desirous to receive the enemy's attack. I cannot promise the post will be successfully defended, but I am certain every exertion will be made by the troops to secure the possession of that honor to themselves and their country, which they so frequently anticipate in reflection. If any more troops are ordered here, and *should I continue in command* of the post for any length of time, I would beg your Excellency to order my brigade to compose part of the garrison. Two regiments of that brigade are perfectly acquainted with the country, and in that respect are better able to answer all the purposes expected from the garrison.

S. H. Parsons.

[Note M.]

Letter from Gen. Parsons to Gen. Washington

IN RELATION TO THE INVASION OF CONNECTICUT BY GEN. TRYON JULY, 1779.

Redding, July 9th, 1779.

Dear General:

I have this moment arrived here, after a tour of sixty miles since eleven o'clock last night. The few militia at New Haven, behaved exceedingly well, repulsed the enemy several times, and considerable loss was suffered by the enemy. They burnt a number of houses at East and West Haven, and plundered New Haven. They have destroyed Fairfield—almost every house; the abuses of women, children, and old men, are unparalleled. They embarked from Fairfield yesterday and passed over the sound, but there is reason to think they design an attack on Norwalk and the other towns. Gen. Wolcot has received an express, informing him that four thousand of the enemy are in possession of Horseneck, and marching eastward. I have wrote to Col. Wayland, and the small number of infantry, desiring them to march to the coast. I hope it will be agreeable to your Excellency's intentions. I hear nothing of Glover's brigade. Is it possible to send one thousand continental troops? They will serve to steady the militia, and render them a formidable body. I will write you from Norwalk, where I shall be to-night.

I am your Excellency's obedient servant.

Samuel H. Parsons.

Gen. Parsons to Gen. Washington,

INFORMING WASHINGTON OF GEN. TRYON'S LANDING AND BURNING OF NORWALK, BATTLE WITH TRYON, RETREAT OF THE ENEMY, ETC.

Wilton, July 11th, 1779.

Dear General:

In my last I informed you that the enemy landed last night. This morning, the enemy, on their advance, were met by the militia, and some skirmishing ensued, but without any considerable effect on either side. At about six o'clock the troops under Gen. Wolcot, and my small detachment of about one hundred and fifty continental troops joined and took possession of an eminence the north end of the town. The enemy advanced in our front and on our left flank, until about nine o'clock, when they were checked in their progress by the vigorous exertions of the parties of militia and continental troops sent out to oppose them, and in turn were compelled to retire from hill to hill, sometimes in great disorder. We continued to advance upon them until near eleven o'clock, when a column having nearly gained our right flank, the militia in the center gave way and retreated in disorder. This gave the enemy possession of our ground. Gen. Wolcot, who commanded, exerted himself upon this occasion to rally the troops and bring them to order again, but without effect, until they had retired about two miles, when some troops being again formed, returned to the aid of the right and left wings, who had retired but a small distance, and in order. With these the enemy were pursued again, and retreated with precipitation to their ships.

I have the pleasure to assure your Excellency the continental troops, without exception, they being all engaged, behaved with the greatest bravery. Capt. Betts, who was the first engaged with the enemy, and who continued longest in the action, deserves particular notice for his great fortitude and prudent conduct in the battle. He continued advancing on the enemy until the center of the main body gave way, and he with his party advanced near a mile at the time, by his prudence was able to effect a regular retreat, without any considerable loss. Capt. Eels, on the right, and Capt. Sherman, on the left, were also engaged, and when obliged to retire, kept their order, and retreated with regularity. A body of the militia—I think they were commanded by Maj. Porter—and another considerable detachment, deserve honorable mention to be made of them.

I am not yet able to ascertain our own or the enemy's loss, but in my next shall be able to give a more particular account. In *my handful of continental troops* I have lost five men killed, a Lieutenant and six privates wounded; I don't know of any missing: some loss the militia have sustained. I am satisfied the loss of the enemy must have been considerable.

About twenty boats landed on the west side of the harbor, at five o'clock, and immediately began to set fire to the buildings. They completed burning the town at about twelve o'clock. This appeared to have been their sole business, as they did not stay to carry off any plunder of considerable value. A few Tory houses arc left, which I hope our people will burn, as the burners are here, and have committed no act by which the public can seize them. I imagine *Stamford* will be the next object to wreak their hellish malice upon. To that place I shall repair to-morrow.

I am fully persuaded that five hundred more men, such as the brave militia I have before mentioned, and the one hundred and fifty continentals, would have given the enemy a total defeat. The numbers of the enemy were about two thousand—our numbers between nine and eleven hundred.

I am, dear General, your obedient servant.

Samuel H. Parsons.

A more full and detailed statement of the movements of Gen. Tryon, and the depredations committed by him upon the sea coast, may be found in letters from General Parsons to General Washington dated July 14th and 20th, 1779 and to General Heath July 12th.

His correspondence with General Washington is large and details with great precision and minuteness the movements of the enemy as well as the plans and continued movements of the few under his command; and likewise exhibits the mutual confidence existing between the writer and the Commander-in-Chief. Time and space, however do not admit a transcript.

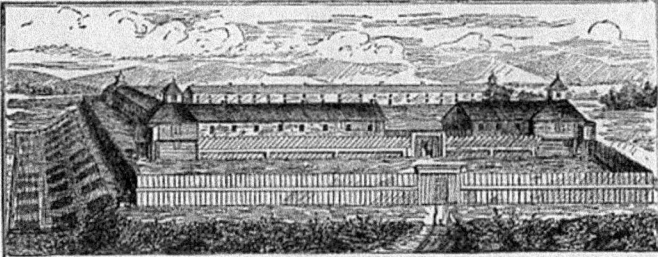

PLAN OF CAMPUS MARTIUS.

If you enjoyed this book, be sure to check out its sister book titled Pioneer History by S. P. Hildreth. For this book and more great stories from our past please visit the Historical Collection at our web site.

Badgley Publishing Company

WWW.BadgleyPublishingCompany.com

www.ingramcontent.com/pod-product-compliance
Lightning Source LLC
Chambersburg PA
CBHW060036100426

42742CB00014B/2614